Pro T-SQL 2019

Toward Speed, Scalability, and Standardization for SQL Server Developers

Elizabeth Noble

Pro T-SQL 2019: Toward Speed, Scalability, and Standardization for
SQL Server Developers

Elizabeth Noble
Roswell, GA, USA

ISBN-13 (pbk): 978-1-4842-5589-6 ISBN-13 (electronic): 978-1-4842-5590-2
https://doi.org/10.1007/978-1-4842-5590-2

Managing Director, Apress Media LLC: Welmoed Spahr
Acquisitions Editor: Jonathan Gennick
Development Editor: Laura Berendson
Coordinating Editor: Jill Balzano

Cover image designed by Freepik (www.freepik.com)

Distributed to the book trade worldwide by Springer Science+Business Media New York, 233 Spring Street, 6th Floor, New York, NY 10013. Phone 1-800-SPRINGER, fax (201) 348-4505, e-mail orders-ny@springer-sbm.com, or visit www.springeronline.com. Apress Media, LLC is a California LLC and the sole member (owner) is Springer Science + Business Media Finance Inc (SSBM Finance Inc). SSBM Finance Inc is a **Delaware** corporation.

For information on translations, please e-mail rights@apress.com, or visit http://www.apress.com/rights-permissions.

Apress titles may be purchased in bulk for academic, corporate, or promotional use. eBook versions and licenses are also available for most titles. For more information, reference our Print and eBook Bulk Sales web page at http://www.apress.com/bulk-sales.

Any source code or other supplementary material referenced by the author in this book is available to readers on GitHub via the book's product page, located at www.apress.com/9781484255896. For more detailed information, please visit http://www.apress.com/source-code.

Printed on acid-free paper

This book is dedicated to #SQLFamily. You all have helped me grow as a data professional. You have given me confidence and encouraged me to pursue my dreams.
I hope this books helps others as much as I have been helped by all of you.

This book is also dedicated to my family and friends for all their love and support, especially while writing this book. Eric and Danny, you can accomplish the challenges that come before you.

Table of Contents

About the Author

 **Elizabeth Noble** is a Director of Database Development or "E" at Pull-A-Part in the metro Atlanta area. It was love at first sight when she was introduced to her first database over 10 years ago. Her passion is to help others improve the quality and speed of deploying database changes through automation. When she is not trying to automate all things, she can be found spending time with her dogs, playing disc golf, or taking a walk. She is also a frequent speaker at SQL Saturdays across the United States and was a first-time speaker at PASS Summit in 2019.

About the Technical Reviewer

 **Warner Chaves** is a SQL Server MCM, Data Platform MVP, and Principal Consultant at Pythian. He started his career with a brief stint in .NET programming that led to working for enterprise customers in Hewlett-Packard's ITO organization. From there, he transitioned to his current position at Pythian, building and managing data solutions for some of the biggest names across many industry verticals. Warner is a frequent speaker at SQLSaturday events around the world and at the PASS Summit, the largest conference dedicated to the Microsoft Data Platform.

Acknowledgments

I would like to thank my husband, Casey, for believing in me and encouraging me to pursue my dreams. I want to thank my Mom for teaching me that growth is the key to life. Thanks to my Dad for helping me remember to take time for myself. I also want to thank Ed, Jeff, Mike, Phil, and Rob for mentoring me and introducing me to #SQLFamily.

I want to thank my friends Angela, Joey, Jude, Lee, LeeAnn, and Tammy for their words of encouragement while writing this book. Thanks to Rie for teaching me both the importance of confidence and empathy. I want to thank Kellyn for believing in me and my ability to author a book.

Introduction

Working with T-SQL allows you to write code and see results relatively quickly. There is also a great deal of flexibility when creating T-SQL statements. In many cases, there is more than one way you can achieve the same outcome from your T-SQL. This book is designed for database developers and data professionals that have a general knowledge of T-SQL but are looking to improve their overall code quality. You should understand T-SQL syntax and know how to write SELECT, INSERT, UPDATE, or DELETE statements before beginning this book. *Pro T-SQL 2019* will prepare you to write consistent code with improved performance. You will also learn how to protect your T-SQL code by using source control and improving your database deployment pipeline. Overall, the goal of this book is to provide you with a framework to write better T-SQL code. As data professionals, we can find ourselves in scenarios where there are high demands or short deadlines. *Pro T-SQL 2019* was written with the intent to help you write code that could save you time and energy in the future.

There are four sections in this book. The first section covers how to improve the readability of your T-SQL code. There is an overview of the various data types for T-SQL along with guidance on how to best use those data types. This first section explains the benefits and disadvantages of the various database objects in SQL Server. Additional chapters discuss standardizing and designing T-SQL code. The second section explains how to write T-SQL code that is efficient. This section includes using set-based design to write T-SQL code and understanding the relationship between hardware and T-SQL design. You will also learn how to use execution plans and new features in SQL Server 2019 to improve the performance of your T-SQL code. The third section discusses how to manage your T-SQL code. The chapters included in this section cover developing coding standards and using source control to store your code. To further manage your T-SQL code, you will also learn some methods to test and deploy your database code. The fourth section addresses how to write T-SQL code so that it is sustainable over time. These chapters include methods to safely add new functionality, to log changes to data within your databases, and to manage data growth over time.

PART I

Building Understandable T-SQL

CHAPTER 1

Data Types

Data types are the building blocks that make the foundation of writing efficient and performant T-SQL. While many data types are either a number or a string, there are also a variety of data types that do not fit into either category. When selecting the right data type, it is important to understand what the data type is and when to use it.

Number Data Types

While numbers may all seem to be the same, T-SQL segments numbers into different kinds of data types. These data types can include whole numbers or numbers with decimal places. Numbers are also categorized by either being exact or approximate. Understanding how to work with various number data types when performing mathematical calculations is critical to ensuring applications handle data as expected.

While it may be easiest to pick the most common seeming data types from each category, there are specific times where it is best to analyze the data that will be stored and select a more appropriate option. When choosing data types, there are various factors to consider. The most important step is to figure out what kind of data will be stored. The next logical step is to consider how the data will be used and stored. In addition, it is important to understand how T-SQL handles calculations involving various data types.

Exact Number Data Types

There are situations when the value of a number is definite and known. These types of numbers can be referred to as exact numbers. Some examples include true or false, quantity of units sold, discount percent, or dollars and cents. One of the keys to writing good T-SQL is selecting the correct data type category to use for a given field. In some cases, the categories have more than one data type available.

© Elizabeth Noble 2020
E. Noble, *Pro T-SQL 2019*, https://doi.org/10.1007/978-1-4842-5590-2_1

When considering what data type to use, you will want to consider the purpose for this data type. This will provide better clarity when determining which data type should be used. You will want to consider both the benefits and drawbacks associated with each data type. You will also want to consider if SQL Server will have to perform any implicit conversions as a result of using this data type in calculations with other data types. The final piece will be to consider how the data type is stored in SQL Server.

BIT

The term BIT is derived from the phrase binary digit. Therefore, the BIT data type can only store one of two values. In the case of SQL Server, there is a third option relating to unknown values. This third option is known as NULL. As such, the only values allowed with the BIT data type are 0, 1, and NULL. This consequently causes the BIT data type to only allow the smallest set of available values.

The BIT data type is great for data types where "either X or Y" is applicable. The information stored can be true or false, on or off, and yes or no. In the case of true or false, this BIT type could be used to indicate if a data record was translated successfully. A common use of indicating on or off with the BIT data type would involve indicating if a certain feature is enabled. One example of a yes or no value would be to record a customer's decision to opt in to receive marketing information from a company.

One of the challenges with the BIT data type is making sure to use them in a way that promotes good database design. This means there are times when you need to consider the overall purpose when selecting the BIT data type. For instance, it may seem like indicating whether an item has specific characteristics may be a good use of the BIT data type. An example could be a column in a table like IsVegetarian. However, it may be better to consider redesigning the database to record those attributes in another table. A BIT can be used to indicate a successful status for a transaction. However, there is often more status to record the state of the transaction in over a period of time. If recording status changes over time is important, then using a BIT to record if a transaction is successful may not be the best option.

An advantage of the BIT data type is the overall storage space required when saving BIT values in a database. As there are 8 bits in a byte, the same holds true for storing records in a database. For each 8 BIT columns in a table, those values are all stored a single byte. If there were 9 to 16 BIT columns in the table, all the BIT values would be stored in a total of 2 bytes. This small amount of storage space required indicates that it would take one table with up to 8 BIT columns and 1 million records to use one MB of space in the database.

TINYINT, SMALLINT, INT, BIGINT

SQL Server also allows you to store whole numbers, that is, numbers that do not have decimals or fractional values. These numbers are known as integers. One example of data stored as integers can be quantities of a given item. There are several types of integer values that can be stored within SQL Server. The first integer type is TINYINT. The TINYINT value can contain any integer value between 0 and 255. Due to the limited size of this data type, this may be useful for limited configuration types or number of locations. This data type is like the BIT data type, but this data type has a slightly wider range. This data type would also be useful to configure the types of statuses in a system or categories of objects. The TINYINT is good for storing these status types as many applications do not need more than 256 statuses.

Now that we've covered TINYINT, let's discuss the possibilities of SMALLINT. The range of SMALLINT covers approximately 70,000 possible values. With this range available, you want to consider what sorts of values you would want to have between 256 and 65,435 unique values. The range for the SMALLINT starts at –32,768 and ends at 32,767. This data type would not be useful for a table that logs every single activity that happens. Many databases or data tables may have more than 70,000 transactions or records over the course of several years. This may cause this data type to be unsuitable for those tables. However, there may be other tables where the SMALLINT data type is ideal.

If you have data tables that do not experience high transactional activity but will be growing for some time, the SMALLINT data type may be beneficial. Understanding your business will help you determine if the SMALLINT is the correct data type for that value being stored.

If you were to create a table to continue to add functionality to your applications, you may want to store a record indicating each new piece of functionality was to your application. An example of this can be feature flags. Your application will likely have more than 256 enhancements over the life of the application. You may also want to store configuration values for the application. Storing these configuration values in a table may benefit from the SMALLINT data type.

Moving on to integers or INT. This is the most frequently use of the whole number data types. Many databases use this number exclusively for any sort of whole number that is being tracked. One of the reasons for this is the entire range covers about 5.4 billion records. The INT data type covers the range from –2,147,483,648 to 2,147,483,647. However, when many data tables are created, their identity column is often started, or seeded, at the integer 1. This causes the table to be limited to approximately 2.15 billion unique identities.

If you believe that your table will need more than 2.15 billion unique identity records, you may want to start the identity with the lowest number possible, –2,147,483,648.

This is often where you may need to perform some mathematical calculations. Some businesses process a couple hundred transactions per second. Other businesses process upward of 10,000 or 20,000 transactions per second. In both cases it's important to consider what kind of growth will be expected in the tables holding this transactional information. If your application has hundreds of transactions per second over several years, the number of records stored will be much smaller than if the application has tens of thousands of transactions per second for the same time period.

DECIMAL/NUMERIC

Now that we have discussed various integers, we should consider what to do with numbers that require decimals. There are various cases where you are going to want decimal places. Some of these cases involve using dollars and cents, and other times you are going to need decimal places for precision in measurements. There are a couple of options available in these scenarios.

First there is the option for DECIMAL or alternatively it is called a NUMERIC data type. This value does not save any currency information with it; however, it does record decimal places. These decimal places can be specified by indicating both the total number of digits that should be stored and the number of digits to the right of the decimal point. You will find that the DECIMAL or NUMERIC data type is acceptable for almost all data types involving numbers. This includes general-purpose numbers, decimals, measurements, and money values.

Considering that the DECIMAL type can represent multiple different types of numbers, we should take a closer look at this data type. There is no difference between DECIMAL and NUMERIC. They are the same data type in SQL Server. There are some specific terms for the DECIMAL data type. The values that make up a DECIMAL data type are precision and scale. Precision relates to the total number of digits that are saved in a DECIMAL data type. Scale refers to the number of digits that are stored to the right of the decimal point.

SMALLMONEY, MONEY

The next data types to discuss are MONEY and SMALLMONEY. The MONEY and SMALLMONEY data types are like the DECIMAL or NUMERIC data type. The SMALLMONEY and MONEY data types can also be used to store values for currency.

SQL Server will save the numeric value and exclude the type of currency associated with the value saved.

The largest difference between the MONEY and SMALLMONEY data types is size and storage space. The SMALLMONEY data type covers a range from –214,000 to positive 214,000 and takes up only 4 bytes of data, whereas the MONEY data type covers a range from –922 billion to 922 billion and takes up 8 bytes of data.

The MONEY data type is accurate to store up to four decimal places. The limitation on decimal places will limit the accuracy to ten thousandths of the monetary value stored. The MONEY data type will save all values to four decimal places. The fixed number of decimal places will impact how rounding affects calculations involving the MONEY data type.

Approximate Number Data Types

Next we will move on to the differences between exact and approximate numbers. Exact numbers exist for things that you know the exact quantity of, for instance, how many items you bought at the store or the exact amount in dollars and cents. Whereas approximate numbers exist for scenarios where the measurements may not be exact. Approximate numbers can be used to store very large or very small numbers. You may also find that your application is recording a measurement that is not exact. You may cut a length of fabric that is close to but not exactly a specific value. For example, the length of fabric may be around 12 inches. Storing the value 12 for inches would be an approximate value. This measurement of 12 inches may be so close that it would be difficult to tell that the length of fabric was not exactly 12 inches.

There are some rounding issues that come into play when dealing with approximate numbers. This is because approximate numbers are known to not be the exact measurement. In SQL Server, there is one option for approximate numbers. This data type is called FLOAT. If the floating number has 24 numbers, the synonymous data type is REAL.

When working with REAL or FLOAT numbers, there can be issues converting this data type to other data types. Converting a FLOAT data type to an INTEGER, all the values in the decimal places will be truncated. You will want to be aware that using approximate numbers may cause unexpected results. One example is when using the DECIMAL or NUMERIC data types. When converting a FLOAT or REAL number to a DECIMAL or NUMERIC data type, you are only able to keep seven decimal places.

Converting Number Data Types

We have covered the types of numbers available, and what happens in working with the various number data types. In addition to storing numbers, you will also want to understand how various number data types interact with one another. First we should consider what happens when we are doing calculations involving fields with the same data type. In these scenarios, if all the fields for the calculation are of the same data type, the data type will remain the same. Therefore, if you were multiplying a quantity times the price and both values are stored as a NUMERIC data type of DECIMAL(5,2), it will give the same data type of DECIMAL as a result. SQL Server will determine the result precision and scale based on the starting precision and scale as well as the type of calculation performed. You will also want to consider how the precision and scale is stored in the application. The application may be expecting a value of DECIMAL(5,2). Based on the calculation performed, the data values returned may be outside the range of the data type specified. This can cause an overflow in calculation.

Things can get a little more interesting when working across various data types. To use the example of quantity times price again, we can examine what happens if you had an INT data type that was calculated with a DECIMAL (5,2) data type. SQL Server would use the process of data type precedents. First we should get familiar with the data type order of precedence related to the data types covered so far. The following list is ordered from highest order to lowest.

1. FLOAT

2. REAL

3. DECIMAL

4. MONEY

5. SMALLMONEY

6. MONEY

7. BIGINT

8. INT

9. SMALLINT

10. TINYINT

11. BIT

In the preceding scenario, we are using both the INT and DECIMAL data types. As you can see, the INT and DECIMAL data types are listed. In the case of the INT and DECIMAL data types, the INT has a lower precedence. Due to the order of precedence, SQL Server will internally convert the INT data type to the DECIMAL data type. This conversion does not change the original data value, only how SQL Server uses this value as part of the calculation. Once this conversion is complete, SQL Server moves forward with the calculation. This works well unless you are performing an action like trying to concatenate a number and string data types.

String Data Types

Now that you know how to work with number data types, we should spend some time on the various string data types. These sorts of data types are used to store alphabetical letters, words, or combinations or letters and numbers. In addition, string data types are used to store character values that are either non-unicode or unicode. The last category of string data types includes images and binary values.

Character String Data Types

There is information that will be stored in the database that is not related directly to numbers. This data can be names, descriptions, addresses, or other character values. Determining which data type to use will depend on what type of information is being stored and how much information needs to be stored.

CHAR and VARCHAR

Two of the character string data types available are CHAR and VARCHAR. These data types are similar and only vary regarding some specific considerations. The data field can be configured to determine how data can be stored. The columns can be configured to toggle case sensitivity, accent sensitivity, sensitivity for kana, or width sensitivity. The sensitivity that is stored is referred to as collation. The type of data that can be stored usually matches the database collation. The collation of a column is the same as the database unless there is a specific override in place. Both data types are used to store text data, and the characters that can be stored in these fields are the same characters allowed by the collation of the column.

When determining which data type to use, keep in mind what kinds of data will be stored. If the data will have similar lengths, like phone numbers or zip codes, then CHAR may be the preferred data type. However, if the column widths can vary significantly as is the case with address lines or notes columns, then VARCHAR will be a better option. Consider limiting the use of VARCHAR(MAX) for situations where you expect to save more than 8000 characters. If VARCHAR(MAX) is specified, then the maximum storage size is 2 GB.

There are some additional considerations to keep in mind when using CHAR and VARCHAR. When using CHAR and VARCHAR for data definition or variable declaration, remember that the default value is one character. However, when using the CAST or CONVERT functions, the default number of characters will be 30. In order to minimize truncating data, make sure to always specify the number of characters explicitly when using the CHAR or VARCHAR data types.

For collations using single-byte encoding characters, such as Latin, the storage size in bytes for CHAR is equal to the number of characters. When working with VARCHAR, the number of characters plus 2 additional bytes is equal the total number of bytes stored. It is also possible to save multi-byte encoding characters in the CHAR and VARCHAR data types. For both data types, the number of characters saved may be less than the total number of bytes.

Starting with SQL Server 2019, it is now possible to save unicode values in CHAR or VARCHAR. However, this is only possible if UTF-8 encoding is enabled.

TEXT

The TEXT data types have been previously used when needing to store very large strings of characters. However, this data type has been deprecated. As this data type has been deprecated, you will want to avoid using the TEXT data type for new development. If you need to use the TEXT data you, you will want to consider the data type VARCHAR(MAX) for new development instead. However, consider if you need this functionality or if using VARCHAR with a smaller number of characters may be more appropriate. The only consideration for using the TEXT data type going forward should be as needed for backward compatibility of your applications. The TEXT data type is primarily used in situations with very large strings that have variable length. In many cases, this would be where the length of data saved is more than 8000 characters. The maximum number of characters that can be saved to the TEXT data type is 2,147,483,647. There may be occasions where the total number of characters that can be stored is less than this number.

Unicode String Data Types

Prior to SQL Server 2019, any Unicode text data would need to be saved as a special data type. This is still true for situations where UTF-8 encoding cannot be enabled.

NCHAR and NVARCHAR

When using Unicode values, there are a couple of options available. These options include storing a fixed or variable-length string. In order to avoid unexpected results, you should understand how these data types work if the number of characters or collation is not specified.

Once you have determined that you need to use the NCHAR or NVARCHAR data types, choosing between them gets easy. If the data being stored will have generally similar lengths, then the NCHAR data type is the correct choice. However, if the values stored will vary significantly, then the NVARCHAR data type may be a better choice. In addition, if the number of characters to be stored is over 4000, it is recommended to use NVARCHAR(MAX).

Typically, it is best practice to specify the number of characters when declaring the NCHAR or NVARCHAR data types. The default number of characters for data definition or variable declaration is one character for NCHAR or NVARCHAR. However, when using the CAST or CONVERT function, the default number of characters is 30 if none are specified. If a collation is not specified for the NCHAR or NVARCHAR data type, the default database collation will be used.

Understanding the amount of space required to store this data type also allows you to make better decisions about if this is the correct data type and the number of characters that need to be stored. Storing NCHAR takes up twice as many bytes as the string length of the byte pairs, while using NVARCHAR the number of bytes stored is twice the string length in byte pairs plus 2 bytes.

NTEXT

Previously, storing very large variable-length Unicode data was accomplished using the NTEXT data type. If this data type is still in use in your systems, you can expect it to store up to 1,073,741,823 characters. However, due the size associated with Unicode values, the total length stored may be less. Going forward, it is no longer best practice to use this data type. Instead, use the NVARCHAR(MAX) data type.

Binary String Data Types

At some point, you may want to store data that is neither a number nor a character. In these cases, the use of binary strings may be appropriate. There are a couple alternatives when using binary string data types.

BINARY and VARBINARY

The options available for storing binary string data involved storing either fixed length or variable-length character strings. Like the other string data types discussed, there are also some considerations when dealing with these data types.

Using binary strings for storing items that are strings without characters may be useful. These can include audio, video, images, or other similar items. Two of the available data types are BINARY and VARBINARY. The best option for storing binary strings with similar lengths is the BINARY data type. Conversely, when storing binary strings with significantly varying lengths of data, the VARBINARY data type is a better choice. If the total length of the binary string is expected to exceed 4000 characters, then it is suggested to use VARBINARY(MAX).

Using the BINARY and VARBINARY data types for data definition or variable declaration will have a default length of one if the number of characters is not specified. When converting the BINARY to VARBINARY with the CAST or CONVERT function, the default number of characters will be 30. Use caution when converting to BINARY or VARBINARY from a variable with a different length as SQL Server may pad or truncate the binary data as necessary.

The BINARY data types stores the same number of bytes as the length of data being stored, whereas VARBINARY uses 2 bytes plus the same number of bytes as the length of data being stored. In both data types, the length can be up to 8000. For VARBINARY(MAX), the maximum storage size is 2 GB.

IMAGE

One of the items that can be stored in a binary string is image. When working with images, it is important to consider how this data should be stored and if so what data type should be used.

This IMAGE data type has been used to store large variable-length binary data. While this data type can have a length of 2,147,483,647, there are times where the allowable length stored may be less. In the case of the IMAGE data type, you should use the VARBINARY(MAX) data type going forward as the IMAGE data type is deprecated.

Date and Time Data Types

Each database transaction occurs at a specific point in time. There may be a need to reference or know when a transaction happened. Your application may record important dates for a person including birthdays or anniversaries. Dates and times can also be used to determine pricing and functionality. By using dates and times, you can determine when functionality should be enabled or disabled. Dates and times can also show when a user account is inactive or access to a given system is enabled or expired. Pricing and billing rates can cover multiple different date ranges. When one set of pricing becomes inactive, another set may be active. Due to regulations, your company may need to record the pricing over a period of time. This includes indicating when the pricing rates may have started and stopped. Depending on the purpose for tracking this information, you may only need to know only the date or time of the transaction. There are other situations where it is best to know both the date and time associated with a certain action.

DATE

When working with transactions, there may be a specific occasion where you want to record when something happened. In some cases, it may only matter on what day in which the transaction happened. The DATE data type can also be used to store aggregated data for a given day. While recording the date of the activity, there may also be some options available as to how that data is displayed. When choosing if the DATE data type is right for you, it is also important to consider not only how much data is stored for the DATE data type but any possible limitations in how the data can be stored.

There will be times when an application or a user needs to know when a specific action happened. When deciding if a DATE data type is the right choice, you will want to consider the need for the information both in terms of user and application usage. In some cases, it is easier to think about when a DATE data type would not be preferable.

For any action where you would want to know a specific time when something happened, the DATE data type would not be a good choice. However, if it is only necessary to know on what day an action occurred, then the DATE data type would be a great option.

For the DATE data types, there are several options as to how a DATE can be displayed. With the date format, the default is YYYY-MM-DD. In this case YYYY represents the four-digit year with the range of 0001 to 9999. MM represents the month number from 01 to 12, and DD stands for the day ranging from 01 to 31, per the number of days in a month. The DATE can be displayed in a variety of numeric and alphabetic formats. However, the format ydm is not supported.

The DATE values that can be stored range from 0001-01-01 to 9999-12-31. The DATE data type has a ten-digit character length with a precision of 10 and a scale of 0. The DATE data type takes up 3 bytes and is stored as an INT.

Dates can be converted to DATETIME, SMALLDATETIME, DATETIME2, or DATETIMEOFFSET. However, the time value will be set to midnight. However, dates cannot be converted to the TIME data type, and any attempts to perform this conversion will fail with an error. In addition, dates do not have a time zone offset and are not daylight saving time aware.

TIME

Another data type related to when an action happened is the TIME data type. It is useful to understand how time is stored and formatted. When using the TIME data type, it is helpful to know the implications of converting the data type to other DATE and DATETIME data types. There are also some limitations when using the TIME data type.

TIME can be used to record a specific time when a transaction or activity occurred. When this happens, the time is recorded independently of the date and the date may not be able to be determined in the future. One way around this issue could be to store the date separately from time. The accuracy of TIME is up to 100 nanoseconds, and the default value for TIME is 00:00:00.

The default format for TIME is hh:mm:ss[.nnnnnnn]. In this format, hh stands for a two-digit hour ranging from 0 to 23, mm is for a two-digit minute ranging from 0 to 59, and ss is for a two-digit second from 0 to 59. The TIME data type allows for varying precision, and if specified, up to seven decimal places can be used for fractional seconds as represented by nnnnnnn. These values can range from 0 to 9999999.

Due to how AM and PM are used to differentiate between morning and evening, there are additional considerations when working with TIME. If AM or PM is not provided and the value for hour is between 00 and 11, the time will be recorded as AM. For hours 12 to 23, the time will be saved as PM. When writing TIME, if 12 AM is entered, this value will be converted to the 0 hour.

The range of TIME is 00:00:00.0000000 to 23:59:59.9999999. The character length can vary from 8 to 16 digits, depending on the precision specified for TIME. In either scenario, TIME will be saved as fixed 5 bytes. If TIME is converted to any data type with a date and time, the day value will be represented as 1900-01-01. If the fractional precision is higher for TIME than the new data type, the value will be truncated. Any attempt to convert the TIME data type to a DATE will fail. Like DATE, TIME is neither time zone nor daylight saving time aware.

SMALLDATETIME, DATETIME, DATETIME2, DATETIMEOFFSET

There are occasions where saving the date or time may not be enough. For these scenarios, it may be best to combine the date and time values together. Sometimes these values can be somewhat simpler, need more precision, or need to be time zone aware.

One such data type is the SMALLDATETIME. This data type is used to record both a specific date and time. It has a default value of 1900-01-01 00:00:00. While the accuracy of this data type is listed as 1 second, it is important to note that the seconds will always be saved as 00 in the database.

As with the date data type, the SMALLDATETIME data type can be displayed in a variety of numeric and alphabetical formats. The range for the SMALLDATETIME is somewhat limited as compared to other DATE and DATETIME data types. The day portion of this data type can span 1900-01-01 to 2079-06-06. While the time entered can range from 00:00:00 to 23:59:59, the value saved in the database will be 00:00:00 to 23:59:00. The overall length of the SMALLDATETIME is up to 19 characters, and the storage size required is a total of 4 fixed bytes.

When converting SMALLDATETIME to other DATETIME data types, keep in mind that any additional precision needed will be recorded with 0s. While it may be tempting to use the SMALLDATETIME, this data type is not ANSI compliant. As stated previously, the seconds for this data type will be rounded depending on the value passed for the seconds. If the seconds passed are less than or equal to 29.998, the minute will be rounded down. Otherwise, the minute will be rounded up. Like the date and time data types, SMALLDATETIME is also not time zone or daylight saving time aware.

There are more options available than just SMALLDATETIME. DATETIME has been an option for a higher level of precision than the previously mentioned data types. There are also several key considerations when using this data type.

While the DATETIME data type can record a specific day and time, it may not comply with the SQL Standard. One of the key issues with this data type has to do with the limitations related to accuracy. The DATETIME data type can record three decimal places for fractional seconds; the third decimal place is always rounded to an increment ending in .000, .003, or .007.

If a value is not specified, the default for DATETIME will be 1900-01-01 00:00:00. There are many numeric and alphabetical formats available when using this data type. The year range for DATETIME is 1753-01-01 to 2999-12-31, and the time can range from 00:00:00.000 to 23:59:59.997. The size of this data type is 8 bytes with a character length ranging from 19 to 26.

While it is possible to convert other data types to DATETIME, it is not recommended as this data type does not meet SQL Standards and is not ANSI compliant. The DATETIME data type is also limited due to the rounding that occurs allowing only increments of .000, .003, and .007. This data type is also not time zone or daylight saving time aware.

The DATETIME2 data type has some additional advantages over the data types previously mentioned. While some of the previously mentioned data types have a fixed size, this data type works a little differently. We will also look at storing and formatting available for this data type.

The DATETIME2 data type allows for a specific date and time to be recorded with an accuracy of up to 100 nanoseconds. The default value for DATETIME2 is 1900-01-01 00:00:00. Due to this level of precision, this is a great data type to use for scenarios where the time must be known to a fraction of a second. As DATETIME2 doesn't have the same rounding issues as DATETIME, it is also more straightforward to work with this data type when writing code.

The DATETIME2 data type supports multiple numeric and alphabetical ways to display the information. The date range for DATETIME is from 1753-01-01 to 2999-12-31, and the time range is from 00:00:00 to 23:59:59.9999999. Multiple precision options are allowed, thus causing the character length to range from 19 for the precision to the second all the way up to 27 for the precision to 0.0000001 nanoseconds.

16

The variation in the precision also affects the storage size of the DATETIME2 data type. One byte is used to store the precision of DATETIME2 plus the number of bytes needed depending on the precision of time. If the precision is less than three decimal places for nanoseconds, then there are another 6 bytes used to store the DATETIME2 value. If the precision is 3 or 4, there is 1 byte to store the precision and 7 bytes to store the value, for a total of 8 bytes. However, the total will be 9 bytes for any values with a precision of more than four decimal places.

Due to the high level of accuracy, the probability of converting values to DATETIME2 is highly likely. If a date is converted to DATETIME2, the time component will be recorded as 00:00:00. If time is converted to DATETIME2, the day will be 1900-01-01. In the case of SMALLDATETIME to DATETIME2, the date and time will be copied. Any additional precision will be represented with 0s. Going from DATETIMEOFFSET to DATETIME2 will cause the time zone to be truncated. When going from DATETIME to DATETIME2, make sure to use explicit conversions to avoid unexpected results. The main limitation of using DATETIME2 is that the data type is not time zone aware or daylight saving aware.

The final data type for dates and times is DATETIMEOFFSET. When discussing the DATETIMEOFFSET, there is some additional functionality that has not been seen before with the other data types. There are also things to keep in mind when formatting, storing, or converting to this data type.

The DATETIMEOFFSET data type records the specific date and time, with a high level of accuracy, for transactions or actions that have taken place. One of the key advantages to this data type is the ability to have an offset on the time, thus allowing databases from multiple geographic locations to not only be aware of when something happened in relation to their local time but also in relation to local time at another location.

The DATETIMEOFFSET is accurate to 100 nanoseconds and has a default value of 1900-01-01 00:00:00. The format of DATETIMEOFFSET is YYYY-MM-DD hh:mm:ss. nnnnnnn +|- hh:mm. The +|- hh:mm portion of this data type is related to the offset. The offset can range from +14 to –14 for the number of hours that a given time can have an offset. As with the other time and DATETIME data types, this date can be formatted or displayed numerically or alphabetically.

The dates can range from 0001-01-01 to 2999-12-31. The time that can be saved ranges from 00:00:00 to 23:59:59.9999999. When the precision is saved as YYYY-MM-DD hh:mm:ss {+|–} hh:mm, the character length is 26. The character length can go up to 34 when the precision is YYYY-MM-DD hh:mm:ss.0000000 {+|–} hh:mm. The storage space required for the DATETIMEOFFSET data type is a fixed 10 bytes.

Other Data Types

In addition to the data types discussed previously, SQL Server has several other data types that are available. Some of these data types can be used in table definition and may have special purposes, while some of the other data types may only be usable as variables or inside stored procedures.

UNIQUEIDENTIFIER

This data type can be a column in a table or used as a variable. The UNIQUEIDENTIFIER takes up 16 bytes and has a maximum number of characters that can be stored in this data type is 36. While non-unicode character strings can be converted to UNIQUEIDENTIFIER, if the total number of characters exceeds 36, those results will be truncated.

This data type is a GUID, or Globally Unique Identifier. The concept is that these unique values will only ever be used once. However, there have been reports of this not being true. Either way, the UNIQUEIDENTIFIER can be populated one of several ways. These include using the functions NEWID() and NEWSEQUENTIALID(). Otherwise, these values can be manually populated if the overall format of the GUID is correct and uses valid hexadecimal values of 0–9 and a–f.

While the UNIQUEIDENTIFIER can be used in place of IDENTITY, I would only recommend it for scenarios where it is absolutely required. Not only does it take up significantly more space than an INT or BIGINT, but UNIQUEIDENTIFIER is limited in the types of constraints that can be used with this data type. UNIQUEIDENTIFER can be an IDENTITY but other table constraints are not allowed.

XML

Various systems and applications send, use, or store XML data. While there is the option to parse this data and save it in tables, there are also times where it may be necessary to store the XML data intact. When storing XML data, there are other considerations that include what data is in the XML.

For the XML data type, the data must be in a valid XML format. In order to be valid, there are several requirements. These include all starting tags must have matching end tags. In addition, nested elements must begin and end within the same parent element. XML elements cannot have more than one attribute and markup characters must be properly specified. If the XML data meets all the preceding requirements, then the XML data is considered well-formed.

The total amount of stored XML data allowed is limited to 2 GB. That data can have non-unicode or Unicode data. Sometimes XML data follows a set guideline and has specified data types. In this scenario, the XML data may have a defined XML schema. For XML data that has a schema, the XML can be considered typed. Often typed XML data will take up less space, and there may be additional functionality with the data that is stored. However, a limitation of this typed XML is that the XML must pass validation. If untyped XML data is chosen, the data does not have to be validated and may not be assigned a schema.

Spatial Geometry Types

When working with data, you may want to store various shapes in your database. While this is not a common request, there is an available data type that can be used to store shapes or drawings based on flat maps.

This data type can support several format instances including points, lines, circular lines, curves, polygons, curved polygons, multiple points, multiple strings, multiple polygons, and a collection of any or none of these objects.

Spatial Geography Types

While you may want to save shapes in SQL Server using a flat-earth method, there are other times that it is necessary to store information based on the shape of the earth. In these cases, using the geography data type will be preferable. Use this data type for countries, roads, or maps where longitude and latitude are important.

Like the geometry data type, the geography data type also supports several options. These options include all the same types as the geometry data type including points, lines, circular lines, curves, polygons, curved polygons, multiple points, multiple strings, multiple polygons, and a collection of any or none of these shapes. However, the geography data type also supports the full globe instance.

SQL_VARIANT

There may be an occasion where you will want to store more than one data type in a column. While this is generally not best practice, make sure to understand how this data type stores information and what kinds of limitations exist for this data type.

The SQL_VARIANT data type allows you to store various data types in the same column. The data saved in this column has a total maximum length of 8016 bytes. However, 16 of those bytes are to store information about the data stored in that record. This leaves a total of 8000 bytes available for the actual data saved in the column.

You can insert data directly into the column or cast the data as a specific data type. If you do not specify the data type at the time of the insert, SQL_VARIANT will try to determine the correct data type. This can cause data to be stored differently than expected. While SQL_VARIANT does seem to choose well with numbers, there are cases where dates may be stored as VARCHAR(8000) if the data type is not specified.

All data types that can be stored in tables can be used for SQL_VARIANT except the following:

- VARCHAR(MAX)

- NVARCHAR(MAX)

- TEXT

- IMAGE

- SQL_VARIANT

- HIERARCHYID

- VARBINARY(MAX)

- XML

- NTEXT

- ROWVERSION

- GEOGRAPHY

- GEOMETRY

- DATETIMEOFFSET

- User-defined types

The way data in a SQL_VARIANT columns is ordered also differs from other data types. SQL_VARIANT groups data into like types called data type families. These data type families have their own order, and values with data types in higher families will be considered greater than values in lower families. If a data that is being compared exists in same family, SQL_VARIANT will implicitly convert the data type that is lower to the data type that is higher and then complete the comparison.

Rowversion

There are instances where you may want to know when an action happened to a table. While there are some methods that can be used to track database changes, there is also a specific data type that can be used to record when a record has been updated.

The ROWVERSION data type allows you to get a relative idea on when a specific record or set of records was updated. This value neither has a date nor time component but is a binary value. The ROWVERSION can be compared to other rowversion values or to the current rowversion value in the database. I can create a table with that has a column named RowVersion with the type ROWVERSION. Upon inserting a record, the ROWVERSION column may be updated to have the value 0x00000000000007D1. I can update one of the columns in the same row, and the ROWVERSION column may be updated to 0x00000000000007D2. While I can tell a change has happened, I cannot determine when the change happened or determine what was changed.

When storing the rowversion value, the total storage space required is 8 bytes. You can specify if ROWVERSION should be either non-nullable or nullable. If the column is not nullable, then the column will act similarly to BINARY(8). Otherwise, the column will behave similarly to VARBINARY(8). Only one ROWVERSION column can be added per table. This column will be updated systematically any time one or more rows is inserted or updated.

HIERARCHYID

Sometimes data is related to the other data in the same column. Oftentimes this has to do with data that is a parent or child of other data. This can involve locations like countries, states, and cities or product information like manufacture, item, and production date.

For these scenarios, the HIERARCHYID may be useful to help categorize how data is interrelated. The data type HIERARCHYID is limited to 892 bytes. However, this data type is a system data type with a variable length. Even though this data type is a system data type, the application using this data type is responsible for determining the correct hierarchy that should be stored.

Table

Some data types cannot exist as columns in tables. The table data type is one of those. When you find yourself wanting to store data for later use, this may be a good data type to consider. However, there are some caveats and limitations to keep in mind with using tables as a data type.

Usually, it is preferable to limit the use of table variables to scenarios where there will not be a significant amount of data returned. Historically, SQL Server has not accurately estimated the total number of rows in a table variable. However, starting with SQL Server 2019 the database engine should give a better estimation when dealing with table variables going forward.

While table variables can be used in stored procedures, batches, or functions, the table variable only exists for the duration of that object. In the case of functions or stored procedures, the table variable no longer exists after the function or stored procedure has completed executing. In the case of batches, the table will exist for the entirety of the batch. As table variables only persist for the entirety of an update, using them may decrease the locks required as part of an update.

Another limitation of tables as data types is that there are no statistics generated on the table variable. This also means that using indexes with table variables is very limited. As a matter of fact, indexes could not be created on table variables until SQL Server 2014. Starting with SQL Server 2014, some indexes can be included when creating a table variable.

Cursor

Another data type that cannot be used as a column in a table is cursor. Overall, this data type can be very limited, but there are occasions where this is the best data type for the task. When considering this data type, it is best to understand the potential performance impact associated with using the cursor data type.

The cursor data type is usually used as a variable. However, this data type can also be used as an output from a stored procedure. In either case, the cursor data type takes a set of data and interacts with each record row by row. Since the cursor data type can hold a set of data, it is also possible for this data type to have no data. This indicates that the cursor data type is nullable.

Most of the uses for this data type have to do with creating and using a cursor. In order to create a cursor, a local variable must be declared as a cursor. Like other local variables, it is possible to either declare the cursor and populate values or declare the cursor and populate values using a set statement. Other functions used to create cursors can be used with this data type. This include open, fetch, close, deallocate, and cursor_status. In addition, there are system stored procedures that have cursor data types.

One of the key factors in understanding the various data types available is knowing which data type to use. In some cases, using the correct data type may come down to saving space. Other times, using an incorrect data type could lead to significant performance issues. You also want to be consistent in how you use and reference your data types both in your T-SQL code and database objects. If SQL Server needs to compare two different types, SQL Server will need to convert at least one of the data types so that both data types are the same. This process is known as implicit conversion. The CPU cost associated with implicit conversion can be significant and should be avoided if possible. The best way to avoid implicit conversion is to use the same data types for fields that will be compared. The biggest challenge is that sometimes it takes several years to realize how an incorrect data type may be negatively impacting application performance.

CHAPTER 2

Database Objects

You often need to know more than just the right data types to write T-SQL that performs quickly and uses hardware efficiently. Data types will help you determine how your data should be stored, but the next step will be to design the process to access that data. One of the largest benefits and drawbacks to using T-SQL is the number of options available to access data. The expectation is that you are already familiar with how to write T-SQL to read, insert, update, or delete data.

In this chapter, I will discuss various methods that can be used to interact with your data. There are objects that will allow you to consistently and quickly pull information together. You may also want a database object that performs small, quick actions and can reuse that code for multiple purposes. Some database objects can store information temporarily for reusability either within the same batch or connection. Other database objects can perform actions as result of activities on the server or database objects. While T-SQL performs best with set-based activities, you may also find yourself needing to loop through data one record at a time.

Depending on your purpose, there can be one or more database objects that meet your needs. While each of these database objects has their place, there are pros and cons for when and how to use each of these objects. Throughout this chapter, I will walk through various scenarios showing both the positive and negative consequences of using each of these database objects. First, I will start with discussing views in T-SQL.

Views

What is a view? Like the definition of the word view, a view in T-SQL is a means of taking several different items and putting them together to form one cohesive image. In this section, I will be discussing some of the options available when using views. As with any tool, there are advantages to using views, and there are risks associated with views if they are used incorrectly.

25

© Elizabeth Noble 2020
E. Noble, *Pro T-SQL 2019*, https://doi.org/10.1007/978-1-4842-5590-2_2

User-Defined Views

The term user-defined view is the full name for the basic version of a view. One of the results of a view is simplicity. It is one way for applications and users to access complex sets of information without needing to understand all the relationships in a database. There is some additional functionality for protection and security that is available when using views. I will go through examples of views that help performance as well as some situations where views may not be the right option.

For standard user-defined views, SQL Server does not store the actual data returned by a view physically. Therefore, each time a view is called, it will use the statement inside the view to pull back the data that currently exists. One of the advantages for this method is it allows users accessing these views to look at code that is cleaner and easier to read. Another feature of views is that users can be granted permission to the view but not the associated tables. This can allow users to have access to some but not all the data from the tables that make up the view.

Let's start out with comparing the performance of a view to the performance of the same query as an ad hoc query or a stored procedure. Listing 2-1 shows the query that will be used as the basis for the comparison.

Listing 2-1. Query for Analysis

```
SELECT meal.MealTypeName, rec.RecipeName, rec.ServingQuantity, ing.
IngredientName
FROM dbo.Recipe rec
     INNER JOIN dbo.MealType meal
     ON rec.MealTypeID = meal.MealTypeID
     INNER JOIN dbo.RecipeIngredient recing
     ON rec.RecipeID = recing.RecipeID
     INNER JOIN dbo.Ingredient ing
     ON recing.IngredientID = ing.IngredientID
```

This query will be used as the basis for comparing how views can affect performance. In the case of this query, the logic is simple. In Listing 2-2, the query shows how to make a view using the following T-SQL code.

Listing 2-2. Creating a View

```
CREATE VIEW dbo.AvailableMeal
AS
SELECT meal.MealTypeName, rec.RecipeName, rec.ServingQuantity, ing.
IngredientName
FROM dbo.Recipe rec
     INNER JOIN dbo.MealType meal
     ON rec.MealTypeID = meal.MealTypeID
     INNER JOIN dbo.RecipeIngredient recing
     ON rec.RecipeID = recing.RecipeID
     INNER JOIN dbo.Ingredient ing
     ON recing.IngredientID = ing.IngredientID
```

Once the view has been created, it becomes much simpler to use the view to pull back the same information as the original query. Listing 2-3 shows how the view can be used to simplify pulling back data from SQL Server.

Listing 2-3. Calling the View

```
SELECT MealTypeName, RecipeName, IngredientName
FROM dbo.AvailableMeal
```

While having a simplified way to access data is nice, another consideration is how the view performs vs. the query. In general, you might expect the view to perform the same as the query that exists inside the view. Figure 2-1 shows the actual query execution plan for the ad hoc query.

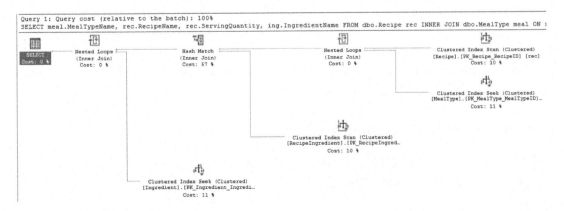

Figure 2-1. Ad Hoc Query Execution Plan

Comparing this to the query execution plan for the view in Figure 2-2, you can see there is no difference between the execution plans.

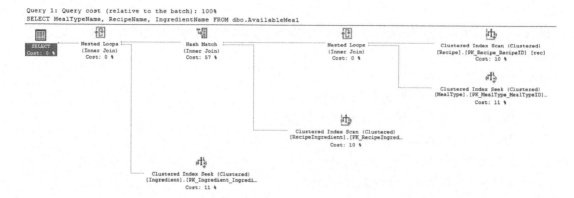

Figure 2-2. Execution Plan for View

One of the issues that can occur when using views is that the execution plan does not clearly show the relationship between the view and the underlying tables. While views can make things simpler to use, there are other ways you may want to use views. As views make interacting with complex queries simpler, it may also make modifying data easier. However, there are some caveats that you need to consider when updating data through views. In Listing 2-4, you can see the query to update data based upon the view.

Listing 2-4. Update Data in View

```
UPDATE dbo.AvailableMeal
SET IngredientName = 'Spicy Italian Sausage'
WHERE RecipeName = 'Spaghetti'
```

Through a view you can update data from the base table. If a view is used to modify data from more than one base table, then the update will fail. The same is true for inserts as it is for updates. In Listing 2-5, you can see what happens when you attempt to insert a record for data in more than one table.

Listing 2-5. Insert Data Through a View

```
INSERT INTO dbo.AvailableMeal (MealTypeName, RecipeName)
VALUES ('Lunch', 'Spinach Quiche')
```

When trying to execute the preceding query, SQL Server returns the error "View or function 'dbo.AvailableMeal' is not updatable because the modification affects multiple base tables." There are other features available when using views. There is a way to prevent an underlying table from being modified when they are referenced by a view. If you want to make sure that users cannot accidentally drop a table, having a view reference table with SCHEMABINDING is an available option. You can implement this additional level of security using a query like the one in Listing 2-6.

Listing 2-6. Create a View with Schema Binding

```
CREATE VIEW dbo.RecipeSecure
WITH SCHEMABINDING
AS

SELECT RecipeName, RecipeDescription, IsActive
FROM dbo.Recipe;
```

When adding SCHEMABINDING to a view, I have changed how SQL Server handles changes to the columns contained within the view. Specifically, I cannot modify columns in the dbo.Recipe table in a way that would impact the view dbo.RecipeSecure. Listing 2-7 shows a query where I am trying to drop a column in the dbo.Recipe table that is referenced by the dbo.RecipeSecure schema.

Listing 2-7. Remove Column in Schemabound View

```
ALTER TABLE dbo.Recipe
DROP COLUMN RecipeDescription;
```

When trying to execute the preceding query, I get the following error "The object 'RecipeSecure' is dependent on column 'RecipeDescription'. ALTER TABLE DROP COLUMN RecipeDescription failed because one or more objects access this column." However, there is also a potential loophole regarding protecting data. Once a view is created, the original column name can be replaced to use a different column as long as the field is aliased with the same column name. Going back to the view created in Listing 2-2, I can try to change the values returned. This can create a scenario where users can access data that they should not be able to access. In Listing 2-8, I have altered the original dbo.AvailableMeal view.

Listing 2-8. Alter View to Change Column

```
ALTER VIEW dbo.AvailableMeal
AS
SELECT meal.MealTypeName,
       rec.RecipeName,
       rec.RecipeDescription AS ServingQuantity,
       ing.IngredientName
FROM dbo.Recipe rec
       INNER JOIN dbo.MealType meal
       ON rec.MealTypeID = meal.MealTypeID
       INNER JOIN dbo.RecipeIngredient recing
       ON rec.RecipeID = recing.RecipeID
       INNER JOIN dbo.Ingredient ing
       ON recing.IngredientID = ing.IngredientID;
```

Previously, I had a user that only had permission to access the data within the view dbo.AvailableMeal. My intention was to allow this user to only have access to the original columns in the view. This same user attempts to query the view at a later date, this same user is now able to see the data in the RecipeDescription column.

Throughout all these features, one of the largest issues remains around nested views. In typical software development, there is a desire to reuse the same software code in multiple scenarios. When creating views, it can become tempting to reuse those views to create other views. Unfortunately, this can create a situation where one view can start performing poorly. Once the view is performing poorly, it can take considerable effort to weave through the various layers of nested views to find the root cause.

Indexed View

I have covered how views can be used to simplify writing queries, to modify data, and to protect database schemas. I have also covered how reusing views to create other views can cause significant performance issues. As you saw in the previous section, views can help make T-SQL simpler, but the execution plan is the same for both the ad hoc query and the view. In some instances, there are joins that do not perform well either as a query or a view. There is the possibility of adding indexes to a view.

If you find yourself in a situation where you need to improve the performance of view, you have the option of adding indexes to a view. When adding indexes to a view, the view is then considered an indexed view. The first index added to a view must be a clustered index. After a clustered index has been added, non-clustered indexes can also be added to the view. However, there is a cost associated with adding indexes to a view. Each time data is modified, the indexes on any related table and the indexed view must also be updated.

The first step in creating an indexed view is to create view. In this example, I will be using the view created in Listing 2-2. The next step will be to add an index to this view. In Listing 2-9, I will add a clustered index to this view.

Listing 2-9. Add Clustered Index to a View

```
CREATE UNIQUE CLUSTERED INDEX CX_AvailableMeal_RecipeNameIngredientName
    ON dbo.AvailableMeal (RecipeName, IngredientName);
```

Comparing the performance between the view before adding a clustered index and after shows an improvement in performance overall. Remember that while there are situations where indexed views can help performance when pulling back the data, there can still be performance issues that happen when data is inserted, updated, or deleted on the affected tables. In Figure 2-3, see the execution plan for when data is inserted into the base table.

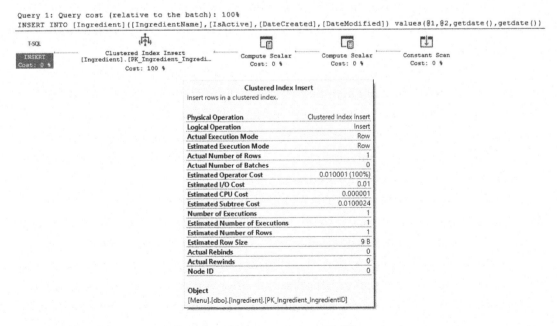

Figure 2-3. *Execution Plan for Insert into Base Table*

As you can see, there is an extra step where the index on the view is updated as part of the insert into the base table.

Functions

In many applications, there are core parts of the functionality that may be recalculated or reused several times. Sometimes you may want to write some simple piece of code once and reuse that code throughout various other database objects. There are other situations where you may want to take complex logic and create a database object that encompasses that logic and returns the required results. This could be done to make T-SQL code appear less complex and therefore less overwhelming. Either way, functions can help you simplify your T-SQL code.

Scalar Functions

You may find yourself in a situation where you need to rerun the same portion of code in many different scenarios. You may be looking up a configuration value, or you may want to rerun the same basic logic in many different parts of your code where only one value is returned. When there are times where you want to pass zero or more parameters and you only want to return a single value, you may be able to use a scalar function. However, you will want to consider what the potential cost on may be when using a scalar function.

Prior to SQL Server 2019, scalar functions worked very differently in SQL Server. Historically, SQL Server did not include cost-based optimization on scalar functions. This often meant that scalar functions were not included as part of the execution plan. Now that SQL Server 2019 has implemented additional features as part of the intelligent query processing, including scalar user-defined function (UDF) inlining, the performance of functions has improved.

An inline function is one that can be included as part of the execution plan. One of the largest advantages of inlining scalar UDFs is the significantly improved performance when it comes to using scalar UDFs. When wanting to simplify complex processes and reuse code, scalar UDFs are the ideal option when the function only needs to return one result.

The difference between scalar UDFs between prior versions of SQL Server and SQL Server 2019 in terms of performance is significant. To compare these execution plans, I will change the compatibility mode to match that of SQL Server 2017 and SQL Server

2019. Compatibility mode 140 will use the optimizer as it works in SQL Server 2017. Putting the compatibility mode of the data to 150 will then use the optimizer available in SQL Server 2019. Listing 2-10 shows the code necessary to create a scalar UDF in T-SQL.

Listing 2-10. Creating a Scalar UDF

```
CREATE FUNCTION dbo.Ingredient_Price
(
     @Cost DECIMAL(6,3),
     @Count DECIMAL(6,3)
)
RETURNS DECIMAL (6,3) AS
BEGIN
       RETURN @Cost / @Count;
END
```

When executing the preceding function in compatibility mode 140, the execution plan ends up appearing to be simpler than the execution plan generated in compatibility mode 150. In Listing 2-11, you can see the code that I executed in both compatibility mode 140 and 150.

Listing 2-11. Code to Execute Function

```
SELECT ing.IngredientName, dbo.Ingredient_Price(ingcos.Cost, srv.
ServingPortionQuantity)
FROM dbo.Ingredient ing
     INNER JOIN dbo.IngredientCost ingcos
     ON ing.IngredientID = ingcos.IngredientID
     INNER JOIN dbo.ServingPortion srv
     ON ingcos.ServingPortionID = srv.ServingPortionID
```

In order to simulate the behavior of SQL Server 2017, I will change the compatibility mode of the database to 140. You can see the T-SQL code needed to change the compatibility mode in Listing 2-12.

Listing 2-12. Change Database Compatibility Mode to Previous Version

```
ALTER DATABASE Menu
SET COMPATIBILITY_LEVEL = 140;
```

The query in Listing 2-13 allows us to force SQL Server to generate new execution plans for all queries using compatibility level 140.

Listing 2-13. Clear Execution Plan for Query from Listing 2-11

```
DBCC FREEPROCCACHE;
```

It is important to note that the preceding T-SQL code should not be run in your Production environments. This code will cause SQL Server to use additional resources to determine how every query should be run the first time the query is called. I saved the actual execution plan from running the preceding query using compatibility mode 140. You can see a copy of this actual execution plan in Figure 2-4.

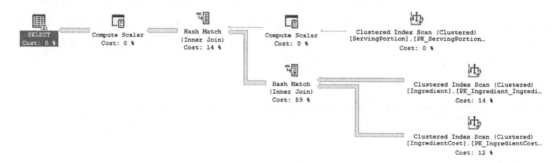

Figure 2-4. *Execution Plan for Compatibility Mode 140*

Looking at the actual execution plan for compatibility mode 150, you can see that the execution plan appears more complex. However, you can also see that the scalar function is included in the execution plan in Figure 2-5.

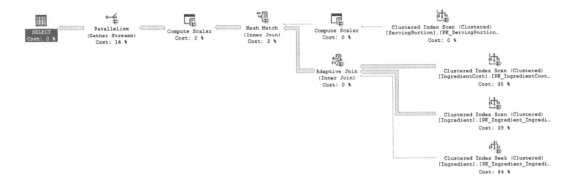

Figure 2-5. *Execution Plan for Compatibility Mode 150*

While the execution plan for SQL Server 2019 may be more complex, the execution time between these two versions of SQL Server is significant. We can also compare the CPU and elapsed times for both compatibility mode 140 and 150. In Table 2-1, you can see the CPU and elapsed times for both query executions.

Table 2-1. *Elapsed and CPU Times for Query Execution*

Compatibility Mode	CPU Time	Elapsed Time
140	3438 milliseconds	4768 milliseconds
150	655 milliseconds	1913 milliseconds

As you can see, the function performs significantly better in compatibility mode 150 vs. 140.

The ability to inline scalar UDFs in SQL Server 2019 does not apply only to single query scalar UDFs. There is also improved functionality when it comes to using multi-statement scalar UDFs. Multi-statement scalar UDFs return a single value similarly to the scalar UDF created in Listing 2-10. The difference with a multi-statement scalar UDF is that additional logic can exist within the function. We may want to improve the function created in Listing 2-10 so that the function can handle a divide by zero error. In Listing 2-14, I have written the T-SQL code to enhance Listing 2-10 by using a multi-statement scalar UDF.

Listing 2-14. Create Multi-Statement Scalar UDF

```
 CREATE OR ALTER FUNCTION dbo.Ingredient_Price
(
     @Cost DECIMAL(6,3),
     @Count DECIMAL(6,3)
)
RETURNS DECIMAL (6,3) AS

BEGIN
     DECLARE @IngPrc DECIMAL (6,3)

     IF @Count = 0
          BEGIN
               SET @IngPrc =  0.00
          END
     ELSE
          BEGIN
               SET @IngPrc = @Cost / @Count;
          END
     RETURN @IngPrc
END;
```

The multi-statement scalar UDF created in Listing 2-14 will benefit from the same scalar inlining as the scalar UDF created in Listing 2-10. Regardless of the scalar UDF you decide to use, SQL Server 2019 has been improved so that you can see improved performance with these functions.

Table-Valued Functions

There will be situations where you find yourself needing to perform complex logic, but you need to return more than one value. When these situations come up, you may want to consider using a table-valued function. Prior to SQL Server 2019, the only function that could run inline was a variation of table-valued functions.

Table-valued functions are useful for those times where you need a table as a result. This could be anything from one row with multiple columns to one column with the potential for multiple rows or many rows and many columns. No matter your purpose, if you want a reusable piece of code that can give you a table output, then table-valued functions may be what you want. Keep in mind that there are two main types of table-valued functions, and while the output can look the same, the performance of each of these types can be incredibly different.

Inline Table-Valued Functions

If you're using a function to perform some complex logic, but you can survive only using a select statement, then you may want to learn more about how inline table-valued user-defined functions can work for you. It is important to note that you do not specifically indicate that a function is inline or multi-statement. It is how you create and declare the function that will determine which type of function you have created.

Like the inline scalar user-defined functions (UDFs) available in SQL Server 2019, table-valued functions can also be inlined. Also be aware that table-valued functions have been able to be inlined for quite some time, while inlining scalar UDFs is quite new. Either way, the advantage is clear. When a table-valued function can be run inline with the rest of the query, the optimizer can provide a better execution plan for the function and the T-SQL code overall.

Historically, the most popular use for inline table-valued functions is to operate similarly to views. Except that in the case of inline table-valued functions, parameters can be used to limit the data returned; whereas views will return all data available to the view for each execution. Let's look at the steps necessary to create an inline table-valued function in Listing 2-15.

Listing 2-15. Create Inline Table-Valued Function

```
CREATE FUNCTION dbo.IngredientsByRecipe (@RecipeID INT)
RETURNS TABLE
AS
RETURN
(
    SELECT meal.MealTypeName, rec.ServingQuantity, ing.IngredientName
    FROM dbo.Recipe rec
        INNER JOIN dbo.MealType meal
        ON rec.MealTypeID = meal.MealTypeID
        INNER JOIN dbo.RecipeIngredient recing
        ON rec.RecipeID = recing.RecipeID
```

```
        INNER JOIN dbo.Ingredient ing
        ON recing.IngredientID = ing.IngredientID
    WHERE rec.RecipeID = @RecipeID
);
GO
```

The process to create an inline table-valued function is straightforward. There can be concerns about the impact functions have on performance. I can see how an inline table-valued function performs; I will need to run a query using this function so that we can see what happens in the execution plan. In Listing 2-16, there is the script that will be run to determine the effectiveness of an execution plan.

Listing 2-16. Query to Call Inline Table-Valued Function

```
SELECT * FROM dbo.IngredientsByRecipe (1);
```

I will show the execution plan generated from the code in Listing 2-16 as it was returned in SQL Server 2019. You can see the execution plan in Figure 2-6.

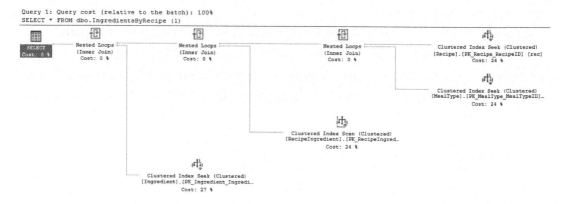

Figure 2-6. *Inline Table-Valued Function Execution Plan*

As you can see, the function appears directly in the execution plan. The optimizer is aware of this inline table-valued function. While inline table-valued UDFs can be used like tables and can accept parameters, there are still limitations associated with using inline table-valued UDFs. These types of functions can only allow for one select statement and one result set. In addition, the data that is returned in these functions cannot be modified in the database. However, data returned from an inline table-valued UDF that is displayed in a select statement can be modified. This is a change to the data that is cosmetic and does not affect the data that is stored in the database.

Multi-statement Table-Valued Functions

When there are times that you must have both code reuse and the ability to update SQL Server, then it may be time to consider using multi-statement table-valued functions. I would caution you to carefully consider whether this approach is necessary as these types of functions can end up having a tremendous performance impact.

Multi-statement table-valued functions are not just inline table-valued functions that can do more. They also cannot be inlined with the query execution. This signifies that the query optimizer does not attempt a best guess when using these types of functions. As a matter of fact, prior to SQL Server 2014, multi-statement table-valued functions were estimated to have one row. For SQL Server 2014 and SQL Server 2016, the estimated number of rows was 100. However, as of SQL Server 2017, there is a possibility that SQL Server will get a proper estimate for the rows returned by using interleaved execution.

What will happen is that the optimization process will pause to allow execution so that the cardinality estimator can determine the actual number of rows that should be returned by the multi-statement table-valued function. While interleaved execution is part of the new adaptive query processing, there are some limitations to keep in mind. If there is a CROSS APPLY used in conjunction with a multi-statement table-valued function, then the interleaved functionality will not work. It has also been reported that if there is a WHERE clause inside the multi-statement table-valued function that depends on an input parameter, then interleaved execution may also not apply.

To get a better idea of how this all works, I will create the multi-statement table-valued function in Listing 2-17. I will create this function in SQL Server 2012, SQL Server 2017, and SQL Server 2019.

Listing 2-17. Multi-statement Table-Valued Function

```
CREATE FUNCTION dbo.IngredientCostByIngredientID (@IngredientID INT)
RETURNS @Output TABLE
(
    IngredientName      VARCHAR(25),
    IngredientCost      DECIMAL(6,3)
)
AS
    BEGIN
        INSERT INTO @Output (IngredientName, IngredientCost)
        SELECT ing.IngredientName, ingcos.Cost
```

```
FROM dbo.Ingredient ing
        INNER JOIN dbo.IngredientCost ingcos
        ON ing.IngredientID = ingcos.IngredientID
    WHERE ing.IngredientID = @IngredientID;
    RETURN;
  END;
GO
```

Now that this function has been created, I can write a script to test the performance of this function in the various versions of SQL Server. The following code is the T-SQL written and executed as shown in Listing 2-18.

Listing 2-18. Code to Execute Function

```
SELECT rec.RecipeName, inglis.IngredientName, inglis.IngredientCost
FROM    dbo.Recipe rec
    INNER JOIN dbo.RecipeIngredient recing
    ON rec.RecipeID = recing.RecipeID
    INNER JOIN dbo.Ingredient ing
    ON recing.IngredientID = ing.IngredientID
    CROSS APPLY dbo.IngredientCostByIngredientID(ing.IngredientID) inglis
WHERE ing.IngredientName = 'Italian Sausage';
```

Next, I will test the execution plans and relative performance across the various versions of SQL Server. In Figure 2-7, I will show the execution plan in SQL Server 2012 by using the compatibility mode 110.

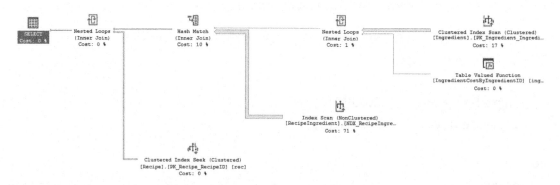

Figure 2-7. *Execution Plan for Compatibility Mode 110*

The execution plan does not appear to have too many different operators. The table-valued function is represented as a single operator. The properties for the table-valued function are shown in Figure 2-8.

Table Valued Function	
Table valued function.	
Physical Operation	Table Valued Function
Logical Operation	Table Valued Function
Actual Execution Mode	Row
Estimated Execution Mode	Row
Number of Rows Read	1
Actual Number of Rows	1
Actual Number of Batches	0
Estimated Operator Cost	0.0000012 (0%)
Estimated I/O Cost	0
Estimated CPU Cost	0.0000012
Estimated Subtree Cost	0.0000012
Number of Executions	1
Estimated Number of Executions	1
Estimated Number of Rows	1
Estimated Row Size	28 B
Actual Rebinds	1
Actual Rewinds	0
Node ID	5

Object
[Menu].[dbo].[IngredientCostByIngredientID] [inglis]
Output List
[Menu].[dbo].
[IngredientCostByIngredientID].IngredientName, [Menu].
[dbo].[IngredientCostByIngredientID].IngredientCost

Figure 2-8. *Properties for Table-Valued Function in Compatibility Mode 110*

Figure 2-8 shows the estimated number of rows as 1. Additional enhancements were made to the database engine in SQL Server 2017. The estimation for the number of rows for a table-valued function was improved. Using the compatibility mode 140 for SQL Server 2017, you can see the execution plan generated in Figure 2-9.

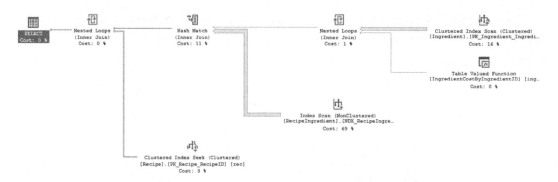

Figure 2-9. *Execution Plan for Compatibility Mode 140*

Figure 2-9 looks like the same as Figure 2-7. The only visible differences are on the percentages displayed for some of the operators. The percentage variance is not significant enough to affect the performance of the execution of this query in both compatibility modes 110 and 140. You can see the execution times in Table 2-2.

Table 2-2. *Comparing Execution Time for Multi-statement Table-Valued Function with Compatibility Modes 110 and 140*

Compatibility Mode	CPU Time	Elapsed Time
110	1172 milliseconds	1529 milliseconds
140	1140 milliseconds	1523 milliseconds

The times displayed here are close enough to be considered comparable. While the execution plans and times are similar, we can also check and see if the properties on the table-valued function are the same. In Figure 2-10, we can see the properties associated with the table-valued function.

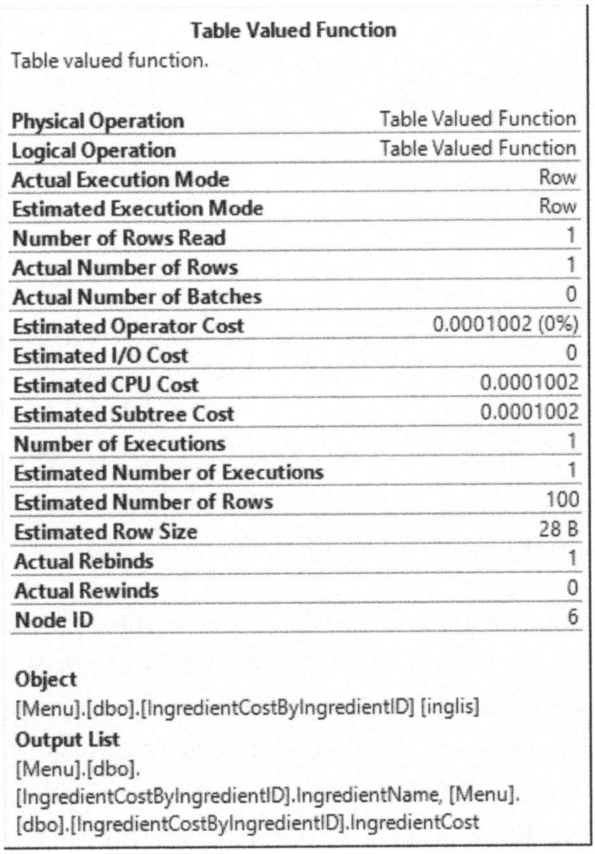

Table Valued Function

Table valued function.

Physical Operation	Table Valued Function
Logical Operation	Table Valued Function
Actual Execution Mode	Row
Estimated Execution Mode	Row
Number of Rows Read	1
Actual Number of Rows	1
Actual Number of Batches	0
Estimated Operator Cost	0.0001002 (0%)
Estimated I/O Cost	0
Estimated CPU Cost	0.0001002
Estimated Subtree Cost	0.0001002
Number of Executions	1
Estimated Number of Executions	1
Estimated Number of Rows	100
Estimated Row Size	28 B
Actual Rebinds	1
Actual Rewinds	0
Node ID	6

Object
[Menu].[dbo].[IngredientCostByIngredientID] [inglis]
Output List
[Menu].[dbo].
[IngredientCostByIngredientID].IngredientName, [Menu].
[dbo].[IngredientCostByIngredientID].IngredientCost

Figure 2-10. *Properties for Table-Valued Function in Compatibility Mode 140*

You can see that the estimated number rows in Figure 2-10 is 100. This is different from the estimated number of rows shown in Figure 2-8. You can also see that the estimated operator cost and estimated subtree cost have all changed slightly.

Now that we have run the query from Listing 2-18, we can now run the same query using the optimizer from SQL Server 2019. Before we do this, we will need to change the compatibility level back to 150 and clear the execution plan cache. Once this has been done and we execute the query from Listing 2-18, we get an execution plan like the one in Figure 2-11.

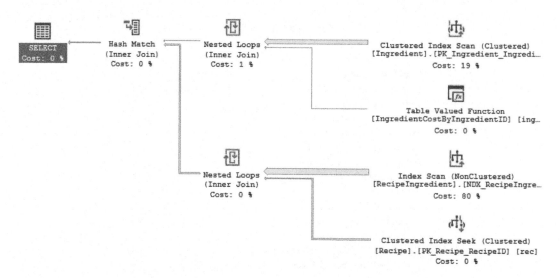

Figure 2-11. *Execution Plan for Compatibility Mode 150*

The execution plan in Figure 2-11 is different from either of the execution plans in Figure 2-7 and Figure 2-9. We can also see that the Index Scan on one of the non-clustered indexes from the dbo.RecipeIngredient table takes the majority of time to execute. As expected, this is the same operator that takes the majority of time in the execution plans for Figures 2-7, 2-9, and 2-11. We can also compare the elapsed and CPU times across compatibility levels 110, 140, and 150. This will allow us to compare the expected execution times from the SQL Server optimizer from SQL Server 2012, SQL Server 2017, and SQL Server 2019. Table 2-3 shows all three compatibility levels and their associated times.

Table 2-3. *Comparing Execution Time for Multi-statement Table-Valued Function with Compatibility Modes 110, 140, and 150*

Compatibility Mode	CPU Time	Elapsed Time
110	1172 milliseconds	1529 milliseconds
140	1140 milliseconds	1523 milliseconds
150	391 milliseconds	644 milliseconds

Table 2-3 shows a dramatically improved execution time as compared to either compatibility level 110 or 140. I can also compare the table-valued function properties from Listing 2-10 which represented the compatibility level associated with SQL Server 2017 to those of compatibility level 150. In Figure 2-12, I have the properties for the table-valued function in compatibility mode 150.

Table Valued Function	
Table valued function.	
Physical Operation	Table Valued Function
Logical Operation	Table Valued Function
Actual Execution Mode	Row
Estimated Execution Mode	Row
Number of Rows Read	1
Actual Number of Rows	1
Actual Number of Batches	0
Estimated Operator Cost	0.0001002 (0%)
Estimated I/O Cost	0
Estimated CPU Cost	0.0001002
Estimated Subtree Cost	0.0001002
Number of Executions	1
Estimated Number of Executions	1
Estimated Number of Rows	100
Estimated Row Size	28 B
Actual Rebinds	1
Actual Rewinds	0
Node ID	3
Object	
[Menu].[dbo].[IngredientCostByIngredientID] [inglis]	
Output List	
[Menu].[dbo].[IngredientCostByIngredientID].IngredientName, [Menu].[dbo].[IngredientCostByIngredientID].IngredientCost	

Figure 2-12. *Properties for Table-Valued Function in Compatibility Mode 150*

Looking at the values in Figure 2-12, there are several values that match those of Figure 2-10. This includes the more accurate estimated number of rows in both Figure 2-10 and Figure 2-12. The estimated operator cost, estimated CPU cost, and estimated subtree cost are also the same in both Figure 2-10 and Figure 2-12.

The performance of the multi-statement table-valued function improves in the newer versions of SQL Server. In addition, you can see that both SQL Server 2017 and SQL Server 2019 have the most accurate estimated and actual rows returned in the execution plan. While there still are performance concerns to keep in mind with multi-statement table-valued functions, there are scenarios where the performance is improved enough that it may be beneficial to use these functions starting with SQL Server 2017.

Other User-Defined Objects

There are many ways of working with complex data and breaking data up into sections that can be easily managed and analyzed. In some cases, data can be saved to temporary tables or table variables. However, there are other options available depending on your needs. One type of feature in SQL Server is using table-valued parameters. This allows for similar performance as temporary table, but it also works similarly to table variables. There is also a method where a temporary result set is created for use in the next statement in a batch.

User-Defined Table Types

When working with databases and stored procedures, you may find yourself in a situation where you want to pass many fields into a stored procedure as a parameter. There is an option to create a user-defined table type that will allow you to specify multiple columns and data types. One advantage of creating a user-defined table type is that this table type can be reused. This user-defined table type can be applied to multiple different stored procedures or other database code. You can see an example of creating a user-defined table type in Listing 2-19.

Listing 2-19. Code to Create User-Defined Table Type

```
CREATE TYPE RecipeMealType AS TABLE
(
     RecipeName VARCHAR(25),
     MealTypeName VARCHAR(25)
);
GO
```

Once a user-defined table type has been created, it can be used as a parameter for a stored procedure or be used for variable declaration. The reusability and consistency that is created with user-defined table types comes with a cost. As the stored procedures now use a single parameter to represent all of the columns and rows stored in this object, it becomes difficult to determine what parameters in a stored procedure represent a single value and what parameters represent a user-defined table type. This object can make code easier to read; it can also make it harder to troubleshoot performance issues in the future.

Table-Valued Parameters

A high percentage of stored procedures can be used to insert, update, or delete data from tables. In some cases, the application may need to send one parameter per column of a table to various stored procedures. While using one parameter per field is straightforward and easy to debug, some can contend that it would be cleaner and simpler to send multiple fields in one parameter. I can understand wanting to simplify the code, but I also believe that too much simplification can make it difficult to troubleshoot code in the future.

However, you may want to use an array type format in a stored procedure or other code. In this case, it would be beneficial to use this data to perform a set-based operation. When doing so, you will need to remember that the user-defined table type that is passed in as a parameter cannot be modified. When this parameter is passed in, the data passed can be treated like a temporary table and used to join to the base table and make any necessary modifications.

As SQL Server is designed to perform best for set-based operations, you may get to the point where you want to take advantage of SQL Server's inherent ability to work best with sets. You may want to consider using table-valued parameters if you are wanting to pass in a table to a stored procedure and use that table relationally with other tables within the same stored procedure.

Since a table-valued parameter is ultimately a variable, SQL Server will not necessarily optimize the execution plan for the actual estimated number of rows. If you find yourself in this situation, you may need to take the values from the parameter and save them into a table variable within the stored procedure. I would advise against using table-valued parameters solely to improve readability of the code. Listing 2-20 shows an example of using a table-valued parameter in a stored procedure.

Listing 2-20. Using a Table-Valued Parameter

```
CREATE PROCEDURE dbo.UpdateRecipeMenuType
    @RecipeMeal RecipeMealType READONLY
AS
SET NOCOUNT ON
UPDATE rec
SET MealTypeID = meal.MealTypeID
FROM dbo.Recipe rec
    INNER JOIN @RecipeMeal recmeal
    ON rec.RecipeName = recmeal.RecipeName
    INNER JOIN dbo.MealType meal
    ON recmeal.MealTypeName = meal.MealTypeName
```

The table-valued parameter in Listing 2-20 is using the user-defined table type created in Listing 2-19. When you want to execute the stored procedure using the table-valued parameter, you can run the code in Listing 2-21.

Listing 2-21. Code to Execute Stored Procedure with Table-Valued Parameter

```
DECLARE @RecipeType AS RecipeMealType;

INSERT INTO @RecipeType (RecipeName, MealTypeName)
SELECT rec.RecipeName, ml.MealTypeName
FROM dbo.Recipe rec
    INNER JOIN dbo.MealType ml
    ON rec.MealTypeID = ml.MealTypeID;

EXEC dbo.UpdateRecipeMenuType @RecipeType;
GO
```

The execution plan from this code is in Figure 2-13. Notice the Table Scan on the table-valued parameter.

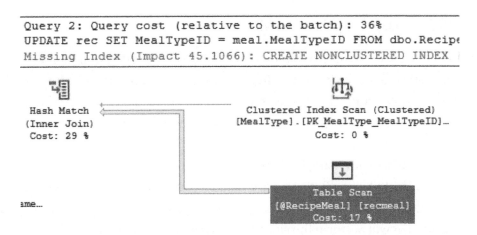

Figure 2-13. *Execution Plan for Stored Procedure with Table-Valued Parameter*

If we kept the indexed view created in Listing 2-9, the execution plan returned gets even more complex. Figure 2-14 shows the resulting execution plan if the indexed view still exists.

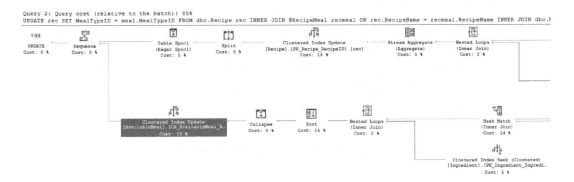

Figure 2-14. *Execution Plan for Table-Valued Parameter with an Indexed View*

While table-valued parameters can streamline your code, keep in mind that there can be a hidden performance impact. One of the best practices when developing new code is to check the execution plan and confirm that SQL Server is processing the code in a method that aligns with the shape of the data.

Common Table Expressions

While this is not a user-defined database object, I have included common table expressions in this section as they are often used for similar purposes as temporary tables, table variables, and table-valued parameters. Their purpose is to help break up complex logic or get a subset of data to be used later in the T-SQL code, batch, or stored procedure.

The primary reason for using basic common table expressions is to improve overall readability of code. In Listing 2-22, I have created a common table expression using the same logic as the view that was created in Listing 2-2. The expectation is that when this code is executed, it will perform the same as the view created earlier.

Listing 2-22. Create a Basic Common Table Expression

```
WITH cte_meal AS
(
    SELECT meal.MealTypeName, rec.RecipeName, rec.ServingQuantity,
    ing.IngredientName
    FROM dbo.Recipe rec
        INNER JOIN dbo.MealType meal
        ON rec.MealTypeID = meal.MealTypeID
        INNER JOIN dbo.RecipeIngredient recing
        ON rec.RecipeID = recing.RecipeID
        INNER JOIN dbo.Ingredient ing
        ON recing.IngredientID = ing.IngredientID
)
SELECT meal.MealTypeName, meal.RecipeName, meal.ServingQuantity, meal.
IngredientName
FROM cte_meal meal
```

In Figure 2-15, you can see that the execution plan generated from Listing 2-22 matches the execution in Figure 2-6. If you recall, the execution plan in Figure 2-6 was generated from the view created in Listing 2-16.

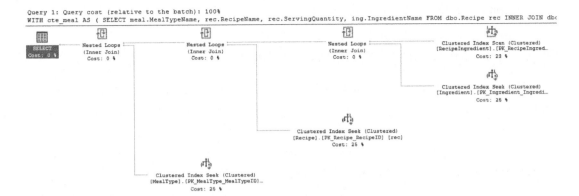

Query 1: Query cost (relative to the batch): 100%
WITH cte_meal AS (SELECT meal.MealTypeName, rec.RecipeName, rec.ServingQuantity, ing.IngredientName FROM dbo.Recipe rec INNER JOIN dbo

Figure 2-15. *Execution Plan for Basic Common Table Expression*

When you use a common table expression, you can also join the common table expression (CTE) to other tables as you would do for a view or a temporary table. You also get the ability to use CTEs to not only SELECT but also INSERT, UPDATE, and DELETE data based from the CTE. Listing 2-23 shows a query with more complex logic when using common table expressions.

Listing 2-23. Using Joins with Common Table Expressions

```
WITH cte_meal AS
(
      SELECT meal.MealTypeName, rec.RecipeName, rec.ServingQuantity, ing.
IngredientName
      FROM dbo.Recipe rec
            INNER JOIN dbo.MealType meal
            ON rec.MealTypeID = meal.MealTypeID
            INNER JOIN dbo.RecipeIngredient recing
            ON rec.RecipeID = recing.RecipeID
            INNER JOIN dbo.Ingredient ing
            ON recing.IngredientID = ing.IngredientID
)

SELECT meal.RecipeName, meal.IngredientName, SUM(ingcos.Cost) AS
'IngredientCost'
FROM cte_meal meal
      INNER JOIN dbo.Ingredient ing
      ON meal.IngredientName = ing.IngredientName
```

51

```
        INNER JOIN dbo.IngredientCost ingcos
        ON ingcos.IngredientID = ing.IngredientID
GROUP BY meal.RecipeName, meal.IngredientName
```

There is also one final piece of functionality related to common table expressions that makes them somewhat unique. You can create recursive common table expressions. In this scenario, a CTE will reference itself to help generate hierarchical data. It may be tempting to try to get recursive CTEs to solve many different issues. I would advise to use caution when implementing recursive CTEs. They can be the correct tool when needed, but they can also cause significant performance challenges. Listing 2-24 is an example of creating a recursive CTE to find child recipes that are required for the parent recipe.

Listing 2-24. Recursive CTE to Find All Required Recipes

```
WITH cte_meal (MealTypeName, RecipeName, ServingQuantity, IngredientName,
RecipeLevel) AS
(
        SELECT meal.MealTypeName, rec.RecipeName, rec.ServingQuantity,
        ing.IngredientName, 1
        FROM dbo.Ingredient ing
                INNER JOIN dbo.RecipeIngredient recing
                ON ing.IngredientID = recing.IngredientID
                INNER JOIN dbo.Recipe rec
                ON recing.RecipeID = rec.RecipeID
                INNER JOIN dbo.MealType meal
                ON rec.MealTypeID = meal.MealTypeID
                LEFT JOIN dbo.Ingredient baseing
                ON rec.RecipeName = baseing.IngredientName
        WHERE baseing.IngredientName IS NULL
        UNION ALL
        SELECT meal.MealTypeName, rec.RecipeName, meal.ServingQuantity,
        ing.IngredientName, meal.RecipeLevel + 1
        FROM cte_meal meal
                INNER JOIN dbo.Recipe rec
                ON meal.IngredientName = rec.RecipeName
                INNER JOIN dbo.RecipeIngredient recing
                ON rec.RecipeID = recing.RecipeID
```

```
        INNER JOIN dbo.Ingredient ing
        ON recing.IngredientID = ing.IngredientID
)

SELECT MealTypeName,
       RecipeName,
       IngredientName,
       RecipeLevel
FROM cte_meal meal
```

As you can see from the partial execution plan in Figure 2-16, the steps SQL Server
needs to take to execute this query get considerably more complex.

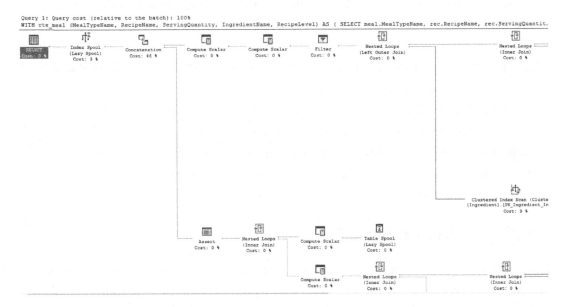

Figure 2-16. *Partial Execution Plan for Recursive CTE*

I have found very few times where I have needed to absolutely use a recursive
CTE. However, when I have had to use a common table expression, I have found them
very helpful.

Temporary Objects

You may find yourself in a situation where you need to create an object but only for a short period of time. Sometimes these objects are created so that you can work with a subset of data when dealing with complex logic. Other times it is easier to break some of the code out to create a temporary object to improve readability or make it easier for others to understand what you are doing. Regardless of the scenario, there is the possibility to create temporary objects in SQL Server.

Temporary Tables

Temporary tables are exactly what they sound like. They take the same shape as tables where they have columns and data types and stored data. The main difference is that temporary tables do not hang around indefinitely. Depending on what you want to do with your temporary tables and how long you need them to last will determine which type of temporary table you would end up creating.

There are other advantages to using temporary tables. These include the ability to use primary keys and indexes for improved performance. Statistics can also be created on temporary tables further improving their performance. One thing to consider is that statistics may not be automatically updated on the temporary table if additional modifications are performed after the temporary table is first created.

Local Temporary Tables

If you find yourself needing to put data aside for additional analysis or processing, then you may have considered using a local temporary table. This type of temporary table can also be useful inside of stored procedures. Local temporary tables are only available within the same session or connection as they were created. Once the session is closed or the connection is terminated, you are unable to access the local temporary table.

While local temporary tables can be used for many different scenarios, it is often recommended to not use temporary tables as the first option when needing to store data temporarily. There is nothing inherently wrong with local temporary tables, but you may find other objects can store data temporarily with less potential performance impact. As with all things related to SQL Server, it is best to implement a solution and test your solution including load testing before pushing the T-SQL code to Production.

Creating temporary tables is easy. While data can be inserted in a temporary table as part of table creation, it is considered best practice to create the temporary table with defined data type before inserting records. In Listing 2-25, there is code to generate a local temporary table. For comparison, this code used to populate this table is the same as the code used in Listing 2-2.

Listing 2-25. Create a Temporary Table

```
CREATE TABLE #TempAvailableMeal
(
        MealTypeName VARCHAR(25),
        RecipeName VARCHAR(25),
        ServingQuantity TINYINT,
        IngredientName VARCHAR(25)
)
```

Once the temporary table has been created, run the query in Listing 2-26 to populate the data in the table.

Listing 2-26. Populate the Temporary Table

```
INSERT INTO #TempAvailableMeal (MealTypeName, RecipeName, ServingQuantity,
IngredientName)
SELECT meal.MealTypeName, rec.RecipeName, rec.ServingQuantity, ing.
IngredientName
FROM dbo.Recipe rec
        INNER JOIN dbo.MealType meal
        ON rec.MealTypeID = meal.MealTypeID
        INNER JOIN dbo.RecipeIngredient recing
        ON rec.RecipeID = recing.RecipeID
        INNER JOIN dbo.Ingredient ing
        ON recing.IngredientID = ing.IngredientID
```

When I ran the process to populate the temporary table, I also got the execution plan for this process. In Figure 2-17, you will see that the execution plan looks like the ones generated for the view and the common table expression. While the shape is similar, some of the activities that are happening and the percent distribution are different.

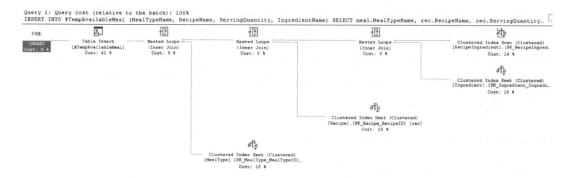

Figure 2-17. *Execution Plan to Create Temporary Table*

Now that we have determined what the execution plan is to create the temporary table, how does the execution plan look after we query from the temporary table? Listing 2-27 shows how to query the existing temporary table.

Listing 2-27. Query the Temporary Table

```
SELECT MealTypeName, RecipeName, ServingQuantity, IngredientName
FROM #TempAvailableMeal
```

So far, we have seen where most of the work for a query happen as the same time as when the data is originally selected. In this case, the insert and the select have been separated into two separate steps. Figure 2-18 is the execution that was generated when the data in the temporary table was queried.

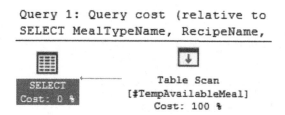

Figure 2-18. *Query the Temporary Table*

While this query used a Table Scan, it is possible to add indexes to a temporary table.

Global Temporary Tables

You may find yourself wanting to create a temporary table that exists for a longer period than just the current session or active database connection. Maybe you want a temporary table that can be accessed by more than one user. In this case, you may want to create a global temporary table. This global temporary table would exist even if the original session or connection that created the global temporary table is still available.

Creating a global temporary table is straightforward. If I wanted to re-create the temporary table in Listing 2-26 but make sure that the table was global, I could run the code in Listing 2-28 to create the global temporary table.

Listing 2-28. Create Global Temporary Table

```
INSERT INTO ##TempAvailableMeal (MealTypeName, RecipeName, ServingQuantity,
IngredientName)
SELECT meal.MealTypeName, rec.RecipeName, rec.ServingQuantity, ing.
IngredientName
FROM dbo.Recipe rec
     INNER JOIN dbo.MealType meal
     ON rec.MealTypeID = meal.MealTypeID
     INNER JOIN dbo.RecipeIngredient recing
     ON rec.RecipeID = recing.RecipeID
     INNER JOIN dbo.Ingredient ing
     ON recing.IngredientID = ing.IngredientID
```

The only change between creating a local and global temporary table is with the table name used during creation. Comparing the code in Listing 2-26 for a local temporary table and Listing 2-28 for a global temporary table, you can see the difference in the table names. In Listing 2-26, the table name is #TempAvailableMeal, while the temporary table name is ##TempAvailableMeal in Listing 2-28. The addition of the second # character at the beginning of the table name indicates that this temporary table is a global temporary table. In addition, global temporary tables operate similarly to local temporary tables. One of the key differences is global temporary tables can be accessed outside of the specific connection that created the temporary table.

Persistent Temporary Table

When working with temporary tables, you may want to create a table that exists in the tempdb database permanently. One thing to keep in mind is if you plan on creating a temporary table that exists permanently, the data will not be saved in the case where SQL Server is restarted. You can create a persistent temporary table by using the same sort of T-SQL as you would to create a table in a user database. An example of this database code can be found in Listing 2-29.

Listing 2-29. Create Persistent Temporary Table

```
USE tempdb;
GO

CREATE TABLE AvailableMeal
(
      MealTypeName VARCHAR(25),
      RecipeName VARCHAR(25),
      ServingQuantity TINYINT,
      IngredientName VARCHAR(25)
);
```

You can use the T-SQL code in Listing 2-29 to create a persistent table, but I would recommend a method that is more consistent with the use of tempdb. Instead you can create a stored procedure that executes when SQL Server starts. This stored procedure will then create any global temporary tables that you may need. You can use the T-SQL in Listing 2-30 to create a stored procedure to create global temporary tables.

Listing 2-30. Create Stored Procedure for Global Temporary Tables

```
CREATE PROCEDURE dbo.CreatePersistentTable
AS

      CREATE TABLE ##AvailableMeal
      (
            MealTypeName VARCHAR(25),
            RecipeName VARCHAR(25),
```

```
        ServingQuantity TINYINT,
        IngredientName VARCHAR(25)
    );
GO
```

Once the stored procedure in Listing 2-30 is created, you will want to modify the stored procedure options so that the stored procedure is executed when SQL Server restarts. The T-SQL in Listing 2-31 will allow you to modify the stored procedure to execute on startup.

Listing 2-31. Update Stored Procedure to Execute on Startup

```
EXEC sp_procoption 'CreatePersistentTable', 'startup', 'true'
```

If you find yourself in the situation where you are considering a persistent temporary table, consider your environment and what potential difficulty is being added in terms of maintenance and knowledge sharing so that everyone is aware a mission critical table may exist on the tempdb database.

Table Variables

There are instances where you want to store data locally, but you know that the number of records you will be storing is limited. If you do not need to have the data available to other connections and it is acceptable to only have the data persist within the batch, then you may want to try out using table variables. When it comes to using table variables, you also have the option to reuse the table variable as many times as you would like if you are willing to keep everything in the same batch.

Prior to SQL Server 2019, the estimated number of rows for a table variable was one record. Like other objects discussed previously in this chapter, SQL Server has made significant strides to improve general performance related to table variable. SQL Server is now capable of generating a more accurate estimated number of rows when it comes to using table variables. Now that SQL Server is estimating the number of rows more accurately, it is also saving that logic in the execution plan.

If you find yourself in a situation where the data that will be pulled back with the table variable can be highly skewed, you may find that the T-SQL code will perform inconsistently. Now that the information about the table variable is getting stored in the execution plan, there is a higher probability of coming across parameter sniffing. While this may be troublesome, remember that SQL Server is also generating an execution plan that can be highly efficient for at least some data values.

Like temporary tables, table variables can be straightforward to create and use. Listing 2-32 shows the method to declare and populate a table variable.

Listing 2-32. Declare and Populate a Table Variable

```
DECLARE @TempAvailableMeal TABLE
(
    MealTypeName VARCHAR(25),
    RecipeName VARCHAR(25),
    ServingQuantity TINYINT,
    IngredientName VARCHAR(25)
)

INSERT INTO @TempAvailableMeal (MealTypeName, RecipeName, ServingQuantity,
IngredientName)
SELECT meal.MealTypeName, rec.RecipeName, rec.ServingQuantity, ing.
IngredientName
FROM dbo.Recipe rec
    INNER JOIN dbo.MealType meal
    ON rec.MealTypeID = meal.MealTypeID
    INNER JOIN dbo.RecipeIngredient recing
    ON rec.RecipeID = recing.RecipeID
    INNER JOIN dbo.Ingredient ing
    ON recing.IngredientID = ing.IngredientID
```

The execution plan for this query looks very similar to the one generated in Figure 2-16 when populating the local temporary table. Figure 2-19 shows the execution plan created when populating the table variable.

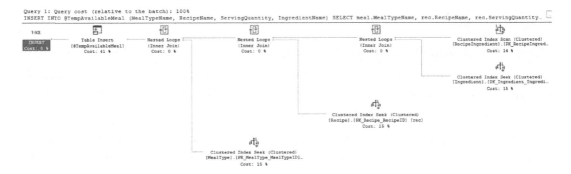

Query 1: Query cost (relative to the batch): 100%
INSERT INTO @TempAvailableMeal (MealTypeName, RecipeName, ServingQuantity, IngredientName) SELECT meal.MealTypeName, rec.RecipeName, rec.ServingQuantity...

Figure 2-19. *Populating the Table Variable*

Now that SQL Server 2019 has been updated to allow for better estimates when using table variables, I expect the execution plans to match often. However, I would double-check the query performance especially if you are planning on adding large quantities of data to the table variable.

Temporary Stored Procedures

If a stored procedure is created in the tempdb database, then this stored procedure is a temporary stored procedure. SQL Server may have made this functionality possible, but keep in mind how developers and applications would interact with this database object. At the very least, having a temporary stored procedure in the tempdb database would make it more difficult to troubleshoot or maintain code related to these stored procedures.

Triggers

SQL Server provides the ability to have specific actions occur as a result of some other activity. The reactions can occur in result to a user logging into the system. There are other reactions that can happen after or prevent changes to the existing database. When dealing with applications and data, the most common type of reaction is in response to changing data in the database. Regardless of the reason, these reactions are defined as triggers. Triggers are a special type of stored procedure that responds to a specific action on the server, database(s), or table(s).

Logon Triggers

When users log onto the server, you may want to record that specific activity. Or in other instances, you may want to limit user activity upon login or implement additional security functionality as a result of a server login. The logon trigger gives you the ability to allow SQL Server to initiate reactions in response to some or all logins onto the server.

There are not many scenarios where logon triggers will be needed for application development. However, there are some things that can be done with logon triggers that could help protect your application. A logon trigger can limit the number of connections allowed by a login. In the case of a breach, this could make sure the database does not get flooded with excess connections. Conversely, limiting the number of connections allowed per login can also limit scalability and futureproofing. The number of acceptable connections today may be much lower than the number of logins needed in the future.

Data Definition Language (DDL) Triggers

When applications or users change the overall database schema, they are using data definition language. In the case of SQL Server, it is possible to react to specific scenarios resulting from changes to the database. While I do not expect this to be a standard part of application development, it may be helpful to be aware of this type of trigger.

If you are concerned about SQL injection causing issues on your server, data definition language triggers can help mitigate the damage. There are options to prevent all sorts of database objects from being dropped. In addition, it is possible to log or record when database objects are created or altered. While you may want to use triggers to set up all sorts of triggers to monitor every activity on the server and the databases, there can be better options available. There are other alternatives available for tracking this type of behavior. This includes SQL Server Audit for both server and database activity. Typically, applications are not concerned with logging changes to the server or database schemas.

Data Manipulation Language (DML) Triggers

If you find yourself needing to implement auditing or logging as a part of your application development, you may find using data manipulation triggers quite helpful. These triggers have several options and respond to a variety of actions based on changes to the actual data in the database. In some cases, you may just want to record when the change happened and what changed. In other instances, it may be more important to change or verify the functionality of the request.

One method for triggers is to have an action performed after something happens. In this case, I want to successfully modify a record in the dbo.IngredientCost table, but I also want to keep a history of that item's cost changes over time. Listing 2-33 shows some T-SQL that will add an entry to a history table after a change is made.

Listing 2-33. Create After Insert DML Trigger

```
CREATE TRIGGER dbo.LogIngredientCostHistory
ON dbo.IngredientCost
AFTER INSERT, UPDATE
AS
      IF (ROWCOUNT_BIG() = 0)
      RETURN;

      INSERT INTO dbo.IngredientCostHistory (IngredientCostID, Cost,
      DateCreated)
      SELECT inserted.IngredientCostID, inserted.Cost, GETDATE()
      FROM inserted;
GO
```

When a record is inserted or updated in the dbo.IngredientCost table, the new cost and the date the cost was changed will be recorded in the dbo.IngredientCostHistory table. To see the performance of this trigger, I test this trigger by running the code in Listing 2-34.

Listing 2-34. Query to Insert Record into IngredientCost

```
INSERT INTO dbo.IngredientCost (IngredientID, ServingPortionID, Cost,
IsActive, DateCreated, DateModified)
VALUES (1, 1, 5.98, 1, GETDATE(), GETDATE())
```

When executing the preceding code, the execution plan includes two steps. The first is to run the code to insert the record into dbo.IngredientCost. The second execution plan shows the plan for the insert that occurs due to the trigger. The execution plans generated from Listing 2-34 are in Figure 2-20.

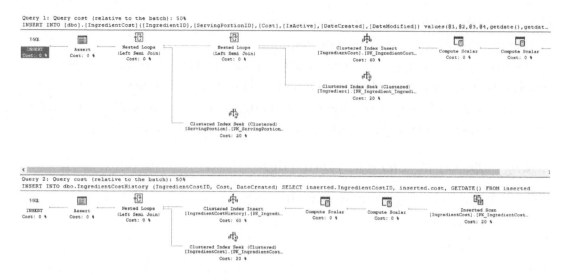

Figure 2-20. *Execution Plan to Insert Record with Trigger*

The execution plan in Figure 2-20 shows what happens when there is a record that is modified in a way to fire the trigger. However, the T-SQL code IF (ROWCOUNT_BIG() = 0) RETURN; from Listing 2-31 prevents the DML trigger from firing if no records were updated. This is considered best practice to minimize resource utilization on the server when no actions are needed. Listing 2-35 shows an update query where there will not be any records to be updated.

Listing 2-35. Update Statement that Will Not Update Any Records

```
UPDATE dbo.IngredientCost
SET Cost = 10.00
WHERE IngredientID <> IngredientID
```

As you can see in Figure 2-21, the execution plan only has one step. That is the execution plan for the update. There is no T-SQL code execution from the trigger.

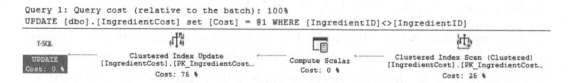

Figure 2-21. *Execution Plan Where No Records Are Updated*

As you can see, SQL Server was aware that there were no records to update returned from the trigger. Without attempting to insert any records into the dbo. IngredientCostHistory table, the only action was to generate an execution plan for the update. Having a trigger execute after an activity is not the only option for data manipulation triggers. There is also the possibility of having a trigger perform an action instead of the original action that was requested. Listing 2-36 shows a trigger that will disable a record when a user issues a delete.

Listing 2-36. Instead of Trigger

```
CREATE TRIGGER dbo.DisableMealType
ON dbo.MealType
INSTEAD OF DELETE
AS
      IF (ROWCOUNT_BIG() = 0)
      RETURN;

      UPDATE meal
      SET IsActive = 0
      FROM dbo.MealType meal
            INNER JOIN deleted del
            ON meal.MealTypeID = del.MealTypeID;
GO
```

As you can see, there is more than one option available when using DML triggers in SQL Server. There is also the possibility of having multiple triggers per database object. You can have up to one INSTEAD OF trigger per INSERT, UPDATE, and DELETE. You can have multiple AFTER triggers on the same table or view as well. Due to the number of triggers allowed, you can also specify which trigger should be run first and last per INSERT, UPDATE, or DELETE. If you have more than one type of AFTER trigger per action type, any of the triggers will be run in a random order.

Since there can be so many layers of triggers on a given database object, testing the functionality of these triggers is important. Like many other concepts discussed in this chapter, understanding how triggers will perform under load helps prepare for how the application will perform.

Cursors

In order to use relational databases effectively, it is often critical to think of processes and data in large chunks, or sets. The goal in almost all scenarios is to write T-SQL that takes advantage of this set-based logic. While this is the ideal method, you may find yourself in a situation where you feel handling data in large sections is not possible. In some of these scenarios, it may mean that it is time to handle the data by each row individually.

If you consider this route, it is imperative to acknowledge that SQL Server is designed to perform best when dealing with one large section of data vs. dealing with lots of individual records one at a time. In some cases where it is tempting to use something that handles row-by-row logic, it may be time to look for another tool to handle your needs better. Such is the case when creating a cursor to connect to several instances of SQL Server one at a time and perform a task. While it is outside the scope of this book, this specific situation may be best resolved by creating an SQL Server Integration Services (SSIS) package to handle connecting to the various SQL Server instances.

There are other times where you may need to use T-SQL to generate a result set where the data returned is the same, but the data must be segmented by location or vendor information. In this example, SQL Server Reporting Services (SSRS) could be used to achieve the same goal. However, your business may decide not to use SSRS. Therefore, using a cursor may be the right choice. I have also seen situations where data needed to be updated with a calculation using a specific, calculated value per record. In this case, it was almost impossible to perform the updates using set-based logic. While SQL Server was able to handle this task, it would have been preferable for the application to handle these changes.

Cursors can help make a repeatable process that touches one record at a time. While cursors can be used to address a variety of issues, it is important to remember that many times there may be a different way to achieve the same outcome without using cursors. If you have decided that you must really use a cursor, the next step is determining which type of cursor to use. While the concept of a cursor is the same regardless of which type is used, the type of cursor will determine the functionality and accessibility of the data within the cursor.

When choosing the right type of cursor for your needs, choose the one with the least amount of functionality that will meet your needs. This will help reduce negative performance as compared to cursor types with more functionality. Whenever you are handling records in SQL Server one at a time, they will almost always perform worse than handling data in groups.

A cursor selects a set of data, fetches one record at a time, and then modifies the current record. Once the required actions have been taken, the next record can be fetched. This is where knowing the various types of cursors available will allow you to choose the correct type.

Forward-Only Cursors

The default type of cursor is called the forward-only cursor. For this type of cursor, the data can only be fetched in one direction. Records fetched in forward-only cursors can insert, update, and delete records that are fetched within the cursor. If a record has been updated previously, it will not be fetched again unless the cursor is closed and reopened. There are also limited cases where you would be able to see the same record within the cursor after it had already been updated. Listing 2-37 shows an example of forward-only cursor.

Listing 2-37. Example of a Forward-Only Cursor

```
SET NOCOUNT ON;

DECLARE @RecipeID INT,
    @RecipeName VARCHAR(25),
    @message VARCHAR(50);

PRINT '-------- Recipe Listing --------';

DECLARE recipe_cursor CURSOR FORWARD_ONLY
FOR
SELECT RecipeID, RecipeName
FROM dbo.Recipe
ORDER BY RecipeID;

OPEN recipe_cursor

FETCH NEXT FROM recipe_cursor
INTO @RecipeID, @RecipeName

WHILE @@FETCH_STATUS = 0
BEGIN
    PRINT ' '
```

```
    SELECT @message = '----- Ingredients For Recipe: ' +
    @RecipeName + '-----'

    PRINT @message

    SELECT ing.IngredientName, srv.ServingPortionQuantity, srv.
ServingPortionUnit
    FROM dbo.Ingredient ing
            INNER JOIN dbo.RecipeIngredient recing
            ON ing.IngredientID = recing.IngredientID
            INNER JOIN dbo.ServingPortion srv
            ON recing.ServingPortionID = srv.ServingPortionID
    WHERE recing.RecipeID = @RecipeID

    FETCH NEXT FROM recipe_cursor INTO @RecipeID, @RecipeName
END
CLOSE recipe_cursor;
DEALLOCATE recipe_cursor;
```

In the case of this forward-only cursor, I am generating a list of recipes with all the ingredients required per menu. In Figure 2-22, you can see what this result looks like when output to the text window.

```
-------- Recipe Listing --------

----- Ingredients For Recipe: Spaghetti
IngredientName            ServingPortionQuantity ServingPortionUnit
------------------------- ---------------------- ------------------
Italian Sausage           2                      lbs
Tomato Sauce              40                      oz


----- Ingredients For Recipe: Tomato Sauce
IngredientName            ServingPortionQuantity ServingPortionUnit
------------------------- ---------------------- ------------------
Tomato                   40                      oz
```

Figure 2-22. *Output from the Forward-Only Cursor*

While this produced the output I wanted, I also must keep in mind the performance impact. In Figure 2-23, you can see part of the execution plan for this cursor.

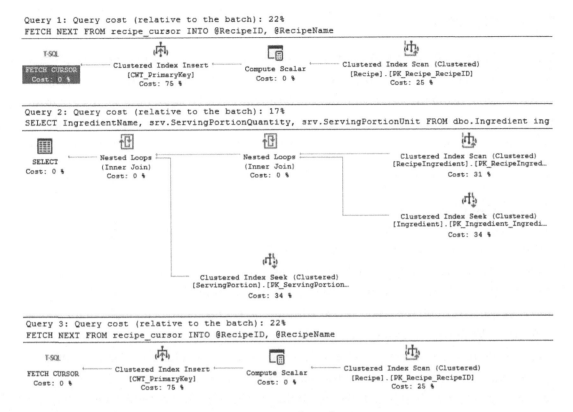

Figure 2-23. *Execution Plan for a Forward-Only Cursor*

It is important to remember that the second and third sections of this figure will rerun for each row processed in this cursor. When the underlying queries are quick and perform efficiently, that may not be an issue. However, if the queries inside of the cursor have any performance issues at all, a cursor can severely exacerbate any of these performance issues.

Static Cursors

Sometimes you will want to be able to move backward and forward when running the cursor. When using a static cursor, the available result set does not change from when the cursor is first opened. The static cursor has the option to be read only or allow reads and writes. When the cursor is read only, data cannot be modified. If the data is modified, there is no guarantee that the cursor will pull back the modified data.

Keyset Cursors

When defining a cursor, there may be a set of columns that create a unique entry. If that set of unique data can be found and you need to be able to interact with records that have changed, using the keyset cursor may be an option. The keyset is a set of keys from the unique set of columns. The cursor can move backward and forward, but the only way to detect changes to the order are the records that belong in the cursor to close and reopen the cursor.

Dynamic Cursors

If the other cursors may not work for your situation, there is a final type of cursor available. This type of cursor should be used as infrequently as possible due to the potential performance implications. The dynamic cursor allows you to move forward and backward through the result set. In addition, it will be aware of changes made to the data. While dealing with transaction levels is outside the scope of this book, there are some additional caveats for dynamic cursors when related to transaction levels. All changes from committed transactions will be visible. However, the only way uncommitted transactions can be seen is if the transaction level of the cursor is set to uncommitted.

Earlier in this section, I showed how to create a forward-only cursor. The interesting thing about creating cursors is that the code does not change significantly when switching between the various types of cursor. The largest difference between the cursor types is what data modifications each cursor can see and how the data is fetched. One of the largest temptations is that cursors work very similarly to application code. Instead of handling large quantities all at once, the cursors loop through data. In application code, this would be the preferred method of accessing data, which makes using cursors even more tempting.

Where I have seen cursors most used is to handle processes that could be better handled by applications. You may find yourself in a situation where a cursor seems like one of the only solutions available. Looking at Listing 2-38, you can get an idea of what a dynamic cursor can look like.

Listing 2-38. Creating a Dynamic Cursor

```
SET NOCOUNT ON;

DECLARE @RecipeID INT,
    @RecipeName VARCHAR(25),
    @message VARCHAR(50);

PRINT '-------- Recipe Listing --------';

DECLARE recipe_cursor CURSOR DYNAMIC
FOR
SELECT RecipeID, RecipeName
FROM dbo.Recipe
ORDER BY RecipeID;

OPEN recipe_cursor

FETCH NEXT FROM recipe_cursor
INTO @RecipeID, @RecipeName

WHILE @@FETCH_STATUS = 0
BEGIN
    PRINT ' '
    SELECT @message = '----- Ingredients For Recipe: ' + @RecipeName + '-----'

    PRINT @message

    SELECT ing.IngredientName, srv.ServingPortionQuantity, srv.
ServingPortionUnit
    FROM dbo.Ingredient ing
        INNER JOIN dbo.RecipeIngredient recing
        ON ing.IngredientID = recing.IngredientID
        INNER JOIN dbo.ServingPortion srv
        ON recing.ServingPortionID = srv.ServingPortionID
    WHERE recing.RecipeID = @RecipeID

    FETCH NEXT FROM recipe_cursor INTO @RecipeID, @RecipeName
END
CLOSE recipe_cursor;
DEALLOCATE recipe_cursor;
```

Changing the cursor type from FORWARD_ONLY to DYNAMIC was as easy as swapping out the phrases for one another. The output of these cursors is also the same. The real difference that could have happened is behind the scenes. If a record had changed while the cursor was running, the forward-only cursor may not have been aware of that change, whereas the dynamic cursor may have been able to scroll to see that change or in certain scenarios the dynamic cursor may have seen the change before it was committed.

Throughout this chapter, I have covered several different types of database objects that are available to use when writing T-SQL. These objects can help make code more readable. While some of these database objects can improve performance in the right circumstances, none of these database objects are designed to resolve every technical challenge. There are situations where using the wrong database objects can have negative performance impact on the database and your application code. Now that you know when to use each database object, it is time to start considering the quality of code you write.

CHAPTER 3

Standardizing T-SQL

Before I start talking about how to write queries for complex scenarios, I want to focus on how to write good T-SQL. This is not about writing code that performs well. This is about writing T-SQL code that reads well. I want to go over how to write code so that it is easily readable to others and to yourself. If you are like me, you'll get to a point in your career where you look at your own code and do not immediately understand all the logic involved.

Writing T-SQL that is understandable helps you and your company. Many other coding languages have standards or best practices, and I believe that T-SQL should be no different. While the primary goal of writing T-SQL may be to implement a piece of functionality, no less important is the secondary goal of making sure that your T-SQL makes sense. Over time, code changes or bugs are found. The more readable and understandable your T-SQL code is, the easier it is to modify or troubleshoot.

Formatting T-SQL

How T-SQL looks when it is written can be as significant as what is written. Like other application code, there is always a chance that someone will need to look at your code in the future or you will need to look at theirs. If I am not writing new code, I am looking at pre-existing code to understand the purpose, to debug the code, to performance tune the query, or to update business logic. Depending on the reason why I am reviewing the code, I will generally determine what is important to me at the time.

If I am looking at the T-SQL code to understand what the code does, I will look at what tables are involved first to understand what application may be using this T-SQL code. I am not concerned with how tables are joined together as I expect that to be functioning correctly. Though incorrect logic on table joins can be a cause of queries returned very unexpected results. Next, I will look at the criteria used to filter the results

© Elizabeth Noble 2020
E. Noble, *Pro T-SQL 2019*, https://doi.org/10.1007/978-1-4842-5590-2_3

of the T-SQL code. Only at the very end of my analysis will I review the column returned in the query. Oftentimes, I am only concerned with the columns if there is special business logic involved. Applying this thought pattern to writing simple queries, you can see that I list the column names on one line in Listing 3-1.

Listing 3-1. Basic Query

```
SELECT IngredientID, IngredientName, DateCreated, DateModified
FROM dbo.Ingredient
```

I format my code this way because I want to be able to quickly see all the action items that are happening through the FROM clause and the WHERE criteria. If I were to create one line per column, it would be harder for me to see how tables were related and what conditions were being applied to those relationships. As you can see in Listing 3-2, I have altered how the columns in the SELECT clause are displayed.

Listing 3-2. Queries with Joins

```
SELECT rec.RecipeName,
       rec.RecipeDescription,
       rec.IsActive AS 'RecipeIsActive',
       ingr.IngredientName,
       ingr.IsActive AS 'IngredientIsActive'
FROM dbo.Recipe rec
       INNER JOIN dbo.RecipeIngredient recingr
       ON rec.RecipeID = recingr.IngredientID
       LEFT OUTER JOIN dbo.Ingredient ingr
       ON recingr.IngredientID = ingr.IngredientID
            AND ingr.IngredientName <> 'Italian Sausage'
```

For this query, the columns are listed line by line. This is because I have altered something about the actual column being pulled back. If there is ever a time I am aliasing a column or adding special logic to a column, I will change how I format the columns in the SELECT statement. For these scenarios, I will create one line or more per column depending on the complexity of the logic. If you also notice on the last two lines of the query, I have two join conditions. I usually indent any join condition after the first one as I want it to be immediately obvious there has been more than one condition applied to a join.

There are many times I am reviewing T-SQL code to troubleshoot why the T-SQL code may be returning incorrect results. When there are issues with the results being returned, I start with a user story indicating what is happening that is incorrect. In these cases, I will go immediately to the WHERE clause to double-check the logic and confirm that it is correct. Once I have confirmed that logic, I look at the join criteria to confirm that the tables are joined correctly. I use the same process to troubleshoot the code as I use to understand T-SQL code; I will look at the SELECT statement last focusing on any primarily columns with any special logic. Looking at the query in Listing 3-3, I can scan first the FROM clause, then the WHERE clause.

Listing 3-3. Queries with Subqueries

```
SELECT
        (
                SELECT rec.RecipeName
                FROM dbo.Recipe rec
                        INNER JOIN dbo.RecipeIngredient recingr
                        ON rec.RecipeID = recingr.RecipeID
                WHERE recingr.IngredientID = ingr.IngredientID
        ) AS 'RecipeName',
        ingr.IngredientName,
        ingr.IsActive,
        ingr.DateCreated,
        ingr.DateModified
FROM dbo.Ingredient ingr
WHERE IngredientName LIKE '%Tomato%'
ORDER BY RecipeName, ingr.IngredientName
```

This allows me to immediately determine this query is dealing with ingredients that are like tomato. With the columns in the SELECT statement listed on individual lines, I am immediately aware that there is some special logic involved in the part of the SELECT statement. I have also indented the subquery portion of the logic which helps that subquery stand out even further. Now that I am trying to troubleshoot potentially inaccurate results, I can quickly dig into what can be causing the issue. Depending on the bug reported, there is a very high possibility the issue is either with the WHERE clause or the first column returned in the SELECT statement. Analyzing the view created in Listing 3-4 shows a different conclusion.

Listing 3-4. Create a View

```
CREATE VIEW dbo.AvailableMeal
AS
SELECT meal.MealTypeName, rec.RecipeName, rec.ServingQuantity, ing.
IngredientName
FROM dbo.Recipe rec
     INNER JOIN dbo.MealType meal
     ON rec.MealTypeID = meal.MealTypeID
     INNER JOIN dbo.RecipeIngredient recing
     ON rec.RecipeID = recing.RecipeID
     INNER JOIN dbo.Ingredient ing
     ON recing.IngredientID = ing.IngredientID
```

In the T-SQL code for this view, I still go first to the FROM clause. I immediately identify that there are several joins. In addition, there is no WHERE clause, and I can also quickly determine there is no special logic in the SELECT statement as all columns are not on their own line(s). Matching the information about this view to any potential bug I am researching, I know the most complex part of this query is the join logic. If the joins are correct, I can quickly rule out the SELECT statement if the view is returning too many results or I can rule out the WHERE clause if the data returned is incorrect. A similar pattern can be followed when creating a function as shown in Listing 3-5.

Listing 3-5. Create a Function

```
CREATE FUNCTION dbo.IngredientsByRecipe (@RecipeID INT)
RETURNS TABLE
AS
RETURN
(
     SELECT meal.MealTypeName, rec.ServingQuantity, ing.IngredientName
     FROM dbo.Recipe rec
          INNER JOIN dbo.MealType meal
          ON rec.MealTypeID = meal.MealTypeID
          INNER JOIN dbo.RecipeIngredient recing
          ON rec.RecipeID = recing.RecipeID
          INNER JOIN dbo.Ingredient ing
```

```
        ON recing.IngredientID = ing.IngredientID
    WHERE rec.RecipeID = @RecipeID
);
```

In the preceding function, I can quickly identify several joins in the FROM statement and one criterion in the WHERE clause. If the function is returning only results for the recipe provided, it is highly likely that any bug that has been found is related to the join conditions.

My process for performance tuning queries is handled differently, and I will discuss those differences further in Part II of this book, Building Performant T-SQL. When it comes to reviewing the T-SQL as part of performance tuning, I will focus on what tables are used. If there is more than one table, I will also look at how those tables are joined together. My final focus will be on what columns are being used and how those relate to indexes that already exist.

I also review T-SQL code when updating logic inside of the T-SQL code. Either new functionality has been added, changed, or removed, I will need to modify the T-SQL code to mirror those modifications. Depending on the modifications, it may be as simple as looking at the fields in the SELECT clause and changing what fields are displayed or how calculations are performed. Other times, I may need to look at the FROM clause and add or remove tables from join conditions. In some cases, I need to update criteria in the WHERE clause to handle the new business requirements. Such is the case in Listing 3-6 which shows the creation of a table-valued parameter. One of the first things I notice is the lack of a WHERE clause in this stored procedure. This is also where some complexity is added when dealing with user-defined table types.

Listing 3-6. Create Table-Valued Parameter

```
CREATE PROCEDURE dbo.UpdateRecipeMenuType
    @RecipeMeal RecipeMealType READONLY
AS
SET NOCOUNT ON
UPDATE rec
SET MealTypeID = meal.MealTypeID
FROM dbo.Recipe rec
    INNER JOIN @RecipeMeal recmeal
    ON rec.RecipeName = recmeal.RecipeName
    INNER JOIN dbo.MealType meal
    ON recmeal.MealTypeName = meal.MealTypeName
```

It is very likely that the user-defined table is being used to filter the data on the join. However, just looking at the code, it is very difficult to tell how the application uses this stored procedure. Because of the user-defined table type, the amount of work required to enhance the logic on this stored procedure is significantly increased. I need to be aware of how data is being passed in the table-valued parameter, but I also need to consider how the data being passed to this table-valued parameter can change over time. As database administrators are often the ones managing the T-SQL code long after the application has been deployed, I find it best to design T-SQL code so that it can be easily supported going forward. As you can see in Listing 3-7, when creating a common table expression I use the same method, but I indent the query inside of the common table expression. Once again, I use this indent to help signify that special logic is happening in a given section.

Listing 3-7. Create a Common Table Expression

```
WITH cte_meal AS
(
      SELECT meal.MealTypeName, rec.RecipeName, rec.ServingQuantity,
      ing.IngredientName
      FROM dbo.Recipe rec
            INNER JOIN dbo.MealType meal
            ON rec.MealTypeID = meal.MealTypeID
            INNER JOIN dbo.RecipeIngredient recing
            ON rec.RecipeID = recing.RecipeID
            INNER JOIN dbo.Ingredient ing
            ON recing.IngredientID = ing.IngredientID
)
SELECT meal.MealTypeName, meal.RecipeName, meal.ServingQuantity, meal.
IngredientName
FROM cte_meal meal
```

When defining my own personal style, I have learned that my overall objective is to have a query fit in a small enough area that I can quickly and efficiently find the part of T-SQL code that I am trying to review. When it comes to designing your own standard, you will want to think about what your overall objective is.

In many companies, junior team members will be hired. Some of these junior team members will be new to SQL Server, and it will take any new hire some time to understand how the applications in your business work. When designing an internal T-SQL coding standard, you will want to take into consideration what formatting conventions should be followed that will help new employees quickly learn your company's systems and data flows.

Another factor in developing a T-SQL formatting standard is creating a standard that employees can easily remember or reference. You want your team members to be able to succeed when implementing a new standard and not be overwhelmed by all the nuances when writing the code. This is especially important if all T-SQL code must be written manually, and your company does not have software that can automatically format the T-SQL code for you.

There are also some formatting considerations for inserts, updates, and deletes. In Listing 3-8, there is a sample INSERT statement. In this example, I have listed all the column names for an INSERT.

Listing 3-8. Query to Insert Data

```
INSERT INTO dbo.IngredientCost (IngredientID, ServingPortionID, Cost,
IsActive, DateCreated, DateModified)
VALUES (1, 1, 5.98, 1, GETDATE(), GETDATE())
```

While listing the column names may seem unnecessary, this formatting standard makes what data is being inserted easily identifiable, but this format also protects the application code from future issues if columns are added or the column order changes. The format to update data is simple as you can see in Listing 3-9. I am still following the same formatting for reserved words and referencing user-defined database objects.

Listing 3-9. Simple Query to Update Data

```
UPDATE dbo.AvailableMeal
SET IngredientName = 'Spicy Italian Sausage'
WHERE RecipeName = 'Spaghetti'
```

You can also see that I consistently pad the operator. I have done this in several examples. Like other decisions I have made for formatting, I believe adding a space before and after the equal sign improves the readability of the T-SQL code. I have also included Listing 3-10 to show how to format deleting data in T-SQL.

Listing 3-10. Query to Delete Data

```
DELETE FROM dbo.Ingredient
WHERE IngredientName LIKE '%tomato%'
```

This example is for a simple delete, and when joins are involved, the format to delete data can become even more involved. Deleting data often seems more significant than other data manipulation activities in SQL Server. There are times where you may want to write a query to systematically delete data from a table. When I first started writing queries to delete data from tables, I would start with writing the SELECT statement. This would help with several factors. I could clearly see what data would be affected. I could also get a row count for the number of records I expected to be affected. Once I had the SELECT statement written, I could easily modify the code to delete the necessary records. The query in Listing 3-11 shows the SELECT statement I would use to prepare for deleting data records.

Listing 3-11. Select Recipes with MealTypeID of 2

```
SELECT rec.RecipeID, rec.RecipeName
FROM dbo.Recipe rec
     INNER JOIN dbo.MealType meal
     ON rec.MealTypeID = meal.MealTypeID
WHERE meal.MealTypeID = 2
```

In this case, I am preparing to delete records from the dbo.Recipe table that have a MealTypeID of 2. Using the result from Listing 3-11, I can confirm what data I am deleting and how many records I can expect to delete. After I reviewed the results from Listing 3-11, I can update my T-SQL code to delete the records. In Listing 3-12, I have replaced the SELECT statement with a DELETE FROM referencing the table alias for dbo.Recipe.

Listing 3-12. Delete Recipes with MealTypeID of 2

```
BEGIN TRAN

DELETE FROM rec
FROM dbo.Recipe rec
     INNER JOIN dbo.MealType meal
     ON rec.MealTypeID = meal.MealTypeID
WHERE meal.MealTypeID = 2

COMMIT
```

Over the years, I have found it best to wrap complex DELETE statements in an explicit transaction. By default, when we execute T-SQL code on SQL Server, we are using an implicit transaction. That means that SQL Server knows to commit the transaction automatically after we execute the transaction. We also have the option of specifying an explicit transaction. This is where SQL Server will not complete the execution of the T-SQL code until we send the COMMIT to SQL Server. Particularly with deletes, but often with any complex code, I have found that it is best to always be careful. I know I will either run the BEGIN TRAN and the query without the COMMIT or end the whole statement with a ROLLBACK when I first execute a query like the one in Listing 3-12. This allows me to verify the number of records affected. This is my last chance to confirm that my query is working as expected. If I were to get a different number of records returned than the one I expected I could issue a ROLLBACK, and SQL Server would undo the code that I had attempted to run. This is only possible while using explicit transactions. It is also worth mentioning that if you are using multiple levels of transactions, referred to as nested transactions, the functionality of the ROLLBACK may work differently than expected.

This leads to another consideration when designing your T-SQL formatting. You will need to know how your T-SQL code will be written and stored. If all T-SQL code will be written manually and cannot be formatted by a third-party tool, then you may need to keep the coding standard very simple and limit criteria for special situations. However, if you have a third-party tool available, you can create a format that is as complex as that tool can handle.

One of the factors that makes a good developer or engineer is discipline. The same is true when writing T-SQL. To certain extent, it does not matter what specific style of formatting you use. What does matter is being consistent with that formatting. Ideally, you should try to get your entire team to agree to a standard method of formatting T-SQL.

When your whole team writes T-SQL code the same way, it makes it much easier to look at someone else's code. You no longer must translate both the format and the coding style which can lead to quicker analysis and quicker problem resolution. Formatting your T-SQL code to make it more readable is all about how the code will look.

You should move toward having consistent formatting for all T-SQL code written at your company. Since the formatting will be the same regardless of who writes the code, it also means that everyone reading the code will become more and more familiar with quickly interpreting their code. As you can see in Listing 3-13, I am creating a user-defined table type.

Listing 3-13. Create User-Defined Table Type

```
CREATE TYPE RecipeMealType AS TABLE
(
     RecipeName VARCHAR(25),
     MealTypeName VARCHAR(25)
);
```

I also use a consistent format in Listing 3-14 when creating a temporary table.

Listing 3-14. Create a Temporary Table

```
CREATE TABLE #TempAvailableMeal
(
     MealTypeName VARCHAR(25),
     RecipeName VARCHAR(25),
     ServingQuantity TINYINT,
     IngredientName VARCHAR(25)
)
```

You can also see I use the same format when creating a table variable in Listing 3-15.

Listing 3-15. Create a Table Variable

```
DECLARE @TempAvailableMeal TABLE
(
     MealTypeName VARCHAR(25),
     RecipeName VARCHAR(25),
     ServingQuantity TINYINT,
     IngredientName VARCHAR(25)
)
```

Comparing Listings 3-8, 3-9, and 3-10, you can quickly see that I use a consistent format when creating tables. This will allow anyone else and myself to see code in this format and quickly know that this code is creating a table.

There are at least two things to consider when it comes to capitalization. There is capitalization related to keywords and capitalization for all other terms. I prefer to uppercase all reserved words. The list of T-SQL reserved words can be quite lengthy. I chose to consider any word that is not part of the database schema as considered a reserved word. I capitalize database objects and column names as they were created. When I create table aliases, I use lowercase. You can see in Listing 3-16 how the reserved words are uppercased and the first letter of each word for a database object name is capitalized.

Listing 3-16. Create a DML Trigger

```
CREATE TRIGGER dbo.LogIngredientCostHistory
ON dbo.IngredientCost
AFTER INSERT, UPDATE
AS
        IF (ROWCOUNT_BIG() = 0)
        RETURN;

        INSERT INTO dbo.IngredientCostHistory (IngredientCostID, Cost,
        DateCreated)
        SELECT inserted.IngredientCostID, inserted.Cost, GETDATE()
        FROM inserted;
```

One of the other factors to consider when determining formatting standards for T-SQL is if and how to use aliasing. Aliasing is a method that allows you to create a shortened name to reference a table. It is also possible to alias column names in your select statements when writing queries. How the aliased values can be used depends on whether a table or a column is being aliased. However, the overall concept is the same. If an alias is created for a table name, the alias must be used in place of the table name for the entirety of the given query. For columns, aliases are often used to rename a column or make the output more user-friendly. Often the column aliases are not referenced.

The only time I will reference a column alias when writing my queries is if I must order by a column that has been aliased, particularly if that column has more logic than only renaming the original column name. It is possible to provide a numeric representation of the column order in the ORDER BY statement instead of proving a column name. While this is a quick method to sort data, this is not recommended to be used as part of permanent application code as the order of columns in the SELECT statement can be changed without the ORDER BY clause getting updated. This would cause the data returned to potentially be ordered differently than intended.

Another debated topic when it comes to T-SQL code formatting is how to format commas when writing code. There are those who prefer to put the commas at the beginning of each line. This can improve readability and help others quickly identify that this is one of multiple lines. Adding the commas at the front of each line does simplify debugging as it is easy to comment out a single line that begins with a comma and the rest of the query will parse correctly. I prefer adding my commas at the end so that I can ignore the commas and focus on the columns being returned in a query.

When it comes to multiple criteria in the WHERE clause, I do prefer the same type of methodology as those that prefer the commas at the beginning. I want the WHERE clause to have the same style as the SELECT statement. However, this does not always mean that the logic for each line is the same as it does for a comma. Some lines in a WHERE clause can have an AND or an OR instead of a single comparison. This additional logic will require you to make some decisions about what is comfortable for you to read. I do like those to stand out that I can be aware of how the logic is being used for each line in the WHERE clause.

There are times when working with T-SQL code that you will write complex code. This code may include subqueries or logic in the WHERE clause involving ANDs or ORs. If there is logic like a subquery or a mixture of ANDs and ORs in the WHERE clause, I will wrap those in parentheses. I will indent all the code inside the parentheses so that it is easy to identify what logic is wrapped together. There are also times where there are multiple join conditions between two tables. If there is more than one join condition between two tables, I will indent every join condition except the first one so that others can easily tell there are multiple join conditions between two tables.

You will also want to consider how to format T-SQL code when adding additional levels of logic to your code. There are various reasons for T-SQL code blocks including TRY... CATCH blocks, IF... ELSE statements, BEGIN...END, or other reasons to segment code. For these scenarios, I indent the interior of the code block. If code blocks end up being nested, I will indent each subsequent code block. I prefer to indent my code blocks so that others reviewing my code can see the parent activity such as the WHILE loop in Listing 3-17. Once you see the first level of indentation, you know that all the logic that has been indented belongs to the same code block.

Listing 3-17. Create a Cursor

```
SET NOCOUNT ON;

DECLARE @RecipeID INT,
    @RecipeName VARCHAR(25),
    @message VARCHAR(50);

PRINT '-------- Recipe Listing --------';
```

```
DECLARE recipe_cursor CURSOR FORWARD_ONLY
FOR
SELECT RecipeID, RecipeName
FROM dbo.Recipe
ORDER BY RecipeID;

OPEN recipe_cursor

FETCH NEXT FROM recipe_cursor
INTO @RecipeID, @RecipeName

WHILE @@FETCH_STATUS = 0
BEGIN
    PRINT ' '
    SELECT @message = '----- Ingredients For Recipe: ' + @RecipeName + '-----'

    PRINT @message

      SELECT ing.IngredientName,
            srv.ServingPortionQuantity,
            srv.ServingPortionUnit
      FROM dbo.Ingredient ing
            INNER JOIN dbo.RecipeIngredient recing
            ON ing.IngredientID = recing.IngredientID
            INNER JOIN dbo.ServingPortion srv
            ON recing.ServingPortionID = srv.ServingPortionID
      WHERE recing.RecipeID = @RecipeID

      FETCH NEXT FROM recipe_cursor INTO @RecipeID, @RecipeName
END
CLOSE recipe_cursor;
DEALLOCATE recipe_cursor;
```

Formatting T-SQL code consistently improves readability for yourself and anyone in the future who will need to review your code. Well-formatted code can help provide clarity when troubleshooting, performance tuning, and code enhancing. Creating a T-SQL formatting standard in your organization can also help when onboarding new employees or training junior database developers. Once T-SQL formatting standards have been determined, you will want to consider what steps need to be taken to create naming conventions for your T-SQL code.

Naming T-SQL

When you write T-SQL, you have options on how to write that code. You will most likely create persistent objects in T-SQL. Regardless of your purpose, following a good naming policy makes it easier for others to understand the purpose of your T-SQL code. Ideally, your team members should be able to determine the purpose of your code based on the object name where the code lives. This is particularly helpful for new or less experienced employees.

The same practices for formatting T-SQL are similar for when choosing your naming convention strategy. One of the aspects that comes with naming conventions is look and feel. This can involve the capitalization used for objects. There are various options available when providing a case for database objects. The main choices are camel case or pascal case. The primary difference between these casing styles is the first letter of the database object. In Listing 3-18, you will see writing a query using camel case.

Listing 3-18. Query with Camel Case

```
SELECT recipeID, ingredientID, dateCreated, dateModified
FROM dbo.recipeIngredient
```

Conversely, you can see in Listing 3-19 what pascal case looks like when writing the same query.

Listing 3-19. Query with Pascal Case

```
SELECT RecipeID, IngredientID, DateCreated, DateModified
FROM dbo.RecipeIngredient
```

In addition, there is also an option where the first letter is not capitalized and there is an underscore between words. I am generally not a fan of non-alphabetic characters in database names, but I do know some people that prefer underscores. If you want another alternative, Listing 3-20 shows how tables and columns would need to be named has been referred to as snake case.

Listing 3-20. Query with Snake Case

```
SELECT recipeID, ingredientID, date_created, date_modified
FROM dbo.recipe_ingredient
```

When determining which case to use for your naming convention, make sure to also be aware of the collation for your database and if any tables have a special collation. Being aware of case sensitivity will help you ensure that your naming conventions and your formatting standards line up.

This can also involve where objects appear in Object Explorer. Some of this has to do with what type of object is being named and who will be looking for these objects. If you are wanting to find objects by their use, you may want to specify schema names that group those objects together. This can be particularly useful for applications or services. Depending on what type of troubleshooting is expected, database objects, particularly stored procedures, can be named with the action they are taking. This would allow for an easy search of stored procedures that are selecting data vs. inserting data. However, there is also another option where the main table affected could be the first word in the stored procedure name. This would allow someone to search in Object Explorer by affected table to see all the stored procedures that exist.

Another consideration is whether reserved words can be used when naming database objects. If reserved words are used in database object names, you will want to add another word to the object name so that brackets are not needed when referencing the object name.

When determining naming conventions, you may also want to consider if there are columns in tables that will have the same names as other columns in tables. Some of these types of columns include specifying the date a record was created, the date a record was last updated, and if the record has been soft deleted. For tables that are specifying status or types, these tables can have columns with a status or type name and an associated description. You may decide that you want all these columns to have the exact same name in all tables with these columns.

When writing my queries, I prefer not to alias my column names, if possible. I also am not displaying more than one date created or updated. Therefore, I would use the exact same name for creation date, modified date, and the soft delete flag. However, I also am usually pulling back the name or description field from multiple tables when I write my queries. Therefore, I prefer those columns to include the table name as part of the column name. This allows others to view the select statement and easily identify which table is being referenced. It also means I am aliasing less columns when I write my queries.

Naming persistent database objects can get tricky as well. Naming tables can be different than naming indexes or views or triggers or functions. Once again, naming these objects is more than just giving them a descriptive name. In addition, it may also be about giving them a name that makes it clear what type of object it is. This is because many database engineers and developers use Object Explorer as their primary tool for finding objects. As I have discussed if table names begin with nouns and stored procedures begin with verbs, I next need to figure out how to differentiate other database objects from tables and stored procedures.

One of the options is to precede the object name with an abbreviation for the object type. In the case of indexes, you can use IX_ for non-clustered indexes and CX_ for clustered indexes. When naming indexes, once you specify the IX_ or CX_ the next item should be the table name where the index exists. After the table name should be the list of columns in the index. The columns should be listed in the same order that they are specified when the index is created. In Listing 3-21, I have created a clustered index. As you can see, the clustered index name begins with CX followed by the table name and then the column name. Each section is separated by an underscore.

Listing 3-21. Create a Clustered Index

```
CREATE CLUSTERED INDEX CX_Ingredient_IngredientName
     ON dbo.Ingredient (IngredientName);
```

Creating a non-clustered index follows the same pattern. In Listing 3-22, you will see the non-clustered index also includes multiple columns.

Listing 3-22. Create a Non-clustered Index with Multiple Columns

```
CREATE NONCLUSTERED INDEX IX_Ingredient_IngredientName_IsActive
     ON dbo.Ingredient (IngredientName ASC, IsActive DESC);
```

The same is true when creating primary and foreign keys. If you do not specify a name when you create a primary or foreign key in T-SQL, SQL Server will assign a name at random. Therefore, it is best practice to specifically name the primary or foreign key. When naming the primary key, you will want the primary key to begin with PK_ which stands for primary key. Similarly, you will want to precede the foreign key with FK_ and then name the rest of the key. The next part of the name is the table name where the primary or foreign key is assigned. This is followed by the column or columns used to define the primary or foreign key. If there is more than one column specified, the columns listed in the primary or foreign key should be listed in order. Listing 3-23 shows an example of how to add and name a primary key after table has been created.

Listing 3-23. Add a Primary Key

```
ALTER TABLE dbo.Ingredient
ADD CONSTRAINT PK_Ingredient_IngredientID
    PRIMARY KEY (IngredientID);
```

As you can see, the primary key name begins with PK followed by the table name and then the column name used for the creation of the primary key.

Similarly, you will want to precede the foreign key with FK_ and then name the rest of the key. The next part of the name is the table name where the primary or foreign key is assigned. This is followed by the column or columns used to define the primary or foreign key. If there is more than one column specified, the columns listed in the primary or foreign key should be listed in order. When creating a foreign key after the table has been created, you can refer to Listing 3-24.

Listing 3-24. Add a Foreign Key

```
ALTER TABLE dbo.RecipeIngredient
ADD CONSTRAINT FK_RecipeIngredient_IngredientID
    FOREIGN KEY (IngredientID)
    REFERENCES dbo.Ingredient(IngredientID);
```

Like creating the primary key, the foreign key follows a similar naming structure. The foreign key begins with FK followed by the table name and then the column name.

I can also precede views with vw_ and triggers with tr_. There are other options available that can be less obvious. For instance, you can define a list of nouns or verbs that will be reserved for only views or triggers. This will give you more flexibility, and it will also keep Object Explorer from having all items in the list begin with the same three characters. This will allow anyone to easily be able to tell these objects are neither tables nor stored procedures. This is particularly true when it comes to views and triggers.

One of the biggest challenges is that if they are not named to make it obvious that they are views or triggers, people can spend a significant amount of time looking for these objects without being able to find them. This is because views are used similarly to tables, and triggers operate similarly to stored procedures. This is because views are used in joins like tables, whereas triggers change objects like stored procedures. Triggers are even trickier because they can cause you to spend a significant amount of time researching stored procedures trying to determine why values are changing.

When naming tables, you want to use only nouns. This helps signify that these objects are for storage and not performing any specific activity. When naming objects, one of the naming conventions that is often overlooked until it is too late is whether objects are singular or plural. It is not really an issue until that first time where an object is pluralized. Once a plural database object is in the overall schema, it becomes obvious very quickly the issues with a plural object. This is because once a plural object exists in the database, it becomes increasingly difficult to write queries without specifically remembering which tables are plural.

You also want to make sure that you choose a descriptive name when naming a table. You will want to describe your table in a way that other database engineers and developers will easily know what type of information is stored in the table. Naming tables with nouns will also indicate that the object is for storage and not performing any specific activities.

Most users become easily familiar with tables and stored procedures. It is easy to choose a naming convention that differentiates these objects either by having stored procedure preceded with a verb or having additional high-level criteria as part of the stored procedure name. Listing 3-25 shows a stored procedure that has a verb at the beginning of a stored procedure name.

Listing 3-25. Stored Procedure Beginning with a Verb

```
EXECUTE dbo.GetRecipeIngredient
```

If I were to see that stored procedure name, I would expect it to retrieve all recipes and all associated ingredients. The stored procedure in Listing 3-26 would pull back all the ingredients for a given stored procedure.

Listing 3-26. Stored Procedure with Selection Criteria

```
EXECUTE dbo.GetIngredientByRecipe
```

As you can see, there are many considerations when it comes to naming your T-SQL database objects. In many of these cases, a good name will help you easily determine the purpose of the database object. In special circumstances, it can also help you identify the type of object. While you would normally name your objects after formatting and commenting the T-SQL, I saved the commenting for last as it covers both the creation of the database object and the T-SQL code that goes inside the database object.

Commenting T-SQL

While the primary goal of writing T-SQL is to allow an application to do a specific action regarding data, almost equally important is ensuring that others will understand your T-SQL code going forward. At the very least, this makes sure that you are not the only one responsible for a certain piece of code or business logic going forward. It also helps all your other team members build confidence in their ability to do their job and their understanding of the code behind the scenes.

In many cases, quickly scanning the T-SQL code or looking at the name of a database object is not enough to understand the purpose of the T-SQL code. In Listing 3-27, there is sample T-SQL code for creating a header section at the top of your database objects.

Listing 3-27. Comment for Header of Persistent Database Object

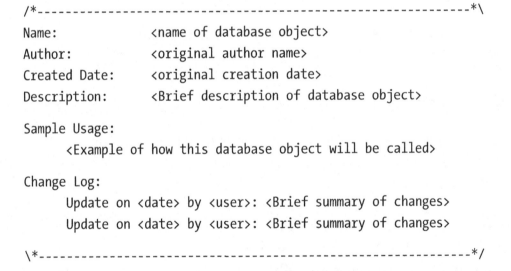

```
/*-----------------------------------------------------------------*\

Name:              <name of database object>
Author:            <original author name>
Created Date:      <original creation date>
Description:       <Brief description of database object>

Sample Usage:
      <Example of how this database object will be called>

Change Log:
      Update on <date> by <user>: <Brief summary of changes>
      Update on <date> by <user>: <Brief summary of changes>

\*-----------------------------------------------------------------*/
```

The purpose of this heading is giving other users a summary of this database object at a glance. Depending on the purpose for reviewing this T-SQL will determine what is important to the user. For those that are not familiar with all the details of the business applications, the description segment will provide a high-level idea of the purpose of the T-SQL database object. Likewise, the sample usage allows those looking into performance issues to understand how the applications are using this piece of T-SQL code. The author of the database object can be useful to determine if the original creator is still with the company to answer more specific questions about the database object. If your databases are in source control, you may decide to omit some of these fields. I will discuss source control further in Chapter 10. In Listing 3-28, you can see how the header information would look while creating the view originally found in Listing 3-4.

Listing 3-28. Create a View with a Commented Header

```
/*---------------------------------------------------------------*\
Name:              dbo.AvailableMeal
Author:            Elizabeth Noble
Created Date:      03/13/2019
Description:       Simple view to display all meals with ingredients

Sample Usage:
     SELECT MealTypeName, RecipeName FROM dbo.AvailableMeal

Change Log:
     Update on 03/31/2019 by enoble: Added header to view

\*---------------------------------------------------------------*/

CREATE VIEW dbo.AvailableMeal
AS
SELECT meal.MealTypeName, rec.RecipeName, rec.ServingQuantity, ing.
IngredientName
FROM dbo.Recipe rec
     INNER JOIN dbo.MealType meal
     ON rec.MealTypeID = meal.MealTypeID
     INNER JOIN dbo.RecipeIngredient recing
     ON rec.RecipeID = recing.RecipeID
     INNER JOIN dbo.Ingredient ing
     ON recing.IngredientID = ing.IngredientID
```

Sometimes it may be enough to write simple T-SQL that is easily readable. However, there are other times where a database object may have T-SQL code that is difficult to understand at a quick glance. I often find one of the challenges in commenting after I've written my code is that my comments are too technical to easily describe what I am trying to accomplish. You will want to make sure that someone unfamiliar with your code can easily understand the purpose of your T-SQL code.

If there is any complex logic, you will want to clearly explain how the complex logic works. This is especially true if you are using T-SQL coding practices that are not best practices. Any explanation as to why non-standard practices were chosen will help save others' time to try and figure out why non-standard practices were used. This can also save your team members' time if you have already determined that standard best practices will not perform well enough in the given situation. Looking back to Listing 3-3, there is a subquery in the SELECT statement. First writing this code, it may be obvious why a subquery was used, but you may forget the reason in the future. In addition, it is probably not obvious to others who read my code why I chose to include a subquery for that column. In Listing 3-29, I show how you can add commenting to help show how adding comments can make it easier for you to quickly understand the purpose or logic of the code that is written.

Listing 3-29. Queries with Subqueries

```
SELECT
      -- This subquery pulls back the recipe name based on
      -- the ingredients in the recipe
      ---- The logic uses a correlated subquery between the
      ---- where clause in the subquery
      ---- and the table in the outer query
      (
            SELECT rec.RecipeName
            FROM dbo.Recipe rec
                  INNER JOIN dbo.RecipeIngredient recingr
                  ON rec.RecipeID = recingr.RecipeID
            WHERE recingr.IngredientID = ingr.IngredientID
      ) AS 'RecipeName',
      ingr.IngredientName,
      ingr.IsActive,
      ingr.DateCreated,
      ingr.DateModified
FROM dbo.Ingredient ingr
WHERE IngredientName LIKE '%Tomato%'
ORDER BY RecipeName, ingr.IngredientName
```

It is often easiest to include comments in your code if you start commenting your T-SQL code even before you begin writing any T-SQL. In Listing 3-30, you can see the header information and the beginning comments. The comments specified indicate the concept behind writing the stored procedure.

Listing 3-30. Create New Stored Procedure

```
/*--------------------------------------------------------------*\
Name:              dbo.GetRecipeNutrition
Author:            Elizabeth Noble
Created Date:      03/13/2019
Description: Lookup nutritional information for a given recipe

Sample Usage:
     DECLARE @RecipeID INT
     SET @RecipeID = 1

     EXECUTE dbo. GetRecipeNutrition @RecipeID

\*--------------------------------------------------------------*/
-- Get the nutrition information for a recipe
-- Since nutrition information is saved per ingredient
-- This will be a summary of nutrition information
-- per ingredient that is specified in the recipe
```

Once you specify the general logic for the query, you can move forward with writing the T-SQL so that these requirements are met. This is often helpful if you usually find yourself rephrasing the code you have already written instead of explaining the overall purpose of the code.

Writing these comments before writing any T-SQL code ensures the comments explain the purpose of the stored procedure instead of how the code executes.

You should now be prepared to start defining SQL formatting standards for yourself and in your own organization. This will allow you and other members of your team to quickly review your organization's T-SQL code. In addition, I have discussed strategies to use when providing additional documentation about your T-SQL code. Commenting your T-SQL code will allow others to understand what the T-SQL code should be doing both regarding business logic and advanced technical logic. I have also covered options available when defining naming conventions for your organization. Well-defined naming conventions should make it easier for anyone accessing the database schema to know where to find database objects.

You should now be familiar with SQL Server data types and the best time to use them. You should also be comfortable with some of the various database objects that are available when writing your T-SQL. Now that you are also more familiar with how to style your code to improve readability and understanding, you are ready to learn more about designing T-SQL code using parameters, complex logic, and stored procedures.

CHAPTER 4

Designing T-SQL

In the earlier chapters in the section on "Building Understandable T-SQL," I have covered the various data types available and how to select the correct data type. I have also discussed several database objects available when you write your T-SQL and the pros and cons of using each database object. In the previous chapter, I explained the importance of making your code readable for yourself and others. I will finish up this section by going over the various options when designing your T-SQL code.

When writing T-SQL for your applications, I am a huge fan of using stored procedures. There are many advantages to using stored procedures including the possibility to make your code more adaptable and reusable. Similarly, using parameters with your code can increase the flexibility of your T-SQL code. You can use stored procedures and parameters when designing solutions for more complex queries. In addition, you may want to consider other techniques when it comes to solving complex issues. There are several items to consider when designing T-SQL code including stored procedures, parameters, and complex query logic.

Using Stored Procedures

When writing T-SQL code, you have several options available. Depending on the implementation you use, we will determine what SQL Server does with that T-SQL code. You can write ad hoc T-SQL where each query is written without uniformity. While this code can be repeated, you will need to be careful to make sure that all formatting is exactly consistent, including whitespace. There is also what is referred to as prepared statements. This type of T-SQL code uses parameters. When the prepared statements are used, the values passed to the parameters are updated. Finally, there are stored procedures. These are database objects that are persistent. Each of these has their pros and cons. However, stored procedures generally are the most consistent when writing T-SQL.

© Elizabeth Noble 2020
E. Noble, *Pro T-SQL 2019*, https://doi.org/10.1007/978-1-4842-5590-2_4

There are several aspects to consider when writing T-SQL code for applications. In order to better understand how you want your applications to use T-SQL, it may be best to understand how SQL Server handles each of the T-SQL options available. When SQL Server executes a query, it must determine how it will go about executing that query. Before doing this, SQL Server will check to see if there is already an execution plan for this query. Depending on how the T-SQL is written will have some impact on how SQL Server verifies that the execution plan is already in place.

To show how stored procedures, ad hoc queries, and prepared statements affect the plan cache, I will walk through some examples. In Listing 4-1, you can see a statement to create the stored procedure.

Listing 4-1. Create a Stored Procedure

```
/*----------------------------------------------------------------*\
Name:           dbo.GetRecipe
Author:         Elizabeth Noble
Created Date:   April 20, 2019
Description: Get a list of all recipes in the database

Sample Usage:
      EXECUTE dbo.GetRecipe

\*----------------------------------------------------------------*/
CREATE PROCEDURE dbo.GetRecipe

AS

      SELECT
            RecipeID,
            RecipeName,
            RecipeDescription,
            ServingQuantity,
            MealTypeID,
            PreparationTypeID,
            IsActive,
            DateCreated,
            DateModified
      FROM dbo.Recipe;
```

In this example, I am creating a stored procedure that cannot be configured. Each time this stored procedure is executed, it will pull back the same types of data. This stored procedure will pull back information about all recipes that have been entered into the database. If you want to see the results for this stored procedure, you can execute the stored procedure as shown in Listing 4-2.

Listing 4-2. Execute the Stored Procedure

```
EXECUTE dbo.GetRecipe;
```

SQL Server will create this execution plan and save the execution plan to the query plan cache. If this stored procedure is run again in the future, SQL Server will check the plan cache to see if this stored procedure already exists in the cache. This plan will sit in the plan cache for as long as SQL Server deems the plan relevant. In Figure 4-1, you can see the execution plan associated with the stored procedure in Listing 4-2.

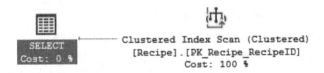

SELECT
Cost: 0 %

Clustered Index Scan (Clustered)
[Recipe].[PK_Recipe_RecipeID]
Cost: 100 %

Figure 4-1. *Execution Plan for Stored Procedure*

If the plan is in the cache, SQL Server will continue to reuse the same execution plan. This works well for stored procedures. However, there are other ways of accessing data in SQL Server. One of these methods is to write ad hoc queries. When writing ad hoc queries, you have the option to hard-code the values or parameterize them. An example of this type of query shown in Listing 4-3 has the same logic as a stored procedure in Listing 4-1.

Listing 4-3. Ad Hoc Query Logic

```
SELECT
    RecipeID,
    RecipeName,
    RecipeDescription,
    ServingQuantity,
    MealTypeID,
    PreparationTypeID,
```

```
        IsActive,
        DateCreated,
        DateModified
FROM dbo.Recipe;
```

The logic in Listings 4-1 and 4-3 is the same. The largest difference is in how SQL
Server handles the two. For both queries, it is a little harder to see. However, what
happens is SQL Server checks the plan cache to see if the same plan exists. The plans
that are stored in the plan cache are not based on the core logic but are based on how the
actual ad hoc query or stored procedure execution is written. In order to look at the plan
cache in SQL Server, you can use the query is available in Listing 4-4. This query is from
Microsoft Books Online.

Listing 4-4. Query to View Plans in the Cache

```
SELECT cplan.usecounts, cplan.objtype, qtext.text, qplan.query_plan
FROM sys.dm_exec_cached_plans AS cplan
CROSS APPLY sys.dm_exec_sql_text(plan_handle) AS qtext
CROSS APPLY sys.dm_exec_query_plan(plan_handle) AS qplan
ORDER BY cplan.usecounts DESC
```

As you will be able to see in Table 4-1 below, the ad hoc query is even stored as an
ad hoc object type, whereas SQL Server can properly tell that the second row is a stored
procedure. In Table 4-1, you can see the results in the plan cache from running the
stored procedure and the same code as an ad hoc query.

Table 4-1. *Plan Cache for Ad Hoc Query and Stored Procedure*

Use Count	Object Type	Query Text
1	Ad hoc	SELECT RecipeID, RecipeName, RecipeDescription, ServingQuantity, MealTypeID, PreparationTypeID, IsActive, DateCreated, DateModified FROM dbo.Recipe;
1	Proc	CREATE PROCEDURE dbo.GetRecipe AS SELECT RecipeID, RecipeName, RecipeDescription, ServingQuantity, MealTypeID, PreparationTypeID, IsActive, DateCreated, DateModified FROM dbo.Recipe;

Where this all can become important is when users or applications are writing code inconsistently. In this case, I modify the query from Listing 4-3 by moving the first column in the select statement to the same row as the SELECT clause. If I modify the query from Listing 4-3, you can see how the query plan cache changes since running the query in Listing 4-5.

Listing 4-5. Ad Hoc Query Modified

```
SELECT RecipeID,
       RecipeName,
       RecipeDescription,
       ServingQuantity,
       MealTypeID,
       PreparationTypeID,
       IsActive,
       DateCreated,
       DateModified
FROM dbo.Recipe;
```

I would hope that SQL Server can tell that the query in Listing 4-3 matches the same code as Listing 4-5. The only thing that has really changed is the formatting of the query itself. Rerunning the query from Listing 4-4, I can check the plan cache in Table 4-2.

Table 4-2. *Plan Cache for Modified Ad Hoc Query*

Use Count	Object Type	Query Text
1	Ad hoc	SELECT RecipeID, RecipeName, RecipeDescription, ServingQuantity, MealTypeID, PreparationTypeID, IsActive, DateCreated, DateModified FROM dbo.Recipe;
1	Ad hoc	SELECT RecipeID, RecipeName, RecipeDescription, ServingQuantity, MealTypeID, PreparationTypeID, IsActive, DateCreated, DateModified FROM dbo.Recipe;
1	Proc	CREATE PROCEDURE dbo.GetRecipe AS SELECT RecipeID, RecipeName, RecipeDescription, ServingQuantity, MealTypeID, PreparationTypeID, IsActive, DateCreated, DateModified FROM dbo.Recipe;

You can see in Table 4-2 that there are now three entries in the plan cache. Instead of SQL Server reusing the execution plan from the first time the ad hoc query was called, SQL Server has generated an entirely new execution plan. Each time SQL Server creates a new execution plan, it uses additional resources to create the plan. This can cause it to take a couple of seconds longer for SQL Server to return the query results. Each query plan executed is saved in the plan cache. Having multiple execution plans saved for each query can fill up the execution plan cache. This can cause other query execution plans to be removed from the plan cache prematurely. The removal of a query plan from the cache will cause SQL Server to expend additional resources to create a new execution for that other query. This is something to consider when determining how your applications will call T-SQL code.

While a stored procedure gives us a consistent way to call that same type of code more than once, stored procedures can be fairly limiting if the exact same base query will be used for every scenario. I will often want to write a general piece of T-SQL code that can be used for various scenarios. In these types of situations, I find myself wanting to write queries or stored procedures that use parameters.

Using Parameters

In addition to using stored procedures to help T-SQL code be more reusable, you can also use parameters with your T-SQL code. Parameters can be used with ad hoc queries, prepared statements, or stored procedures. It is also possible to use parameters as an input or output. Regardless of where parameters are used, parameters are what allow you to write queries that can be used in a variety of situations. In Listing 4-6, you can see that this is a stored procedure that will return recipe information based on the RecipeID that has been provided in the stored procedure.

Listing 4-6. Create Stored Procedure with a Parameter

```
/*-------------------------------------------------------------*\
Name:           dbo.GetRecipeByRecipeID
Author:         Elizabeth Noble
Created Date:   April 20, 2019
Description: Get recipe information when a recipe ID is provided
```

```
Sample Usage:
      DECLARE @RecipeID INT;

      SET @RecipeID = 1;

      EXECUTE dbo.GetRecipeByRecipeID @RecipeID

\*------------------------------------------------------------*/
CREATE PROCEDURE dbo.GetRecipeByRecipeID
      @RecipeID    INT
AS
      SELECT
            RecipeID,
            RecipeName,
            RecipeDescription,
            ServingQuantity,
            MealTypeID,
            PreparationTypeID,
            IsActive,
            DateCreated,
            DateModified
      FROM dbo.Recipe
      WHERE RecipeID = @RecipeID;
```

The preceding stored procedure allows you to pass in any RecipeID and the stored procedure will return a predefined set of recipe information based on that RecipeID. This also allows the T-SQL code to be called in a much simpler method. Looking at Listing 4-7, I have written code to execute the stored procedure passing a hard-coded value as part of the execution.

Listing 4-7. Execute Stored Procedure with Hard-Coded Value

```
EXECUTE dbo.GetRecipeByRecipeID 1;
```

While it is possible to use this method to call the stored procedure, using variables would be a much more dynamic way to execute this stored procedure. One such method is to declare a variable with a specific data type and then set that variable to a specific value. This more closely simulates how an application might call a stored procedure. The application code would generally have a variable already declared and use the same variable when executing the stored procedure. The process of declaring a variable, setting that variable to a value, and executing the stored procedure using that variable can be seen in Listing 4-8.

Listing 4-8. Execute Stored Procedure with a Variable

```
DECLARE @RecipeID INT;

SET @RecipeID = 1

EXECUTE dbo.GetRecipeByRecipeID @RecipeID;
```

To get a comparison of the plan cache for the stored procedure in Listing 4-6 vs. an ad hoc query, I will execute the ad hoc query that will use the same overall logic as Listing 4-6. However, this value will not be parameterized. In Listing 4-9, you can see the query with the hard-coded value for the RecipeID.

Listing 4-9. Run Ad Hoc Query with Hard-Coded Value

```
SELECT
     RecipeID,
     RecipeName,
     RecipeDescription,
     ServingQuantity,
     MealTypeID,
     PreparationTypeID,
     IsActive,
     DateCreated,
     DateModified
FROM dbo.Recipe
WHERE RecipeID = 1;
```

Another method for executing the same stored procedure would be to use a query like the one in Listing 4-9 but to use a parameter as part of the where clause. This will perform that same overall logic as Listings 4-7, 4-8, and 4-9. In Listing 4-10, I have used the same code by declaring a variable and parameterized the query overall.

Listing 4-10. Run Ad Hoc Query with a Parameter

```
DECLARE @RecipeID INT;

SET @RecipeID = 1

SELECT
      RecipeID,
      RecipeName,
      RecipeDescription,
      ServingQuantity,
      MealTypeID,
      PreparationTypeID,
      IsActive,
      DateCreated,
      DateModified
FROM dbo.Recipe
WHERE RecipeID = @RecipeID;
```

While all these queries are pulling back the same data, the way SQL Server handles these four queries can be surprisingly different. In my test case, I cleared the plan cache and then executed the T-SQL code in Listings 4-7, 4-8, 4-9, and 4-10. Even though each of these queries is returning the same results, you will see in Table 4-3 how SQL Server has calculated or used execution plans for each of these queries.

Table 4-3. *Comparison of Plan Cache for Variables and Hard-Coded Values*

Use Counts	Object Type	Text
2	Proc	CREATE PROCEDURE dbo.GetRecipeByRecipeID @RecipeID INT AS SELECT RecipeID, RecipeName, RecipeDescription, ServingQuantity, MealTypeID, PreparationTypeID, IsActive, DateCreated, DateModified FROM dbo.Recipe WHERE RecipeID = @RecipeID;
1	Ad hoc	DECLARE @RecipeID INT; SET @RecipeID = 1 EXECUTE dbo. GetRecipeByRecipeID @RecipeID;
1	Ad hoc	DECLARE @RecipeID INT; SET @RecipeID = 1 SELECT RecipeID, RecipeName, RecipeDescription, ServingQuantity, MealTypeID, PreparationTypeID, IsActive, DateCreated, DateModified FROM dbo.Recipe WHERE RecipeID = @RecipeID;
1	Ad hoc	SELECT RecipeID, RecipeName, RecipeDescription, ServingQuantity, MealTypeID, PreparationTypeID, IsActive, DateCreated, DateModified FROM dbo.Recipe WHERE RecipeID = 1;
1	Prepared	(@1 tinyint)SELECT [RecipeID], [RecipeName], [RecipeDescription], [ServingQuantity], [MealTypeID], [PreparationTypeID], [IsActive], [DateCreated], [DateModified] FROM [dbo].[Recipe] WHERE [RecipeID]=@1

In Table 4-3, you can see that the stored procedure has been executed twice. The SELECT statement with the hard-coded value and the SELECT statement with the parameter value each have their own execution plan. This may not have a large impact when you are discussing only a handful of queries. However, if your entire environment has a significant number of queries that are not stored procedures, you may want to check your plan cache to see how they are being handled.

This is not the only topic you need to consider when writing your queries. Another potential option has to do with what is commonly referred to as parameter sniffing. Parameter sniffing does not sound as dangerous as it can be. The key takeaway when

understanding what parameter sniffing is and how it affects you is to consider how
your data is shaped. For many companies, not all data stored in a data table is evenly
distributed. In Listing 4-11, you can see the stored procedure that I am creating to test for
parameter sniffing.

Listing 4-11. Stored Procedure to Find Recipe and Ingredient by Meal Type

```
/*----------------------------------------------------------------*\
Name:               dbo.GetRecipeAndIngredientByMealTypeID
Author:             Elizabeth Noble
Created Date:       April 20, 2019
Description: Get all recipes and their ingredients by meal type

Sample Usage:
      EXECUTE dbo.GetRecipeAndIngredientByMealTypeID 1

\*----------------------------------------------------------------*/
CREATE PROCEDURE dbo.GetRecipeAndIngredientByMealTypeID
      @MealTypeID     INT
AS

      SELECT
            rec.RecipeName,
            ingr.IngredientName,
            ingr.IsActive,
            ingr.DateCreated,
            ingr.DateModified
      FROM dbo.Recipe rec
            INNER JOIN dbo.RecipeIngredient recingr
            ON rec.RecipeID = recingr.RecipeID
            LEFT OUTER JOIN dbo.Ingredient ingr
            ON recingr.IngredientID = ingr.IngredientID
      WHERE rec.MealTypeID = @MealTypeID
      ORDER BY rec.RecipeName, ingr.IngredientName;
```

In the case of recipes, you may have a significant difference in the quantity of
the types of recipes that are stored in the tables. If you had hundreds or thousands
of breakfast recipes but only a handful of dinner recipes, you may find yourself in a

scenario where parameter sniffing would affect your application performance. In our scenario of meal types, you may execute a stored procedure wanting breakfast recipes. The first time you call your stored procedure, SQL Server will use the parameter provided to generate an execution plan. That execution plan will end up stored in the plan cache. To test for parameter sniffing, you may want to execute the stored procedure with a given parameter as shown in Listing 4-12.

Listing 4-12. Execute Stored Procedure with a Parameter with Many Records

```
EXECUTE dbo.GetRecipeAndIngredientByMealTypeID 3;
```

For this stored procedure execution, I get the following execution plan as shown in Figure 4-2.

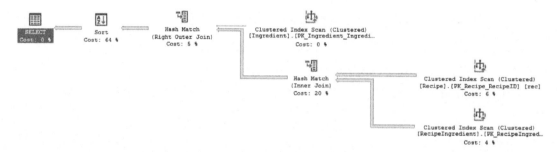

Figure 4-2. *Execution Plan for Stored Procedure with a Parameter That Has Many Records*

If you come back later and want to rerun the stored procedure for dinner recipes, SQL Server will reuse the original execution plan to pull back the data. However, the first execution plan that SQL Server created may perform worse when trying to find recipes with the meal type of dinner. If I were to clear the plan cache and rerun the stored procedure in a different order, I can verify that the issue is related to parameter sniffing. In Listing 4-13, you can see the T-SQL code used to generate a new execution plan now that the plan cache has been cleared.

Listing 4-13. Execute Stored Procedure with a Parameter with Few Records

```
EXECUTE dbo.GetRecipeAndIngredientByMealTypeID 2;
```

When I execute this stored procedure, I find that a different plan cache is created. You can see the other execution plan that is created in Figure 4-3.

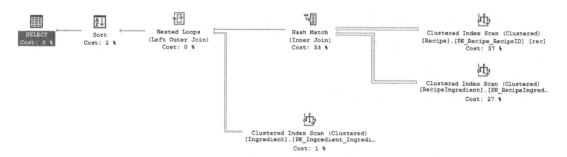

Figure 4-3. *Execution Plan for Stored Procedure with a Parameter That Has Many Records*

If I run the same T-SQL from Listing 4-12, I now get the same execution plan. This is a sign that this query is encountering parameter sniffing. There are several options available to handle parameter sniffing. Ideally, you may be able to redesign your query to use different indexes.

Unfortunately, it may not always be possible to modify the query in this manner. This may cause you to look for other options like updating the query using the WITH RECOMPILE query hint. The downside of using this method is that the query must be compiled each time the query is executed. This incurs both an additional cost in terms of hardware and time for each query execution. That is when you may want to look for better alternatives. It is possible to modify the query to the cached plan for certain parameters which are more common and recompile the stored procedure for all other scenarios. The stored procedure in Listing 4-14 has been modified to use recompile for some values.

Listing 4-14. Execute the Stored Procedure

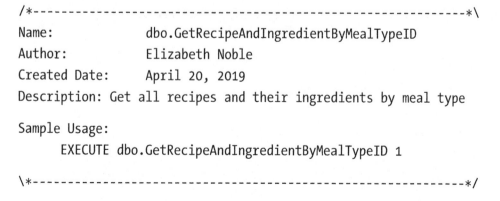

```
/*---------------------------------------------------------------*\
Name:          dbo.GetRecipeAndIngredientByMealTypeID
Author:        Elizabeth Noble
Created Date:  April 20, 2019
Description: Get all recipes and their ingredients by meal type

Sample Usage:
    EXECUTE dbo.GetRecipeAndIngredientByMealTypeID 1

\*---------------------------------------------------------------*/
```

```
CREATE PROCEDURE dbo.GetRecipeAndIngredientByMealTypeID
     @MealTypeID      INT
AS

DECLARE @QueryString     NVARCHAR(1000);

     -- Original query to be executed
     SELECT @QueryString = N'
     SELECT
          rec.RecipeName,
          ingr.IngredientName,
          ingr.IsActive,
          ingr.DateCreated,
          ingr.DateModified
     FROM dbo.Recipe rec
          INNER JOIN dbo.RecipeIngredient recingr
          ON rec.RecipeID = recingr.RecipeID
          LEFT OUTER JOIN dbo.Ingredient ingr
          ON recingr.IngredientID = ingr.IngredientID
     WHERE rec.MealTypeID = @MelTypID
     ORDER BY rec.RecipeName, ingr.IngredientName'
 -- If the parameters do not provide a stable execution plan
 ---- Add OPTION(RECOMPILE) to the query
IF (@MealTypeID <> 2)
BEGIN

     SELECT @QueryString = @QueryString + N' OPTION(RECOMPILE)';
END

-- Execute the query string
EXECUTE [sp_executesql] @QueryString,
     N'@MelTypID INT',
     @MelTypID = @MealTypeID;

GO
```

In Listing 14-14, the execution plan is considered stable when MealTypeID of 2 is provided. When the stored procedure is run with a MealTypeID of 2, the stored procedure will execute the T-SQL code without generating a new execution plan. However, if a different value is provided for the MealTypeID, then SQL Server will generate a new execution plan each time. This type of scenario works well when most of the time the query is executed; it will receive the parameter of MealTypeID of 2. This keeps SQL Server from generating an execution plan every time the stored procedure is called. If one or two times out of every ten times the stored procedure is executed and the parameter is not set as MealTypeID of 2, then SQL Server will generate a new execution plan. This method allows you to minimize the cost of recompiling the execution and limiting this to happen much less frequently. While SQL Server is working as intended, it is the shape of the data that is contributing to the performance issue.

Using Complex Logic

There are some basic operations in SQL Server that are not significantly complex. These basic operations can include inserting, reading, updating, and deleting table from single tables. Some of these operations may involve a couple of joins, but at some point in time, there may be a need for more complex logic. One of the challenges that happens while working with T-SQL is dealing with complex logic.

When dealing with complex logic, it is important to keep a couple of things in mind. The first step in dealing with complex logic is breaking down the request into smaller parts. Part of this logic will be to figure out what data you need to start with and how to whittle that data down into a smaller data set. You will also want to focus on taking all the requirements and breaking those requirements down into simplified steps.

Many of these query requests can involve either dealing with databases that were not designed to take advantage of the strengths for relational databases and systems that were not designed to be integrated or interacting with legacy applications. Oftentimes, we do not have control over what we are requested to do, and we are lucky if we get to design how the data is stored in the database.

These types of scenarios can also involve various types of coding methodologies that do not necessarily coincide with best practices. This includes needing to loop through data including recursion. There are also times that you may want to use correlated subqueries or work with various strings such as XML or JSON. While many of these options may seem like they are the perfect solution, many of these options are overly complex. This is where the balancing act between making T-SQL code easy to understand and having T-SQL code that performs well can be tricky. My goal here is to show how using what seems like more advanced query techniques may be contributing to poor performance in your applications.

It is often tempting with writing T-SQL to write your code in a way that matches the specific acceptance criteria or business request. Sometimes this will work well, and you will end up with code that performs very well. In other instances, not only can trying to write to solve complex problem be difficult and frustrating, but if the T-SQL code is not written in a way that works best for SQL Server, you have the potential to come across significant performance issues. I have found that SQL Server generally works best if you can keep your code simple and straightforward. This also means that using new functionality in SQL Server may not always yield the best results in terms of performance, even if the code is easier to write.

The most common case I see where the T-SQL code that is written does not always consider how SQL Server performs best is involving loops. SQL Server allows many options for looping through data, and while the code will return the correct results, I often find the cost on SQL Server more significant than figuring out a different way of interacting with the same data. Looking back at Listing 2-29, I have pasted the same logic in Listing 4-15.

Listing 4-15. Creating a Dynamic Cursor

```
SET NOCOUNT ON;

DECLARE @RecipeID INT,
    @RecipeName VARCHAR(25),
    @message VARCHAR(50);

PRINT '-------- Recipe Listing --------';

DECLARE recipe_cursor CURSOR DYNAMIC
FOR
SELECT RecipeID, RecipeName
FROM dbo.Recipe
ORDER BY RecipeID;

OPEN recipe_cursor
```

```
FETCH NEXT FROM recipe_cursor
INTO @RecipeID, @RecipeName

WHILE @@FETCH_STATUS = 0
BEGIN
    PRINT ' '
    SELECT @message = '----- Ingredients For Recipe: ' + @RecipeName +
    '-----'

    PRINT @message

        SELECT ing.IngredientName, srv.ServingPortionQuantity,
        srv.ServingPortionUnit
        FROM dbo.Ingredient ing
            INNER JOIN dbo.RecipeIngredient recing
            ON ing.IngredientID = recing.IngredientID
            INNER JOIN dbo.ServingPortion srv
            ON recing.ServingPortionID = srv.ServingPortionID
        WHERE recing.RecipeID = @RecipeID

        FETCH NEXT FROM recipe_cursor INTO @RecipeID, @RecipeName
END
CLOSE recipe_cursor;
DEALLOCATE recipe_cursor;
```

This query will give us the exact results we want, but SQL Server will have to repeat the logic inside the cursor for each row that the cursor will be analyzing. When the query logic inside the cursor is written well, there can be minimal impact. However, the real challenges happen when the T-SQL code inside the query either performs slowly or uses a significant amount of hardware. Then the server and even the applications can feel the pain every time the code inside the cursor is executed. While it is easy to blame cursors specifically, there are other scenarios like WHILE loops that have the same potential for issues.

Another of the larger struggles here is that even if the code performs well when it is first created, there is still the potential for the performance of this code to decrease over time as the database grows or the shape of the data changes. In those situations, what once appeared to be a great solution can quickly become one of the largest headaches. There are some options available to get the same output but write the T-SQL code in a manner that is more efficient and less resource intensive. In Listing 4-16, you will see some comments that are trying to outline the steps needed to get the same data output as would be returned in Listing 4-15.

Listing 4-16. Simplifying T-SQL Code Logic with Comments

```
-- Create Report Heading for All Recipes
-- Repeat the following per recipe
---- Create Section Subheading per Recipe
---- List All Ingredients Per Recipe
```

When working with queries where the logic is not straightforward, I will start by breaking down the overall request into smaller pieces. Ideally, the process of breaking the acceptance criteria down will allow me to focus on where I can start minimizing data. I will look at the query from two different perspectives. The first is determining how I can start paring the data down to only the data I will need in my result. I usually try to do that as early as possible in my query design. I will also try to look for the sections where I know the T-SQL code needed will be simple.

When referring to Listing 4-15, I can tell that I need a way to pull all ingredients per recipe. I also want to find a way to insert some sort of header between each recipe. I will eventually want to figure out how to insert the header row. However, I will first write a query to pull back all recipes and their ingredients. I have written that query in Listing 4-17.

Listing 4-17. Get All Ingredients for All Recipes

```
-- Create Report Heading for All Recipes
-- Repeat the following per recipe
---- Create Section Subheading per Recipe
---- List All Ingredients Per Recipe
    SELECT
            rec.RecipeName,
            ing.IngredientName,
            srv.ServingPortionQuantity,
            srv.ServingPortionUnit
    FROM dbo.Ingredient ing
            INNER JOIN dbo.RecipeIngredient recing
            ON ing.IngredientID = recing.IngredientID
```

```
        INNER JOIN dbo.Recipe rec
        ON recing.RecipeID = rec.RecipeID
        INNER JOIN dbo.ServingPortion srv
        ON recing.ServingPortionID = srv.ServingPortionID
    ORDER BY rec.RecipeName, ing.IngredientName
```

Once I have a starting point of data, I can continue to add additional pieces of logic. I will start with the main part of the data I am trying to pull back and branch out from there. In this example, I start adding header information as shown in Listing 4-18.

Listing 4-18. Get All the Data Pulled Together

```
-- Create Report Heading for All Recipes
PRINT '-------- Recipe Listing --------';
-- Repeat the following per recipe
---- Create Section Subheading per Recipe
    SELECT
            '----- Ingredients For Recipe: ' + rec.RecipeName + '-----' AS
            'SectionHeader'
    FROM  dbo.Recipe rec
---- List All Ingredients Per Recipe
    SELECT
            rec.RecipeID,
            rec.RecipeName,
            ing.IngredientName,
            srv.ServingPortionQuantity,
            srv.ServingPortionUnit
    FROM dbo.Ingredient ing
        INNER JOIN dbo.RecipeIngredient recing
        ON ing.IngredientID = recing.IngredientID
        INNER JOIN dbo.Recipe rec
        ON recing.RecipeID = rec.RecipeID
        INNER JOIN dbo.ServingPortion srv
        ON recing.ServingPortionID = srv.ServingPortionID
    ORDER BY rec.RecipeName, ing.IngredientName
```

After adding some header information, I am ready to start getting the output to match the current output. In Listing 4-19, you can see all the code that was required to match the original output.

Listing 4-19. Rewritten Query to Avoid Using a Cursor

```
SET NOCOUNT ON;
-- Create Report Heading for All Recipes
PRINT '-------- Recipe Listing --------';
PRINT "
-- Create a temporary table to store the recipe information
    CREATE TABLE #RecipeList
    (
        OrderedList             INT,
        RecipeID                INT,
        SectionHeader           VARCHAR(100)
    );
-- Repeat the following per recipe
---- Create Section Spacing per Recipe
    INSERT INTO #RecipeList (OrderedList, RecipeID, SectionHeader)
    SELECT
        0 AS 'OrderedList',
        rec.RecipeID,
        " AS 'SectionHeader'
    FROM  dbo.Recipe rec
    WHERE rec.RecipeID < 3

---- Create Section Subheading per Recipe
    INSERT INTO #RecipeList (OrderedList, RecipeID, SectionHeader)
    SELECT
        10 AS 'OrderedList',
        rec.RecipeID,
        '----- Ingredients For Recipe: ' + rec.RecipeName AS
        'SectionHeader'
    FROM  dbo.Recipe rec
    WHERE rec.RecipeID < 3
```

```
---- Add the column headings for ingredients per recipe
    INSERT INTO #RecipeList (OrderedList, RecipeID, SectionHeader)
    SELECT
        15 AS 'OrderedList',
        rec.RecipeID,
        CAST('IngredientName' AS CHAR(25)) + ' ' +
            CAST('ServingPortionQuantity' AS CHAR(22)) + ' ' +
            CAST('ServingPortionUnit' AS CHAR(19)) AS 'SectionHeader'
    FROM  dbo.Recipe rec
    WHERE rec.RecipeID < 3

    INSERT INTO #RecipeList (OrderedList, RecipeID, SectionHeader)
    SELECT
        20 AS 'OrderedList',
        rec.RecipeID,
        '------------------------ --------------------- -------------
        -----' AS 'SectionHeader'
    FROM  dbo.Recipe rec
    WHERE rec.RecipeID < 3
---- List All Ingredients Per Recipe
    INSERT INTO #RecipeList
    (
        OrderedList,
        RecipeID,
        SectionHeader
    )
    SELECT
        25 AS 'OrderedList',
        rec.RecipeID,
        CAST(ing.IngredientName AS CHAR(25)) + ' ' +
            CAST(srv.ServingPortionQuantity AS CHAR(22)) + ' ' +
            CAST(srv.ServingPortionUnit AS CHAR(19)) AS
            'SectionHeader'
    FROM dbo.Ingredient ing
        INNER JOIN dbo.RecipeIngredient recing
        ON ing.IngredientID = recing.IngredientID
```

```
        INNER JOIN dbo.Recipe rec
        ON recing.RecipeID = rec.RecipeID
        INNER JOIN dbo.ServingPortion srv
        ON recing.ServingPortionID = srv.ServingPortionID
WHERE rec.RecipeID < 3
ORDER BY rec.RecipeName, ing.IngredientName

SELECT
        SectionHeader
FROM #RecipeList
ORDER BY RecipeID, OrderedList

DROP TABLE #RecipeList
```

The original cursor gave the output shown in Figure 4-4 when the results were written to text.

```
-------- Recipe Listing --------

----- Ingredients For Recipe: Spaghetti
IngredientName              ServingPortionQuantity ServingPortionUnit
------------------------    ---------------------- ------------------
Italian Sausage             2                      lbs
Tomato Sauce                40                     oz


----- Ingredients For Recipe: Tomato Sauce
IngredientName              ServingPortionQuantity ServingPortionUnit
------------------------    ---------------------- ------------------
Tomato                      40                     oz
```

Figure 4-4. *Output from Cursor*

To confirm that our rewrite from Listing 4-19 is correct, I captured the results to text when executing the same query. The output in Figure 4-5 appears to be the same.

```
-------- Recipe Listing --------


----- Ingredients For Recipe: Spaghetti
IngredientName                ServingPortionQuantity ServingPortionUnit
----------------------------- ---------------------- ------------------
Italian Sausage               2                      lbs
Tomato Sauce                  40                     oz

----- Ingredients For Recipe: Tomato Sauce
IngredientName                ServingPortionQuantity ServingPortionUnit
----------------------------- ---------------------- ------------------
Tomato                        40                     oz
```

Figure 4-5. *Output from Modified Query*

However, these outputs are only the same when they are exported to text. When dealing with small sets of data, the extra code and level of work may not seem to be required. As is usually the case, most performance issues do not become apparent until the performance is significantly and negatively impacted. In the case of these two methods, when working with two records, the performance appeared the same. However, when handling over 10,000 recipes, it becomes immediately clear that the query from Listing 4-19 performs significantly better.

In this chapter, I have covered how and why you would want to use stored procedures. This includes creating code that is reusable and consistent. I have also shown you how to use parameters. For the most part, parameters will help make your code more adaptable and dynamic. Parameters are helpful for many different scenarios. While parameters are very useful in many different situations, you will also need to make sure your T-SQL is not being negatively affected by parameter sniffing. I also covered a common situation where you may need to solve complex problems using T-SQL. You will often find your T-SQL performs better when you keep the code more straightforward. This may mean that the code is not as readable or clean, but SQL Server will have a better idea how to get an optimal execution plan.

This also concludes the current section on writing understandable T-SQL. This is T-SQL that uses the best data type for each scenario. This is usually a data type that takes up the least amount of space possible and provides the necessary accuracy. You will also want to understand the various SQL Server database objects available that you can use to build your T-SQL. You will need to determine the benefits vs. the challenges of using one database object vs. another. In some cases, you will need to decide if code readability or database performance is more important. Another aspect of writing understandable T-SQL is formatting, naming, and commenting your T-SQL so that others can quickly understand what you have written.

When working with T-SQL, there will be times where you want to write T-SQL that can be called consistently more than once. This T-SQL code may also become more flexible using parameters. When faced with writing T-SQL that is not straightforward, it will help you break the code into segments to simplify what needs to be written. Once you feel comfortable writing T-SQL that is understandable, you will be ready to start focusing on writing T-SQL that is efficient and minimizes performance impact on SQL Server.

PART II

Building Performant T-SQL

CHAPTER 5

Set-Based Design

Knowing how to design T-SQL is part of the foundation for writing professional code. Once you can write T-SQL code that can be easily understood, you can start to focus on improving the performance of your T-SQL code. If you learned T-SQL informally as part of your job or your primary function is writing code for software applications, you may not consciously consider set-based design when writing your T-SQL code. You may be an experienced database developer and want to learn more about set-based design.

In this chapter, I want to discuss how to work with your data. The first step is to get familiar with the various ways to interact with your data. Once you understand the different ways you can interact with your data, you want to start thinking about how to put the data in the best format for your queries. Then you should be able to write those queries in a way that takes advantages of SQL Server's natural strengths.

Introduction to Set-Based Design

We live in a world where data is everywhere. Almost anything we do can generate data that needs to be saved. The first challenge in collecting data is determining how to store data. The second challenge is accessing that data. One of the reasons you will use SQL Server is to take advantage of the relationships between data. This is because SQL Server is a relational database management system (RDBMS). While our focus is writing T-SQL, it is important to also understand how the data is stored in SQL Server.

Going back to my example of a database for recipes, let's look at what types of data can be associated with this type of information:

- Name
- Cost
- Ingredients
- Number of Servings

- Preparation Time

- Cooking Time

- Type of Cuisine

- Cooking Method

- Type of Meal

I can group data together by how they describe other items. For instance, I can group information about recipes as shown in Table 5-1.

Table 5-1. *General Attributes for Ingredients*

Recipe	Ingredient	Cooking Method
Name	Name	Name
Cuisine	Unit of Measure	
Number of Servings	Cost	
Ingredients		
Quantity of Ingredient		

Once that information is grouped, the data can be stored by those groupings. If I were to start populating data for ingredients, the data could be stored in a table as shown in Table 5-2.

Table 5-2. *General Ingredient Information*

Ingredient Name	Unit(s)	Measurement	Cost
Diced Tomatoes	28	Ounces	$1.84
Tomato Paste	10	Tablespoon	$0.79
Tomato Sauce	8	Ounces	$0.55
Minced Garlic	60	Tablespoon	$5.99

The data organized in the table is a data set. Looking at the data in the first column, Ingredient Name, there are three records that contain the word tomato. There are also two rows that are measured in ounces.

One of the things that can be difficult when working with SQL Server is the use of set-based transactions. People come to SQL Server from other fields and professions. These include software development, networking, system administration, or general business operations. In each of these cases, a person may not have developed the skill set for thinking in set-based operations.

What are set-based operations? What do they mean? Why are they so important? Set-based operations are looking at data in terms of chunks or segments instead of looking at records or data row by row. To show you a comparison, Table 5-3 shows each data record individually.

Table 5-3. *Ingredients by*
Individual Row

Ingredient Name
Diced Tomatoes

Ingredient Name
Tomato Paste

Ingredient Name
Tomato Sauce

Ingredient Name
Minced Garlic

If I were to select the data from Table 5-3 in this manner, it would be far less efficient than trying to select the data as a set. Table 5-4 shows what it would look like to select the data as a set.

Table 5-4. *Ingredients as One Data Set*

Ingredient Name
Diced Tomatoes
Tomato Paste
Tomato Sauce
Minced Garlic

Viewing the data like this allows you to also see the similarities between the data.

You are trying to figure out how to handle implementing a process or a task with multiple rows at the same time. You want to consider doing the same thing to all those rows at the same time. In the preceding example, I can quickly determine which records have the word tomato in common. The data is giving us a hint that if we want to look at or change something about ingredients with tomatoes, there may be more than one way to accomplish this goal. This type of scenario may indicate your logic should be structured in a way that it can function correctly by using algebraic logic instead of hard-coded values.

Procedural code is described as not only telling a system what to do but how to do it. In many companies the software developers or software engineers are the ones responsible for writing the T-SQL code. One of the things I have found is when writing application code, this code is designed to work best procedurally. Much of the code performs well when interacting with data iteratively. The cost of context switching between procedural application code and database T-SQL code can be significant. Overall the process of writing set-based code causes a very different thought process than dealing with the code iteratively.

Why are we even interested in using set-based design? Why is it worth the trouble? This has to do with how the SQL Server engine works and how data is retrieved for queries. When a query is issued, SQL Server needs to retrieve the data record. SQL Server goes to the buffer cache to see if this data is available. Figure 5-1 shows the process SQL Server goes through to retrieve data as part of a query request if the data is cached in the buffer pool.

Figure 5-1. *Data Retrieval from a Single Query*

If the query is written procedurally, that is, to execute every time a new row is retrieved, SQL Server will need to go to the buffer cache for each record. The process of retrieving a single row at a time can increase the workload on SQL Server. In Figure 5-2, you can see the additional workload required to retrieve one row at a time.

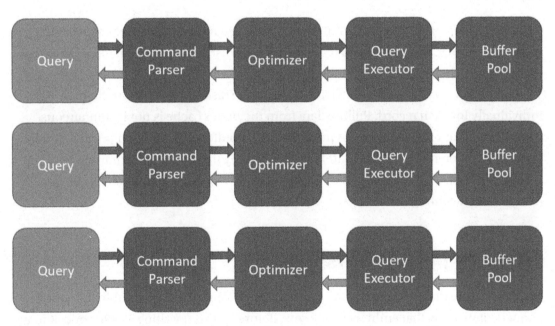

Figure 5-2. *Data Retrieval when Query Retrieves One Row at a Time*

Figure 5-2 shows the query process to retrieve a single record at a time with the data stored in the buffer pool. However, if the query is written for set-based design, then there will be one call to the buffer pool. On a small set of data, this may not be a very large impact. When dealing with data sets of thousands or millions of records, the difference in execution time can be drastic. There is also something else at play here that has to do with how the data is stored in the buffer cache. When SQL Server executes a query and pulls back data, it only pulls back data that exists in the buffer cache. Starting in

SQL Server 2019, there is a feature called the hybrid buffer pool. The hybrid buffer pool allows both data stored on RAM and in persistent memory (PMEM) to be treated as being part of the buffer cache. Otherwise, if the data is not available in RAM or PMEM, then SQL Server will need to go to disk to retrieve the data. The data retrieved will then be stored in memory. Figure 5-3 shows how this data would be retrieved from disk and stored in the buffer cache.

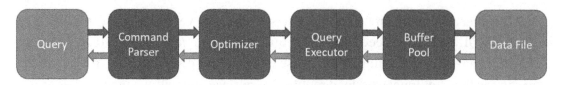

Figure 5-3. *Data Retrieval from Disk to the Buffer Cache*

When the query is executed, that data may not even be in the buffer cache at that point in time. SQL Server must go to the subsystem disk I/O to find that data. Once that data is found, that data is stored in the buffer cache.

If each row is pulled individually, that call to the disk I/O will have to happen individually for each record. Pulling data from the buffer cache is not instantaneous. Getting data from the disk I/O and putting it in the buffer cache to then be retrieved by the query is even more resource intensive. Ultimately this creates a scenario where you want to focus on set-based design to have the best possible performance for the queries that you are executing.

Thinking in Data Sets

Now that I have discussed what data sets are, I want you to be comfortable thinking about data in a way that embraces data sets. Before you start writing T-SQL code, it may save you time and energy by first understanding what information is stored, how the data is stored, and selecting or using that data in groups of similar characteristics. Working with data sets is also easier to accomplish when the underlying tables are designed to work best with data sets.

The real trick is learning how to think in terms of data sets. This means how to think about handling multiple records at once instead of a single record. This really requires an approach that is less arithmetic and more algebraic. In general, performing SELECT statements is the easiest way to get comfortable with set-based transactions. Consider the data shown in Table 5-5.

Table 5-5. *Ingredient Data*

Ingredient Name	Unit(s)	Measurement	Cost
Diced Tomatoes	28	Ounces	$1.85
Tomato Paste	10	Tablespoons	$0.79
Tomato Sauce	8	Ounces	$0.55
Minced Garlic	60	Tablespoon	$5.99

This is a list of possible ingredients for a recipe along with the number of units, the unit of measure, and the cost per unit. By looking at the preceding data, I can find similarities between the data in some of the columns.

I can create a data set that gets all records where the measurement is tablespoon. Those records are shown in Table 5-6.

Table 5-6. *Ingredients with Measurement of Tablespoon*

Ingredient Name	Unit(s)	Measurement	Cost
Tomato Paste	10	Tablespoons	$0.79
Minced Garlic	60	Tablespoon	$5.99

I could instead get the data set for all ingredients where the cost was less than $1.00 as shown in Table 5-7.

Table 5-7. *Ingredients with a Cost Less Than $1.00*

Ingredient Name	Unit(s)	Measurement	Cost
Tomato Paste	10	Tablespoons	$0.79
Tomato Sauce	8	Ounces	$0.55

Now that I have a set of data, I can consider how I want to interact with that data set. Knowing that I can group like data together and perform an action on that entire set of data is the key to using T-SQL code effectively. If I want to find out that cost per unit, I can divide the cost by the number of units. To calculate the cost per unit for each record,

I can calculate the cost per unit manually for each record. In this case, the cost per unit for tomato paste would be $0.79/10. This would give the result of $0.08 per tablespoon. Alternatively, I can use the columns in the data sets to do the same calculation. To calculate the cost per unit as a data set, I can specify Cost/Unit(s). The result of handling the data in this fashion would be an output like the one shown in Table 5-8.

Table 5-8. *Calculated Value for Cost per Unit of an Ingredient*

Ingredient Name	Cost per Unit
Tomato Paste	$0.08 per tablespoon
Tomato Sauce	$0.07 per ounce

One of the greatest challenges working with SQL Server is learning how to think in data sets. The simplest way to think of data sets is to view the process of retrieving data as performing an action on a column or a subset of a column. If you can find some sort of pattern on how to perform that action on a subset of the data, then you are thinking in terms of data sets.

Looking at the ingredient table, I could create a data set where all ingredients had the word tomato in the ingredient name. All the available values in the Ingredient table are in Table 5-9.

Table 5-9. *General Listing of Ingredients*

IngredientID	Ingredient Name	Unit(s)	Measurement	Cost
1	Diced Tomatoes	28	Ounces	$1.85
2	Tomato Paste	10	Tablespoons	$0.79
3	Tomato Sauce	8	Ounces	$0.55
4	Minced Garlic	60	Tablespoon	$5.99

I have a couple different ways to do this. I can write a query that looks where the IngredientID is 1, 2, or 3. You can see the results of this logic shown in Table 5-10.

Table 5-10. *Ingredients Containing the Work Tomato*

IngredientID	Ingredient Name	Unit(s)	Measurement	Cost
1	Diced Tomatoes	28	Ounces	$1.85
2	Tomato Paste	10	Tablespoons	$0.79
3	Tomato Sauce	8	Ounces	$0.55

Going back to the preceding table, I want to add a new record for Tomato Soup.
I show the new record added to Table 5-11.

Table 5-11. *Adding Tomato Soup to Ingredients*

IngredientID	Ingredient Name	Unit(s)	Measurement	Cost
1	Diced Tomatoes	28	Ounces	$1.85
2	Tomato Paste	10	Tablespoons	$0.79
3	Tomato Sauce	8	Ounces	$0.55
4	Minced Garlic	60	Tablespoon	$5.99
5	Tomato Soup	10.75	Ounces	$1.58

If I want to still show all records that have tomato and I use the same logic as earlier
which is to use the IngredientID to display the desired values, I will not get the results
I expect. If I did not change how the data was pulled back and used the same data to
pull back records like I did in table, then I would get the following result set as shown in
Table 5-12.

Table 5-12. *Ingredients with Tomato Using Hard-Coded IngredientID*

IngredientID	Ingredient Name	Unit(s)	Measurement	Cost
1	Diced Tomatoes	28	Ounces	$1.85
2	Tomato Paste	10	Tablespoons	$0.79
3	Tomato Sauce	8	Ounces	$0.55

Table 5-13 shows the expected results by changing my logic to look at the ingredient name to find all ingredients containing the word tomato.

Table 5-13. *Ingredients with Tomato Searching on the Ingredient Name*

IngredientID	Ingredient Name	Unit(s)	Measurement	Cost
1	Diced Tomatoes	28	Ounces	$1.85
2	Tomato Paste	10	Tablespoons	$0.79
3	Tomato Sauce	8	Ounces	$0.55
5	Tomato Soup	10.75	Ounces	$1.58

In that case, I would want to run a query where the ingredient name was like tomato. As you can see in this example, there are not only limitations with regard to data sets that affect performance but can also affect functionality.

One of the largest challenges in using data sets has to do with inserting data records. In most cases, when you insert a data record, you are inserting a single record at a time. This can cause it to become a habit to only deal with inserting one individual record at a time. When you are designing new table or moving data, you may have situations where you can think of an insert in terms of a data set. This will often happen when you are creating a query to insert data into another table.

While it does not seem like these situations will come up very often, I am frequently using data sets when I am populating temporary tables, table variables, and common table expressions.

Inserting data as a set uses the foundation of selecting data as data set. Once you a select data as a set, you can insert data as a set. I have used inserting data into an object like a temporary table for a couple of different reasons. One of the more common situations where I insert data sets is when I am joining several different tables and implementing criteria that make complicated calculations or functions. Looking at Table 5-14, you can see some examples of data that will be inserted into dbo. RecipeIngredient.

Table 5-14. *Ingredients in a Recipe by Each Record*

RecipeID	IngredientID	IsActive
Spaghetti	Diced Tomatoes	True

RecipeID	IngredientID	IsActive
Spaghetti	Tomato Paste	True

RecipeID	IngredientID	IsActive
Spaghetti	Tomato Sauce	True

RecipeID	IngredientID	IsActive
Spaghetti	Minced Garlic	True

While all these entries could be inserted individually, it is also possible to insert multiple records at once. In this case, it may look something like Table 5-15.

Table 5-15. *Ingredients in a Recipe as a Data Set*

RecipeID	IngredientID	IsActive
Spaghetti	Diced Tomatoes	True
Spaghetti	Tomato Paste	True
Spaghetti	Tomato Sauce	True
Spaghetti	Minced Garlic	True

Another scenario where I have found using bulk inserts into temporary objects is when those records may require additional modifications by joining to other queries that include multiple table joins.

If you are changing how your application code works and inserting new tables or changing how the value should be populated, you may find yourself needing to perform bulk updates. While you can perform bulk updates by updating one record at a time with hard-coded values, you will want to see if there is a way to update all the records in the data set by using the same code logic. However, this can be where data sets really help you out.

You can write one query to find all the records that you need to update and systematically perform all those updates. In addition to the advantages in terms of performance and functionality, this type of process also ensures that your data is being handled consistently.

Overall, the process for updating data as a data set is very much like the methods discussed for selecting and inserting data. In Table 5-16, you can see information stored in the dbo.Recipe table.

Table 5-16. *Recipes with Servings and Meal Type*

Recipe	Serving Quantity	Meal Type
Spaghetti	8	Dinner
Spinach Frittata	6	Breakfast
Roasted Chicken	4	Dinner
Dinner Rolls	12	Bread

While this is how the recipes are currently saved, I may decide that I want to change how meal types are stored. I may want to change the meal type by the main ingredient rather than by the time of day the meal was served. In that case, I could update the records one at a time as shown in Table 5-17.

Table 5-17. *Recipes as Individual Records*

Recipe	Serving Portion	Original Meal Type	New Meal Type
Spaghetti	8	Dinner	Meat

Recipe	Serving Portion	Original Meal Type	New Meal Type
Spinach Frittata	6	Breakfast	Egg

Recipe	Serving Portion	Original Meal Type	New Meal Type
Roasted Chicken	4	Dinner	Meat

Recipe	Serving Portion	Original Meal Type	New Meal Type
Dinner Rolls	12	Bread	Grain

If I used a simple form of logic to determine what records should be updated, I may be able to write the updates to run in the manner shown in Table 5-18.

Table 5-18. *Recipes as Data Sets by Meal Type*

Recipe	Serving Portion	Original Meal Type	New Meal Type
Spaghetti	8	Dinner	Meat
Roasted Chicken	4	Dinner	Meat

Recipe	Serving Portion	Original Meal Type	New Meal Type
Spinach Frittata	6	Breakfast	Egg

Recipe	Serving Portion	Original Meal Type	New Meal Type
Dinner Rolls	12	Bread	Grain

While these updates could be done in a with hard-coded values, there are times that it may be better to join the table you are updating to other related tables. This type of interaction between the tables may make it easier to perform your updates.

You could use the ingredients in the recipe to determine how to update the meal types on your recipes. It helps to think about the logic you would want to use. If you wanted to update the meal type to a generic category based upon the main ingredient per recipe, you would first need to figure out what the main ingredient was per recipe. You would also need to determine general categories for your meal type. In the preceding scenario, I might have Meat, Egg, Fruit, Vegetable, Grain, and Sugar. Once I have both pieces of information, I may create a temporary table to map the ingredients to a specific category, unless I have designed the ingredient table to record that specific category per ingredient.

In general, I found anytime that I am dealing with data one record of the time, I am often having to perform some type of manual interaction. I have found that manual interactions are the most likely to have issues or errors. I much prefer writing code in data sets, so that I can be more assured that my logic is being consistent.

Writing Code for Data Sets

Previously, I discussed how to start thinking about your data as data sets instead of individual records. I frequently use data sets when selecting, updating, or deleting data. While most application code may insert single records at a time, there are many common scenarios where inserting data as data set may also be helpful. In this next section, I will walk through various scenarios where you may want to think about your data as sets instead of individual records.

The most frequent use for data sets is when you want to view a portion of data. Ideally, these data sets are selected based upon specific criteria. This is not only good for performance but also can help make sure you are only looking at the specific data that you want. For most scenarios, it does not even make sense to retrieve and display one individual record at a time. Oftentimes, if you find yourself in a situation where you are selecting one record at a time, it is a good indication that you may want to see if that T-SQL code can be rewritten to use set-based logic.

There are some more complex ways that queries can be selected. In some cases, you may find yourself wanting to combine or compare two different data sets. If you want to join two data sets together, you have the option of UNION or UNION ALL. There is only one small but important difference between the two of these. When you UNION data, each record returned will be distinct between the SELECT statements that are joined together. Listing 5-1 shows a UNION between two queries.

Listing 5-1. Union of Two Queries

```
SELECT IngredientID, IngredientName
FROM dbo.Ingredient
WHERE IngredientName LIKE '%Tomato%'

UNION

SELECT IngredientID, IngredientName
FROM dbo.Ingredient
WHERE Measurement = 'Ounces'
```

Table 5-19 shows the data currently stored for ingredients. In Table 5-19, I have five ingredients that are all active.

Table 5-19. *General Ingredients*

IngredientID	IngredientName	Measurement	IsActive
1	Italian Sausage	Pound	1
2	Tomato Sauce	Tablespoon	1
3	Diced Tomatoes	Ounces	1
4	Tomato Paste	Ounces	1
5	Minced Garlic	Ounces	1

Using Table 5-20, the first query from the preceding figure would return the following values.

Table 5-20. *Ingredients with Tomatoes*

IngredientID	IngredientName
2	Tomato Sauce
3	Diced Tomatoes
4	Tomato Paste

The data from the second query from Table 5-21 would be the following.

Table 5-21. *Ingredients Measured in Ounces*

IngredientID	IngredientName
3	Diced Tomatoes
4	Tomato Paste
5	Minced Garlic

A union would give us the following result set as shown in Table 5-22.

Table 5-22. *Union of Results from Tables 5-21 and 5-22*

IngredientID	IngredientName
2	Tomato Sauce
3	Diced Tomatoes
4	Tomato Paste
5	Minced Garlic

However, for a UNION ALL, every record returned in both queries will be returned regardless of whether there are duplicate values in the multiple queries. If we were to run the same query but use a UNION ALL, the T-SQL code would look like Listing 5-2.

Listing 5-2. Union All of Two Queries

```
SELECT IngredientID, IngredientName
FROM dbo.Ingredient
WHERE IngredientName LIKE '%Tomato%'

UNION ALL

SELECT IngredientID, IngredientName
FROM dbo.Ingredient
WHERE Measurement = 'Ounces'
```

Since we are returning all data, even if they are duplicate, the result for a UNION ALL would look like the values in Table 5-23.

Table 5-23. *Union All of Results from Tables 5-21 and 5-22*

IngredientID	IngredientName
2	Tomato Sauce
3	Diced Tomatoes
4	Tomato Paste
4	Tomato Paste
5	Minced Garlic

As you can see, the UNION ALL would return two rows that were identical. There are times where each of these scenarios may be desirable.

There are times where the query logic is complex enough that I may not quickly understand all the T-SQL code or other times where I am troubleshooting very large data sets. If I write a simpler query that returns all the data that I want, I will often write an INTERSECT between those two queries to find where the records match. Using the same general query as earlier, I want to show you what the data returned will look like when using INTERSECT as compared to the other options. In Listing 5-3, you can see the query to find the intersection between the two queries.

Listing 5-3. Intersect of Two Queries

```
SELECT IngredientID, IngredientName
FROM dbo.Ingredient
WHERE IngredientName LIKE '%Tomato%'

INTERSECT

SELECT IngredientID, IngredientName
FROM dbo.Ingredient
WHERE Measurement = 'Ounces'
```

We already know what results returned for each query individually from the preceding figures. The actual results for the preceding T-SQL code are shown in Table 5-24.

Table 5-24. *Intersect of Results from Tables 5-21 and 5-22*

IngredientID	IngredientName
4	Tomato Paste

In addition, if I am trying to find missing records or verify that there are matching records, I will use an EXCEPT between two queries. Listing 5-4 shows what the T-SQL code would look like if you were trying to exclude the results from one query from the results of the other query.

Listing 5-4. Except of Two Queries

```
SELECT IngredientID, IngredientName
FROM dbo.Ingredient
WHERE IngredientName LIKE '%Tomato%'

EXCEPT

SELECT IngredientID, IngredientName
FROM dbo.Ingredient
WHERE Measurement = 'Ounces'
```

In this case, the first query returns all results where the ingredient name includes the word tomato. However, the except statement indicates that if a record is returned in both the first and second query, then the record will be excluded from the result set. The results of this query is in Table 5-25.

Table 5-25. *Except of Results from Tables 5-21 and 5-22*

IngredientID	IngredientName
2	Tomato Sauce
3	Diced Tomatoes

Using an EXCEPT statement may not be the preferred method to exclude results from a data set, but it is the method that I am more accustomed to using. Therein lies the benefits and challenges of T-SQL code, for almost any scenario there is almost certainly more than one way to write T-SQL code. Depending on the reason you are writing database code will determine the level of flexibility you have in writing your code. If you are executing a query for a single time, you may be able to use a less efficient method to access this data. However, if you are writing your code for an application, you will want to balance how you write your T-SQL code to be both efficient and readable.

Listing 5-5 is an example of how to use data sets when inserting data.

Listing 5-5. Inserting Data as a Set

```
CREATE TABLE #TempIngredientNutrition
(
        IngredientID     INT         NOT NULL,
        IngredientName   VARCHAR(25) NOT NULL,
        Calories         TINYINT     NOT NULL,
        Sugar            TINYINT     NOT NULL,
        Fiber            TINYINT     NOT NULL,
        Protein          TINYINT     NOT NULL
)

INSERT INTO #TempIngredientNutrition
(
        IngredientID,
        IngredientName,
        Calories,
        Sugar,
        Fiber,
        Protein
)
SELECT
        ing.IngredientID,
        ing.IngredientName,
        nutr.Calories,
        nutr.Sugar,
```

```
        nutr.Fiber,
        nutr.Protein
FROM dbo.Ingredient ing
        INNER JOIN dbo.IngredientNutrition nutr
        ON ing.IngredientID = nutr.IngredientID
```

As shown in Listing 5-6, this is what the insert statements would look like if there were inserted record by record.

Listing 5-6. Inserting Data Record by Record

```
CREATE TABLE #TempIngredientNutrition
(
        IngredientID        INT         NOT NULL,
        IngredientName      VARCHAR(25) NOT NULL,
        Calories            TINYINT     NOT NULL,
        Sugar               TINYINT     NOT NULL,
        Fiber               TINYINT     NOT NULL,
        Protein             TINYINT     NOT NULL
)

INSERT INTO #TempIngredientNutrition
(
        IngredientID,
        IngredientName,
        Calories,
        Sugar,
        Fiber,
        Protein
)
VALUES (1, 'Italian Sausage', 180, 5, 1, 18)

INSERT INTO #TempIngredientNutrition
(
        IngredientID,
        IngredientName,
        Calories,
        Sugar,
```

```
        Fiber,
        Protein
)
VALUES (2, 'Tomato Sauce', 60, 7, 2, 1)

INSERT INTO #TempIngredientNutrition
(
        IngredientID,
        IngredientName,
        Calories,
        Sugar,
        Fiber,
        Protein
)
VALUES (3, 'Diced Tomatoes', 20, 2, 3, 1)
```

As you can see, inserting data record by record takes up considerably more code and can be quite a bit more tedious.

One of my favorite uses for data sets is to update data. In many situations, I am not updating a specific record, but I am updating multiple records that share the same characteristics. If I want to make all these ingredients inactive from the table, I have a couple different ways I can do this. For instance, I can write one update statement per record to set the IsActive value to zero as shown in Listing 5-7.

Listing 5-7. Updating Data Record by Record

```
UPDATE dbo.Ingredient
SET IsActive = 0
WHERE IngredientID = 1

UPDATE dbo.Ingredient
SET IsActive = 0
WHERE IngredientID = 2

UPDATE dbo.Ingredient
SET IsActive = 0
WHERE IngredientID = 3
```

```
UPDATE dbo.Ingredient
SET IsActive = 0
WHERE IngredientID = 4

UPDATE dbo.Ingredient
SET IsActive = 0
WHERE IngredientID = 5
```

This would require five unique transactions. In addition, SQL Server would have to access the data page that each of these records was on five times. As shown in Listing 5-8, I could also write a query that would allow me to update all five records at once.

Listing 5-8. Updating Data as a Range

```
UPDATE dbo.Ingredient
SET IsActive = 0
WHERE IngredientID BETWEEN 1 AND 5
```

In fact, if all five of these records lived on the same data page, I would only need to access that page once. A much more likely scenario would be a request to deactivate all ingredients that contained the word tomato in the ingredient name. This is type of pattern you want to find. If there is a pattern like this, you can write a query like the one in Listing 5-9.

Listing 5-9. Updating Data as a Data Set

```
UPDATE dbo.Ingredient
SET IsActive = 0
WHERE IngredientName LIKE '%Tomato%'
```

This query accomplishes two goals. It lets you update more than one record in a given query. This T-SQL code also uses the data set for all ingredients that contain the word tomato to determine which records should be updated.

This is not the limit to using data sets for updating multiple records. I have had many situations where I need to update hundreds or thousands of records. While I could write a query to identify each record individually and then manually pull those IDs to update all those records individually or in a set. There are easier ways to update those multiple records and minimize the risk of errors due to human intervention. The query in Listing 5-10 shows you can update data while joining tables together.

Listing 5-10. Updating Data with Joins to Create a Data Set

```
UPDATE ing
SET ing.DateModified = GETDATE()
FROM dbo.Ingredient ing
     INNER JOIN dbo.RecipeIngredient recing
     ON ing.IngredientID = recing.IngredientID
     INNER JOIN dbo.Recipe rec
     ON recing.RecipeID = rec.RecipeID
WHERE rec.RecipeName = 'Spaghetti'
```

When using joins during your updates, I would recommend that you confirm what data you are updating. This can be done by converting the update statement to a select statement as shown in Listing 5-11.

Listing 5-11. Verifying the Data Set with a Select Statement

```
SELECT ing.IngredientID,
       ing.IngredientName,
       ing.IsActive,
       ing.DateCreated,
       ing.DateModified
FROM dbo.Ingredient ing
     INNER JOIN dbo.RecipeIngredient recing
     ON ing.IngredientID = recing.IngredientID
     INNER JOIN dbo.Recipe rec
     ON recing.RecipeID = rec.RecipeID
WHERE rec.RecipeName = 'Spaghetti'
```

You can check the records and verify the record count. Before performing the update, I suggest wrapping the UPDATE statement in a BEGIN TRAN... ROLLBACK to verify the record count.

Just like working with updates, you can also use data sets when deleting data. I have found that deleting data using data sets can be significantly more efficient, but it can also be somewhat risky if the data is not verified prior to deleting.

One of the largest temptations overall in writing T-SQL code is not taking advantage of data sets. Often, this is a result of being more comfortable writing procedural code or not having developed the ability to think in terms of data sets. My goal throughout this next section is to guide you through various ways to write code that embraces using data sets.

CHAPTER 6

Hardware Usage

I have covered the elements of set-based design when considering how to design your queries. There are other things to take into consideration when working with SQL Server. You are working with a system that involves more than its pieces. There are many aspects to SQL Server. There is the data that is stored. There is accessing the data. There is also the process of how to access the data. SQL Server is not only software, but it's also how that software interacts with your computer's or server's hardware.

When it comes to working with hardware, there are several different parts that SQL Server uses. Some of these may seem straightforward and others may be surprising at first. SQL Server is known as a relational database management system (RDBMS). As part of a relational database management system, SQL Server's purpose is to allow for efficient storage and retrieval of data. This implies that one of the most important pieces of hardware is the memory on the system that is running SQL Server. When it comes to long-term storage of data, the hard drives become the most significant. We will refer to these as storage for the purposes of this chapter as storage is not only limited to hard disks. However, there are other elements that are less obvious such as CPU.

Considering Memory with T-SQL Design

When you first start working with data in SQL Server, it may come as a surprise that memory is one of the most important factors. Much of this has to do with what memory is used for within SQL Server. One of the reasons for this is because of the speed and versatility for memory. Another factor is related to the cost of memory vs. the cost of storage. This difference in costs increases the importance of using memory effectively. There are many different types of things that are stored in memory. The process SQL Server will use to access the data needed to meet a query's criteria is saved in memory as an execution plan. The data retrieved for a query's results are also stored in memory. You can also have database objects that exist in memory such as table variables or temporary tables.

147

© Elizabeth Noble 2020
E. Noble, *Pro T-SQL 2019*, https://doi.org/10.1007/978-1-4842-5590-2_6

First, let me consider why memory is so important when dealing with SQL Server. You often hear the term OLTP (online transaction processing). What this really means is you want a system that can perform a high volume of write and update activity. These are the types of activities that happen frequently within our applications. When referring to write and update activity, using the database for recipes would involve each time a recipe was accessed, each change that was made to recipe, or every new ingredient that was added to the system.

While there is a significant amount of data being stored within the system, often someone only wants to deal with a very small subset of that data. The skill comes when trying to determine what data should remain readily available. This will increase the speed required to add new entries, to update existing entries, or to access pre-existing entries. This is where a better understanding of hardware can assist you.

We most commonly think of memory as the RAM available on our servers or in our machines. However, there are other types of memory available. Even closer to the CPU and faster than RAM are L2 cache and L3 cache. L2 and L3 cache exist on the processor and have a lower latency than RAM. This latency can be ten times less than RAM. However, the L2 cache or L3 cache available to SQL Server is significantly smaller the amount of data that is usually required for your applications to run effectively. The latency on the L2 cache can be half as much as the L3 cache, but the speed comes at the size of the cache. L2 cache is frequently measured in hundreds of kilobytes, and L3 cache is usually in tens of megabytes. How can we access data as quickly as possible and as cheaply as possible? This is where proper use of memory excels.

SQL Server is designed to take advantage of memory. There is a process called caching that keeps information in memory. There are two types of caching that are important when it comes to SQL Server. The first of these has to do with caching execution plans. This is where SQL Server saves directions on how it would execute a stored procedure or ad hoc query again in the future. The goal is to take advantage of the knowledge SQL Server already has calculated when it comes to the best way to execute a specific query. The second form of cache that has to do with query design can almost be more important. It has to do with how information is stored in memory. This is called the buffer pool.

While both the execution plan and the data can be saved in cache, there are certain calculations performed by SQL Server to determine how much should be allocated in memory to either the plan cache or the buffer pool. In addition, there are complex calculations that are used to determine how long to keep something in the plan cache or the buffer pool. The real goal is to make certain that stored procedures or queries that are not frequently accessed are dropped from the plan cache, so they do not take up unnecessary space. In the same way, when it comes to the buffer pool, the goal is to only keep data in the buffer pool that is being actively used and to clear out data that is no longer needed by the application. In both scenarios, items are not cleared from cache until the cache is full and space is needed for new execution plans or data. Another solution is available in SQL Server 2014 with the introduction of buffer pool extensions. The buffer pool extension allows you to extend the buffer pool to use RAM and solid state drive (SSDs). Considering that SSDs can be more cost-effective than purchasing additional RAM, this can help with I/O bottlenecks.

When it comes to the plan cache, there are some specific considerations that need to be remembered. By default, SQL Server is optimized to deal with stored procedures and prepared statements. This optimization for stored procedures is also a factor when using the plan cache. In a perfect world, your plan cache would have a significant amount of stored procedures in the cache and very few ad hoc queries. However, this is not always the case for every business. Your company may use ORM or other technologies like LINQ to write ad hoc queries inside application code. While these are convenient for the developers to write, they put an additional cost on SQL Server. This can be especially true if those queries are not converted into prepared statements.

What can happen is the plan cache can get full of ad hoc queries. This can cause stored procedures that are more critically needed by the application to be dropped from the plan cache. If there are stored procedures that are dropped out of the plan cache by the application, then when the stored procedure is called the next time, SQL Server will need to recalculate its execution plan. This will require an additional cost on the system. There are various ways to handle situations where there are a high number of ad hoc queries in your plan cache. However, that is outside the scope of this book.

One of the other issues I have seen when interacting with SQL Server has to do with the buffer pool and the data that is being held in the buffer pool. I have heard more than once that when dealing with very large tables, you will always be stuck having to deal with accessing large quantities of data. This can be true that when the table design, the indexes, the queries, or any combination of the preceding is not optimized, then this exact scenario can happen. However, there are ways to prevent this.

The main aspect to consider when working with memory and with SQL Server is when you write queries those queries will return the correct results and complete in an acceptable amount of time for your applications. However, depending on the overall table design or how the queries are written, these queries may be accessing far greater amounts of data than is necessary. This may not seem like a significant issue at first.

It typically will not be an issue when the data tables are new and not full of data. The query in Listing 6-1 is a query used to return some data in the application.

Listing 6-1. Query to Get Recipe Ingredients

```
SELECT rec.RecipeName,
       rec.RecipeDescription,
       rec.ServingQuantity,
       ing.IngredientName,
       ml.MealTypeName,
       ml.MealTypeDescription,
       prp.PreparationTypeName,
       prp.PreparationTypeDescription
FROM dbo.Recipe rec
       INNER JOIN dbo.RecipeIngredient recing
       ON rec.RecipeID = recing.RecipeID
       INNER JOIN dbo.Ingredient ing
       ON recing.IngredientID = ing.IngredientID
       INNER JOIN dbo.MealType ml
       ON rec.MealTypeID = ml.MealTypeID
       INNER JOIN dbo.PreparationType prp
       ON rec.PreparationTypeID = prp.PreparationTypeID
WHERE ing.IngredientName LIKE 'Tom%'
       AND ing.IsActive = 1
```

When the tables are new and there is not much data, you will see logical reads as shown in Table 6-1.

Table 6-1. *Logical Reads when Data Table Is Small*

Number of Recipes	Number of Ingredients	Number of Recipe Ingredients	Records Returned	Logical Reads
32,242	4	3	4	351

The logical reads of 351 refers to the number of data pages read in order to execute this query. As your tables grow SQL Server must sift through more and more data, you may start seeing significant performance impact related to this behavior. When this happens, the number of logical reads can increase significantly as shown in Table 6-2.

Table 6-2. *Logical Reads when Data Table Is Larger*

Number of Recipes	Number of Ingredients	Number of Recipe Ingredients	Records Returned	Logical Reads
32,242	263,010	3,040,002	196	7858

As you can see, a query that originally seemed to perform well may start experiencing performance issues as the application matures and acquires more data.

In these situations, the data that is frequently accessed by the application may be getting cleared out of the buffer pool. When there is a stored procedure that runs that must sift through a significant amount of data, you can usually see this when you look at the logical reads associated with the query. You may be working with a query that only returns five results; however, it must go through 2 million logical reads to return the results. This is a sign that you are potentially using more of your buffer pool than you intended.

This type of behavior can cause a significant amount of data in the buffer pool to be cleared out. There is value called page life expectancy in SQL Server that shows the amount of time on average that data pages stay in the buffer pool. I have come to use page life expectancy as an indicator that there are queries that may be reading far more data in SQL Server than are returned in the result set. This can cause those same queries to use more memory than the query needs. Often when I am working with queries that are working with the application, they normally do not involve more than ten records at a time. If the query is used for some form of reports, it is still usually not more than a couple thousand records at a time. Even if I am getting results where I am looking at 200,000 records at a time, I would still not want to be handling tens of millions of logical reads in order to get those results.

The real key is to try to limit the amount of data SQL Server must process. When writing your queries, this can be handled based on your join logic or this can also be handled with your where clause criteria. You want to make sure that you are accessing as little data as possible. Accessing the smallest amounts of data needed allows you to minimize your use of memory when it comes to your T-SQL. The query previously referenced in Listing 6-1 is being used to return some data. However, there are some extra columns and joins that are included in this query that are not needed. I can update the query to remove the extra columns in Listing 6-2.

Listing 6-2. Query to Get Only Recipe and Ingredients

```
SELECT rec.RecipeName,
       ing.IngredientName
FROM dbo.Recipe rec
       INNER JOIN dbo.RecipeIngredient recing
       ON rec.RecipeID = recing.RecipeID
       INNER JOIN dbo.Ingredient ing
       ON recing.IngredientID = ing.IngredientID
WHERE ing.IngredientName LIKE 'Tom%'
       AND ing.IsActive = 1
```

While it did not affect the original performance of the query, now that the data table has more data, there is an obvious performance impact. Even though I expect the query to involve less logical reads, I should verify this hypothesis by executing the query. In Table 6-3, you can see the logical reads now that the query has been modified.

Table 6-3. *Logical Reads with Only Necessary Columns*

Number of Recipes	Number of Ingredients	Number of Recipe Ingredients	Records Returned	Logical Reads
32,242	263,010	3,040,002	196	6990

Comparing the results from Table 6-2 to Table 6-3, you can see that the logical reads has decreased . As a result, SQL Server should access less data pages in the buffer pool to perform this query. This should help other applications using this instance of SQL Server perform better.

While memory could be considered the most powerful and beneficial hardware available to SQL Server, there are monetary costs associated with memory. Memory can make up for T-SQL that has not been optimized. But there often comes a point where tables are significantly large and the queries are not fully optimized, at that time it is tempting to get more memory to solve the performance issues. In many cases, this ends up being a short-term solution to a long-term problem. On top of that, the cost associated with purchasing additional memory is not always an option for the business. One way to prevent this or resolve this issue is to look at the stored procedures and prepared statements in your system and look for queries that can be improved by reducing the logical reads associated with those queries.

Considering Storage with T-SQL Design

I have covered how to interact with the data that you plan on accessing frequently; you will also want to consider how the bulk of your data is stored. When it comes to working with storage, it is important to consider what activities cause you to have to access data on disk. These are the types of activities that we want to figure out how to minimize or improve. In some cases, when I see a significant amount of disk I/O, it may be a sign that there is some other part of T-SQL design that needs to be improved. This may be the symptom instead of the cause.

In the previous section, I talked about data being stored in the buffer pool. What happens if we need data that is not in the buffer pool? This can be where things within SQL Server get a little more complex. SQL Server only interacts with data that is inside the buffer pool. Therefore, if data is needed that is not in the buffer pool, the first step will be to determine what data has been used less frequently. Then remove this data from the buffer pool. These first steps already give us a hint into the memory usage. If there is something that fills up the buffer pool unnecessarily, we now know that critical data may be cleared out of the buffer pool to make room for this new data.

Once the data has been deemed to not be a priority, SQL Server can then go to disk and get the data that it needs. This data will then be stored in the buffer pool until a future point where it is deemed that this data is no longer needed. In terms of the speed of hardware, there is already a slowness introduced with this process. If the data did not exist in the buffer pool, there is also the time associated with determining what records need to be dropped from the buffer pool. Dropping those records from the buffer pool and going to disk incurs additional cost in terms of time to retrieve that data from disk.

If this data was only needed for a job that runs once every 4 to 6 hours, most of this data may be deemed irrelevant for every other process. This introduces a high churn of data that is being removed from the buffer pool. New data can be grabbed from disk and saved to the buffer pool. Then this new data may be removed from the buffer pool and be replaced with even newer data that has been retrieved from disk.

In addition to this overhead associated with dealing with significant amount of data, there are other activities that interact with the disk or storage. When new data is being written to the system, that data will get stored in the transaction log. Data will continue to be added to the transaction log until the transaction log is cleared. Flushing the log can occur when the transaction is committed and the information is written to disk. In cases where there is a significant amount of data that is being added, updated, or deleted from the system, this can incur a significant use of storage.

Knowing how this data is stored and how SQL Server can easily find that data through indexes and other data pages is stored on disk is important. When information is added to an index or an index needs to be updated, this information will also incur storage cost. This is not only in terms of the time needed to store the data but also the time involved to go to disk and make these additions or changes.

When working with T-SQL, you want to consider how your queries are affecting your data storage. This can mean multiple things as we have seen in the previous section. You will want to make sure that you are not accessing, inserting, updating, or deleting more data than you need at a given time. That is not the only factor that comes into play when writing T-SQL. There are some things you can do to monitor storage use associated with your queries. Most of these involve looking at the number of physical reads, read-ahead reads, or the I/O cost associated with the query.

If you have confirmed that you are dealing with the minimal amount of data that you want to interact with, there may be nothing you can do to decrease the storage cost associated with your T-SQL queries. In some cases, just like with memory finding large storage usage may point to other issues. These issues can include things like how the data is saved on disk; it can also include how the indexes are designed.

In some cases, you may find that frequent index updates are causing a significant amount of storage cost. This may be due to indexes constantly needing to reorganize based on how the index is designed. There are also cases involving page splits where you may see a significant storage cost associated with this activity. The way that your tables are ordered or your indexes are designed may cause a significant amount of page splits. You may see an increase in storage costs associated with this activity as well.

For additional information regarding how storage costs work, it may help to understand how the SQL Server storage engine operates. When dealing with T-SQL queries, there is one aspect that depends on the storage engine more frequently. This has to do with accessing data that is currently not in the buffer pool.

The storage engine has several different functions. These functions involve accessing data that is not in the buffer pool. Another function of the storage engine has to do with how data is handled when locks are required. The third function of the storage engine involves commands that are not related to running T-SQL that is used by applications.

The storage engine can experience performance bottlenecks when accessing data. These bottlenecks can in turn cause performance issues when it comes to accessing the data that is stored. One example is when queries are accessing rows in data tables or interacting with indexes. At other times, the storage engine may need to handle page allocations related to retrieving data for the buffer pool. If your company has decided to implement row versioning, there may also be a possibility that this could cause performance issues with storage. While this is outside the scope of this book, if you are using row versioning and you experience issues related to storage performance, you may want to do some additional research to confirm that row versioning is not the cause.

When accessing data rows or indexes, SQL Server will utilize the storage engine. The data being accessed may be stored in the buffer pool. It is up to the storage engine to keep track of where these rows live in the B-tree. The same process happens with regard to managing, adding, updating, or removing entries from indexes within SQL Server. This is collectively called row and index operations maintenance within the storage engine.

SQL Server uses indexes to organize data and allow data to be retrieved easily and quickly. When it comes to tables that are larger than a couple of data pages, SQL Server tries to use indexes to help traverse the various data pages and find the data it needs quickly. However, there can be scenarios where the necessary indexes do not exist. This causes SQL Server to have to read more data pages, sometimes all the data in a table, to determine which rows are needed in order to satisfy the query requirements.

When writing queries to access data, SQL Server keeps track of the data that needs to be accessed by referring to that data as reads. If the data is available in memory, the act of accessing that data is referred to as a logical read. There are also times that accessing data may require SQL Server to go to disk or storage to access the data pages. If the data is accessed from disk, the data is referred to as physical reads. If the pages are moved to the buffer pool, then that action is referred to as read-ahead read. In either case, SQL Server will need to go to disk to access the requested records. When you write a query and it needs to retrieve records that do not exist in the buffer pool, SQL Server will need to access those records on disk. This can be a very normal process for SQL Server. However, in cases where the query requires more records to be read than are needed for the query results, this can cause more activity on disk than is required. One way to monitor the amount of time spent retrieving data from disk is with latch waits. This is the amount of time that SQL Server spends accessing data that does not exist in the buffer pool.

In addition to SQL Server managing data access within the storage engine, the storage engine also manages activities relating to locking data. This type of activity can be affected by the concurrency method configured on the server, application, or transaction. In many cases, the concurrency level configuration is usually managed by a different team than the people that are responsible for writing the T-SQL code. The storage engine is also responsible for handling how locks are handled in SQL Server.

Additional factors that can contribute to performance issues related to storage have to do with other areas of query design that may interact with the hard drive, for instance, database actions that require a large amount of activity to get recorded to the transaction. This can include inserting, updating, or deleting a large quantity of data. SQL Server is designed to handle recording these changes to the transaction log promptly. However, these modifications will need to be recorded to disk as well. Depending on fragmentation or other processes utilizing the hard disk, this may cause additional performance issues.

Tempdb is another part of SQL Server that can have a noticeable amount of overhead related to storage. There may be queries that are causing quite a bit of activity to happen within tempdb. In many cases, the effects to the rest of the system can be mitigated by putting tempdb on a separate drive. In those causes, any storage overhead on tempdb should only affect other queries also relying on tempdb.

Writing T-SQL queries is fundamentally linked to how SQL Server interacts with data that has been stored. There are some aspects of this interaction that can be controlled like making sure that you are accessing the least amount of data as possible. There are other factors such as how SQL Server accesses data or manages locking that may be outside of your control. Either way, it is important to be aware of how all these pieces come together and may affect your query performance.

Considering CPU with T-SQL Design

SQL Server does not only work with memory and with storage but also interacts with the server CPU. This is one of the final pieces to consider when designing your queries. When it comes to licensing SQL Server, the CPU can be a significant cost. Some of this may be due to not understanding the best CPU needed for SQL Server. This can cause servers to be purchased with a CPU that seems like it would be more beneficial than other CPUs out there. However, more cores on the CPU may not mean better performance. It may operate slower for SQL Server but have more cores. Therefore, some CPUs may be more expensive than other CPUs on the market, but they may also be less effective than other CPUs when those CPUs are used by SQL Server. There are several different places that CPUs can be used with SQL Server. There is the matter of performing calculations as part of your T-SQL code.

As we saw previously in the chapter, there are times where a significant use of memory can cause I/O issues. The same can be said when there is a significant amount of I/O activity; this can lead to CPU issues. When talking about considering memory in your overall T-SQL design, I discussed there were two types of caching. In that section, I mainly focused on buffer caching or the buffer pool. In this section, I will talk a little bit about how caching of execution plans can contribute to CPU performance issues.

When SQL Server determines how to execute a query, it creates an execution plan. For SQL Server to know how to execute a query, it must utilize the CPU. This is considered a CPU cost. The expectation is that this type of cost should not cause performance issues as frequently executed prepared statements and stored procedures will already have their plans saved in the cache and do not need to have these execution plans re-created with any amount of significant frequency.

That does lead into what causes SQL Server to determine that a new execution plan is needed. This is directly related to understanding what SQL Server does when it creates an execution plan. Part of creating an execution plan is creating a value that allows SQL Server to quickly find a previously created execution plan. In the plan cache, this value is known as the plan hash. While you may have several queries that look similar or return the same results, SQL Server may not give them the same plan hash. Only queries that look the same have the same plan hash.

This dependency on the plan hash helps determine if a new execution plan needs to be created. This causes us to become dependent on using parameters. These parameters can exist either in stored procedures or prepared statements. If the query that is being executed has the same plan hash and the plan hash in the plan cache, SQL Server will not re-create a new execution plan. This process of creating an execution plan is called compilation. This can be one of the many reasons that your queries may be using more CPU resources than you expected.

It is also possible that SQL Server may determine it needs to create a new execution plan for a query where there is already an associated plan hash in the execution cache. This scenario is generally caused when SQL Server identifies that the data involved in the query has changed significantly enough to require a new execution plan. This can be the result of frequent data changes, or it can be the result of parameter sniffing; either way, it will lead to something that SQL Server identifies as a recompilation. Just like there was a cost associated with a query compilation, there is also a cost on the CPU associated with recompilations.

If there is a significant amount of I/O being handled for a query, this may spill over into causing CPU performance issues. While it is possible that a query may be accessing more data than is necessary, it may not be due to the overall T-SQL query design. It is possible that it could be due to out-of-date statistics. While the concept of managing statistics is outside the scope of this book, you want to be aware of the effect that statistics have on your execution plans. Statistics are what give SQL Server a quick glance at the overall distribution of data within a specific data table or index. The concept is that proper statistics help SQL Server make a best guess as to how to create an execution plan. If these values are out of date or stale, then SQL Server may decide on an execution plan that would not be as efficient as it could be if SQL Server had up-to-date statistics. Due to the out-of-date statistics, you can see that there is a significant difference between the estimated and actual number of reads. This can cause a performance impact on the CPU. You can see now that the statistics have been updated and the estimated and actual number of rows returned remains relatively consistent.

There is also the possibility that SQL Server is having to traverse more of the hard disk or storage than it originally anticipated. This can be due to situations involving fragmentation. In the case of higher than normal CPU activity, it could be possible that this is due to index fragmentation. This means that SQL Server may have only estimated a certain amount of work required to retrieve data by assuming that the index was not fragmented. However, since the index is fragmented, SQL Server is having to do potentially more work than it anticipated to access the requested data.

Another common issue that can happen with your T-SQL query design involves data types. There are many different places in SQL Server where you will define data types. These can be defined in tables, temporary tables, parameters, stored procedure, parameters, and even the data types that are specified through your application code. As discussed previously in Chapter 1, SQL Server can convert one data type to another in the background; this process is called implicit conversion. While SQL Server can handle implicit conversion and has a structured process to do so, forcing SQL Server to perform an implicit conversion can also have a CPU cost associated with that activity. The code in Listing 6-3 is an example of an implicit conversion.

Listing 6-3. Query with Implicit Conversion

```
DECLARE @IsActive NVARCHAR(1);

SET @IsActive = 1;

SELECT RecipeID,
      RecipeName,
      RecipeDescription,
      ServingQuantity,
      MealTypeID,
      PreparationTypeID
      IsActive,
      DateCreated,
      DateModified
FROM dbo.Recipe
WHERE IsActive = @IsActive;
```

The implicit conversion is created in Listing 6-3 as the data type for the variable @IsActive is set to an NVARCHAR. The data type for the field IsActive in the dbo. Recipe table is a BIT. Therefore, SQL Server will have to perform an implicit conversion to compare these two values. In Figure 6-1, you can see the impact of an implicit conversion on an execution plan.

Clustered Index Scan (Clustered)
Scanning a clustered index, entirely or only a range.

Physical Operation	Clustered Index Scan
Logical Operation	Clustered Index Scan
Actual Execution Mode	Row
Estimated Execution Mode	Row
Storage	RowStore
Number of Rows Read	32242
Actual Number of Rows	30994
Actual Number of Batches	0
Estimated I/O Cost	0.334236
Estimated Operator Cost	0.369859 (100%)
Estimated CPU Cost	0.0356232
Estimated Subtree Cost	0.369859
Number of Executions	1
Estimated Number of Executions	1
Estimated Number of Rows	32242
Estimated Number of Rows to be Read	32242
Estimated Row Size	73 B
Actual Rebinds	0
Actual Rewinds	0
Ordered	False
Node ID	0

Predicate
[Menu].[dbo].[Recipe].[IsActive]=CONVERT_IMPLICIT(bit,
[@IsActive],0)
Object
[Menu].[dbo].[Recipe].[PK_Recipe_RecipeID]
Output List
[Menu].[dbo].[Recipe].RecipeID, [Menu].[dbo].
[Recipe].RecipeName, [Menu].[dbo].[Recipe].RecipeDescription,
[Menu].[dbo].[Recipe].ServingQuantity, [Menu].[dbo].
[Recipe].MealTypeID, [Menu].[dbo].[Recipe].PreparationTypeID,
[Menu].[dbo].[Recipe].IsActive, [Menu].[dbo].[Recipe].DateCreated,
[Menu].[dbo].[Recipe].DateModified

Figure 6-1. Index Scan in Execution Plan Showing Implicit Conversion

An implicit conversion can have a significant and negative overall performance impact on the query; you will want to make sure you avoid implicit conversions when writing your T-SQL queries.

Some companies may also be utilizing data compression. One of the benefits of data compression is the ability to keep more data in memory as the amount of data that is taken up by the compressed data is smaller than the uncompressed data. There are also some drawbacks to using data compression in SQL Server. One of these drawbacks has to do with the CPU cost incurred as part of the overall data compression process. This does not mean that you should not use data compression. I only mention this so that you can be aware of any potential issues should they arise.

160

That brings us to the overall concept of parallelism. The most common way that you can easily see CPU usage is when it comes to parallelism with your queries. Parallelism is a concept where instead of a query executing on a single thread, a query can execute on more than one thread. In this scenario, this can mean that your CPU may have four cores. Each core may have two threads. If a query were only to run on one thread, it would run on one quarter of a core of your CPU. However, if the query was running in parallelism, it may be able to run on more than one thread. For instance, if it ran on four threads, this query could then take the full number of cores in your CPU. This would cause the overall CPU process to increase.

There are many factors involved for SQL Server to determine whether parallelism should be used when executing a query. Much of this involves how SQL Server is configured. While configuring SQL Server is outside the scope of this book, I want you to be aware of how it works when SQL Server creates an execution plan. SQL Server gives the execution plan and overall cost. SQL Server also has a configured value that indicates a minimum cost that should exist before SQL Server decides to implement parallelism. This cost is referred to as the cost threshold for parallelism. If the execution plan has a cost that is greater than the cost threshold of parallelism, then SQL Server can determine if there is a better execution plan that runs in parallel.

If SQL Server does decide to create an execution plan using parallelism, SQL Server will also need to determine the maximum number of threads that are allowed for a given execution plan. There is also a configured value that indicates the maximum number of threads that can be used for parallelism. This value is referred to as the maximum degrees of parallelism. MAXDOP is the abbreviation for maximum degrees of parallelism. This does not mean that SQL Server must use the same number of threads as specified in the maximum degrees of parallelism. It only means this is the maximum amount of threads that can be allowed for an execution plan to run in parallelism.

SQL Server will determine the number of threads to use for an execution plan that will run in parallelism at the time of execution. This will be done based on the number of threads that are not utilized at the beginning of the execution of the query. One factor that can affect CPU performance when it comes to parallelism can occur if more threads come into use while the query is running in parallelism. The general idea for parallelism is that more CPU process will be used overall but for a much shorter duration. If there are more queries that come into the queue and need to be run requiring more threads to be active, it may cause the CPU to operate at a higher than normal level for a longer period.

One of the main reasons you will want to make sure your T-SQL is not negatively impacting CPU usage has to do with the monetary cost related to CPUs. Since SQL Server 2012, the licensing for SQL Server has been related to the number of cores using SQL Server. In later versions of SQL Server, that has been modified to be the number of cores available to the server even if they are not explicitly allocated to SQL Server. One of the common solutions when companies start experiencing performance issues is to add more hardware. While this may solve performance issues in the short term, it can also be a very expensive solution depending on what hardware needs to be added. As the license per core can be over $1000, it is ideal to try and minimize the need for additional CPUs by reducing performance bottlenecks related to CPU usage.

There are many aspects to consider when designing your T-SQL queries. Some of these factors include being aware of the impact T-SQL can have on the physical hardware that runs SQL Server. When writing your T-SQL queries, you will want to be mindful of the amount of data being accessed in order to make the best use of the memory available. Another added benefit to minimizing the data that is decreasing storage resources. Making sure that your statistics are up to date and that proper indexes are in place will benefit the CPU usage. Being aware of how your queries are affecting your hardware will not only minimize the need for additional hardware but also allows your current hardware to better support your applications.

CHAPTER 7

Execution Plans

When I first started writing T-SQL, I focused on using the right syntax. I worked to try memorizing things like if the GROUP BY clause came before the ORDER BY clause. As I became more familiar with writing T-SQL, I had new challenges like making sure that my results were accurate. Over time, I got to the point that not only was I writing queries with complex logic, I also had to write several simpler queries to verify my results. I got to the point where I started debugging T-SQL code that had been written by other database developers. I also became responsible for researching various application issues.

In many cases, the result of this research came down to some T-SQL code that was running at the same time as an application crash or a spike in hardware usage. At this point in time, the pressure was on to figure out what was causing the performance issue as quickly as possible. In the beginning, I learned to rely on my understanding of the needs of the business and the database design. While this can be very helpful, it does require a significant amount of domain knowledge that can take years to acquire. There are better, faster, and easier ways to find the pain points in your queries.

In this chapter, you will learn how to view and understand SQL Server execution plans. You will also see demonstrations on how your existing and new indexes can affect your execution plans. You will also learn about how SQL Server will join data together in the execution plan. By the end of this chapter, you will have the knowledge to know how to use execution plans to improve the performance of your T-SQL.

Reading Execution Plans

My ultimate goal when writing to T-SQL is to make sure that I get accurate results. In some cases, the queries I write are simple and straightforward. As a data engineer, I find myself needing to performance tune queries related to reporting or writing new

© Elizabeth Noble 2020
E. Noble, *Pro T-SQL 2019*, https://doi.org/10.1007/978-1-4842-5590-2_7

queries for reporting. Because these are queries to provide reports on transactional data, I often must incorporate more joins and more logic than I would need if I were to write queries for application. While this is not ideal, this is a very common scenario for many companies out there.

Many companies have begun to realize the importance of the data in their systems, or they want additional monitoring to ensure the applications are working as intended. In either case, it is highly likely that you will come across a query in your environment that is negatively affecting your applications. At that time, you will want to know what you can do to resolve the issue. In this section, you will learn why execution plans are important and when you need to use them. You will learn how to read execution plans including commonly used symbols. You will also learn about properties and warnings in execution plans.

My first mentor once told me that in order to write good T-SQL, I needed to understand how SQL Server worked. It is some of the wisest advice I have received, and I am still working to understand SQL Server internals better each day. Taking this advice in mind, one way that we can have a better understanding of SQL Server is to understand how SQL Server will execute any queries that we have written. While I will not cover all the internals related to executing a query, I will show you the instructions that SQL Server has determined should be used to execute your T-SQL code. These instructions can be found in the execution plan for as long as the plan is still in the plan cache.

Once you have decided that you want to start investigating an execution plan for some T-SQL code, you should confirm that you have access in SQL Server to view execution plans. You have several options. If you are going to be getting the actual execution plan when the T-SQL code is executed, you will need to make sure you have permissions to execute that code and that you have SHOWPLAN access for the databases that exist in the T-SQL code. You can also get the execution plan from the plan cache, but you will need to be able to query the dynamic management view `sys.dm_exec_cached_plans`. Now that you know how to verify that you have access, I want to go over the different types of execution plans available.

There are various ways to retrieve execution plans, and depending on your needs at the time will help determine which is the best model to use. When you are trying to troubleshoot performance issues, the best option is to retrieve the execution plan from `sys.dm_exec_cached_plans`. This is the method you will want to use if you want the best idea of the execution plan that was used previously. You may not be able to find the query or stored procedure here if the execution plan has been cleared from the plan cache. In addition, depending on when the performance issue happened, the plan that was in cache may have been cleared. This may mean you can find an execution plan, but it may not be the same one used previously.

If you find that the execution plan is not in the plan cache or that the execution plan has been changed since the performance issue, you can try to find the current execution plan. There are two options available when using this method. One option is to get a hypothetical idea of what SQL Server would use as an execution plan. This can be done without running the actual T-SQL code on the server. This is called the estimated execution plan. The largest challenge using this method is that just because SQL Server has estimated an execution does not give you any guarantee that this will be the actual execution plan that SQL Server uses when the query is run. I do not usually use estimated execution plans in my day-to-day operations. I have used estimated execution plans only a handful of times, and that was when I was hesitant to run the T-SQL code for fear of causing an outage in Production.

The next best option besides reviewing an execution plan in the plan cache is to see what the execution plan would look like right now if you ran the execution plan. Requesting an actual execution plan when you execute your T-SQL code will cause the execution plan to be available after the query execution completes. There is also a newer option available in SQL Server 2014 and higher, that is, the ability to see the flow of data through the execution plan as the query is executing. Instead of viewing the actual execution plan, you will ask SQL Server to show you the live query statistics. While this option may be helpful in slower queries where there is one specific pain point, I often find that many queries complete too quickly to use this method to effectively diagnose many issues I am trying to resolve.

How and when you retrieve an execution plan are factors that you can control when it comes to working with execution plans. There is also the option of what the execution plan should look like once you retrieve it. My usual method is looking at the graphical output for the execution plan. The process of reviewing execution plans for T-SQL code is the same regardless of whether you are writing new T-SQL or performance tuning some existing code. An example of a graphical execution plan can be found in Figure 7-1.

```
Query 1: Query cost (relative to the batch): 100%
SELECT * FROM dbo.Recipe
```

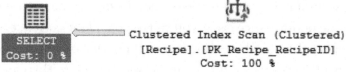

Clustered Index Scan (Clustered)
[Recipe].[PK_Recipe_RecipeID]
Cost: 100 %

Figure 7-1. *Graphical Execution Plan*

The graphical execution gives a high-level view of how a query is executed. This makes the execution plan easier to read at a glance, but it also means that there is additional information that needs to be accessed when getting into the details in the execution plan. Figure 7-2 shows some details that can be viewed when putting your mouse over various objects in the execution plan.

Clustered Index Scan (Clustered)
Scanning a clustered index, entirely or only a range.

Physical Operation	Clustered Index Scan
Logical Operation	Clustered Index Scan
Estimated Execution Mode	Row
Storage	RowStore
Estimated I/O Cost	0.334236
Estimated Operator Cost	0.369859 (100%)
Estimated CPU Cost	0.0356232
Estimated Subtree Cost	0.369859
Estimated Number of Executions	1
Estimated Number of Rows	32242
Estimated Number of Rows to be Read	32242
Estimated Row Size	73 B
Ordered	False
Node ID	0

Object
[Menu].[dbo].[Recipe].[PK_Recipe_RecipeID]
Output List
[Menu].[dbo].[Recipe].RecipeID, [Menu].[dbo].
[Recipe].RecipeName, [Menu].[dbo].[Recipe].RecipeDescription,
[Menu].[dbo].[Recipe].ServingQuantity, [Menu].[dbo].
[Recipe].MealTypeID, [Menu].[dbo].[Recipe].PreparationTypeID,
[Menu].[dbo].[Recipe].IsActive, [Menu].[dbo].[Recipe].DateCreated,
[Menu].[dbo].[Recipe].DateModified

Figure 7-2. *Operator Details from a Graphical Execution Plan*

In addition to the properties in this tool tip, in newer versions of SQL Server Management Studio, you also have access to even more extended properties as shown in Figure 7-3.

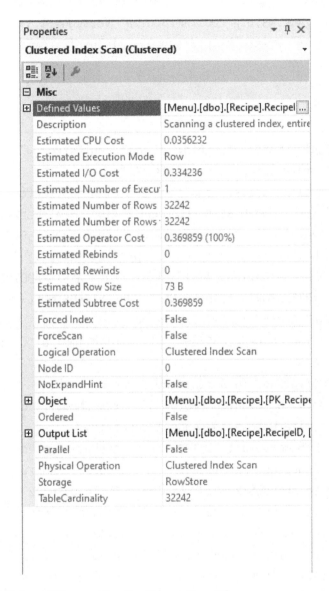

Figure 7-3. *Additional Properties for Execution Plans*

There is an option to interact with the execution plan in an XML format. You can see an example of this in Listing 7-1.

Listing 7-1. XML Execution Plan

```
<?xml version="1.0" encoding="utf-16"?>
<ShowPlanXML xmlns:xsi="http://www.w3.org/2001/XMLSchema-instance"
xmlns:xsd="http://www.w3.org/2001/XMLSchema" Version="1.539"
Build="15.0.1900.25" xmlns="http://schemas.microsoft.com/sqlserver/2004/07/
showplan">
  <BatchSequence>
    <Batch>
      <Statements>
        <StmtSimple StatementCompId="1" StatementEstRows="32242"
StatementId="1" StatementOptmLevel="TRIVIAL"
CardinalityEstimationModelVersion="140" StatementSubTreeCost="0.369859"
StatementText="SELECT *&#xD;&#xA;FROM dbo.Recipe" StatementType="SELECT"
QueryHash="0x52229A4EACC7DD80" QueryPlanHash="0x426A0BAA5E7F4138"
RetrievedFromCache="true" SecurityPolicyApplied="false">
          <StatementSetOptions ANSI_NULLS="true" ANSI_PADDING="true" ANSI_
WARNINGS="true" ARITHABORT="true" CONCAT_NULL_YIELDS_NULL="true" NUMERIC_
ROUNDABORT="false" QUOTED_IDENTIFIER="true" />
          <QueryPlan CachedPlanSize="24" CompileTime="0" CompileCPU="0"
CompileMemory="96">
            <MemoryGrantInfo SerialRequiredMemory="0"
SerialDesiredMemory="0" GrantedMemory="0" MaxUsedMemory="0" />
            <OptimizerHardwareDependentProperties
EstimatedAvailableMemoryGrant="13107" EstimatedPagesCached="3276"
EstimatedAvailableDegreeOfParallelism="2" MaxCompileMemory="271384" />
            <RelOp AvgRowSize="73" EstimateCPU="0.0356232"
EstimateIO="0.334236" EstimateRebinds="0" EstimateRewinds="0"
EstimatedExecutionMode="Row" EstimateRows="32242" EstimatedRowsRead="32242"
LogicalOp="Clustered Index Scan" NodeId="0" Parallel="false"
PhysicalOp="Clustered Index Scan" EstimatedTotalSubtreeCost="0.369859"
TableCardinality="32242">
```

```
        <OutputList>
          <ColumnReference Database="[Menu]" Schema="[dbo]"
Table="[Recipe]" Column="RecipeID" />
          <ColumnReference Database="[Menu]" Schema="[dbo]"
Table="[Recipe]" Column="RecipeName" />
          <ColumnReference Database="[Menu]" Schema="[dbo]"
Table="[Recipe]" Column="RecipeDescription" />
          <ColumnReference Database="[Menu]" Schema="[dbo]"
Table="[Recipe]" Column="ServingQuantity" />
          <ColumnReference Database="[Menu]" Schema="[dbo]"
Table="[Recipe]" Column="MealTypeID" />
          <ColumnReference Database="[Menu]" Schema="[dbo]"
Table="[Recipe]" Column="PreparationTypeID" />
          <ColumnReference Database="[Menu]" Schema="[dbo]"
Table="[Recipe]" Column="IsActive" />
          <ColumnReference Database="[Menu]" Schema="[dbo]"
Table="[Recipe]" Column="DateCreated" />
          <ColumnReference Database="[Menu]" Schema="[dbo]"
Table="[Recipe]" Column="DateModified" />
        </OutputList>
        <IndexScan Ordered="false" ForcedIndex="false"
ForceScan="false" NoExpandHint="false" Storage="RowStore">
          <DefinedValues>
            <DefinedValue>
              <ColumnReference Database="[Menu]" Schema="[dbo]"
Table="[Recipe]" Column="RecipeID" />
            </DefinedValue>
            <DefinedValue>
              <ColumnReference Database="[Menu]" Schema="[dbo]"
Table="[Recipe]" Column="RecipeName" />
            </DefinedValue>
            <DefinedValue>
              <ColumnReference Database="[Menu]" Schema="[dbo]"
Table="[Recipe]" Column="RecipeDescription" />
            </DefinedValue>
```

```
                    <DefinedValue>
                        <ColumnReference Database="[Menu]" Schema="[dbo]"
Table="[Recipe]" Column="ServingQuantity" />
                    </DefinedValue>
                    <DefinedValue>
                        <ColumnReference Database="[Menu]" Schema="[dbo]"
Table="[Recipe]" Column="MealTypeID" />
                    </DefinedValue>
                    <DefinedValue>
                        <ColumnReference Database="[Menu]" Schema="[dbo]"
Table="[Recipe]" Column="PreparationTypeID" />
                    </DefinedValue>
                    <DefinedValue>
                        <ColumnReference Database="[Menu]" Schema="[dbo]"
Table="[Recipe]" Column="IsActive" />
                    </DefinedValue>
                    <DefinedValue>
                        <ColumnReference Database="[Menu]" Schema="[dbo]"
Table="[Recipe]" Column="DateCreated" />
                    </DefinedValue>
                    <DefinedValue>
                        <ColumnReference Database="[Menu]" Schema="[dbo]"
Table="[Recipe]" Column="DateModified" />
                    </DefinedValue>
                  </DefinedValues>
                  <Object Database="[Menu]" Schema="[dbo]" Table="[Recipe]"
Index="[PK_Recipe_RecipeID]" IndexKind="Clustered" Storage="RowStore" />
                </IndexScan>
              </RelOp>
            </QueryPlan>
          </StmtSimple>
        </Statements>
      </Batch>
    </BatchSequence>
</ShowPlanXML>
```

While this method may be more difficult to read, it does contain all information related to the execution plan. The query that generated this table was a SELECT statement on one table. As you can also see, having all the data in one place makes for quite a bit of code that needs to be reviewed.

Once you have set up SQL Server Management Studio to give you an execution plan, you will want to know what to look for when reviewing the execution plan. You will need to know how to interpret the flow in the execution plan to better understand how SQL Server will execute the query. There are also some general shapes you will want to be familiar with as they may help you find potential issues at a glance. Included in the execution plan you may find additional text that quickly shows issues that have been determined to be negatively affecting the execution of your query. Having a better understanding of all these elements will help you figure out the pain points for your queries so that you can determine where to focus your efforts.

Once you have an execution plan, you can get a better idea of exactly how SQL Server will execute that query. When we read English, we are accustomed to reading from left to right and from top to bottom. To compare this to execution plans, the uppermost left corner represents the result of the query. If we compare this to reading a book, as you move from left to right, you are drilling down into steps that SQL Server took to get the result set. The same is true when moving from top to bottom. Looking at the example in Figure 7-4, you can see an execution plan with multiple steps.

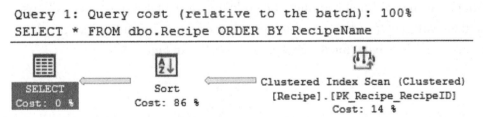

```
Query 1: Query cost (relative to the batch): 100%
SELECT * FROM dbo.Recipe ORDER BY RecipeName
```

Figure 7-4. *Execution Plan with Multiple Steps*

If I read from left to right, I can see the representation for the results returned with the SELECT. When I move to the right, I can see that SQL Server used the compute scalar immediately before getting the result set. This means that if I move to the right-most object, this is the first action SQL Server took when executing the query. In this case, the first step SQL Server performed when executing this query is a clustered Index Scan. This is important to know because you may hear references to reading execution plans left to right. In these cases, the person is referring to reading the execution plan in the same way SQL Server executes the query.

When I first started working with execution plans, I was quickly overwhelmed with the amount of information available in them. I wanted to understand everything from the beginning. However, this was far too much for me to remember. Through my years of troubleshooting any issues, I learned to start my analysis by finding differences. With the execution plans, it did not take long to quickly see difference right away. I noticed that the arrows between two objects did not always stay the same size. There are two different arrows side by side in Figure 7-5 for comparison.

Figure 7-5. *Arrows from Execution Plans*

I learned that the difference in the thickness of the lines indicated the relative amount of records SQL Server was accessing for each step. While there are some queries that are going to return more records than others and therefore have thicker lines, you will find execution plans where one step has a very thick line and the next step will have a thin line. This usually indicates the step with the thicker line could be written more efficiently in order to pull back less data. Looking at the thickness of the lines is one of the things you can check when you look at execution plans.

There are times when you will want your data ordered in a specific way. For instance, you may want to show a list of recipes alphabetically or by creation date. The recipes can either be sorted within the application code or within SQL Server. If you choose to order the data within SQL Server, you may see a Sort operator in your execution plan. You can see an example of what the Sort operator looks like in Figure 7-6.

Sort
Cost: 92 %

Figure 7-6. *Sort Operator*

You will see Sort operators in your execution plans. There are occasions where the Sort operator is necessary. However, you will want to look for instances where the Sort operator may not be needed. This can include Sorts that are required for Merge Joins. In these cases, you will want to see if there is an index that can be used for the join that already has the data sorted. One of the largest issues to watch out for is when there is a warning related to the Sort operator.

One of the most helpful features of execution plans is when they return a warning. Ideally, you want to write T-SQL that performs well. This also means the T-SQL should not return execution plans with warnings. There will be times when you get a warning as part of your execution plan. The warning will look like Figure 7-7.

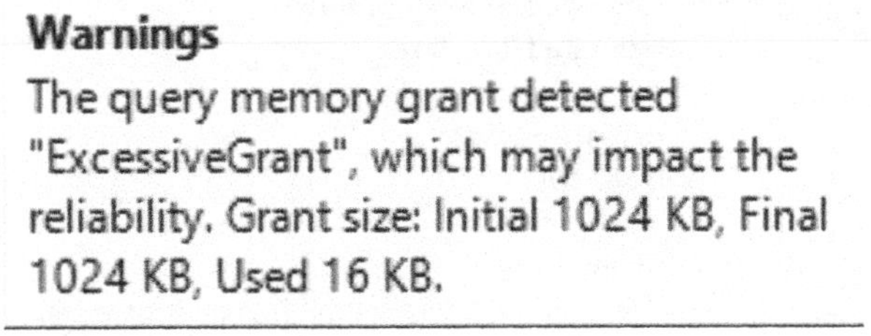

Warnings
The query memory grant detected "ExcessiveGrant", which may impact the reliability. Grant size: Initial 1024 KB, Final 1024 KB, Used 16 KB.

Figure 7-7. *Warning in an Execution Plan*

The main advantage of seeing a warning is that SQL Server has identified a potential issue with your T-SQL code. It would benefit you to investigate any warnings that are returned and see if you can take steps to resolve them.

Execution plans have other elements that will alert you to potential performance issues. While warnings can give you a specific advice about issues with your T-SQL, there are other items in your execution plan that do not provide the same level of guidance. When creating an execution plan, SQL Server uses statistics to make a guess as to the number of rows that will be returned. SQL Server will also keep track of the actual number of rows returned in each step of the execution plan. If you mouse over the operators, you will be able to see something like what is in Figure 7-8.

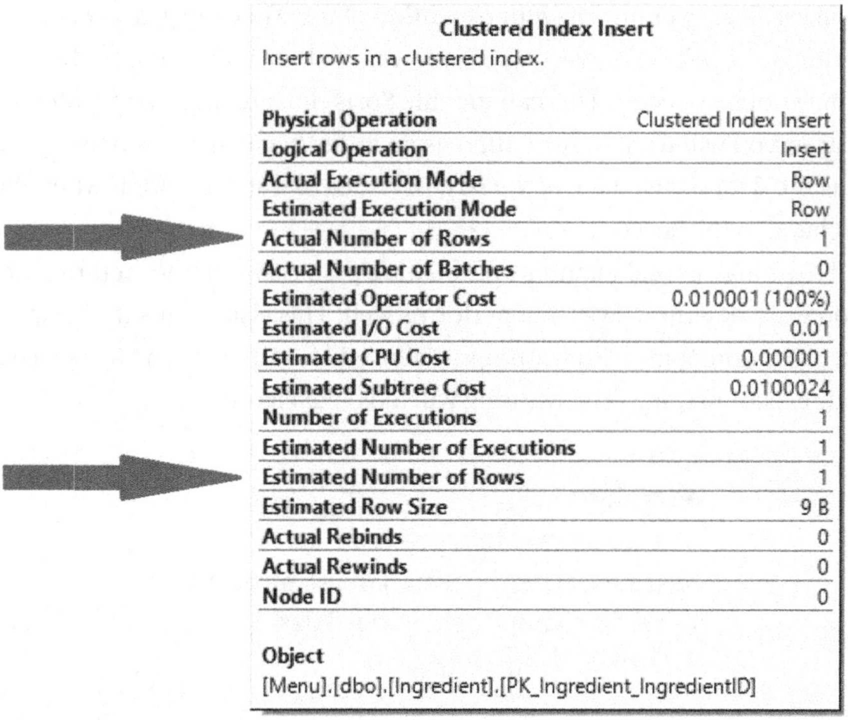

Figure 7-8. *Estimated vs. Actual Number of Rows*

The first arrow points to the actual number of rows returned for this step of the execution plan. The second arrow points to the estimated number of rows returned. In this case, the number of rows matches. If the number of rows matches or is close in range, you will not have performance issues related to estimates. If the two numbers are significantly different, then you may get an execution plan that does not perform as well as it could. This could be happening because the statistics are out of date, and SQL Server cannot accurately determine the number of rows that will be returned. Another possibility is that SQL Server may have created the execution plan for a different set of values. Regardless of the reason, if you see a large variation between the estimated and actual number of rows returned, this is something that you should investigate.

By reading execution plans, you can quickly identify where there are performance issues in your queries and what steps you can take to solve those issues. This includes knowing how to access execution plans and know the difference between estimated and actual execution plans. Execution plans also have several features that will help you quickly identify possible performance issues. By looking at the size of the arrows, you can tell the relative amount of data passing through each step in an execution plan. The Sort operator may provide insights into data that is sorted for more reasons than returning an ordered result set. You can also look at the estimated and actual number of rows returned to help determine if SQL Server has enough information to give you a good execution plan. Once you have gotten familiar with these aspects of execution plans, you may want to investigate how SQL Server is using your indexes.

Index Usage in Execution Plans

In terms of managing T-SQL, one of the largest differences I have seen across companies is how indexes are managed. In some cases, the development teams own writing all the T-SQL code including index creation. There are also companies where the database team handles all index creation and maintenance. Since database administrators usually have less access to development than the developers, I believe it may be most helpful to have the two teams work together. The database administrators can find indexes that are performing poorly and may have more experience designing indexes for multiple T-SQL queries. On the other hand, the developers may have a better idea of how the tables are designed and how the T-SQL code uses those tables.

There are many queries, health checks, and monitoring tools that exist that can help you identify issues with your indexes. You can either use queries to find what stored procedures use the same database objects or you may have a specific query in mind to improve performance. Once you get the execution plan from the cache or generate the current actual execution plan, you can start looking into potential performance issues. As discussed in the previous section, you know that you can check the relative amount of data records for each step, look at various operators and warnings, and verify the estimated and actual number of rows returned. You can also look at how indexes are being used as part of your execution plan.

When working with data in SQL Server, the preference is that data is found as quickly as possible. When data is saved in a clustered index, the data is sorted based on the columns of the index. This means that when SQL Server searches through a clustered index, the data is stored in order. In the best scenario, SQL Server would look through the data and find the data quickly. If this happens, you will see a Clustered Index Seek in the execution plan. The Clustered Index Seek in the execution plan will look like Figure 7-9.

```
Clustered Index Seek (Clustered)
  [Recipe].[PK_Recipe_RecipeID]
         Cost: 100 %
```

Figure 7-9. *Clustered Index Seek*

Seeing a Clustered Index Seek lets you know that your T-SQL code is written well enough to find the data quickly. If you do not see a Clustered Index Seek in your execution plan, you may want to see if there is a way to rewrite your T-SQL to use a Clustered Index Seek.

While it is ideal for your data to use a Clustered Index Seek, you may see something in your execution plan that looks similar but not the same. It is possible for SQL Server to use the clustered index but not find the data quickly. In this case, SQL Server may need to look through a significant percentage of the index. If this happens, you may see a Clustered Index Scan in the execution plan as shown in Figure 7-10.

```
Clustered Index Scan (Clustered)
  [Recipe].[PK_Recipe_RecipeID]
          Cost: 14 %
```

Figure 7-10. *Clustered Index Scan*

This does mean that SQL Server looked through the data as sorted by the clustered index but had to scan through the table to find all the records needed to satisfy the query requirements.

SQL Server uses the term seek to indicate that the requested data could be found without searching a significant portion of the reference index. When the entire table or a significant part of the table needed to be searched, SQL Server refers to this as a scan. While seeks or scans can apply to clustered indexes, they can also apply to non-clustered indexes. Non-clustered indexes are not sorted in the same order as the clustered index or the table, if the table is a heap. The non-clustered index is sorted in the order of key columns specified in the index. If there is a clustered index on the table, the non-clustered index will have a pointer back to the clustered index. If there is no clustered index, then the non-clustered index will point back to the row ID in the table.

If the execution plan uses a non-clustered index, there are a couple of different ways the SQL Server can search through the data records. If SQL Server knows where to find the data in the non-clustered index, you will see an Index Seek in the execution plan. The Index Seek will look like Figure 7-11.

```
Index Seek (NonClustered)
[RecipeHistory].[pk_RecipeHistory_R...
       Cost: 80 %
```

Figure 7-11. *Index Seek*

If a Clustered Index Seek cannot be used based on the T-SQL code that is written, the next best option is an Index Seek. If a seek is not possible, SQL Server ends up using an Index Scan. Like the Clustered Index Scan, this means that SQL Server needed to go through the index to find the necessary data records. If the execution plan uses an Index Scan, Figure 7-12 shows how the Index Scan will appear in your execution plan.

```
Index Scan (NonClustered)
[RecipeHistory].[pk_RecipeHistory_R...
       Cost: 100 %
```

Figure 7-12. *Index Scan*

Also, like Clustered Index Scans, if you see an Index Scan, you may want to see what can be done in terms of rewriting T-SQL to use an Index Seek instead.

Keep in mind what kind of data is needed when writing your T-SQL queries. While including additional data fields can have additional hardware overhead, it can also affect how SQL Server searches the data records. If SQL Server needs to use an Index Seek or an Index Scan to find the required data records, that does not mean that all the data fields need to exist in the non-clustered index. If additional data columns are required, SQL Server may need the non-clustered index to get the additional data columns from the clustered index. When this happens, you will see a Key Lookup in your execution plan like the one in Figure 7-13.

Key Lookup (Clustered)
[RecipeHistory].[ix_RecipeHistory_D...
Cost: 17 %

Figure 7-13. *Key Lookup*

When you see a Key Lookup, that lets you know that not all of the information needed for your query existed in the non-clustered index. In these scenarios, it signifies that the index may need to be modified to include those columns. Before deciding to add these data fields as included columns, you should be aware that including the columns in the index may have an additional cost associated with writing or updating the index.

A table that does not have a clustered index is also known as a heap. If there are no other indexes on the table, SQL Server will have to search row by row to find the data records it needs for query results. There are many other factors that can be involved, but this can cause SQL Server to scan the entire table. This can be seen in the execution plan as Figure 7-14.

Table Scan
[Vendor]
Cost: 100 %

Figure 7-14. *Table Scan*

Some tables that are very small may not need to have indexes, and using a Table Scan may be acceptable. If there are many records in the table, then a Table Scan is not ideal. When this is the case, you may want to investigate if there are any possible indexes that can be added to the table.

If there is a non-clustered index on the heap, it is possible that SQL Server can use those non-clustered indexes as part of the execution plan. If this is the case, you will see an Index Seek or an Index Scan. When either an Index Seek or Index Scan is in the execution plan, it is possible that the columns used in the query do not exist in the non-clustered index. If additional columns need to be looked up in the table, you will see a RID Lookup in the execution plan. You can see this in Figure 7-15.

```
RID Lookup (Heap)
[RecipeHistory] [rh]
   Cost: 100 %
```

Figure 7-15. *RID Lookup*

Like the Key Lookup, you will want to see if you can alter any non-clustered indexes to include the necessary columns from the T-SQL code. It is also possible that the query can be modified to exclude the columns that are causing the RID Lookup.

As an example, I have written a query to pull back all ingredients that begin with the name tomato. In order to do this, I will need to run the query in Listing 7-2.

Listing 7-2. Query to Get Ingredients

```
SELECT IngredientName, DateCreated
FROM dbo. Ingredient
WHERE IngredientName LIKE 'Tomato%';
```

The first time I ran this query, there was only a primary clustered index on IngredientID in this table. The execution plan from the T-SQL code in Listing 7-2 is shown in Figure 7-16.

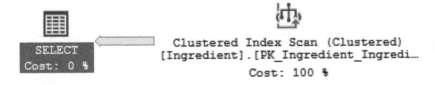

Figure 7-16. *Execution Plan with Only Clustered Index*

There are no non-clustered index on the table. The only option SQL Server has is to search through the entire clustered index to find the requested records. You can see this by looking over the properties associated with the Clustered Index Scan. The properties for this query execution can be found in Figure 7-17.

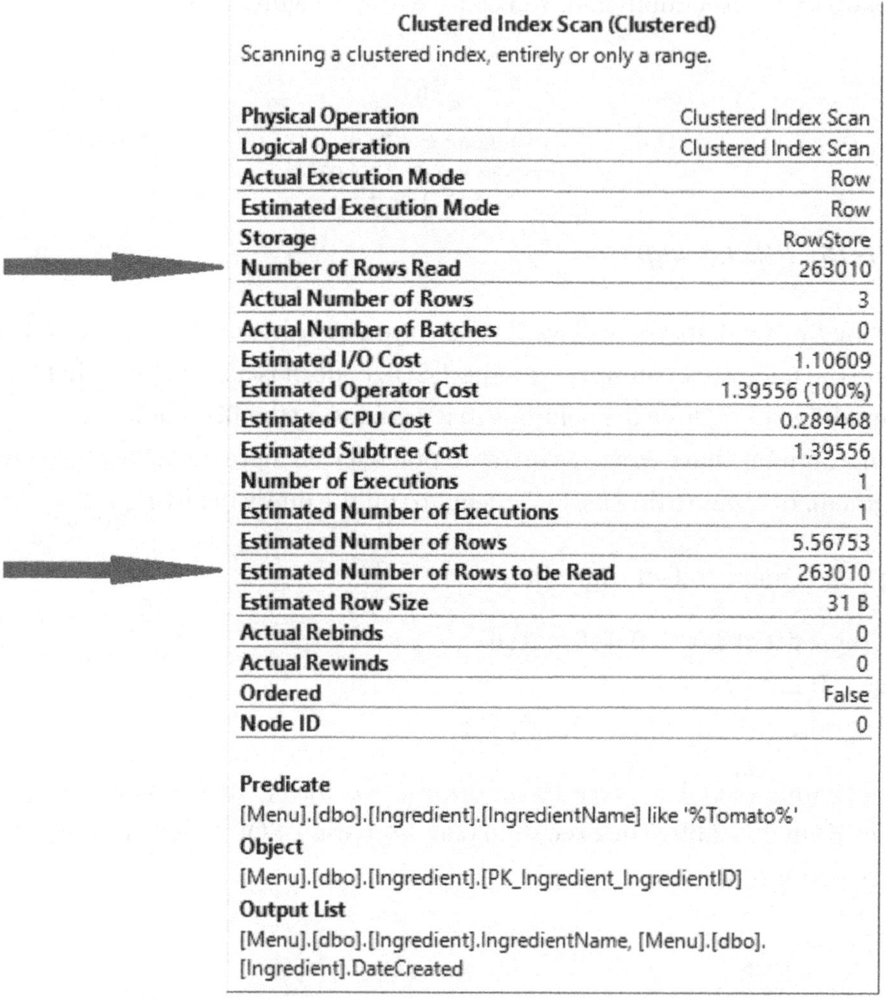

Clustered Index Scan (Clustered)	
Scanning a clustered index, entirely or only a range.	
Physical Operation	Clustered Index Scan
Logical Operation	Clustered Index Scan
Actual Execution Mode	Row
Estimated Execution Mode	Row
Storage	RowStore
Number of Rows Read	263010
Actual Number of Rows	3
Actual Number of Batches	0
Estimated I/O Cost	1.10609
Estimated Operator Cost	1.39556 (100%)
Estimated CPU Cost	0.289468
Estimated Subtree Cost	1.39556
Number of Executions	1
Estimated Number of Executions	1
Estimated Number of Rows	5.56753
Estimated Number of Rows to be Read	263010
Estimated Row Size	31 B
Actual Rebinds	0
Actual Rewinds	0
Ordered	False
Node ID	0

Predicate
[Menu].[dbo].[Ingredient].[IngredientName] like '%Tomato%'
Object
[Menu].[dbo].[Ingredient].[PK_Ingredient_IngredientID]
Output List
[Menu].[dbo].[Ingredient].IngredientName, [Menu].[dbo].
[Ingredient].DateCreated

Figure 7-17. *Reads with Clustered Index*

Looking at the estimated and actual number of rows to be read, the rows to be read are the same for both. The total for each was 263,010 rows read. The actual number of rows is 3. SQL Server must search 263,010 rows to find the 3 rows that matched the criteria.

In this scenario, we have a query that is reading significantly more rows than the number of rows returned. I cannot rewrite the query to use a non-clustered index since none exist. My best option is to write a non-clustered index to improve performance. The new non-clustered index is Listing 7-3.

Listing 7-3. Create Non-clustered Index

```
CREATE INDEX IX_Ingredient_IngredientName
    ON dbo.Ingredient (IngredientName);
```

Now that I have created the non-clustered index, I am going to run the query again to see if I get a new execution plan. The new execution plan is in Figure 7-18.

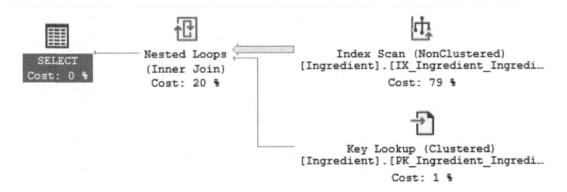

Figure 7-18. *Execution Plan with Non-clustered Index*

In Figure 7-18, the Clustered Index Scan has been replaced with an Index Scan and a Key Lookup. While this may seem like I have decreased the performance of the execution plan, I can verify this by looking at the number of rows read. In Figure 7-19, you can see the properties associated with the Index Seek.

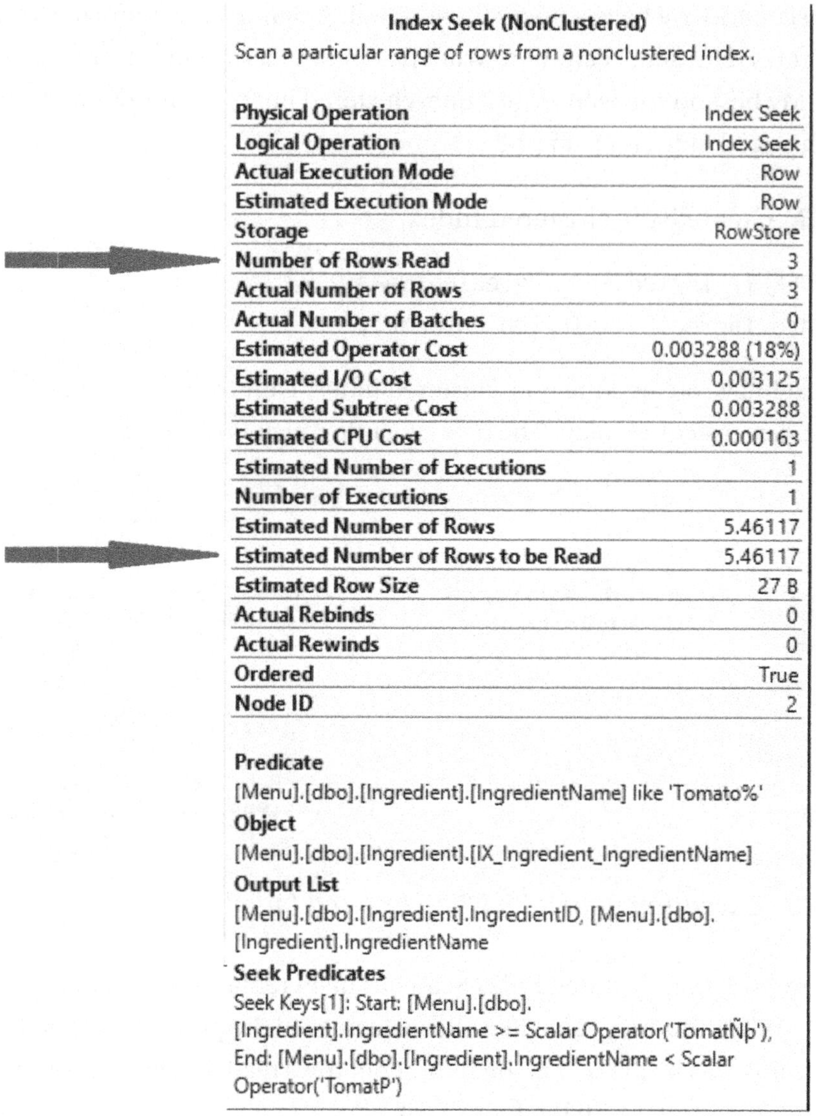

Index Seek (NonClustered)
Scan a particular range of rows from a nonclustered index.

Physical Operation	Index Seek
Logical Operation	Index Seek
Actual Execution Mode	Row
Estimated Execution Mode	Row
Storage	RowStore
Number of Rows Read	3
Actual Number of Rows	3
Actual Number of Batches	0
Estimated Operator Cost	0.003288 (18%)
Estimated I/O Cost	0.003125
Estimated Subtree Cost	0.003288
Estimated CPU Cost	0.000163
Estimated Number of Executions	1
Number of Executions	1
Estimated Number of Rows	5.46117
Estimated Number of Rows to be Read	5.46117
Estimated Row Size	27 B
Actual Rebinds	0
Actual Rewinds	0
Ordered	True
Node ID	2

Predicate
[Menu].[dbo].[Ingredient].[IngredientName] like 'Tomato%'
Object
[Menu].[dbo].[Ingredient].[IX_Ingredient_IngredientName]
Output List
[Menu].[dbo].[Ingredient].IngredientID, [Menu].[dbo].
[Ingredient].IngredientName
Seek Predicates
Seek Keys[1]: Start: [Menu].[dbo].
[Ingredient].IngredientName >= Scalar Operator('TomatÑþ'),
End: [Menu].[dbo].[Ingredient].IngredientName < Scalar
Operator('TomatP')

Figure 7-19. *Properties for Index Seek*

Now that the non-clustered index has been created, I can see that the actual number of rows read has decreased from 263,010 to 3. I would expect that the Key Lookup would have the same number of reads, but I can look at the properties to confirm. In Figure 7-20, you can see the properties returned.

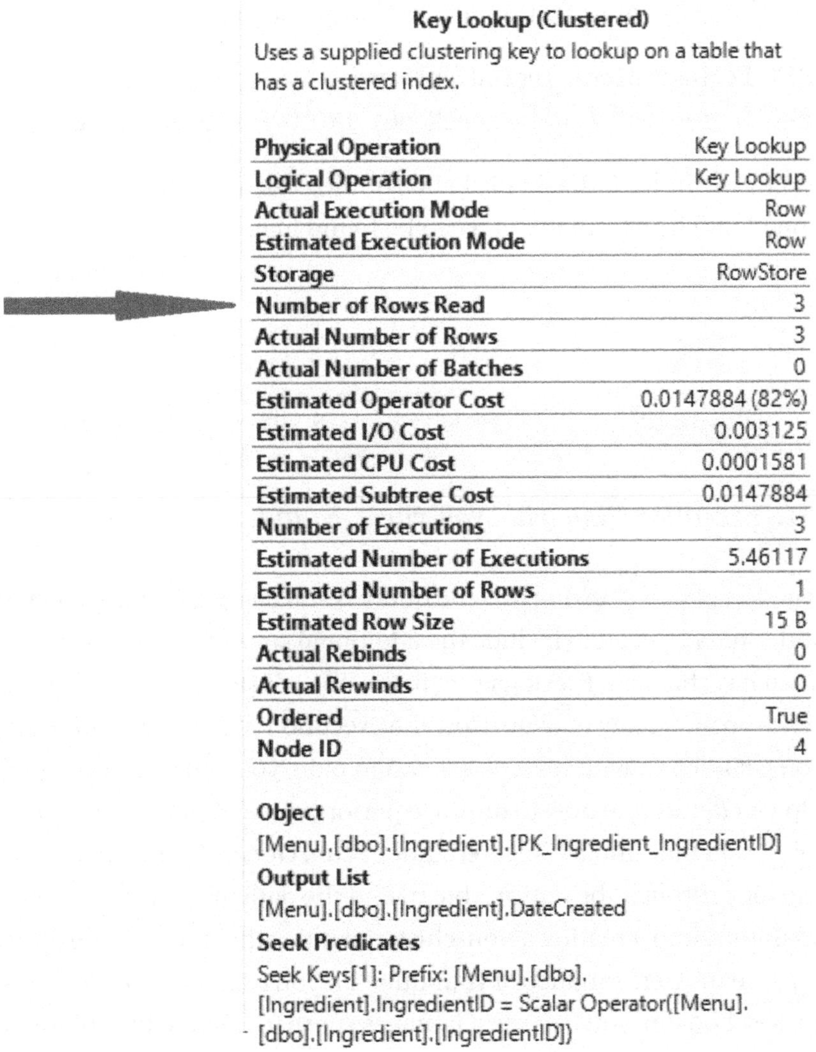

Key Lookup (Clustered)

Uses a supplied clustering key to lookup on a table that has a clustered index.

Physical Operation	Key Lookup
Logical Operation	Key Lookup
Actual Execution Mode	Row
Estimated Execution Mode	Row
Storage	RowStore
Number of Rows Read	3
Actual Number of Rows	3
Actual Number of Batches	0
Estimated Operator Cost	0.0147884 (82%)
Estimated I/O Cost	0.003125
Estimated CPU Cost	0.0001581
Estimated Subtree Cost	0.0147884
Number of Executions	3
Estimated Number of Executions	5.46117
Estimated Number of Rows	1
Estimated Row Size	15 B
Actual Rebinds	0
Actual Rewinds	0
Ordered	True
Node ID	4

Object
[Menu].[dbo].[Ingredient].[PK_Ingredient_IngredientID]
Output List
[Menu].[dbo].[Ingredient].DateCreated
Seek Predicates
Seek Keys[1]: Prefix: [Menu].[dbo].
[Ingredient].IngredientID = Scalar Operator([Menu].
[dbo].[Ingredient].[IngredientID])

Figure 7-20. *Properties of the Key Lookup*

Reviewing the Key Lookup, there were also three rows read in the Key Lookup. The T-SQL code without the non-clustered index had reads of 263,010. The total number of rows read with the non-clustered index is six.

I could get rid of the Key Lookup by including the DateCreated column as part of the non-clustered index or remove the column from the original query.

Listing 7-4. Non-clustered Index with Included Column

```
CREATE INDEX IX_Ingredient_IngredientName
    ON dbo.Ingredient (IngredientName) INCLUDE (DateCreated);
```

After adding the index in Listing 7-4 and running the query from Listing 7-2, I can get the execution plan. The execution plan can be found in Figure 7-21.

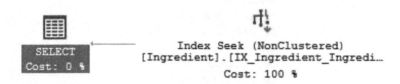

Figure 7-21. *Execution Plan with Non-clustered Index and Included Column*

The execution plan is showing that the query is still using the non-clustered index. Since this index has changed to include the additional column in the select statement, the execution plan has changed. Previously, with the non-clustered index, the execution plan had an Index Scan and a Key Lookup. Now the execution plan is using an Index Seek.

Once you get familiar with reading execution plan, you can start using execution plans to help you determine how to improve performance. When you look at your execution plan, you may find a Clustered Index Scan. Generally, this implies that SQL Server had to look through the entire table to find the data that meets the query criteria. As shown in this section, creating a non-clustered index that includes the join criteria can help improve the performance of your query. If you find that SQL Server is having to perform a Key Lookup, you can see if it makes sense to include the columns being selected as part of the non-clustered index. Understanding how SQL Server uses indexes can help improve your query performance. Understanding how SQL Server compares data from more than one data set can also help you improve query performance.

Logical Join Types in Execution Plans

In addition to reading execution plans and understanding indexes, your T-SQL code can also be used to determine how an execution plan will be generated. In some cases, how tables are joined together is just as important as how data is stored in the tables. There are times where how you are joining your columns together may also affect your execution plan. Some T-SQL in the WHERE clause can impact what types of logical joins are used in the query execution. If multiple queries are combined, it is also possible that it may change how the query is executed. Ultimately, there is a relationship between how the T-SQL code is written and how SQL Server decides to execute the query.

There are several different logical joins in SQL Server. Some of these logical joins are easily visible in T-SQL. This includes the INNER JOIN, LEFT OUTER JOIN, RIGHT OUTER JOIN, and FULL OUTER JOIN. These are not the only logical joins that exist in SQL Server. With some T-SQL commands, SQL Server will compare one table to another looking for records that match or not. In these scenarios, SQL Server does not perform a full join but a SEMI JOIN. This type of join is not specified as a T-SQL command, but some T-SQL commands like EXISTS or NOT EXISTS will indicate a SEMI JOIN. Available semi joins include the LEFT SEMI JOIN, LEFT ANTI-SEMI JOIN, RIGHT SEMI JOIN, and RIGHT ANTI-SEMI JOIN. Finally, there are some logical joins that are related to combining two or more query results in the same transaction. This can include CONCATENATION which is often associated with a UNION ALL or the UNION logical join which can happen with a UNION in T-SQL. Based on the logical join, SQL Server will determine what physical joins can be used. In this way, logical joins can be used to affect query performance.

There are physical join operators that can be associated with logical joins. The four physical join operators are called merge join, hash join, nested loop, and adaptive join. When using an INNER JOIN, any of these four types of physical join operators can be used as part of the execution plan. Depending on how the data is stored in the table and the relative sizes of the tables may affect which physical operator is used. If the data from both tables being compared is sorted, then the records from the two tables can be compared side by side. This would let SQL Server quickly find the records that do or do not match, depending on the query requirements. When this happens, it is called a Merge Join. A Merge Join physical operator that would appear in the execution plan as shown in Figure 7-22.

Merge Join
(Inner Join)
Cost: 33 %

Figure 7-22. *Merge Join*

There are times where the tables being joined together are not sorted. If that is the case, SQL Server can still compare the rows between each of the tables. However, SQL Server will need to convert the records to something that can be compared easily. This can be done by hashing. If SQL Server hashes the columns being compared in both tables and compares them, the physical operator will be a Hash Match. If you see Figure 7-23 in your execution plan, then you know how SQL Server is performing a Hash Match physical join.

Hash Match
(Inner Join)
Cost: 57 %

Figure 7-23. *Hash Match*

If there are two tables where one table is smaller than another, then SQL Server may decide to compare the values or one table one row at a time to all rows of the other table. When this happens, SQL Server will be using a Nested Loop as shown in Figure 7-24.

Nested Loops
(Inner Join)
Cost: 0 %

Figure 7-24. *Nested Loop*

Starting in SQL Server 2017, there is a new physical join operator that can be used when SQL Server determines an execution plan for a query. This new physical join operator is intended to help in situations where the data stored in a given table may vary significantly based on the criteria in the WHERE clause. This type of physical join allows SQL Server to determine if a Hash Match or Nested Loop should be used depending on the data selected for the query. This is referred to as an Adaptive Join. In SQL Server 2017, Adaptive Joins were only available with columnstore indexes. This has changed for SQL Server 2019.

Going through the logical joins that are available, the next one on the list is the LEFT OUTER JOIN and the RIGHT OUTER JOIN. In some ways, these two types of logical joins are the same but also different. For instance, Nested Loops can only use a LEFT OUTER JOIN. If a query is written using a RIGHT OUTER JOIN, SQL Server will incur an additional cost to convert a RIGHT OUTER JOIN to a LEFT OUTER JOIN. Except this specific scenario, all physical join types support the use of LEFT OUTER JOIN. In previous versions of SQL Server, it was possible for SQL Server to generate two different execution plans depending on whether a LEFT OUTER JOIN or a RIGHT OUTER JOIN was used in the query. This was due to the limitations around how joins can be reordered.

The next type of logical join is the FULL OUTER JOIN. Of all the join types, this one has the most specifics about when one physical join type may be used over another. In the first example, I am going to order the table by the identifier as shown in Listing 7-5.

Listing 7-5. Primary Key to Sort Data by RecipeIngredientID

```
ALTER TABLE dbo.RecipeIngredient
ADD CONSTRAINT PK_RecipeIngredient_RecipeIngredientID
PRIMARY KEY CLUSTERED (RecipeIngredientID)
```

Once the table has been ordered by the RecipeIngredientID, I will join the RecipeIngredient table to the Recipe table. The T-SQL code for this join is shown in Listing 7-6.

Listing 7-6. Outer Join Between Recipe and RecipeIngredient

```
SELECT rec.RecipeName
FROM dbo.Recipe rec
     LEFT OUTER JOIN dbo.RecipeIngredient recing
     ON rec.RecipeID = recing.RecipeID
```

In this scenario, the two tables are not ordered in the same way. The RecipeIngredient table is sorted by the RecipeIngredientID, whereas the Recipe table is sorted by the RecipeID. You can see in Figure 7-25 that the physical operator is a Hash Match.

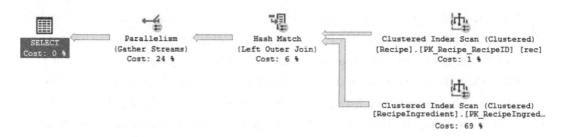

Figure 7-25. *Execution Plan Using Hash Match*

We have seen what happens when the tables are ordered differently. If I run the T-SQL code in Listing 7-7, both tables will be ordered by the same column, RecipeID.

Listing 7-7. Change Primary Key to Sort Data by RecipeID

```
ALTER TABLE dbo.RecipeIngredient
ADD CONSTRAINT PK_RecipeIngredient_RecipeIDIngredientID
PRIMARY KEY CLUSTERED (RecipeID, IngredientID)
```

Looking at Figure 7-26, you can see that the execution plan has changed to use a Merge Join.

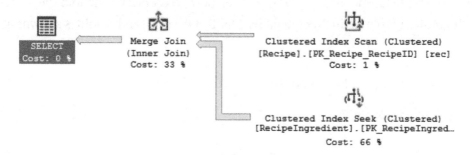

Figure 7-26. *Execution Plan Using Merge Join*

Now that these two tables are ordered in the same manner, SQL Server has determined that it is more cost-effective to use a Merge Join. In the preceding example, SQL Server will take the two ordered data sets and compare the records to determine which records match. All the preceding examples assume equality between the columns being compared. As a general guide, SQL Server will always use a Nested Loop if none of the joins in the query are equal. You can see an example of query that meets this criteria in Listing 7-8.

Listing 7-8. *Full Outer Join with Inequality*

```
SELECT TOP 500 rec.RecipeName
FROM dbo.Recipe rec
     FULL OUTER JOIN dbo.RecipeIngredient recing
     ON rec.RecipeID <> recing.RecipeID
```

If I re-create the primary key referenced in Listing 7-5, the data between the two tables will be sorted differently. Due to the amount of data that will be compared between the two tables, I decided to limit the result to the first 500 records. After running this query, I get the execution plan returned in Figure 7-27.

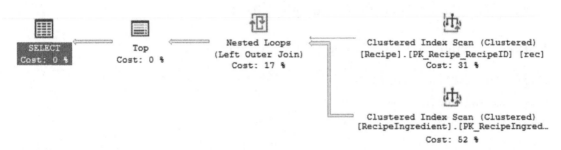

Figure 7-27. *Execution Plan Using Nested Loop*

Now that the only join in the T-SQL code is an inequality, SQL Server uses a Nested Loop physical join. Almost every query where there are no joins that are equal must use a Nested Loop except one specific scenario. If the data being compared is sorted and there is an inequality, SQL Server can use a Merge Join. Creating the primary key from Listing 7-7 will order the data the same between the two tables. The execution plan in Figure 7-28 is returned when executing the query from Listing 7-8.

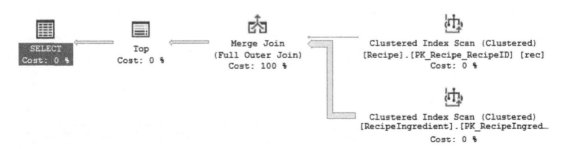

Figure 7-28. *Execution Plan Using Merge Join*

Figure 7-28 shows us that it is possible to have a Merge Join when there is an inequality. However, only when the tables are sorted and there is an inequality is where you can see a Merge Join with a FULL OUTER JOIN. In addition to T-SQL joins that relate to logical joins, there are other logical join types that SQL Server can use.

Another logical join type involves situations where SQL Server compares data between two tables but without doing a full join between the tables. Depending on the T-SQL code used, this can be referred to as a SEMI JOIN or an ANTI SEMI JOIN. Like the LEFT OUTER JOIN and RIGHT OUTER JOIN, SQL Server has some of the same limitations matching the SEMI JOIN and ANTI SEMI JOIN to physical join operators. When working with either a SEMI JOIN or an ANTI SEMI JOIN, there is a concept of left or right. This left or right has to do with which side is being compared. Listing 7-9 finds all ingredients that are not in the recipe with an ID of 2.

Listing 7-9. All Ingredients Except Those in RecipeID 2

```
SELECT ing.IngredientName
FROM dbo.Ingredient ing
WHERE NOT EXISTS
      (
              SELECT *
              FROM dbo.RecipeIngredient recing
              WHERE ing.IngredientID = recing.IngredientID
                   AND recing.RecipeID = 2
      )
```

When this query was run, the data in RecipeIngredient was sorted by RecipeID, then IngredientID. In Figure 7-29, the execution plan shows a LEFT ANTI SEMI JOIN.

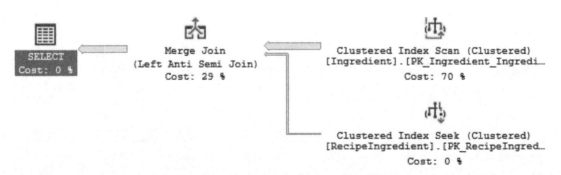

Figure 7-29. *Execution Plan with Left Semi Anti Join*

The semi anti join is due to the NOT EXISTS in the query from Listing 7-9. In the preceding scenario, SQL Server has chosen a left join. Since the table RecipeIngredient is ordered by RecipeID and then IngredientID and the T-SQL code is only looking at one RecipeID, the values evaluated are IngredientIDs that are ordered in the same way as the Ingredient table. This is what allows SQL Server to use a Merge Join for this query. In the query in Listing 7-10, I am looking for all ingredients that exist in a certain subset of recipes.

Listing 7-10. *All Ingredients in All Recipes up to RecipeID 200*

```
SELECT ing.IngredientName
FROM dbo.Ingredient ing
WHERE EXISTS
        (
            SELECT *
            FROM dbo.RecipeIngredient recing
            WHERE ing.IngredientID = recing.IngredientID
                AND recing.RecipeID < 200
        )
```

As shown in execution plan in Figure 7-30, you can see a RIGHT SEMI JOIN.

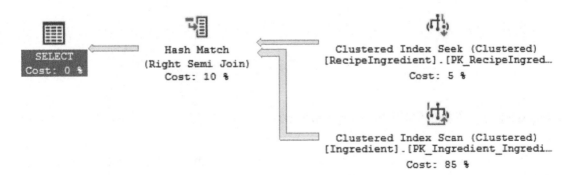

Figure 7-30. *Execution Plan with Right Semi Join*

The use of the RIGHT SEMI JOIN is due to the EXISTS in the T-SQL from Listing 7-10. The use of right is stating the SQL Server is evaluating the results returned from the EXISTS statement to the list of ingredients. While the use of EXISTS or NOT EXISTS can indicate that there will be a SEMI JOIN or an ANTI SEMI join, that may not always be what happens. Listing 7-11 is a query that will return all ingredients that exist for the recipe with an ID of 2.

Listing 7-11. *All Ingredients in RecipeID 2*

```
SELECT ing.IngredientName
FROM dbo.Ingredient ing
WHERE EXISTS
        (
                SELECT *
                FROM dbo.RecipeIngredient recing
                WHERE ing.IngredientID = recing.IngredientID
                    AND recing.RecipeID = 2
        )
```

The execution plan in Figure 7-31 shows how SQL Server has determined to execute this query.

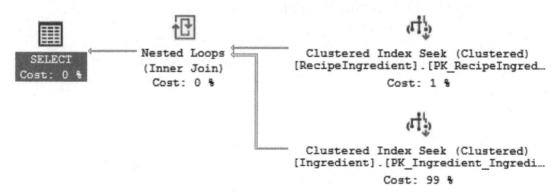

Figure 7-31. *Execution Plan with No Semi Joins*

For this execution, SQL Server has decided to convert this T-SQL to act like an INNER JOIN instead of a SEMI JOIN. This is because SQL Server has calculated that this will give the best execution out of those evaluated.

There are ways to combine data that consist of comparing values between two data sets and selecting items that match or do not match between them. There is also the possibility of combining entire data sets as part of the logical join types. This can include the use of UNION or UNION ALL in your T-SQL code. The query shown in Listing 7-12 shows the use of a UNION between the two tables.

Listing 7-12. All Ingredients with Tomato

```
SELECT ing.IngredientName
FROM dbo.Ingredient ing
WHERE ing.IngredientName LIKE 'Tomato%'

UNION

SELECT ing.IngredientName
FROM dbo.Ingredient ing
WHERE ing.IngredientName = 'Tomato'
```

In this query, the list of ingredients that begin with tomato or the ingredient are equal to tomato will be returned. When this query is executed in the SQL Server, the execution plan in Figure 7-32 is returned.

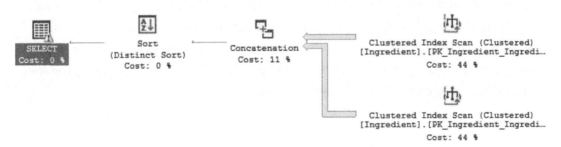

Figure 7-32. *Execution Plan with Concatenation*

In the case of this query, SQL Server is not joining the data together as it has in the other examples from this chapter. Instead, there is only one operator, Concatenation, that indicates how SQL Server is combining this data.

Overall, the goal is to use the physical join that is the most effective for the data that is being joined. Merge Joins can perform very well, but they are limited to data that has been ordered by indexes or ORDER BY or GROUP BY statements. As expected, Index Merge Joins will perform even better than Merge Joins that do not use an index. When data is not sorted and particularly if one of the two sides of the data being joined is small, SQL Server may use a Nested Loop. You will want to confirm that the cost of looping through the other table does not incur a significant cost. Just as a Merge Join using an index performs better than a Merge Join without an index, the same is true for a Nested Loop. For both a Merge Join and Nested Loop, see if you can alter your T-SQL code to use an index. This does not mean creating an index if one does not exist; instead, you can check the indexes on the table and see if any will apply for your specific query. If the tables are not sorted and particularly if the numbers of records being joined on either side are both large, the Hash Match can be the ideal solution.

Throughout this chapter, we have gone over various aspects of working with execution plans. We started with some of the ways you can access and view execution plans. We also discussed how estimated execution plans, actual execution plans, and executions in the plan cache differed. When looking at execution plans, there are some items such as arrow sizes, estimated number of rows, and actual number of rows that can give you some hints regarding the next steps you can take to improve the performance on your T-SQL code. After looking into these items, you may also be able to check how the execution is using indexes. It is helpful to not only focus on what indexes are being used but how SQL Server is searching through those indexes. When joining tables, you will use T-SQL code that can reference certain logical join type behavior. These logical join types can affect what types of physical join types will be used as part of the execution plan. By writing your T-SQL code differently, you may be able to impact the execution plan generated by SQL Server. Using all the information covered in this chapter should help you get more comfortable with reviewing your T-SQL code and improving the speed and hardware usage associated with your T-SQL.

CHAPTER 8

Optimize T-SQL

In this part of the book, I have gone over many aspects of writing T-SQL code. I started with going over the use of set-based design in queries. When designing queries, it will also be important to design queries that use hardware effectively. One way that you can check the performance of your queries is using execution plans. Once you have an execution plan of a query you are wanting to improve, you can start focusing on how to optimize the query. There are some options available when it comes to optimizing T-SQL.

You have many options available to you when you start working on performance tuning your queries. In the past, one option you would have would be to manually identify poorly performing queries and improve them. When identifying queries that need to be optimized, there are many different factors that you can take into consideration. Starting in SQL Server 2017, additional functionality has been added that allows SQL Server to automatically improve the performance of certain aspects of executing T-SQL. With SQL Server 2019, there have been even more enhancements to help queries run better and faster without changing the underlying T-SQL code.

Optimizing Logical Reads

I have seen T-SQL code that appears to run well. The code executes in a timely fashion and returns the correct results. When you look at one of your SQL Server monitoring tools, you may notice some unexpected behavior that indicates there is a performance issue on your system. In some cases, you may find queries that are reading pages from memory that are not included in the result set. Reading the data pages can be identified as logical reads. You will want to look at the execution plan for the T-SQL code to figure out what could be causing this discrepancy. This does not only involve looking at what T-SQL code is executing but also trying to determine what can be done to improve performance.

© Elizabeth Noble 2020
E. Noble, *Pro T-SQL 2019*, https://doi.org/10.1007/978-1-4842-5590-2_8

The advantage of optimizing this query to use less reads is that this should decrease the number of data pages that are read into memory as part of this query execution. Put another way, the downside of reading more data than is needed for the query result is that pages that are used more frequently by the applications may be cleared from memory too soon. Unfortunately, we often are only aware of performance issues when we find out that an application is running slowly or an application is crashing. At these times, it can be difficult to diagnose the specific query causing issues. If you do not have access to monitoring software, this situation can become even more difficult to troubleshoot. When I first started investigating performance issues, I would check SQL Server Agent's job history. Sometimes you will find a process running at the same time as the Production issue. While this does not confirm that the SQL Server Agent job is the cause, it may be worth investigating.

For these situations, it would be preferable to know the exact stored procedure or prepared statement that is causing performance issues. Aside from third-party software, Query Store or extended events that were previously set up, you may have very few options available. In addition, I would rather identify queries that may cause performance issues before there is an outage. If I do not have access to third-party tools, I will use DMVs to try and find queries before they become an issue. I will often use any combination of the preceding actions with Performance Monitor to help track SQL Server over time and confirm if my performance tuning is effective.

If you do not have third-party tools or you want to get more familiar with DMVs to find T-SQL that needs performance tuning, you can query `sys.dm_exec_query_stats`. This DMV tracks statistics about T-SQL code that is executed and is still part of the plan cache. This will only return results for queries that have not been cleared out of the plan cache. If you believe that this DMV is missing some stored procedures that you would expect to see, you may want to do some research on your plan cache and determine if the cache is getting filled with ad hoc queries. You will need to join this data to `sys.dm_exec_sql_text` to find the T-SQL code associated with the statistics.

When trying to find queries with high logical reads, you will want to look at T-SQL code based on various criteria. Looking at the average logical reads is usually my main target when looking for queries to performance tune. I prefer this metric as it often identifies T-SQL code that runs frequently on the server and probably has more reads than I would expect. If there is a process that runs frequently on the server, I would not expect the average number of reads to be very high as a frequent process would imply the T-SQL code is directly related to an application. There are also some queries that do not run very often but use a high number of logical reads when they do run. In my experience, if the total logical reads are high and the overall execution count is low, I will prioritize these queries below T-SQL code that has a higher average logical read value and a high number of executions.

Once you have identified the T-SQL code that needs to be performance tuned, you will want to look at both the code and the execution plan to get familiar with what data the query is retrieving and how SQL Server is retrieving the data. In Listing 8-1, you can see the query that I will be optimizing.

Listing 8-1. Original Query for Recipe and Preparation Details

```
DECLARE @RecipeID            INT = -1;
DECLARE @PreparationTypeID   INT = -1;
DECLARE @MealTypeID          INT = -1;
DECLARE @StartDate           DATETIME = NULL;
DECLARE @EndDate             DATETIME = NULL;

SELECT recing.RecipeID,
       recing.IngredientID,
       ic.IngredientCostID
INTO #TmpRecipe
FROM dbo.Recipe rec
     INNER JOIN dbo.RecipeIngredient recing
     ON rec.RecipeID = recing.RecipeID
     INNER JOIN dbo.Ingredient ing
     ON recing.IngredientID = ing.IngredientID
     INNER JOIN dbo.IngredientCost ic
     ON ing.IngredientID = ic.IngredientID
WHERE (rec.PreparationTypeID = @PreparationTypeID OR
@PreparationTypeID = -1)
     AND (rec.RecipeID = @RecipeID OR @RecipeID = -1)
     AND (rec.MealTypeID = @MealTypeID OR @MealTypeID = -1)
     AND ing.IsActive = 1
     AND (rec.DateCreated > @StartDate OR @StartDate IS NULL)
     AND (rec.DateCreated < @EndDate OR @EndDate IS NULL);
```

```
SELECT IngredientCostID
INTO #UniqueIngredientCost
FROM IngredientCostHistory
GROUP BY IngredientCostID
HAVING COUNT(*)>3;

SELECT rec.RecipeName,
      rec.RecipeDescription,
      ing.IngredientName,
      rec.PreparationTypeID,
      p.PreparationTypeName,
      p.PreparationTypeDescription,
      ic.Cost
FROM #TmpRecipe tr
      LEFT JOIN #UniqueIngredientCost uic
      ON tr.IngredientCostID = uic.IngredientCostID
      LEFT JOIN dbo.IngredientCostHistory ic
      ON uic.IngredientCostID = ic.IngredientCostID
      INNER JOIN dbo.Recipe rec
      ON tr.RecipeID = rec.RecipeID
      INNER JOIN dbo.Ingredient ing
      ON tr.IngredientID = ing.IngredientID
      INNER JOIN dbo.PreparationType p
      ON rec.PreparationTypeID = p.PreparationTypeID
WHERE uic.IngredientCostID IS NOT NULL
ORDER BY
      CASE WHEN
      (
            rec.RecipeID = @RecipeID
            AND rec.PreparationTypeID = @PreparationTypeID
      )
            THEN 0
            ELSE 1
      END,
      rec.RecipeName DESC,
      ing.IngredientName ASC
```

```
DROP TABLE #TmpRecipe
DROP TABLE #UniqueIngredientCost
```

You will also want to get the execution plan from the plan cache so that you can see how SQL Server is executing the T-SQL code. The partial execution plan in Figure 8-1 shows one part of the execution plan that may benefit from optimization.

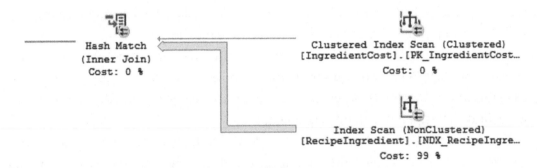

Figure 8-1. *Partial Execution Plan for Listing 8-1*

The execution plan has one thick line that results in a thin line after the Hash Match. This is a good indication that the query may be able to be optimized to use less reads overall. Based on this information, I need to investigate how the data from dbo.Recipe is combined with dbo.RecipeIngredient. Looking at either the T-SQL code or the output of the T-SQL code, I can get a better idea of what the purpose of this query is. This query is returning all ingredients where the cost has changed three times along with information about what recipes use these ingredients.

Knowing this helps us begin the process of optimizing the logical reads on this query. I know that this query is based on ingredients that have had their cost changed more than three times. It may be possible to reduce the number of reads if I focus on trying to find only recipes that contain ingredients where the price has been changed more than three times. While the table dbo.RecipeIngredient is ordered by RecipeID and then by IngredientID, this does not help when the T-SQL code in Listing 8-1 is only looking for recipes that have specific ingredients. The execution plan indicates that there is a non-clustered index that SQL Server is using to retrieve the data. This T-SQL code to create this index is in Listing 8-2.

Listing 8-2. Query for Index on RecipeIngredient

```
CREATE NONCLUSTERED INDEX NDX_RecipeIngredient_IsActive_IngredientID
ON dbo.RecipeIngredient (IsActive, IngredientID)
```

The non-clustered index does not change the order of the data in the table, but the index does keep the data for the index ordered. In this case, the index orders all the data first by the value of the IsActive column, then by the IngredientID. The non-clustered index also must be able to reference back to the clustered index for situations where SQL Server decides to use this non-clustered index but also may need some additional data from the table. SQL Server does this by including the columns for the clustered index as part of this index. This helps us because this means the RecipeID from this index can be used to find all RecipeIDs with this ingredient.

This all sounds great, but it does not look like this index is currently giving us the best performance. While we could work on tuning the indexes, I have found that on very large tables and on highly transactional systems, you may not be able to add or alter indexes as they exist. Sometimes those indexes are there doing exactly what they need to be doing, making sure a critical part of the application performs well. Modifying these indexes may cause even more headaches. We are fortunate that in this scenario we can add one line of the code to the T-SQL from Listing 8-1 and decrease the number of reads. The index is ordered by the IsActive flag. If I modify the query to reference the IsActive flag, I may be able to get the index to work more efficiently. You can see the code `AND (recing.IsActive = 1 OR recing.IsActive = 0)` in Listing 8-3.

Listing 8-3. Optimized Query for Recipe and Preparation Details

```
DECLARE @RecipeID          INT = -1;
DECLARE @PreparationTypeID INT = -1;
DECLARE @MealTypeID        INT = -1;
DECLARE @StartDate         DATETIME = NULL;
DECLARE @EndDate           DATETIME = NULL;

SELECT recing.RecipeID,
     recing.IngredientID,
     ic.IngredientCostID
INTO #TmpRecipe
FROM dbo.Recipe rec
```

```
        INNER JOIN dbo.RecipeIngredient recing
        ON rec.RecipeID = recing.RecipeID
        INNER JOIN dbo.Ingredient ing
        ON recing.IngredientID = ing.IngredientID
        INNER JOIN dbo.IngredientCost ic
        ON ing.IngredientID = ic.IngredientID
WHERE (rec.PreparationTypeID = @PreparationTypeID OR @PreparationTypeID = -1)
        AND (rec.RecipeID = @RecipeID OR @RecipeID = -1)
        AND (rec.MealTypeID = @MealTypeID OR @MealTypeID = -1)
        AND ing.IsActive = 1
        -- Adding the code below to try to use index
        ---- NDX_RecipeIngredient_IsActive_IngredientID
        ------ Index exists on the dbo.RecipeIngredient
        -------- and is ordered by IsActive then IngredientID
        AND (recing.IsActive = 1 OR recing.IsActive = 0)
        AND (rec.DateCreated > @StartDate OR @StartDate IS NULL)
        AND (rec.DateCreated < @EndDate OR @EndDate IS NULL);

SELECT IngredientCostID
INTO #UniqueIngredientCost
FROM IngredientCostHistory
GROUP BY IngredientCostID
HAVING COUNT(*)>3;

SELECT rec.RecipeName,
        rec.RecipeDescription,
        ing.IngredientName,
        rec.PreparationTypeID,
        p.PreparationTypeName,
        p.PreparationTypeDescription,
        ic.Cost
FROM #TmpRecipe tr
        LEFT JOIN #UniqueIngredientCost uic
        ON tr.IngredientCostID = uic.IngredientCostID
        LEFT JOIN dbo.IngredientCostHistory ic
        ON uic.IngredientCostID = ic.IngredientCostID
        INNER JOIN dbo.Recipe rec
```

```
        ON tr.RecipeID = rec.RecipeID
        INNER JOIN dbo.Ingredient ing
        ON tr.IngredientID = ing.IngredientID
        INNER JOIN dbo.PreparationType p
        ON rec.PreparationTypeID = p.PreparationTypeID
WHERE uic.IngredientCostID IS NOT NULL
ORDER BY
        CASE WHEN
        (
                rec.RecipeID = @RecipeID
                AND rec.PreparationTypeID = @PreparationTypeID
        )
                THEN 0
                ELSE 1
        END,
        rec.RecipeName DESC,
        ing.IngredientName ASC

DROP TABLE #TmpRecipe
DROP TABLE #UniqueIngredientCost
```

Now that I have changed the code, I need to get a new execution plan to confirm that these changes worked as I intended. Figure 8-2 shows that same general area of the execution plan, but this is what it looks like after the T-SQL code change.

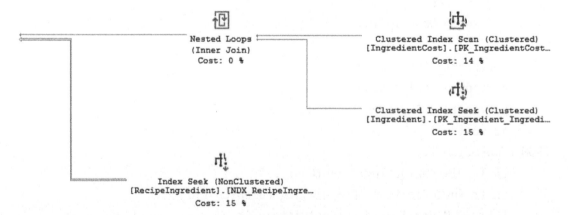

Figure 8-2. *Partial Execution Plan for Listing 8-3*

There are a couple of changes that happened. Looking at the execution plan overall, you can see that all the lines are much thinner than they were before. While the order of some steps has changed, the largest different is related to the non-clustered index. In Figure 8-1, SQL Server was performing an Index Scan on this index. Now that I have specified the IsActive column as part of my query, SQL Server is now using an Index Seek on this same non-clustered index. Not all attempts to optimize your T-SQL code are this simple. However, it is possible for you to make dramatic improvements in your T-SQL code when you understand how your data is stored and how the indexes on your tables reference that data.

Optimizing Duration

My goal when working with SQL Server is to have the queries executing T-SQL code run as quickly as possible. I tend to focus on logical reads as I want to minimize the number of data pages going into the cache that are not needed by the query that is being executed. However, there are other issues that can happen in SQL Server that can have negative effects downstream.

Prior to SQL Server 2019, one of the most common reasons for slow queries was parameter sniffing. The Adaptive Join in SQL Server 2019 has helped minimize issues associated with parameter sniffing. If an execution plan has an Adaptive Join, SQL Server will determine at execution time whether to use a Merge Join or a Nested Loop. The flexibility of the Adaptive Join allows the execution of T-SQL code to execute one way if there is a small set of data and use a different physical join if there is a larger set of data. This will cause the execution of the query to perform better regardless of the data being retrieved.

Working to find the queries that have the slowest durations can be challenging especially if you are trying to find real-time data regarding query performance. Thankfully, SQL Server does keep track of query performance for T-SQL code that exists in the query plan cache. You can use the same DMV from the previous section, `sys.dm_exec_query_stats`, but instead of looking for records with the highest total logical reads or average logical reads, you will want to look at worker time. You can either start with total worker time or average worker time. Depending on what time of day your queries are running may help you decide which to focus on first. If one of the queries with the highest worker time is running during the most active time for your business, I would address that query first. However, if you have T-SQL code with the highest average worker time running frequently throughout the busy time of your day, you may see more benefit by working on this code first. Either way, you will want to look up the plan in sys.dm_exec_sql_text that matches the plan from sys.dm_exec_query_stats to find the associated query text.

One of the challenges with SQL Server is that the same solution does not always work for every situation. I have come across some queries where breaking the data up into smaller segments will improve performance. There are other times where it may be more efficient to combine several steps into a single T-SQL statement. The query in Listing 8-4 shows a series of T-SQL statements.

Listing 8-4. Original Query for Recipe Information for All Recipes

```
DECLARE @RecipeID INT = NULL;

CREATE TABLE #TempIngredient
(
     RecipeID          INT,
     IngredientName    VARCHAR(25),
     Cost              DECIMAL(6,3)
);

INSERT INTO #TempIngredient
SELECT recing.RecipeID, ing.IngredientName, ingcos.Cost
FROM dbo.RecipeIngredient recing
     INNER JOIN dbo.Ingredient ing
     ON recing.IngredientID = ing.IngredientID
     LEFT JOIN dbo.IngredientCost ingcos
     ON ing.IngredientID = ingcos.IngredientID
          AND ingcos.IsActive = 1
          AND ingcos.Cost > 5.00
ORDER BY recing.RecipeID, recing.IngredientID;

SELECT rec.RecipeName, meal.MealTypeName, ting.IngredientName, ting.Cost
FROM dbo.Recipe rec
     INNER JOIN dbo.MealType meal
     ON rec.MealTypeID = meal.MealTypeID
     INNER JOIN #TempIngredient ting
     ON rec.RecipeID = ting.RecipeID
```

```
WHERE (rec.RecipeID = @RecipeID OR @RecipeID IS NULL)
ORDER BY rec.RecipeName, ting.IngredientName;

DROP TABLE #TempIngredient;
```

Overall, the goal of Listing 8-4 is to return the recipe, type of meal, ingredient, and ingredient cost for all or a specific recipe. When looking at the execution plan, we will want to drill into the specific part of the execution plan with the highest percentage as shown in Figure 8-3.

Figure 8-3. *Partial Execution Plan for Listing 8-4*

The insert into the temporary table is the most significant part of the first T-SQL statement. The same statement also took up a higher percentage of the overall execution plan. Therefore, the highest cost associated with this query is inserting data into the temporary table. I can rewrite this query to the one shown in Listing 8-5.

Listing 8-5. Optimized Query for Recipe Information for All Recipes

```
DECLARE @RecipeID INT = NULL;

SELECT rec.RecipeName, meal.MealTypeName, ing.IngredientName, ingcos.Cost
FROM dbo.Recipe rec
     INNER JOIN dbo.MealType meal
     ON rec.MealTypeID = meal.MealTypeID
     INNER JOIN dbo.RecipeIngredient recing
     ON rec.RecipeID = recing.RecipeID
     INNER JOIN dbo.Ingredient ing
     ON recing.IngredientID = ing.IngredientID
     LEFT JOIN dbo.IngredientCost ingcos
     ON ing.IngredientID = ingcos.IngredientID
          AND ingcos.IsActive = 1
WHERE (rec.RecipeID = @RecipeID OR @RecipeID IS NULL)
ORDER BY rec.RecipeName, ing.IngredientName;
```

The preceding T-SQL statement has all the code required to generate the same output as the one from Listing 8-4. Depending on the indexes that exist on your tables and the join criteria, sometimes you will see better performance when selecting all your data in one query. Other times, you may optimize your queries by getting subsets of data and combining them into one query. A portion of the execution plan for Listing 8-5 can be seen in Figure 8-4.

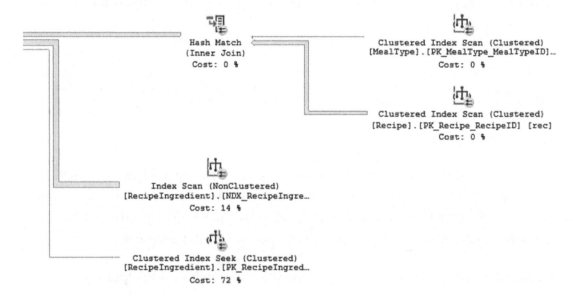

Figure 8-4. *Partial Execution Plan for Listing 8-5*

As shown in Figure 8-4, the step taking up the largest percentage of the execution plan has changed. Based on the actual execution plan, the largest percentage is spent performing a Clustered Index Seek on the primary key of the RecipeIngredient table. As this is a seek relating to the primary key of the table, it seems unlikely that there is a better alternative for performance tuning this query.

There are other factors that can contribute to slowness of running queries. In many scenarios, the best way to optimize these queries involves using indexes. You want to check execution plans for Key Lookups. These Key Lookups indicate that SQL Server is having to go from the non-clustered index to the clustered index to find additional fields that are needed as part of the query. In some cases, you may be able to change the values returned or the join conditions of your query to resolve the Key Lookups. Otherwise, you will need to see if the indexes can be changed in order to improve performance.

Creating and maintaining indexes is a topic that could be covered entirely in a book by itself, but there are some things you can do when working with indexes. If you are at a point where you think you may need to consider adding indexes, you will first want to be aware of what indexes currently exist on the tables in question. While it is outside the scope of this book, you will want to determine if there are indexes that are no longer in use and can be dropped. Of the indexes that are remaining, you will want to evaluate these carefully. One of these indexes may be able to be modified to allow it to continue to be effective for other T-SQL code but also to optimize the current query. You can create or modify an index so that additional columns are stored with the index. However, the index is not sorted by these columns. These columns can be referred to as a covering column. If a column is needed for a join or a WHERE clause, I would consider adding it to the index. Before deciding to add the column to the index, make sure you are familiar with how SQL Server uses indexes to search for data. The approach with some indexes involves adding a column as an included column on the index. This will allow SQL Server to return the column results without a Key Lookup, but it will not affect how SQL Server uses the index to retrieve data records.

Optimizing the duration of your T-SQL code can yield many benefits. Among these is improved performance of your applications. In some cases, you may be able to improve the duration of your queries by rewriting the code in a way that is more efficient. In other situations, you may want to consider if there are ways the code can be written differently to make better use of the existing indexes. Another option is to modify existing indexes or create new ones. If you choose to modify indexes, use caution as sometimes indexes can exist that cause more harm than they help. Regularly review the duration of your T-SQL code to see if you can find any queries that need performance tuning.

Automatic Database Tuning

In the previous sections, I have discussed what you can do to optimize your T-SQL code regarding logical reads and duration. Over the past several releases of SQL Server, there have been many changes that can either help you optimize SQL Server or optimize your queries automatically. In some cases, this involves recording information about the performance of your queries. At other times this can be either SQL Server managing your execution plans or your indexes. While the topics covered in this section are related to optimization that SQL Server can perform for you, it is helpful to understand these concepts so that you can have a better idea as to how SQL Server will handle your T-SQL code.

Query Store

When executing queries in SQL Server, one of the key benefits is the use of execution plans. In Chapter 6, I discussed briefly how memory is used in SQL Server, and in Chapter 7, I explained how execution plans are saved in their own plan cache. One of the challenges with execution plans happens when an execution plan gets cleared from the plan cache. Not only was there a cost associated with generating a new execution plan, but there is also the risk that the new execution plan could perform poorly as compared to the original.

Starting with SQL Server 2016, there is new functionality on how execution plans can be managed. Instead of only having execution plans available in the plan cache, there was the option to save historical information about the execution plans that had been generated. This new feature was called Query Store. In order to use Query Store, you will have to enable it as shown in Listing 8-6.

Listing 8-6. Query to Enable Query Store

```
ALTER DATABASE Menu
SET QUERY_STORE (OPERATION_MODE = READ_WRITE);
```

Enabling Query Store allows SQL Server to keep track of the execution plans over time. In addition to keeping track of execution plans, Query Store also records execution statistics. Starting in SQL Server 2017 and Azure SQL Database, Query Store also tracks information regarding wait statistics for specific query executions. In SQL Server 2016, you would have to manually manage the Query Store to determine if there were better execution plans for your T-SQL code. If you found a query that would benefit from an execution plan in the Query Store, you would need to manually force a plan for that query. This would cause additional maintenance over time as you would need to go back and undo forced plans as the data in your database may change over time.

Automatic Plan Correction

Building on top of the functionality introduced in SQL Server 2016 with Query Store is a new feature introduced in SQL Server 2017. The next step was to see if SQL Server could use the access to historical information about execution plans, execution statistics, and wait statistics for those query executions to the benefit of SQL Server. Like Query Store, this is functionality that can be configured so that no human intervention is required. In order to make that happen, this new functionality also had to include a way to verify the results.

Now that SQL Server could look at the query store, it could determine systematically if a new execution plan performed better or worse than the prior execution plan. This new functionality is referred to as Automatic Plan Correction. This feature is not enabled by default. Before it can be enabled, Query Store will need to be enabled as shown in Listing 8-6. Once Query Store has been enabled, you can run the code shown in Listing 8-7 to enable Automatic Plan Correction.

Listing 8-7. Query to Enable Automatic Plan Correction

```
ALTER DATABASE Menu
SET AUTOMATIC_TUNING (FORCE_LAST_GOOD_PLAN = ON);
```

Once Automatic Plan Correction has been enabled, SQL Server can compare the new and previous execution plans to determine if the comparison meets the criteria where SQL Server can force the execution plan. In order to make sure that SQL Server did not spend extra effort micro tuning performance, the threshold was set at a benefit of decreasing the CPU cost by 10 seconds or more. The other option was if the number of errors in the execution was less than the previous version. If the new execution plan cost less than 10 extra seconds on the CPU, then SQL Server could force the previous plan automatically. Similarly, if the new execution plan had more errors than the previous plan, then SQL Server could force the previous execution plan.

After SQL Server forced an execution plan automatically, it would continue to monitor performance to confirm that the newly forced execution plan was working as expected. If SQL Server determines that the forced execution plan is no longer providing the performance benefit expected, then SQL Server can undo forcing the execution plan. Automatic Plan Correction does not alter your T-SQL code; this feature only helps manage which execution plan is currently being used for your T-SQL code.

If you would prefer to manually manage your execution plans, you can do so. You will want to make sure that you do not run the T-SQL code shown in Listing 7-8. If you choose to manual plan choice correction, then you will need to regularly monitor which queries need to have plans forced. You will also need to manually undo forcing query execution plans over time as the shape of your data and the associated statistics may change over time. Query Store can be used to monitor execution plans over time starting in SQL Server 2016. With SQL Server 2017, there is also the option of using the DMV sys.dm_tuning_ recommendations to find queries that can benefit from forcing an execution plan.

While automatic or manual plan correction is outside the scope of T-SQL, it is helpful to know what SQL Server can do with your T-SQL queries. I would still suggest that you design your T-SQL to run efficiently for a variety of scenarios, but it is nice to know that when there are times that issues like parameter sniffing are unavoidable, there are other options within SQL Server to help your overall query performance.

Automatic Index Management

In addition to allowing SQL Server to manage your execution plans and choose the best available plan, you also have the option of allowing SQL Server to systematically monitor and manage your indexes. This feature is currently only available in Azure SQL Database. Enabling Automatic Index Management allows SQL Server to not only create new indexes that it deems necessary, but SQL Server can also identify indexes that are unused or that seem to be like other indexes that have been created.

Like Automatic Plan Correction, SQL Server will monitor the performance of new indexes. If there are deemed to be less efficient, SQL Server will remove those indexes. The same process will be used if SQL Server modifies or drops indexes. It will still be possible to manually manage your indexes while using Azure SQL Database. However, allowing Azure SQL Database to promptly find and resolve indexing issues may save you money as less resources may be required to perform the same tasks.

Intelligent Query Processing

Along with the ability for SQL Server to automatically manage execution plans and indexes, there are other new features that can help automatically optimize T-SQL code performance. As discussed in Chapter 6, memory is a key resource used by SQL Server. When using memory with SQL Server, we want to be sure that memory is being used as efficiently as possible. Working with data sets is also critical to working with SQL Server. If SQL Server can convert a collection of rows into a batch and then perform any necessary actions, this will help optimize the query. The shape of the data is not always consistent in a data table. In those scenarios, it may be helpful to have an execution plan that is flexible depending on the types of data pulled back. These features can help improve the efficiency of the T-SQL code that is being executed.

Memory Grant Feedback

When executing a query, SQL Server will try to estimate the amount of memory required for that transaction. The amount of memory allocated to a query based on the estimate is referred to as a memory grant. While it is ideal that the SQL Server estimate the memory correctly, there are times where the amount of memory estimated does not match the amount of memory used. Memory Grant Feedback first became available in SQL Server 2017. The original memory grants were for batch mode operations. That is a type of operation where records are processed as a unit instead of row by row.

In order to make sure that memory grants were managed correctly, thresholds were defined for the variance between the memory grant and the actual memory usage. If the memory used was less than 1 MB, no additional analysis was required. If the memory grant was twice the amount of memory used, then the memory grant for the specific query could be recalculated. Similarly, the memory grant could be recalculated if the memory needed to execute the query was more than the memory grant.

Batch Mode on Rowstore

Having memory grants for batch mode operations was a necessary foundation for the next stage in the development of batch mode operations. Batch mode operations are where SQL Server can perform an action to group of records all at once instead of one record at a time. When batch mode was originally introduced in SQL Server 2012, it was only available for columnstore indexes. Starting with SQL Server 2019, batch mode operations were also allowed to be used for a collection of rows. In this case, a collection of rows is also called a rowstore. Memory grants for batch mode operations allowing batch mode operations for heaps and indexes are the foundation for an additional type of query optimization.

Adaptive Joins

SQL Server uses statistics to help estimate the best plan. However, data is not always evenly distributed in a table. This can cause SQL Server to select an execution plan that may not be the best choice. The chance of this happening has decreased in SQL Server 2019 due to new functionality that allows SQL Server to choose between the physical join operator of a Nested Loop and a Hash Match depending on the current execution of the query. This new functionality is called an Adaptive Join.

Adaptive Joins were originally introduced in SQL Server 2017. However, adaptive joins can only be used as part of a batch mode operation. In SQL Server 2017, batch mode operations were only supported for columnstore indexes. Now that batch mode operations are also supported for heaps and B-tree indexes, Adaptive Joins can also be used on these database objects. Executing the query from Listing 8-5 generated an execution plan that contained an adaptive join. When you see the execution plan, you will see a physical operator for an Adaptive Join. On the graphical execution plan, you cannot tell what type of operator was used behind the scenes. However, if you mouse over the Adaptive Join in the execution plan, you will see a list of properties like the one shown in Figure 8-5.

Adaptive Join

Chooses dynamically between hash join and nested loops.

Physical Operation	Adaptive Join
Logical Operation	Inner Join
Actual Join Type	HashMatch
Actual Execution Mode	Batch
Estimated Join Type	HashMatch
Is Adaptive	True
Estimated Execution Mode	Batch
Adaptive Threshold Rows	2163.53
Actual Number of Rows	3039259
Actual Number of Batches	3380
Estimated Operator Cost	0 (0%)
Estimated I/O Cost	0
Estimated CPU Cost	0.0100299
Estimated Subtree Cost	6.29443
Estimated Number of Executions	1
Number of Executions	4
Estimated Number of Rows	1002990
Estimated Row Size	41 B
Actual Rebinds	0
Actual Rewinds	0
Node ID	6

Output List
[Menu].[dbo].[Recipe].RecipeName, [Menu].[dbo].
[MealType].MealTypeName, [Menu].[dbo].
[RecipeIngredient].IngredientID
Hash Keys Probe
[Menu].[dbo].[RecipeIngredient].RecipeID
Outer References
[Menu].[dbo].[Recipe].RecipeID, Expr1026

Figure 8-5. *Adaptive Join Properties from Listing 8-5*

213

The original query from Listing 8-5 was to return a list of all recipes, the meal type associated with the recipe, the list of ingredients, and the cost associated with the ingredients. In Figure 8-5, you can see that the Adaptive Join type listed under the properties is the Hash Match. In Figure 8-6 is a partial screenshot from the live query statistics for the execution of Listing 8-5.

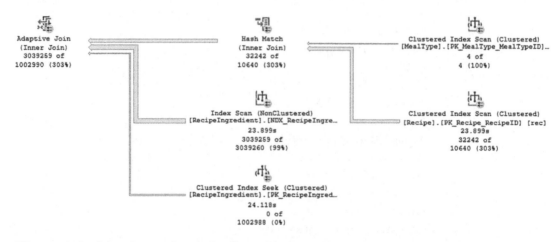

Figure 8-6. *Live Query Statistics from Listing 8-5*

You can see the total number of records processed by each step as the time spent on some of the steps. Looking at the live query statistics, you can see the percent of records returned vs. the estimate. In this case, some records like Clustered Index Scan on the table MealType or the Index Scan on the table RecipeIngredient were estimated correctly. While other operations like the Clustered Index Scan, Hash Match, and Adaptive Join were underestimated. While these variances may cause performance issues, the reason I am pointing these values out is to compare them to the query execution after I change the value passed to the @RecipeID variable.

If I limit the same query to one recipe, I may write T-SQL like what is shown in Listing 8-8.

Listing 8-8. Query for Recipe Information for a Specific Recipe

```
DECLARE @RecipeID INT = 1350;

SELECT rec.RecipeName, meal.MealTypeName, ing.IngredientName, ingcos.Cost
FROM dbo.Recipe rec
     INNER JOIN dbo.MealType meal
     ON rec.MealTypeID = meal.MealTypeID
     INNER JOIN dbo.RecipeIngredient recing
     ON rec.RecipeID = recing.RecipeID
     INNER JOIN dbo.Ingredient ing
     ON recing.IngredientID = ing.IngredientID
     LEFT JOIN dbo.IngredientCost ingcos
     ON ing.IngredientID = ingcos.IngredientID
         AND ingcos.IsActive = 1
WHERE (rec.RecipeID = @RecipeID OR @RecipeID IS NULL)
ORDER BY rec.RecipeName, ing.IngredientName;
```

The singular difference between Listing 8-5 and Listing 8-8 is the first line. In Listing 8-5, the @RecipeID was set to NULL so that all recipes would be returned. In Listing 8-8, the @Recipe is set to one specific value. We can execute this query and look at the execution plan to see if SQL Server will handle this query execution differently now that there may be only one recipe affected. In Figure 8-7, you can see the properties for the Adaptive Join when executing Listing 8-8.

Adaptive Join

Chooses dynamically between hash join and nested loops.

Physical Operation	Adaptive Join
Logical Operation	Inner Join
Actual Join Type	NestedLoops
Actual Execution Mode	Batch
Estimated Join Type	HashMatch
Adaptive Threshold Rows	2163.53
Is Adaptive	True
Estimated Execution Mode	Batch
Actual Number of Rows	102
Actual Number of Batches	1
Estimated I/O Cost	0
Estimated Operator Cost	0 (0%)
Estimated CPU Cost	0.0100299
Estimated Subtree Cost	6.29443
Estimated Number of Executions	1
Number of Executions	4
Estimated Number of Rows	1002990
Estimated Row Size	41 B
Actual Rebinds	0
Actual Rewinds	0
Node ID	6

Output List

[Menu].[dbo].[Recipe].RecipeName, [Menu].[dbo].
[MealType].MealTypeName, [Menu].[dbo].
[RecipeIngredient].IngredientID

Hash Keys Probe

[Menu].[dbo].[RecipeIngredient].RecipeID

Outer References

[Menu].[dbo].[Recipe].RecipeID, Expr1026

Figure 8-7. *Adaptive Join Properties from Listing 8-8*

The Actual Join type shown in Figure 8-7 is a Nested Loop. The difference between the Adaptive Join types in Figures 8-5 and 8-7 shows how the Adaptive Join can help optimize queries that previously were affected by parameter sniffing. The details of the live query statistics from Listing 8-8 are shown in Figure 8-8.

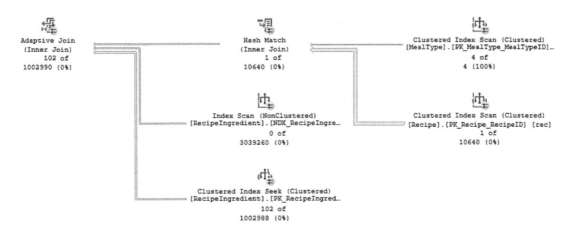

Figure 8-8. *Live Query Statistics from Listing 8-8*

In Figure 8-8, the same physical operators are present as in Figure 8-6. However, the actual number of rows processed vs. the estimated number of rows is significantly different. In the case of Figure 8-8, almost all the steps are severely overestimated. However, the query from Listing 8-8 will still benefit the performance due to the use of the Adaptive Join.

There are many ways that you can work toward optimizing for T-SQL code. Unless you are testing a new query, often the first step is to identify what T-SQL code needs to be optimized. After determining what query needs optimization, you may want to analyze execution plans to help determine if there is a step that stands out as needing optimization. You may also want to analyze information associated with the query such as average logical reads or average execution time. Combining this information together may help you identify what can be tuned to improve performance.

In addition, there are features in SQL Server that can help automatically make your T-SQL code perform better. This includes allowing SQL Server to analyze your new execution plans and confirm that they are performing better than the previous execution plan. If the previous execution plan is expected to perform better, SQL Server can make sure that plan is automatically selected. If you are using Azure SQL Database, you also have a similar option available when it comes to managing indexes. The use of Adaptive Joins allows SQL Server to make your execution plans more flexible. When an Adaptive Join is part of an execution plan, SQL Server can decide the correct physical operator to use depending on the values passed for that specific query execution. Whether you are manually optimizing your T-SQL code or letting SQL Server determine how to improve query execution, you have several tools available that should make your T-SQL code perform better.

PART III

Building Manageable T-SQL

CHAPTER 9

Coding Standards

Earlier in Chapter 3, I discussed various steps you can take to standardize your T-SQL. This included being consistent when you format your T-SQL code, name your database objects, and comment your T-SQL code. While developing standards that allow for consistency when writing, naming, and documenting T-SQL, there is more to creating a comprehensive T-SQL coding standard.

In this chapter, I will discuss various advantages to implementing coding standards. I will also go over what types of factors you should consider when defining coding standards. When developing coding standards, you will also want to determine how to implement those coding standards. I will cover the basic process needed to institute these coding standards.

Why Use Coding Standards

There are many different things you can do to improve your code quality. When improving your code quality, you want to think about your end goal. I want my T-SQL code to run efficiently, can be debugged quickly, and is easy to understand. This is often the result of creating consistency in how you design and write your T-SQL code. One option is to implement coding standards.

Oftentimes, there are specific T-SQL practices that you know you want people to follow. Some of these behaviors are easily agreed upon and most people use them by default. However, there can be other T-SQL best practices that you know are not common in general or in your organization. You want to create a set of guidelines that allows everyone to easily know what they should be doing.

There are also certain things in T-SQL that you know you do not want to see in T-SQL code no matter the reason. Once again, some of these topics are not common, but others may also be pervasive. Either way, you want to clearly define this all as part of your

© Elizabeth Noble 2020
E. Noble, *Pro T-SQL 2019*, https://doi.org/10.1007/978-1-4842-5590-2_9

coding standards. Using coding standards can minimize the back and forth regarding what types of T-SQL code is allowed or preferable vs. other code.

You can use coding standards to set boundaries for what is and is not allowed. I have come across times where software engineers or database developers want to use specific T-SQL because it is easier to read and write. However, there are times where the T-SQL code that makes sense easily to a human does not perform as well with SQL Server. While I want those same individuals to be able to come to me ask question about the current process, there are times where I have too many higher priority requests, and I do not have time to address their concerns.

It would be nice to have these guidelines agreed on prior to the standards being needed. This also should provide some reassurance that each topic has been discussed and multiple parties have come to the same conclusion that certain T-SQL code is either performing well for many scenarios or could be at a high risk to cause performance issues.

I know when I come into work my day is already full. Not only from the things I know I need to do but the last-minute requests and the one-off questions. The real goal to implementing coding standards is to make your life easier. That includes being able to rest easy knowing that quality T-SQL code is in your database. Ideally, you should be able to spend that time working on future database design enhancements or getting rid of technical debt.

Another factor affecting our lives is decision fatigue. This is the concept where a person gets worn down having to make decision after decision throughout the day. With the advent of technology, we experience that kind of fatigue every day. When it comes to making decisions regarding T-SQL coding, this type of decision fatigue can be even more overwhelming. There are many ways to accomplish the same thing in SQL Server. One of the other advantages to implementing T-SQL Coding Standards is that it can minimize the decisions a database developer needs to make when writing new code.

When you first implement coding standards, make sure to get buy-in from all parties. In many cases, you will not be able to have a unanimous decision. If you can, get a majority vote for any change you would like included in the coding standards. Another method is to make sure every individual agrees on the final standard before those standards are approved and implemented.

One of the main challenges with T-SQL in the workplace is that many people that are responsible for writing T-SQL are not database experts. This can not only cause frustration, but it can also contribute to poorly performing queries. One of the nicest and hardest aspects about T-SQL is how easy it is to write your first query. SQL is an abbreviation for Structured Query Language, and that is how simple queries are written. You can read them almost like a sentence.

However, this can give the false impression that what is happening with SQL Server behind the scenes is also simple. Most of us work in a high stress, fast paced environment. This often means we do not have time to stop and explain every decision we make. This can include why or why not certain T-SQL code should not be used. That is where the strength of T-SQL Coding Standards really shines. It allows you to have the conversation once to set up the ground rules. After those rules or standards are in place, T-SQL developers and engineers can write their code in any way they want if it meets the predefined standards.

I have heard software developers say that having defined coding standards when writing applications can be very helpful. It allows them to easily jump into any code, whether they wrote it or not, and immediately feel comfortable. This is because while they may know they have never looked at this set of code, their brain already sees similarities with other code they have written. It gets rid of the instantaneous response that the code they are looking at is not theirs. The benefit is that they can immediately jump into reviewing the code or making the necessary changes.

Now that you have determined that you want to define coding standards, the next step is to implement these coding standards. This is where things can get tricky. It will be tempting to want every stored procedure that goes through script review to adhere to these standards. However, some of the code you will see is already out in Production. I have found there are times, especially when others are under strict deadlines, that it is especially frustrating when a stored procedure is rejected merely because it does not follow coding standards.

A possible compromise is to give a conditional approval and request that a new user story be created so that the T-SQL code can be updated to fit the new coding standards. This gives the developer reassurance that they can meet the deadlines of their current sprint, and it also lets you know that this T-SQL code should be corrected in a future release to meet coding standards.

An easy way to handle these new user stories is to add them to the following sprint. This allows them to get cleaned up while you still remember what needs to be changed. This also makes sure that the others performing script reviews know that the effort to get all T-SQL code compliant with the coding standards is important to all parties.

What to Include in Coding Standards

Ideally, coming up with coding standards will provide you with a framework that minimizes your overall challenges with reviewing and deploying T-SQL code. You want coding standards to cover how T-SQL code should look, how T-SQL code should function, how T-SQL code should perform, and how T-SQL code should be understood.

Some of the basics of coding standards have already been discussed in Chapter 3. This includes formatting T-SQL code by creating standards as to how the T-SQL is written. You will also want standards indicating how to name T-SQL database objects. It is also useful to have standards indicating how T-SQL code should be commented.

T-SQL Design

Using SQL coding standards, you can define database design through coding standards. This can include how database objects should be organized including schemas. Coding standards can also indicate how data should be stored in the database. You can indicate what types of columns should be included in primary keys. It is also possible to indicate how tables should be clustered or when it is best to use clustered or non-clustered indexes.

ANSI STANDARD

One consideration is whether to keep your T-SQL code in compliance with ANSI standards. While SQL Server has some functionality that can be used, not all of this functionality is compliant with ANSI standards. In many cases, the SQL Server specific commands and functions can be rewritten using ANSI standard code. Making sure you write your T-SQL code as ANSI standard allows you to easily move to another relational database management system that is also ANSI standard compliant.

Normal Form

While covering T-SQL Coding Standards, you may also want to define design elements. This includes what and how data should be grouped together in tables and what information should be in those tables. There are various levels of normal forms, and you can use your T-SQL Coding Standards to indicate what those are. There are various types of database normalization that are commonly discussed. These include first normal form (1NF), second normal form (2NF), third normal form (3NF), and fourth normal form (4NF).

Each type of normal form builds on the one before it. The lowest-level normal form is the first normal form. This includes requiring that each table has a Primary Key and that each record only holds a single value.

Table Size

When creating tables, it is tempting to want to put all columns related to a specific item into the same table. This can cause tables to have many, many columns. One of the challenges of having a table with a significant number of columns is how the data is stored. This can ultimately lead to performance issues. It is possible to design your tables to prevent this kind of issue. In addition, properly designed tables make the overall database design more adaptable as applications change over time.

Name Value Pair

Working with SQL Server, the goal is to think about set-based actions. Keeping this is mind, you will want to be careful designing tables. You want to make sure that you do not minimize the number of columns to keep the table width small. You want to consider what kinds of columns are valuable. If you are using one column to define the value type and another column to define the actual value, you have designed a name-value pair relationship.

This type of design may be easier to understand and create simpler tables, but this design does not embrace the benefits of using SQL Server. When using name-value pairs, it becomes increasingly difficult to use indexes. Therefore, SQL Server will need to look through more data to pull back the necessary values.

Primary Key

When creating and designing tables, you will want to think about what type of data will be stored. This not only has to do with how the data is ordered but also the table's relationship to other tables. In many cases, it is ideal to require primary keys as part of your coding standards. While a primary key is not required in all scenarios, it should help clarify what fields are used to define relationships to other tables.

Foreign Key

SQL Server is a relational database management system, and one of the main benefits of SQL Server is the relationships between tables. However, you need to specify the relationships between tables so that SQL Server can ensure that valid data is saved across the tables. When this happens, SQL Server checks the relationship between the table storing the values and the referencing table. SQL Server does this using a foreign key. Because SQL Server knows that it can trust the relationship, SQL Server can often filter out data more efficiently and find data faster. Therefore, it may be a good idea to specify that foreign key relationships are part of your T-SQL Coding Standards.

Non-clustered Index

I have found that non-clustered indexes are a more highly debated topic than I would have ever expected. One of the challenges of using non-clustered indexes is that there is a cost associated with recording the data as part of the index or updating the index as the values change. However, SQL Server uses indexes to quickly find the data referenced by various queries. You will want to make sure that the benefit of using non-clustered indexes outweighs the cost.

One of the ways that you can do this is to make sure that you properly define your indexes. Due to the cost associated with maintaining indexes, you will want to make certain that any index you create is regularly being used by the available queries. You may also want to define how to determine which columns should be part of the index and which columns should be pulled back as part of the index.

Constraint Definition

Your tables can have one or more columns. Each of those columns holds some type of information. When it comes to that information, you may know that only certain values can be stored in that column. Using foreign keys can keep the data integrity in some situations, but there are other times that it may not make sense to use a foreign key. In those cases, you can specify a constraint on the record. The constraint can limit what type of information can be stored in those columns.

However, forcing SQL Server to manage those constraints puts an extra load on SQL Server. So, you may want to consider minimizing the use of constraints to limit what type of data can be stored in the database and rely on the application code to provide good data. Another use of constraints is to specify default values for certain fields. This can happen for columns where you know the most likely value that will exist when a record is created. For instance, you may want to specify a default value of True for an IsActive column as most records created will be active at the time they are created. Once again, this can be handled by the application, but you may also decide to enforce this as part of your T-SQL Coding Standards.

It is important to consider T-SQL Coding Standards that encourage good design practices. This includes determining how closely you will adhere to ANSI standards. There are other topics to include such as choosing the minimum normal form allowed as part of your database design. This decision may affect other aspects of your T-SQL design including primary keys, foreign keys, and non-clustered indexes. You may also consider how you want to handle constraints. Once you have determined the T-SQL Coding Standards you want to enforce for good T-SQL design practices, you may want to decide what coding standards are needed with regard to the overall performance of T-SQL.

T-SQL Performance

After determining the T-SQL Coding Standards related to database design and implementation, you will want to determine what standards you need to help minimize and address any performance issues that may come up. This includes creating T-SQL Coding Standards that help make sure SQL Server does not get bogged down with unnecessary information. You will also want to consider how T-SQL code needs to be or not be written to minimize performance overhead.

Select Necessary Data

SQL Server can store quite a bit of data, and SQL Server can also retrieve large quantities of data. There are many scenarios where applications are retrieving data. When first learning about a database and the associated tables, it is often tempting to select all the columns in a table. While this is the easiest method to return data, it is not usually ideal.

First is the syntax used to select all rows by using the asterisks. The issue with this method is if the columns in the underlying object change, the code may not work as expected. Even worse, the code may not provide an error and users would not know they were getting bad data.

The second issue that can happen is more common. When you pull back all columns, there is considerably more work put on SQL Server. Not only must SQL Server return everything for all rows of data returned, but it is likely that SQL Server will not be able to use any indexes to return this data. This is the equivalent to reading this entire book each time you want to study one specific section. You would learn what you needed, but you would also spend a considerable amount of time reading topics that you were mostly likely going to disregard since they were not relevant for your needs at that time.

Sargeable

You want SQL Server to be able to easily search the database to find the information you are trying to access. There are some ways that you can write T-SQL that can let SQL Server take advantage of indexes and quickly find the necessary data. However, there are other methods of writing T-SQL that can give the same results but may take longer and require SQL Server to look through more data. The difference between these two scenarios is that the first scenario refers to making sure your T-SQL is sargeable, whereas the second option is when the T-SQL is not sargeable. This usually happens in the WHERE clause of the T-SQL statement. In Listing 9-1, I have written a query to find all recipes that were created in August 2019.

Listing 9-1. Query Using Non-sargeable Criteria

```
SELECT RecipeName, RecipeDescription
FROM dbo.Recipe
WHERE DATEPART(MM, DateCreated) = 8
      AND DATEPART(YY, DateCreated) = 2019
```

You can see that I have used the DATEPART function on the date created to determine both the month and the year each record was created. In order for SQL Server to determine which records are in August 2019, SQL Server will need to check every record in the table. You can see this is true in the execution plan in Figure 9-1 with the Index Scan.

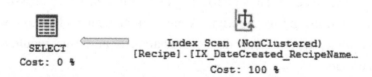

SELECT
Cost: 0 %

Index Scan (NonClustered)
[Recipe].[IX_DateCreated_RecipeName…
Cost: 100 %

Figure 9-1. *Execution Plan from Non-sargeable Criteria*

When execution plans are this simple, it can sometimes be difficult to get an idea of how performant these queries really are. One way that we can get a better idea is to look at the properties associated with this execution plan. There is a lot of information in Figure 9-2, but we will focus on the Number of Rows Read.

Index Scan (NonClustered)
Scan a nonclustered index, entirely or only a range.

Physical Operation	Index Scan
Logical Operation	Index Scan
Actual Execution Mode	Row
Estimated Execution Mode	Row
Storage	RowStore
Number of Rows Read	32242
Actual Number of Rows	1
Actual Number of Batches	0
Estimated I/O Cost	0.120903
Estimated Operator Cost	0.156526 (100%)
Estimated CPU Cost	0.0356232
Estimated Subtree Cost	0.156526
Number of Executions	1
Estimated Number of Executions	1
Estimated Number of Rows	2686.83
Estimated Number of Rows to be Read	32242
Estimated Row Size	58 B
Actual Rebinds	0
Actual Rewinds	0
Ordered	False
Node ID	0

Predicate
datepart(month,[Menu].[dbo].[Recipe].[DateCreated])=(8)
AND datepart(year,[Menu].[dbo].[Recipe].[DateCreated])=
(2019)
Object
[Menu].[dbo].[Recipe].
[IX_DateCreated_RecipeNameRecipeDescription]
Output List
[Menu].[dbo].[Recipe].RecipeName, [Menu].[dbo].
[Recipe].RecipeDescription

Figure 9-2. *Properties for Index Scan from Non-sargeable Criteria*

The number of rows read for the Index Scan from Listing 9-1 is 32,242. To get a better idea of whether this query is performing well, I will also write a query with sargeable values. In Listing 9-2, I am still querying the dbo.Recipe table for records created in August 2019, but I am now using greater than or equal to and less than to specify an exact date range.

Listing 9-2. Query Using Sargeable Criteria

```
SELECT RecipeName, RecipeDescription
FROM dbo.Recipe
WHERE DateCreated >= '8/1/19'
      AND DateCreated < '9/1/19'
```

While this may look less clean or harder to read, the importance is in writing a query where SQL Server can quickly determine what records meet the criteria requested in the query. Figure 9-3 shows the execution plan for the query from Listing 9-2.

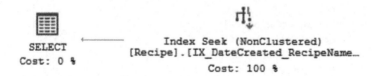

Figure 9-3. *Execution Plan from Sargeable Criteria*

At a glance, the execution plan in Figure 9-3 looks very similar to the execution plan in Figure 9-1. When comparing execution plans that look similar, they can be said to have the same shape. While these execution plans have a similar shape, the items that make up the execution plan are different. In Figure 9-1, we saw there was an Index Scan. In Figure 9-3, we can see that this execution plan is using an Index Seek. There is also a thinner line between the Index Seek from the SELECT in Figure 9-3 than there is in the Index Scan from the SELECT in Figure 9-1. All of this is a graphical representation of the overall performance of each query. However, we can also get some facts and figures to compare the performance to the queries in Listings 9-1 and 9-2. In Figure 9-2, we found the actual number of rows read was 32,242. We can compare this value to the actual number of rows read from Figure 9-4.

Index Seek (NonClustered)

Scan a particular range of rows from a nonclustered index.

Physical Operation	Index Seek
Logical Operation	Index Seek
Actual Execution Mode	Row
Estimated Execution Mode	Row
Storage	RowStore
Number of Rows Read	1
Actual Number of Rows	1
Actual Number of Batches	0
Estimated I/O Cost	0.003125
Estimated Operator Cost	0.0032831 (100%)
Estimated CPU Cost	0.0001581
Estimated Subtree Cost	0.0032831
Estimated Number of Executions	1
Number of Executions	1
Estimated Number of Rows	1
Estimated Number of Rows to be Read	1
Estimated Row Size	50 B
Actual Rebinds	0
Actual Rewinds	0
Ordered	True
Node ID	0

Object
[Menu].[dbo].[Recipe].
[IX_DateCreated_RecipeNameRecipeDescription]
Output List
[Menu].[dbo].[Recipe].RecipeName, [Menu].[dbo].
[Recipe].RecipeDescription
Seek Predicates
Seek Keys[1]: Start: [Menu].[dbo].[Recipe].DateCreated >=
Scalar Operator(CONVERT_IMPLICIT(datetime2(7),[@1],0)), End:
[Menu].[dbo].[Recipe].DateCreated < Scalar Operator
(CONVERT_IMPLICIT(datetime2(7),[@2],0))

Figure 9-4. *Properties for Index Seek from Sargeable Criteria*

The actual number of rows read for Listing 9-2 is 1 as shown in Figure 9-4.
Comparing 1 row read for Listing 9-2 to 32,242 rows read for Listing 9-1, it becomes very
clear which query is more efficient.

We can also look at the total CPU usage for both queries to see how each query
performs. If I run both queries in Listings 9-1 and 9-2 at the same time, 98% of the total
execution plan of both queries is spent on the query in Listing 9-1. I can also use SET
STATISTICS TIME ON to find the CPU time and elapsed time. The CPU time is the total

amount of time the query execution spent on the CPU or CPUs. The elapsed time is the total time for the query to execute. I ran both queries several times and found that the average CPU time for Listing 9-1 was 15 milliseconds and the average elapsed time for Listing 9-1 was 17 milliseconds. Each time the CPU time and elapsed time for Listing 9-2 was 0 millisecond. Comparing both the CPU time and the elapsed time, we can clearly see that Listing 9-2 performs better than Listing 9-1. It is also important to note that the total elapsed time could be less than the total CPU time if there are multiple CPUs.

Implicit Conversion

The data in SQL Server has a data type. These data types are discussed further in Chapter 1. When using these data types, it is important to make sure you keep the data types consistent. Otherwise, SQL Server must undergo an implicit conversation. This is where SQL Server converts one data type to another behind the scenes. This can cause additional load on SQL Server. In addition, there is a risk that the implicit conversion will fail. I see this most when an identification type column saves mostly integer values but occasionally strings.

SET NOCOUNT ON

There are many small tweaks that you can make to your T-SQL that will allow for some minor performance improvements. When you run T-SQL code by default, it will count the number of rows affected and can report those back. The cost of counting these records can be a few extra milliseconds. Therefore, a possible enhancement to the coding standards is to turn this functionality off, particularly when it involves stored procedures. The way to accomplish this is to make sure that SET NOCOUNT ON is included inside of a stored procedure. You can see this in Listing 9-3.

Listing 9-3. Stored Procedure Using SET NOCOUNT ON

```
CREATE PROCEDURE dbo.UpdateRecipeMenuType
    @RecipeMeal RecipeMealType READONLY
AS
SET NOCOUNT ON
UPDATE rec
SET MealTypeID = meal.MealTypeID
FROM dbo.Recipe rec
```

```
INNER JOIN @RecipeMeal recmeal
ON rec.RecipeName = recmeal.RecipeName
INNER JOIN dbo.MealType meal
ON recmeal.MealTypeName = meal.MealTypeName
```

When SET NOCOUNT ON is included before the query code is executed, the stored procedure can execute in a couple fewer milliseconds.

NULL Values

Most of the T-SQL Coding Standards exist to help improve overall performance for SQL Server. However, some T-SQL coding standards exist to help improve query results or make it easier for people to write code that works as expected. One of the issues with NULL is that it does not work intuitively. NULL is treated as an unknown value in SQL Server. That means that NULL is neither True nor False. Therefore, where there are fields that can contain NULL values, the way these fields must be treated is different.

In addition, NULL values may indicate that tables were not designed efficiently. Before ending up in these scenarios, it may be beneficial to consider how the table should be designed. You will want to make sure that the table really needs to include nullable columns. This is also due to how data is stored and how indexes are created. You will want to consider how this data will be used.

NOLOCK

There are also factors involved in T-SQL Coding Standards. Some of these include things that you may consider best practices. Some of the very common best practices include highly debated topics like if or when to use the NOLOCK hint in queries. One of the reasons I mention this specifically is that there are at least two very distinct groups involving NOLOCK. On the one hand, many database administrators view not using NOLOCK is a best practice. On the other hand, there are many developers that see the opposite side that the use of NOLOCK is a best practice. This difference in perspective is based on a trade-off between data accuracy and performance.

The idea behind NOLOCK is to improve query performance by reducing the number of locks. In the case of NOLOCK, the reduction in lock activity is on the SELECT statement. Actions such as INSERT, UPDATE, and DELETE are not affected by NOLOCK. However, using NOLOCK on a SELECT statement can return results more quickly when a data modification action is holding a lock on that same table that the SELECT statement is trying to access.

We can get an idea of how these viewpoints are correct by looking at an example. In Listing 9-4, I have written a query to insert a record into the dbo.Recipe table inside of an explicit transaction.

Listing 9-4. Insert Record into dbo.Recipe

```
BEGIN TRAN

INSERT INTO dbo.Recipe
(
        RecipeName,
        RecipeDescription,
        ServingQuantity,
        MealTypeID,
        PreparationTypeID,
        IsActive,
        DateCreated,
        DateModified
)
VALUES
(
        'Baked Acorn Squash',
        'Acorn squash with butter and brown sugar',
        4,
        4,
        1,
        1,
        GETDATE(),
        GETDATE()
)
```

In Listing 9-4, I have started an explicit transaction using BEGIN TRAN, but I have not specified a COMMIT or ROLLBACK. This will leave the transaction open with a lock on dbo.Recipe. To simulate application performance, I will open a separate query window and run a query to try and find all records created in this table after August 1, 2019. You can see a sample of this query in Listing 9-5.

Listing 9-5. Query to Find Recent Recipes

```
SELECT RecipeName, RecipeDescription
FROM dbo.Recipe
WHERE DateCreated > '8/1/19';
```

Due to the lock on dbo.Recipe from the query in Listing 9-4, it seems like my query is continuing to run. The query in Listing 9-5 is waiting for the locks to be released before any data can be returned. In order to get results more quickly, I can change how SQL Server treats the locks on the table. In Listing 9-6, I have modified the query from Listing 9-5 and included a query hint of WITH (NOLOCK).

Listing 9-6. Query to Find Recent Recipes Using NOLOCK Hint

```
SELECT RecipeName, RecipeDescription
FROM dbo.Recipe WITH(NOLOCK)
WHERE DateCreated > '8/1/19';
```

When I run the query in Listing 9-5 in a separate query window, I get nearly instantaneous results. You can see an example of these results in Table 9-1.

Table 9-1. *Recipes Created After August 1, 2019*

RecipeName	RecipeDescription
Lee's Hamburgers	The best hamburgers
Acorn Squash	Acorn squash with butter and brown sugar

Looking at the preceding results, you can see that the record inserted in Listing 9-4 is included in the results. However, this record has not been committed to SQL Server. I could roll back the transaction from Listing 9-4 and undo the insert. This would cause the results from Table 9-1 to be inaccurate. This discrepancy where queries return results that are not fully committed to the database is known as a dirty read. This is the largest risk when using NOLOCK in your queries. Before deciding that you should use NOLOCK in your T-SQL code, make sure that the business, including your end users, understands the potential risks of using this hint.

RECOMPILE

Besides NOLOCK, another possible query hint that is often considered is RECOMPILE. You may find yourself dealing with a query that is affected by parameter sniffing as discussed in Chapter 4. This means that the query creates an execution plan that may perform well for some values, but when other parameter values are used, the performance can degrade significantly. One of the workarounds that can be easily and quickly implemented is the query hint RECOMPILE. In Listing 9-7, you can see the additional line needed when creating a stored procedure to allow the stored procedure to recompile on execution.

Listing 9-7. Adding WITH RECOMPILE to a Stored Procedure

```
/*-------------------------------------------------------------*\
Name:           dbo.GetRecipeAndIngredientByMealTypeID
Author:         Elizabeth Noble
Created Date:   April 20, 2019
Description: Get all recipes and their ingredients by meal type

Sample Usage:
    EXECUTE dbo.GetRecipeAndIngredientByMealTypeID 1

\*-------------------------------------------------------------*/
CREATE PROCEDURE dbo.GetRecipeAndIngredientByMealTypeID
    @MealTypeID     INT
WITH RECOMPILE
AS

    SELECT
        rec.RecipeName,
        ingr.IngredientName,
        ingr.IsActive,
        ingr.DateCreated,
        ingr.DateModified
    FROM dbo.Recipe rec
        INNER JOIN dbo.RecipeIngredient recingr
        ON rec.RecipeID = recingr.RecipeID
        LEFT OUTER JOIN dbo.Ingredient ingr
```

```
        ON recingr.IngredientID = ingr.IngredientID
    WHERE rec.MealTypeID = @MealTypeID
    ORDER BY rec.RecipeName, ingr.IngredientName;
```

While this is a quick fix, it can increase the CPU load on the server. I would suggest trying to redesign the query if possible. If not, you may need to change the stored procedure to only recompile for the values that fall outside of the majority.

For your T-SQL Coding Standards, it is important to include guidelines related to writing T-SQL that performs well. You will also want to include some rules for what actions are or are not allowable in order to try and fix poorly performing T-SQL. The last part of your T-SQL Coding Standards is a catch-all generally related to security, futureproofing, and maintainability.

T-SQL Usability

Having T-SQL Coding Standards that encourage good database design and address performance issues is a good start. However, you are also going to want some coding standards to help with other aspects of T-SQL. Some of this includes having T-SQL Coding Standards for potential security issues. There are other coding standards that you can put in place that are best practices but may not affect performance. They may be in place either to help keep your T-SQL functioning even if the underlying data structure changes or encourage T-SQL commands that help make your T-SQL code easier to read or understand.

Linked Server

Linked servers are one of those things that may be overlooked as part of the coding standards. It seems unlikely that you will need to use linked servers, but linked servers have a way of seeming necessary when you least expect it. That is why it is a good idea to include specifications about how to handle linked servers as part of your T-SQL Coding Standards. Due to the general security risks associated with using linked servers, it is recommended that you do not use linked servers unless necessary. I would suggest clearly defining exactly what is considered necessary. This will help reduce any contention should you find yourself wanting to implement linked servers.

Column Definition

One of the key factors of writing T-SQL is specifying what columns you are using or affecting. While this is related to making sure you only interact with the data you need, there are other benefits to requiring your T-SQL code to explicate state column names. When inserting data into SQL Server, it is possible to not state the column names or order you are using for the insert. If you are inserting data into every column in the table and you are inserting the data in the same order as the columns in the table, you will not have any issues. However, this can cause stored procedures or other T-SQL code to stop functioning if columns are added or removed from the table or if the column order is changed in the future. Therefore, a good habit is to explicitly state your column names on all T-SQL. For these examples, this specifically includes selects and inserts.

BETWEEN

There are also situations where you have multiple choices on how to write T-SQL code, and all those options seem to perform about the same. This can happen when you are trying to get a subset of data that covers a continuous range. Defining a T-SQL Coding Standard in this situation does not necessarily correlate to improving the performance of SQL Server. This is more closely related to improving the consistency of the T-SQL code. An example of how to write T-SQL using BETWEEN is shown in Listing 9-8.

Listing 9-8. Query with BETWEEN

```
SELECT *
FROM dbo.Recipe
WHERE RecipeID BETWEEN 100 AND 20000
```

In terms of readability, you may decide that all ranges that cover inclusive values should be written using BETWEEN. This may be preferable to using greater than or equal to and less than or equal to get the same range.

Stored Procedure Parameters

While improving code readability is important, there are times that improving readability of T-SQL may make debugging the code harder when it comes to performance issues. This type of situation can happen depending on how you configured your stored procedure parameters. You can either define each parameter individually or you can create a user-defined table that you can use to pass in a multitude of variables. If you choose to use a user-defined table, your T-SQL code may be cleaner, but it may take more time to debug performance issues going forward. In addition, your stored procedure will work differently as you are working with a table variable instead of handling each data field individually.

UNION

You will have times where you want to combine data from two different queries. This type of combination involves appending one data set to another. When these two data sets share the same number of columns with the same data types, there is the possibility to use a UNION statement to combine this data. The advantage of using a UNION is that the queries are readable and you can easily tell by reading the T-SQL code what is happening. The challenge with using UNION is that the performance of a UNION may be worse than the performance of each query independently. In addition to UNION, there is also the UNION ALL functionality. The main difference between a UNION and a UNION ALL is how the data is returned. In a UNION statement, a distinct set of records is returned, whereas in a UNION ALL statement, the actual number of records from each separate query is included in the result set. When designing your coding standards, you will want to decide if UNION and UNION ALL statements are allowed. You may also want to decide if there are specific scenarios where they would or would not be allowed.

CAST

When writing code, you find yourself in a situation where you want to change the data type from one value to another. Changing data types can be important with performing mathematical functions on integer values. Due to how SQL Server performs mathematical operations, if you divided one integer by another integer, you will get an integer as the answer. If you want SQL Server to provide a decimal as a result, you will need to change the data type from an integer to a decimal. Similarly, you may want to display a string of text as part of a SQL Server query. However, if you include an integer in the string, you will get an error when SQL Server tries to execute the query. However, if you change the integer to a varchar data type, you will be able to parse the string correctly.

Cursor

Cursors are a source of controversy when it comes to databases. In Chapter 5, I went over set-based operations which is where SQL Server performs best. The issue with cursors is that they do not take advantage of those set-based operations. This can cause considerable overhead when it comes to handling data. To compound the challenges with cursors, they are written in a way that is more alike to how application code is written than T-SQL. This can make it very tempting to use cursors as it may be easier to understand how to write the code to get the desired results. Like other factors of developing your T-SQL Coding Standards, you may not be able to rule out cursors entirely. If so, try to create some criteria where you believe cursors would be beneficial and limit cursor usage to only those situations.

ORDER BY

It is often tempting to want SQL Server to get all of the data exactly how your application needs the data. While SQL Server can do this, you want to consider if it is worth the cost to SQL Server to do all the work you are requesting. Such can be the situation when you want data to be sorted for your application. SQL Server can sort the data using the ORDER BY statement, but it may be a better use of resources to have the application sort this data. If you decide that is how you want to handle sorting data, then it may be a good idea to include in your T-SQL Coding Standards that data should not be sorted in SQL Server. If you know there are specific situations where this will be unavoidable, then you can state in your coding standards the exact scenarios where using an ORDER BY is allowed in your T-SQL code.

Case Statement

T-SQL code can be versatile. While you may choose to keep your T-SQL code limited to application functionality, database code is also used for other purposes such as reporting. In many applications, you may be both processing transactions and allowing your users to search and filter data. This type of activity can be a reporting activity. Oftentimes, users do not want to see data in the same manner the data is stored. For instance, you may have a table that includes a status type. A given record may have several statuses over time. However, a user may want to see one line with all of the statuses for that specific record. This is where you would want to use a case statement so that you could convert multiple rows into various columns. Performing this type of activity is not a purely transactional use of T-SQL, and you may want to limit this type of behavior as part of your coding standards.

TRY... CATCH

Including error handling in T-SQL code can be helpful and may be considered best practice in your workplace. You want your application to gracefully handle procedures that fail. One of the situations you may find yourself in is in the unfortunate event that a stored procedure is a deadlock victim. The TRY... CATCH block can allow the deadlock stored procedure to either rerun or exit gracefully.

```
DECLARE @IngredientID       INT = 1;
DECLARE @ServingPortionID   INT = 1;
DECLARE @Cost               DECIMAL(5,2) = 5.98
DECLARE @IsActive           BIT = 1;
DECLARE @DateCreated        DATETIME = GETDATE();
DECLARE @DateModified       DATETIME = GETDATE();

BEGIN TRY
    BEGIN TRAN
        INSERT INTO dbo.IngredientCost
        (
            IngredientID,
            ServingPortionID,
            Cost,
            IsActive,
            DateCreated,
            DateModified
        )
        VALUES
        (
            @IngredientID,
            @ServingPortionID,
            @Cost,
            @IsActive,
```

```
                @DateCreated,
                @DateModified
        )

    COMMIT TRANSACTION
END TRY

BEGIN CATCH
    PRINT 'Insert Failed'

    ROLLBACK TRANSACTION
END CATCH
```

Once you have determined what you want to include in your T-SQL Coding Standards, the next step is to get buy-in from your coworkers or other departments that will also be writing T-SQL. Getting everyone to agree to a set standard can solve many issues. First, it helps those that are onboarding to the company. When they review code, they will see a consistent code style. This will allow them to focus on what the T-SQL is doing instead of trying to interpret how the T-SQL code is written.

If you create a thorough and well-defined coding standard, there should be less back and forth during script reviews when there is T-SQL that is not believed to be best practice. With the T-SQL Coding Standard in place, all parties know what is allowable and what code is deemed as undesirable or bad practice. New hires will also know what T-SQL is acceptable. Everyone can be held to the same standard, and it allows others to see that the rules for writing T-SQL are fair.

CHAPTER 10

Source Control

Writing T-SQL code that is manageable is a worthwhile goal to build upon a solid foundation of understandable and maintainable code. Chapter 3 discussed how you can standardize your T-SQL code. This continued in Chapter 9 with the concept of implementing SQL Coding Standards. The purpose of this foundation was to create a consistent code base for your database. While developing a consistent code base can help improve code quality, this effect is diminished if you are unable to maintain your T-SQL code.

Developing manageable T-SQL code covers many different aspects of writing database code. The previous chapter focused on coding standards as a way to help guide you and others to writing T-SQL code that performs well. Having database code that performs well and is easy to read can not only help your applications but also your development process. The next step in that path is to consider how you are storing your code.

One option is to consider using source control to save T-SQL code associated with creating various database objects. You may be wondering why source control is important or what it can do to help make T-SQL code development better. Knowing that you want to implement source control is different from defining a process for managing source control. Setting up guidelines on how source control can be handled puts you in a good place to begin creating your first database project in source control.

Why Use Source Control

There are several aspects to having maintainable code. This includes making sure that you can find the T-SQL code for any database object. You also want to know that you are modifying the correct version of the code. Serious issues can occur when the wrong version of T-SQL code is modified and deployed. It will also help you to know what version of code needs to be deployed at any point in time. All of these items can benefit from incorporating source control for your databases.

© Elizabeth Noble 2020
E. Noble, *Pro T-SQL 2019*, https://doi.org/10.1007/978-1-4842-5590-2_10

Keeping T-SQL code together in a way that can be easily accessed can be a challenge. Source control can help keep all your T-SQL code together and organized. While you may think that source control is only something software developers should use, that is no longer the case. One of the easiest ways to get development teams working together with database administrators is to adopt similar processes. There are additional tools available when your T-SQL code is saved in source control. These tools can help streamline your coding and script reviews by automatically rejecting code that does not meet T-SQL formatting or coding standards.

There are other issues that can happen when writing T-SQL code. You may have times where multiple people or teams need to change the same database objects. Depending on how your company handles deploying code, you may end up with some database objects that have multiple layers of changes. Source control can help manage those changes and make sure they are implemented correctly. Source control can allow you to work from the most up-to-date code.

When you are making changes to database code, you have the option to make those changes locally. If you choose to use SQL Server Data Tools and keep all your database code in the same project, you can build your code to verify that the code will execute. This is an advantage over deploying code manually to SQL Server. As part of the build process, the database project will verify that the fields in your views, functions, stored procedures, or other custom objects exist within the database.

Some changes to T-SQL code can be complex and involved, other times you may be working with database objects or code that is critical to running your company. To start working on changing code, you will want to make sure you are working with the most up-to-date code. Prior to source control, I would pull the code that was in Production. However, this object I am reviewing may have been altered as part of a user story since the last Production deployment. What is worse is that this code may not have been deployed to the development environment or may still be awaiting a script review. Using source control allows me to get the most recent version of the T-SQL code consistently.

When you make those changes, you may want a place where you can go through the process of changing code, testing code, and repeating this process until you get to the desired output. Source control can pull the most recently saved T-SQL code down to your local machine. You can then work on making your modifications to the T-SQL code on your local desktop. When you are ready to save that work, you can save your changes to the centralized location. This centralized repository becomes your source of record for all database changes.

If you keep all your databases in the same solution, you can add references between databases if there are dependencies. This ensures that if you make any changes to the underlying database object, you will receive an alert if any of the dependent objects no longer function. This can be especially useful when you are adding or removing columns, or you are changing column names. There may come a time when you want to re-factor a table or some other database object. If your applications and databases are saved in the same solution, you will have the option to automatically re-factor the code. This can help in situations where your applications have SQL code saved directly in the application.

Another benefit of using source control is that it is easier to quickly find what T-SQL code has changed. Prior to using source control, I would have to manually review an entire database object to confirm what changed. The best process I found was to visually compare the current Production stored procedure to the new version of the stored procedure. While this was somewhat effective, it was also possible for me to easily miss something. I would also review all the T-SQL code from top to bottom to make sure I understood every line.

Prior to performing a script review, I will read through the associated user story to see what the code is expected to do. I may have been tempted to only script review the lines of code that seemed to be explicitly related to the current user story. After getting the database added into source control, I could easily see all code that had changed as part of the script review. This allowed me to quickly see all T-SQL code that changed. This can be especially helpful if you work in an environment where fixing technical debt is not officially condoned, but developers have some freedom to fix technical debt while working on a user story that affects the same database code.

I could also use source control to easily compare T-SQL code to previous versions. As part of the comparison, sections of the code that had been modified were highlighted. Even more helpful was that code that was added vs. modified or removed was highlighted in two different colors. One drawback of source control is that I no longer reviewed the whole script. Any pre-existing issues with the T-SQL code that were not modified did not have a chance to be corrected. This applies to both formatting standards and also to coding standards.

Having access to your T-SQL code can make it easier to get scripts together for deployments. Source control also helps protect unapproved T-SQL code from getting deployed in error. Without source control for T-SQL, getting ready for a deployment can be a hassle. I have worked with various companies that handle deployments differently.

I have experienced deployments where scripts were copied from tickets and added to a release page. I have been on deployments where the SQL scripts were bundled and prepped by the development team. Both methods will work, and every method has its downfall.

For the first method, I had one deployment where the same stored procedure was changed in three different user stories. When it came time to deploy the code, neither I nor the developers knew for certain which version should get deployed. In the second method, the actual deployment time was much shorter, and there was error logging. However, for both methods there was not a single source of truth when it came to database code. In either scenario, if I needed to undo a deployment that was several months old, it would take time to sift through deployment scripts to find which version of the T-SQL code needed to be deployed for the rollback.

You will need to be able to access scripts for different databases and deployments but also keep track of changes over time. You may change some T-SQL code for applications or reporting that may get overwritten with newer code. However, the business may decide they want to go back to the original code. When that code is saved in source control, it is much easier to search through the versions of the specific database object and find the specific occurrence. There are other times where an issue may get reported from Production several deployments after the original change went out. After I have determined the specific T-SQL code that is causing the bug, I may need to report to management the effects of this issue over time. With source control I can save time by finding when the change was implemented.

Another advantage of source control is allowing you to have one more tool to help in the case of disaster recovery. If you were to lose all your hardware and backups, how would it take you to get your business up and running again? While you may know that your backups need to be tested on a regular basis, you may not have had the opportunity to test them lately. Depending on how your company has developed their disaster recovery plan and what happens when disaster strikes could mean you lose access to your current Production servers and all the associated data. If this unlikely situation happens, you may find yourself in a situation where you are wondering how you will get your applications running again. As a plan of last resort, if your databases are in source control along with the necessary data in your base tables, you have a chance of getting your company's systems up and running.

How to Use Source Control

One of the things I found out when first implementing source control were the types of discussions that needed to happen internally prior to implementing source control. I found that the database team, the development teams, and the QA teams needed to come to an agreement as to how code would be managed going forward. Some of these discussions had to deal with how the different teams functioned. There are differences in how you want to manage your database code. This can include guidelines for when to use local vs. centralized repositories, how to save your changes to source control, how to resolve bugs that have been deployed, and what should be included with your database code.

Prior to using source control, you may have written T-SQL scripts and save them locally. When testing your T-SQL scripts, you may have executed them locally on the SQL Server machine. Up until this point, you have done most of your work locally. Afterward, you may have executed them once these scripts were ready to deploy to the development environment. You may haved then modified the objects in your development environment, a database schema in a more centralized location. While this is an easy place to start when writing code, it does create some risk. If the scripts were saved locally on your machine and your machine died, you may have lost any work associated with the scripts. There is also the possibility that when you deployed code to the development environment, it broke functionality somewhere else. In addition, if you and a fellow coworker were both working on the same database object, you may find your changes overwritten with your coworker's code.

This is where the benefits of writing code locally and then saving those changes in a centralized repository can be helpful. To a large extent, that is the idea behind source control. Source control allows you to work with code locally on your machine. You can create database objects or change database objects, and when you build the code locally, you have an additional check that the database project can build successfully. Once you have tested and confirmed your database code, you can check it in a centralized server. This central repository can receive code changes from you and any other members of your team that are authorized to make changes to this database project. This allows a certain degree of separation between your work environment, your coworkers' work environment, and the collection of all code changes together.

Depending on the type of software you use for source control will determine how you manage writing and updating your T-SQL code. When I first started working with databases in source control, Git had not become the primary software used for source control. I started with Team Foundation Server (TFS). In the company where I worked, we typically did not work with multiple branches. The database project is the first place we implemented branching. At the time of implementation, all of development fell under the same reporting structure and deployment cycle.

You can make changes to your source control. Each time you save these changes to central repository, it is called a check-in. When checking in code, you can add comments to the check-in. In my company, we usually indicate the user story number and a brief comment about what has changed. When you begin working on code in source control, you can have the code automatically checked out. This will allow others to know that you are making changes to the code.

Like a check-in in TFS, you can commit code in Git. Both actions save the changes that have been made to the branch you are currently using. While the functionality appears the same, these can work differently depending on what version control software you are using and what tool you are using with the software. Git and GitHub allow you to save changes before they are committed permanently to the repository. Staging changes is the term for when you save changes that are not immediately committed to the repository. Staging changes for your commit can be done through the command line.

When we discussed how to manage checking in code and managing branches, the design was based on our internal development process, script review process, and deployment cycle. We wanted to allow developers to be able to check in T-SQL code frequently and have that code available in their development environment. We also wanted to make sure that the database administrators had time to review code before the code was deployed to the QA environment. We wanted to make sure that QA did not spend time testing T-SQL code that had not been approved.

Due to this break between development and QA, we opted to create a branch specifically for code that had been script-reviewed and approved. As part of the script review process, the database administrators were responsible for merging the code. There were challenges with this process. Even though all code was meant to be deployed in the same sprint, there were times that items were merged out of order from how they were created in the development branch. This led to files getting overwritten. All of this became even more difficult to manage after the teams were split up and the development cycles became staggered.

With the desire for more companies to move to any combination of Agile, Kanban, Scrum, Continuous Integration, or Continuous Delivery, it has become increasingly important to have a source control solution that is more flexible. This new solution needed to allow for multiple different teams to simultaneously work on the same code base without negatively affecting deployments. That is where the popularity of Git originates.

The concept of using Git is that there is more control over how and when your code is merged. In my company, each team is rarely working on the same application as another team, so there are few conflicts when it comes to managing code. However, almost every application relies on shared databases. In addition, the database team is frequently working on the same databases. There are also different deployment cycles across the various teams. That is where you can see the power of Git.

Unfortunately, there are still challenges with using source control. These challenges exist for either TFS, Git, or any other versioning control software. Using version control is not something that has historically been common for data professionals. While there are benefits to making that change, there is also a learning curve when it comes to using and managing source control. As with many things the happy path works well, but when it comes to more complex scenarios, source control can become overwhelming.

There are features available in Git that require more training than using TFS. These same features are also what help make Git's source control more flexible. As is the case, while the increased functionality is nice to have, it can also make using the software more complex. There is a main repository where a group of code can be saved together. If you are using SQL Server Data Tools, this is where you have the option of choosing if each database project will have its own repository, all databases will share the same repository, or all applications and databases will share the same repository. These decisions are not only based on preference and desired functionality. As you will see in Chapter 12, how you organize your repository will also determine how your code is deployed.

Inside of the repository, there is the concept of one or more branches. There is one branch that should be the main branch. Think of it similarly to what set of code would you regularly go to if you needed to deploy these changes. This branch is called the master. Any time you want to make changes to the master branch, it is generally best to create a new branch to write your T-SQL code. This allows the main branch to remain unaffected by code that is in development and is not ready to be deployed. In this way, the master branch can match the code that is currently deployed to Production.

When you create a branch, this takes a copy of the current repository. You can work with this copy and make any changes necessary. When using Git, you may decide that each person will work off their own branch. This helps everyone develop their code individually without being affected by someone else's code. While this is a benefit for development and testing a specific piece of functionality, this is also where source control can get complicated.

As these check-ins happen per branch, you may find yourself in a situation where you need to deploy two different branches during the same deployment. This is where you will want to try to combine this code. In order to combine this code together, you want to take the changes in the branch and add the changes back to the master branch. To combine a feature branch to the master branch is called a merge. One aspect that can happen as part of this merge is called the conflict. This can happen when many people have been working on the same database object over the same period of time or there has been a delay in merging a previous feature branch with the master branch. Make sure to work with your development teams to get a better understanding of how to avoid merge conflicts and how they can be resolved.

One thing that happens more often than some of us would like to admit is when code is deployed and then does not work as intended. I have been in situations where those bugs were found during the deployment. Other times those bugs are not found until days, weeks, or months after a deployment. In either scenario, the key is to figure out how to quickly restore the database to a more functional state. One of the discussions I had with developers and QA was how to handle this on deployment night. A bug can be manually fixed by a T-SQL script. Depending on how you manage your database code deployments, it is possible that this bug fix can be undone in a future deployment. If you put the bug fix into source control, you can make sure this bug fix will not be undone going forward.

As a result, we concluded to adopt what we called a rollforward strategy. If we could quickly find and resolve the issue, then we would check those changes into source control and deploy them up through the environments. This rollforward strategy was only permitted on the night of the deployment. When we adopted the strategy, the concept was that we were going to deploy all code that had been merged to a master branch. If you choose to deploy a different version of the database project than the most recent version, you will not be able to use this method.

We also adopted a method to use a hotfix. These were changes that were needed as soon as possible due to a critical loss in functionality of an application. As there may be various items in development, we could not go ahead and just deploy the most recent database code. In these cases, I would still check the modified T-SQL code into source control. That code may have been deployed to development and tested in our QA environment, but the code would be manually deployed to production. The concept being that the next time the database code was deployed, this database object would already exist.

Designing how to save database code also involves conversations with the development, QA, and release management teams. There are pros and cons to the various methods that exist. You can save all of your database projects in the same solution with all of your application code. While this may take longer for your projects to build, if you create the right relationships, you can be certain that changes in your database will not affect functionality of your applications. Depending on the number of applications that exist in your company, this may be a difficult task. There is also the option of having all your databases saved in the same solution. If you have crossed database dependencies, this method will help protect your databases. This is particularly helpful when you make changes to one database object, and you are not certain if these changes will break functionality in a different database. The final option is to create one solution per database. The advantage of this method is that you can develop each database independently. The downside is that you may make changes to a database that breaks functionality for another database.

Prior to setting up your first database in source control, I would recommend discussing the topics in this section with the other teams at your company. You will want to make sure everyone is in agreement when it comes to writing, testing, and saving changes to your database code. Get others on board when it comes to how to fix database code once it has been deployed. Also consider how you want your database projects to interact with one another and your applications. Once you take all of this under consideration, you are ready to create a database project.

Setting Up Source Control

You are ready to set up source control now that you decided you would like to implement source control for your database, and you figured out some general guidelines on how you want to set up your database projects. One of the first things to do is get whatever IDE you are using to connect to source control. Once you are connected to version control, you will want to create a way to store the source control for your databases. You will want to figure out how to make and save changes to your database code after you have a place for your database source control.

In this section, I will be using Visual Studio 2017, SQL Server Data Tools, Git, and GitHub to get a database into source control. If you are using Visual Studio 2015 or 2017, you will be able to connect to TFS without any additional steps. If you want to use Git and GitHub in either of these versions of Visual Studio, you will need to install a GitHub extension manually. As of this writing, the following URL can walk you through this process: `https://social.technet.microsoft.com/wiki/contents/articles/38935.visual-studio-2017-install-and-use-GitHub-extension.aspx`. You can connect Visual Studio to version control by using Team Explorer as shown in Figure 10-1.

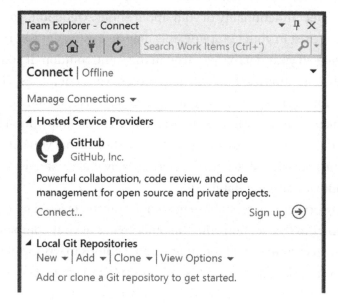

Figure 10-1. *Connect Visual Studio to Version Control*

In this example, I have added the Git extension to Visual Studio, and I am ready to connect to GitHub. If you do not already have a GitHub account, you can create one by selecting Sign up. In my case, I already have a GitHub account. Once I select Connect..., I get a pop-up window as shown in Figure 10-2.

Create a GitHub Repository   ✕

GitHub

Name   MenuDatabase

Description Database project for Menu

Local path   C:\Users\eliza\Source\Repos   Browse

Git ignore   VisualStudio ▼

License   GNU General Public License v2.0 ▼

            sqlzelda ▼
            ☑ Private Repository

            (✓) Create

Figure 10-2. *Create Git Repository*

In this step, I am creating a Git repository and connecting it to my GitHub account. I have decided to name the repository MenuDatabase. I have given the repository the description of Database project for Menu. I also specified a local path where my local code repository should be saved. I have selected the default for Git ignore of Visual Studio. I've also selected a license of GNU General Public License v2.0. It is beyond the scope of this book to go into detail regarding Git ignore or the available licensing options. The last part I specified is a private repository. The main difference between a public and private repository is whether you would like others to be able to access, download, and make suggestions regarding your code.

Now that I have created a new repository and linked it to my GitHub account, I can see the information shown in Figure 10-3.

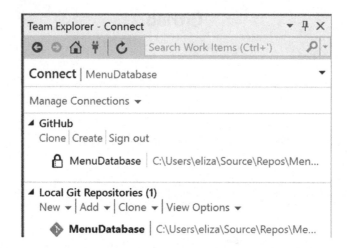

Figure 10-3. *Repository in Team Explorer*

You can see in Team Explorer that I have both a repository on GitHub and a local Git repository. Visual Studio will suggest some third-party tools that you may want to install. The dialog window is shown in Figure 10-4.

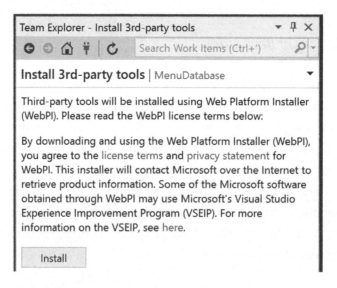

Figure 10-4. *Install Third-Party Tools for GitHub*

You should only need to download these third-party tools once. When installing third-party tools, check and confirm that they are from a trusted source. Installing this third-party tools will give you access to GitHub actions as shown in Figure 10-5.

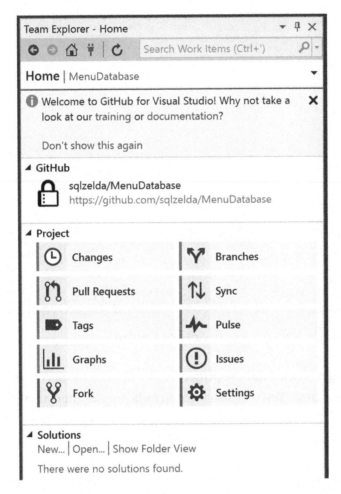

Figure 10-5. *GitHub Action Menu*

The actions available include changes, branches, pull request, and syncing, to name a few.

Before we get into using any of these GitHub actions, I would like to first create a new database project. I have installed SQL Server Developer Tools prior to creating this database project. To create a database project, select New then Project from the File menu. Figure 10-6 shows the dialog box that will pop up.

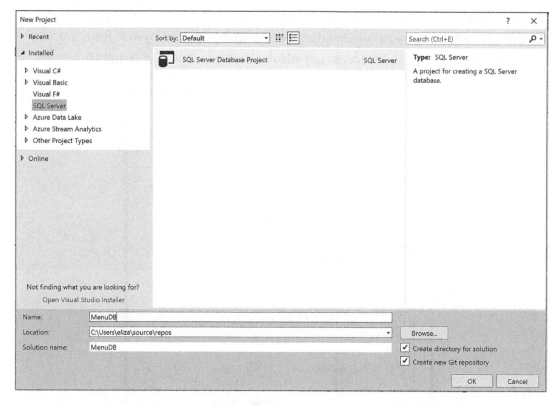

Figure 10-6. *Create New Project in Source Control*

When creating a blank database project, you will need to specify the name, local file path, and solution name. You will also want to indicate whether you need a directory created for the solution and if this solution should be added as a new Git repository. You can see the new database project in Figure 10-7.

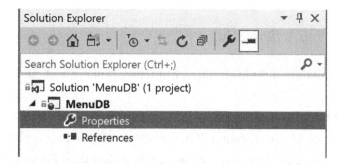

Figure 10-7. *Solution for Database Project*

As shown earlier, we have a solution for a database project. However, there is no database at this time. In the previous chapters in this book, I have been using the Menu database. I can add the Menu database to source control as shown in Figure 10-8.

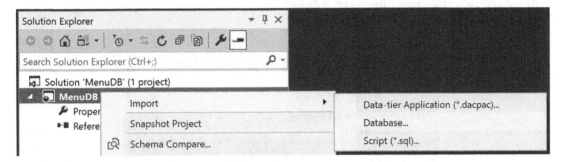

Figure 10-8. *Add Database to the Project*

You can select either a database, a T-SQL script, or a data-tier application (DACPAC) to import. In my example, I have chosen an existing database to import. By selecting this option, a dialog box pops up as shown in Figure 10-9.

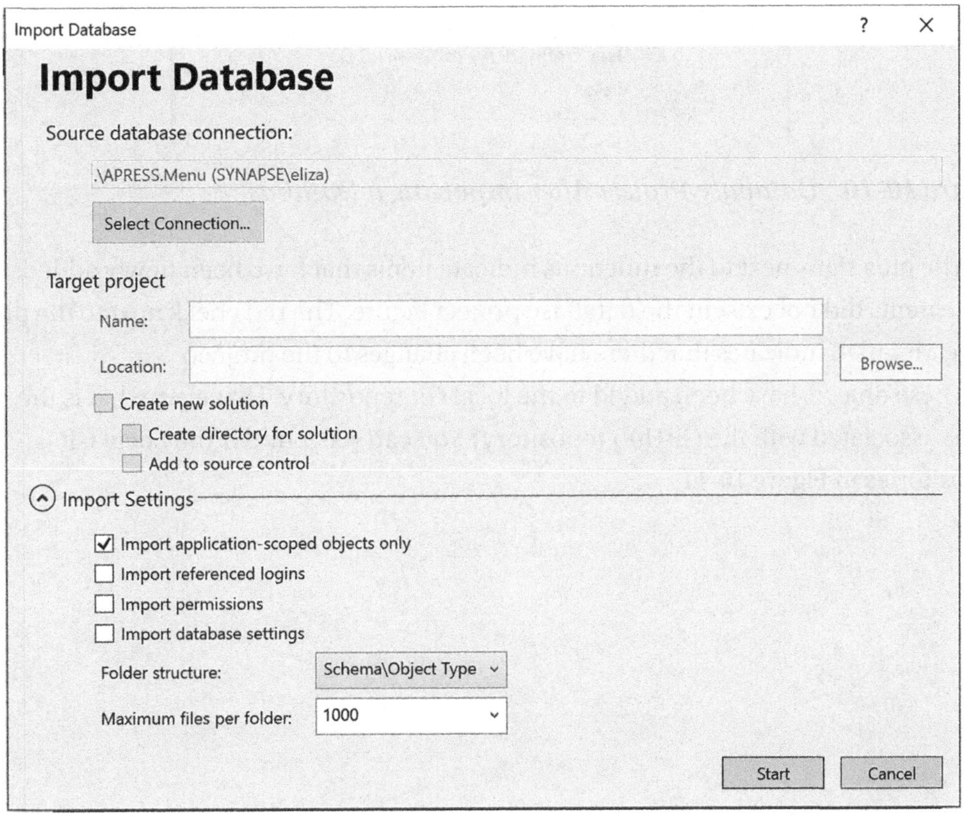

Figure 10-9. *Connect to SQL Server, Select Database, and Configure Settings*

I have kept the setup simple. I created a connection to the SQL Server instance and desired database. I also specified that I wanted to import application-scoped objects only along with specifying an overall folder structure. After this project is created, you can see the new database objects in Solution Explorer as shown in Figure 10-10.

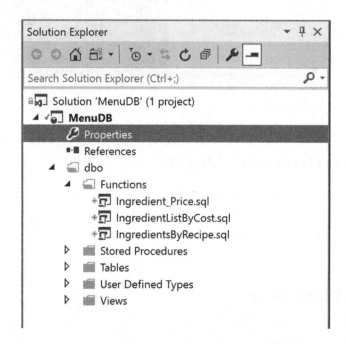

Figure 10-10. *Database Project After Importing a Database*

The plus signs next to the functions indicate items that have been newly added. These items did not exist in the database project before. The red check next to the project name MenuDB indicates that there have been changes to the project.

These objects have been added to the local Git repository. However, what is the status associated with the GitHub repository? You can see it under the Local Git Repositories in Figure 10-11.

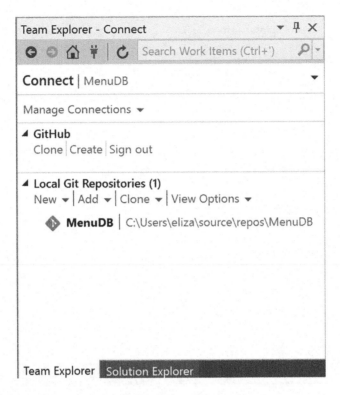

Figure 10-11. *MenuDB as a Local Git Repository*

I can also see that this new database project has not been created in GitHub yet. By going to the action menu in Figure 10-12 and selecting Changes, I can begin the process of getting a GitHub repository created.

Figure 10-12. *Access Changes to GitHub*

The window to commit the changes is shown in Figure 10-13.

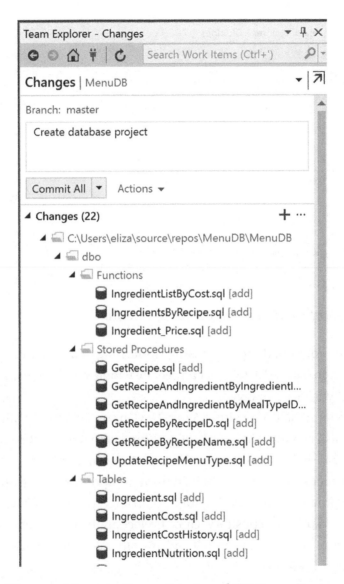

Figure 10-13. Changes Menu to Commit to Local Git Repository

I can choose to commit all or some of these changes. In this case, I am making a new project, and I would like all of the code that has been imported to be saved with one commit. This will be the starting point for the repository going forward.

After committing these items, I get a message confirming that the commit has been successful. You can see this in Figure 10-14.

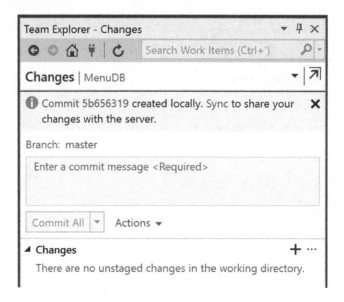

Figure 10-14. *Confirmation Window for Successful Commit*

Along with the commit, there is a message indicating that I can Sync my changes to the GitHub server. In Figure 10-15, you can see the window that appears after clicking the hyperlink to Sync these changes.

I have the option of selecting either Azure DevOps or GitHub. For GitHub, there is an option to Publish this repository or Push this project to Remote Repository. For my example, I will Publish this repository to GitHub. The act of publishing this repository will create a new repository. I have specified the new repository name on GitHub as MenuDB. I have provided a description for the GitHub repository. I have also specified that this should be a private repository. Once I select publish, these changes will be synced to GitHub and available to myself and any other accounts that are added as contributors to this repository.

Figure 10-15. *Select Where to Sync the Solution*

It may be worth noting that the same options shown earlier are the same options we were able to select previously in Figure 10-3. The Synchronization submenu will update and show you that the repository was successfully created as shown in Figure 10-16.

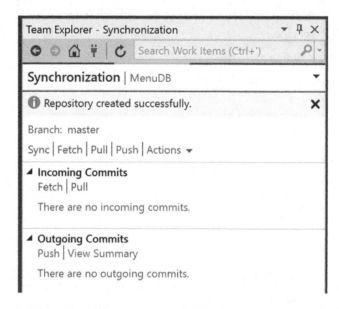

Figure 10-16. *Database Project Has Been Added to GitHub Repository*

You can see that the repository has been successfully created. This window also shows you that there are no incoming or outgoing commits for this project. Once you get the repository created, you will want to get accustomed to pulling incoming changes before you begin making changes to the database objects. Pulling changes down from the centralized Git repository will allow you to have the most updated code before you begin making changes. After pulling down incoming commits, you can then push outgoing commits. I am also unable to commit any changes as all changes have already been committed.

When setting up a new database project and a repository, there are several items that are getting created. I have already confirmed that I have a local Git repository. In the preceding steps, I have published this same repository to GitHub. Now I have both a local and a remote repository for my database project. Previously in Figure 10-13, I committed all the database code to the master branch. I also received confirmation that the commit was successful as shown in Figure 10-14. Looking at the Solution Explorer in Figure 10-17, you can see that the icons next to many of the database objects have changed. Previously in Figure 10-10, you could see green plus signs next to the function names and a red check next to the project name.

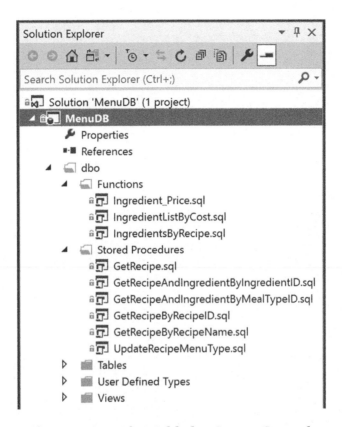

Figure 10-17. *Database Project After Added to Source Control*

Now that all items have been committed, you can see blue locks next to all the items. This signifies that all items have been properly checked into source control.

Implementing source control is a big step into getting your database projects to be more manageable. Knowing why source control can not only help you but help you convince others to help champion a source control initiative at your company. You are also ready to reach out to other departments and put procedures in place that ensure everyone feels comfortable implementing source control. I have also walked through the beginning steps of getting your database added to source control. This is the beginning of a journey that will have some hiccups but also save you time in the long run. Now that you have implemented source control, you are ready for the next steps in managing your T-SQL code. The next chapter will focus on the various methods you can use to test your T-SQL code and confirm that you are complying with various coding standards.

CHAPTER 11

Testing

When you need to write or modify some T-SQL code, you may be tempted to just start writing the code. In many cases, the necessary database code is simple enough that no additional analysis is needed. Eventually, there always comes a scenario where the data being queried or the T-SQL code is complex enough where you want to make certain that your code is working as expected. During these times, you might find that you want to test your T-SQL changes. While you can start testing T-SQL code at any time, you may find it helpful to start the habits early on before dealing with complex scenarios.

You may be ready to start testing your code, but you do not know where to start. What type of testing you will do will depend on what you are trying to accomplish. You can implement testing to confirm that a single piece of functionality is working as expected. It is also possible to test interactions between two or more pieces of code. This type of testing can also be useful when trying to confirm the downstream effects of implementing changes to your T-SQL code. There is also testing that can be done to help ensure that the code you write matches your coding standards. While any type of testing is valuable, the most significant benefits come when using all three in conjunction.

Unit Testing

You have gotten your next task, and you are ready to start writing some T-SQL. You also want to implement functionally testing your code. When you are testing a single piece of code, this is called unit testing. Understanding what unit tests are and why you should use them can help improve your T-SQL code quality. Once you know what unit tests are, you will want to work toward learning when unit testing is beneficial. This will get you ready to start writing your first unit tests for SQL Server.

The concept of unit testing is basic. You have a single change that you want to make to your T-SQL code. Unit testing allows you to test and confirm the functionality for a single piece of code. One of the common methods with unit testing is to create a scenario

267

E. Noble, *Pro T-SQL 2019*, https://doi.org/10.1007/978-1-4842-5590-2_11

that fails, write the T-SQL code, run the unit test, and repeat until the unit test passes. This is test-driven design. Whether you are implementing new functionality or resolving a bug in T-SQL, unit tests can help verify your code.

When creating unit tests, you will need to think differently than you normally would when you set out to write T-SQL code. We are creating unit tests to confirm that the code we are writing works as expected. In order to verify that your T-SQL code is working as expected, you will want your unit test to indicate a Pass. When creating your unit test, your first execution of the unit test should Fail. Starting with a failing unit test would indicate that the desired functionality does not exist.

There are many different implementations of running unit tests. Unit tests can be written inside of Visual Studio. You can also use a free third-party unit testing framework that creates database objects in T-SQL. Another option is using a paid third-party tool to create and run your unit tests. There are benefits and drawbacks to each of these options.

Another factor in determining how you will implement unit testing is in how you would like to run your unit tests. Depending on your environment, you may decide that you would prefer to manually run your unit tests. However, you may also decide that you want an automated way to run your unit tests. The easiest method that has the least amount of overhead is manually running your unit tests. This can either be running these tests with a stored procedure or through a GUI.

You can use unit tests to verify just about anything with your database schema. Most of those unit tests will be for testing functionality for your database objects like stored procedures, views, and functions. I may be biased, but I hope you have far more stored procedures than views or queries. Do not be concerned if you do not have any unit tests in place now. You can create unit tests as you need them. This may mean that you do not have complete code coverage for your unit tests, but it prevents you from spending time implementing unit tests for code that is not modified frequently.

Before I write my first unit test, I need to know what functionality I will be developing. In my case, I need to change the stored procedure dbo.GetRecipe to only display recipes that are active. When I first started unit testing my T-SQL code, I would run my unit tests manually. In this case, I would look for recipes that are currently not active. I can create a unit test to check for inactive records. If my unit test finds any inactive records, my unit test would fail. If my unit test does not find any inactive records, my unit test would succeed or pass. I would run the query shown in Listing 11-1 to find any recipes that are not active.

Listing 11-1. Find Inactive Recipes

```
SELECT
        RecipeID,
        RecipeName,
        IsActive
FROM dbo.Recipe
WHERE IsActive = 0;
```

When running this query, I might get the following results as displayed in Table 11-1.

Table 11-1. *Inactive Recipes*

RecipeID	RecipeName	IsActive
2	Lee's Burgers	False
5	Brandin's Fried Rice	False

Once I get the results in Table 11-1, I know what records will be affected by dbo.
GetRecipe changing to pull back active recipes instead of all recipes. The unmodified
stored procedure is shown in Listing 11-2.

Listing 11-2. Original Stored Procedure

```
/*------------------------------------------------------------*\
Name:           dbo.GetRecipe
Author:         Elizabeth Noble
Created Date:   April 20, 2019
Description: Get a list of all recipes in the database

Sample Usage:
    EXECUTE dbo.GetRecipe

\*------------------------------------------------------------*/
CREATE OR ALTER PROCEDURE dbo.GetRecipe

AS
```

```
SELECT
        RecipeID,
        RecipeName,
        RecipeDescription,
        ServingQuantity,
        MealTypeID,
        PreparationTypeID,
        IsActive,
        DateCreated,
        DateModified
FROM dbo.Recipe;
```

When executing this stored procedure, I expect to see all recipes in the table being returned. After executing this stored procedure, I get the following records as shown in Table 11-2.

Table 11-2. *All Recipes*

RecipeID	RecipeName	IsActive
1	Spaghetti	True
2	Lee's Burgers	False
3	Spinach Frittata	True
3	Roasted Chicken	True
4	Dinner Rolls	True
5	Brandin's Fried Rice	False

You can see in Table 11-2 that both active and inactive recipes are returned when executing the stored procedure. In this way, we have created a basic unit test, the query in Listing 11-1, and confirmed that this test failed when running the stored procedure in Listing 11-2 since the inactive records were also returned with the result set.

The next step is to figure out how to get the unit test to pass. For this example, the change is simple. I need to add a line at the end of the stored procedure where only active recipes are returned as shown in Listing 11-3.

Listing 11-3. Stored Procedure After Modification

```
/*--------------------------------------------------------------*\

Name:           dbo.GetRecipe
Author:         Elizabeth Noble
Created Date:   April 20, 2019
Description: Get a list of all recipes in the database

Sample Usage:
      EXECUTE dbo.GetRecipe

\*--------------------------------------------------------------*/
CREATE OR ALTER PROCEDURE dbo.GetRecipe

AS

      SELECT
            RecipeID,
            RecipeName,
            RecipeDescription,
            ServingQuantity,
            MealTypeID,
            PreparationTypeID,
            IsActive,
            DateCreated,
            DateModified
      FROM dbo.Recipe
      WHERE IsActive = 1;
```

Once this stored procedure has been created, you can execute the stored procedure to confirm that the new functionality is working as expected. In this case, you would want to verify that RecipeIDs 2 and 5 are no longer being returned. Based on the preceding code, we would expect the result set from Listing 11-3 to match what is shown in Table 11-3.

Table 11-3. *All Active Recipes*

RecipeID	RecipeName	IsActive
1	Spaghetti	True
3	Spinach Frittata	True
3	Roasted Chicken	True
4	Dinner Rolls	True

We have confirmed that the changes we made to Listing 11-3 have correctly removed the inactive recipes from the result set.

This method of testing your code is a good place to start, but it can be difficult to follow consistently. You may have some tables that can store data in various states. For instance, if I wanted to find the information about the frequency with which a recipe was prepared based on an ingredient on sale, the logic to test the results gets more complex. That is where the benefit of using third-party tools can be helpful.

Finding individual sample sets for your data can be time consuming and error prone. In addition, you may spend more time trying to find the right test case rather than writing or testing the T-SQL code. Another challenge is that you skip over important test cases due to the time and energy spent manually finding test data that already exists in the database. However, using T-SQL to find specific test cases in your data is not your only option. You could manually insert test data and perform your tests on the records that have been inserted. This method would allow you to determine what were the best scenarios for the code you were testing. In most cases, this sample data would not remain in a centralized location. You may still need to rewrite specific examples each time you test a new piece of functionality.

There are different types of unit testing tools available to you. Unit testing can be handled by adding additional T-SQL objects to your database. Another option is to pay for third-party tools that can help manage your unit tests. Another option is to use Visual Studio to create and manage unit tests. While all these options are valid and have their own benefits, I want to focus on what you can accomplish by creating unit tests natively in Visual Studio. Figure 11-1 shows the first step to create a unit test in Visual Studio.

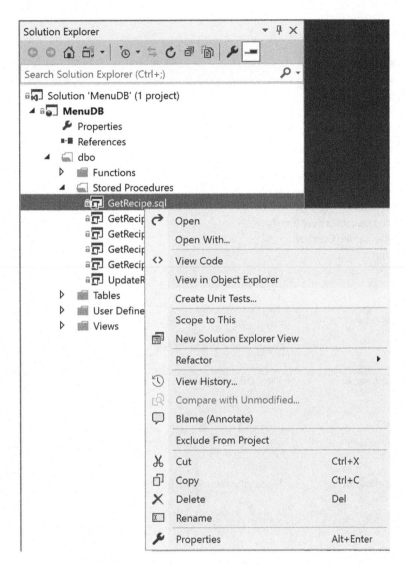

Figure 11-1. *Create Unit Test*

Once you select the option to create a unit test, Visual Studio will walk you through the process of creating your first unit test. A dialog box will open as shown in Figure 11-2.

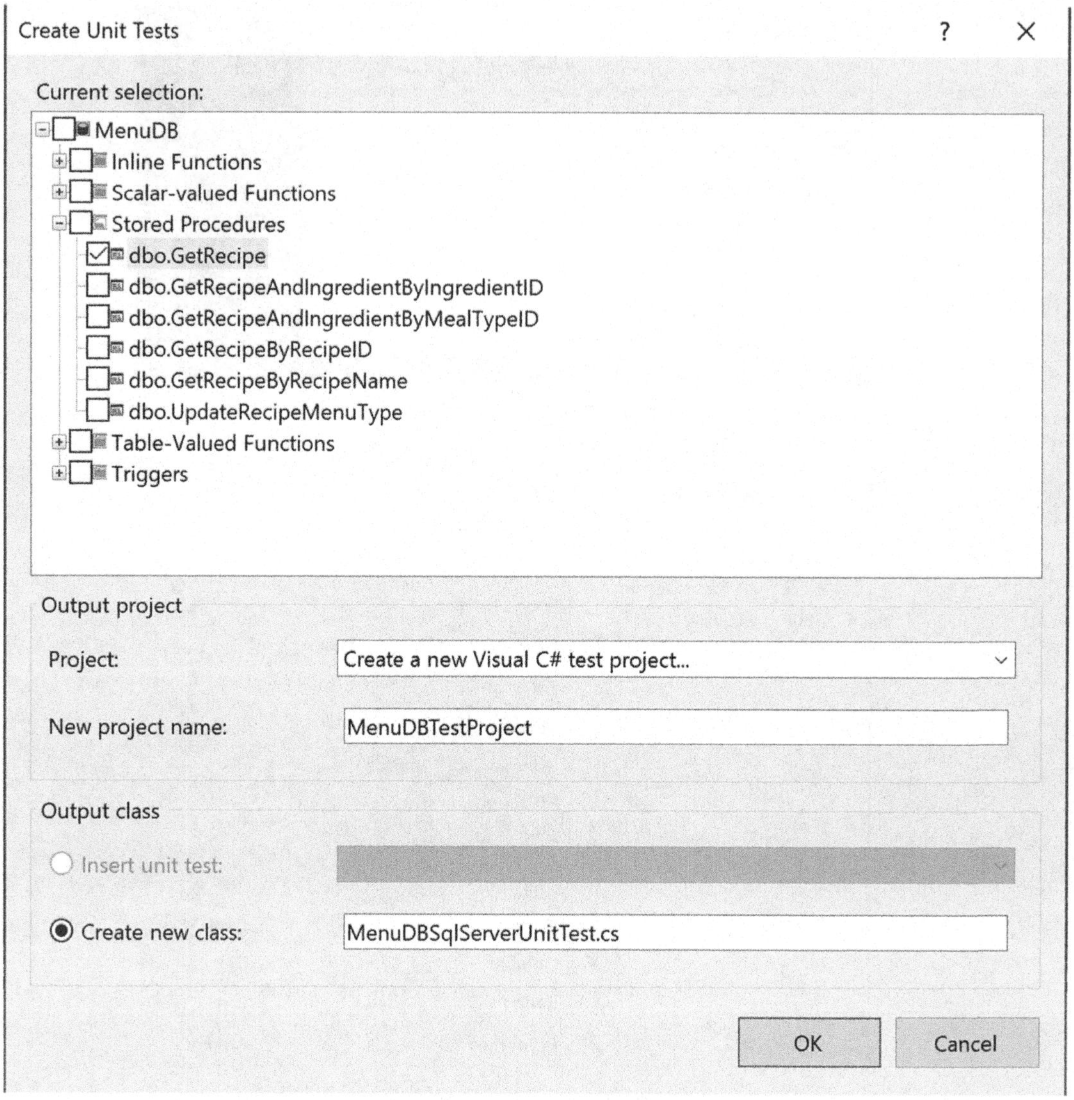

Figure 11-2. Create Unit Test Dialog Box

The top portion of the window allows me to select which objects should be used to create unit tests. For this example, I will work on creating a new unit test for the dbo. GetRecipe stored procedure. I am also creating my first unit test associated with this database project. I can select that I want to create a new Visual C# test project. However, you do not need to know C# to start creating your own unit tests in Visual Studio. I have given this new project a name and decided to create a new class. I can reuse this class for other unit tests going forward.

Once I select OK on the dialog window, I will get another pop-up as shown in Figure 11-3.

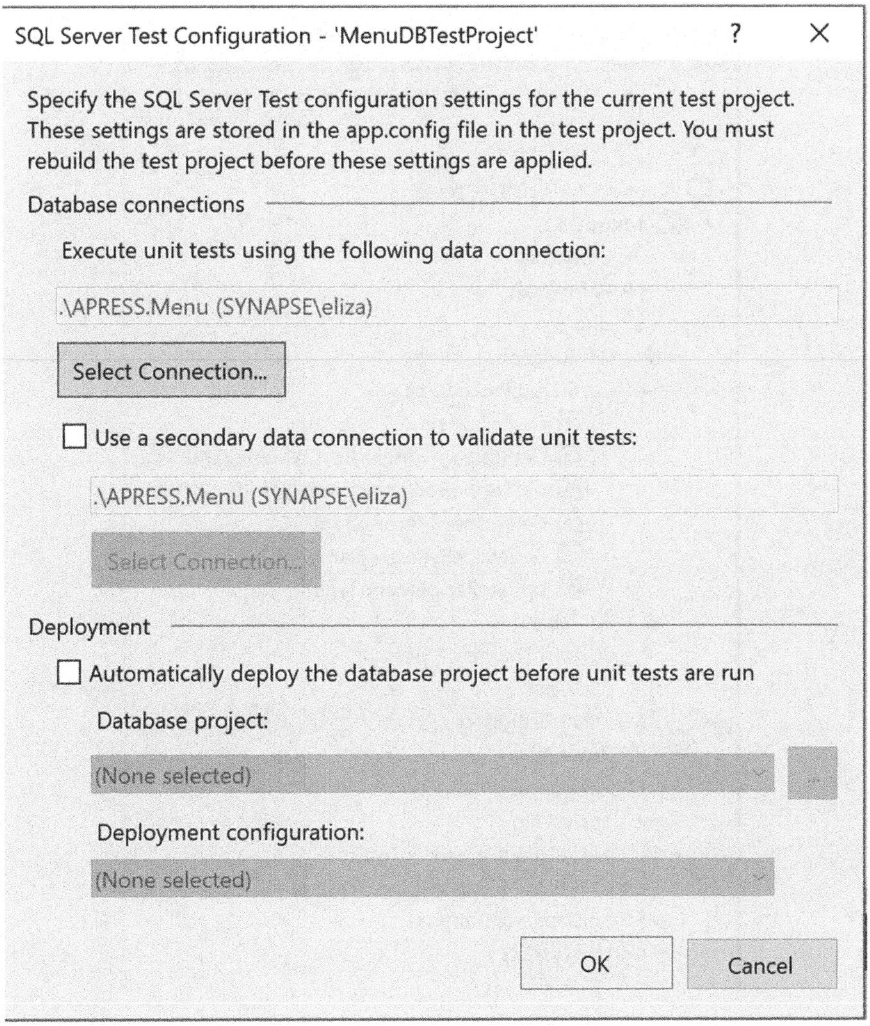

Figure 11-3. *Set Connection String*

There are a couple of options that can be set here. Most of this has to do with selecting a data source we are using where we can perform the unit tests. I have selected the pre-existing Menu database to run the unit tests. I have the option to automatically deploy the database before running the unit tests. However, I would prefer to only deploy the database if the unit tests passes.

Once I have set the connection string and configured the additional settings, Visual Studio will add a new project to the existing solution. You can see in Figure 11-4 how your database project will look along with the unit testing project.

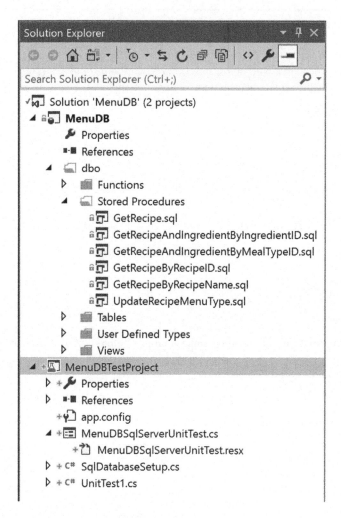

Figure 11-4. *Unit Testing in Source Control*

In Figure 11-4, none of the objects in the original MenuDB project have been altered. You can see all the objects created for the unit testing project are available to be checked into source control. After the unit testing project has been created, some additional windows will open in Visual Studio. One of these windows allows you to set test conditions. By default, a test condition will be configured for Inconclusive. You can leave this test condition or remove it. In Figure 11-5, I have selected the drop-down of available test conditions.

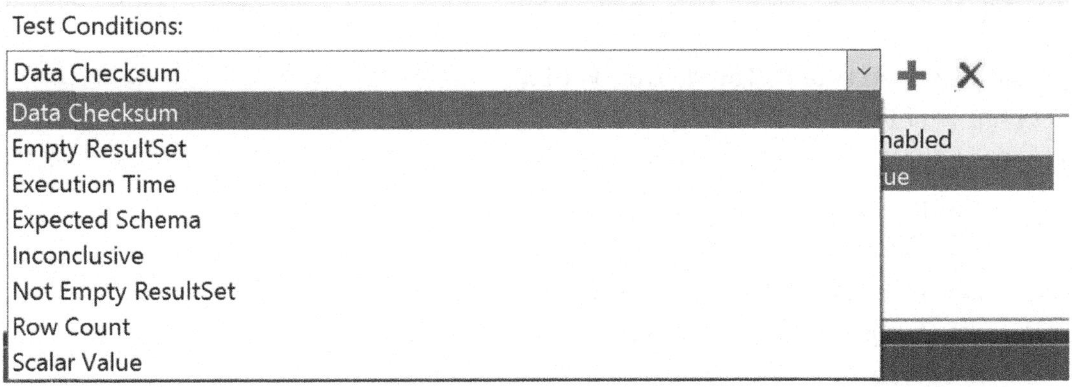

Test Conditions:

Data Checksum	∨	✚ ✕

Data Checksum		
Empty ResultSet		nabled
Execution Time		ue
Expected Schema		
Inconclusive		
Not Empty ResultSet		
Row Count		
Scalar Value		

Figure 11-5. *Available Unit Test Options*

I am still trying to create a unit test to verify that inactive recipes are not being returned by the dbo.GetRecipe stored procedure. Like the manual unit test I wrote previously, I am going to select the condition of Empty ResultSet. You can see this test condition in Figure 11-6.

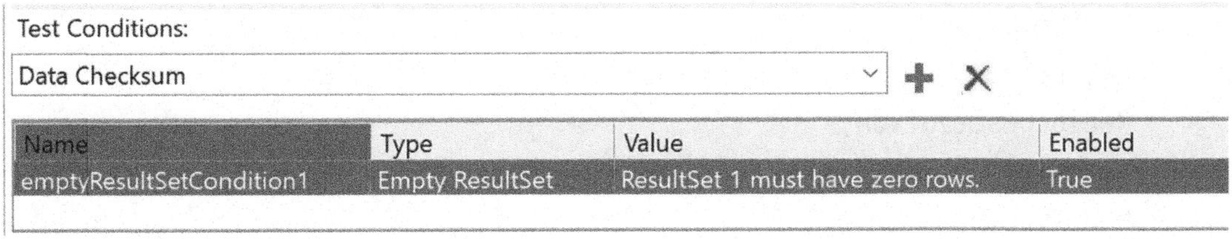

Test Conditions:

Data Checksum	∨	✚ ✕

Name	Type	Value	Enabled
emptyResultSetCondition1	Empty ResultSet	ResultSet 1 must have zero rows.	True

Figure 11-6. *Unit Test to Check for Empty ResultSet*

Now that I've created a test condition, I need to write some T-SQL code for this unit test. I have selected Empty ResultSet as my test condition. For this unit test to pass when it is run, the T-SQL code inside the unit test must not return any results.

After I change the stored procedure, I do not want any inactive recipes to be returned. In this case, my passing test case would be to have no inactive recipes returned. This also matches the test conditions that were created in Figure 11-6. Listing 11-4 shows the code I will be using for my unit test.

Listing 11-4. Code to Run Unit Test

```
-- database unit test for dbo.GetRecipe
DECLARE @RecipeList TABLE
(
     RecipeID          INT,
     RecipeName        VARCHAR(25),
     RecipeDescription VARCHAR(50),
     ServingQuantity   TINYINT,
     MealTypeID        TINYINT,
     PreparationTypeID TINYINT,
     IsActive          BIT,
     DateCreated       DATETIME2(7),
     DateModified      DATETIME2(7)
);

INSERT INTO @RecipeList
(
     RecipeID,
     RecipeName,
     RecipeDescription,
     ServingQuantity,
     MealTypeID,
     PreparationTypeID,
     IsActive,
     DateCreated,
     DateModified
)
EXECUTE [dbo].[GetRecipe];

SELECT RecipeID
FROM @RecipeList
WHERE IsActive = 0;
```

I first create a table variable. The next section of the unit test inserts the results from the stored procedure dbo.GetRecipe into the table variable. The final step is to select only the inactive records from the table variable. Once I add the preceding code to MenuDBSQLServerUnitTest.cs and save the file, I am ready to run my first unit test. You can go to the Test menu to run the unit tests as shown in Figure 11-7.

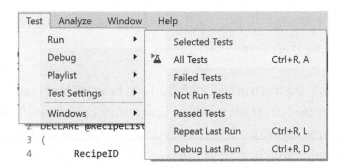

Figure 11-7. *Manually Run Unit Test*

I am using test-driven design for my unit tests, and I am testing this unit test before changing the original stored procedure. For this scenario, I am expecting the unit test to fail. You can see the results of running this unit test in Figure 11-8.

Run All | Run... ▼ | Playlist : All Tests ▼

MenuDB (2 tests) 1 failed

◢ ⊗ MenuDBTestProject (2)   1 sec

  ◢ ⊗ MenuDBTestProject (2)   1 sec

    ◢ ⊗ MenuDBSqlServerUnitTest (1)   1 sec

      ⊗ dbo_GetRecipeTest   1 sec

    ▷ ✓ UnitTest1 (1)   < 1 ms

Figure 11-8. *Failed Unit Test*

The original stored procedure still returns inactive recipes. This caused the unit test to fail. Once I updated the stored procedure dbo.GetRecipe with the T-SQL code from Listing 11-3 and repeat the unit test, I will get the results in Figure 11-9.

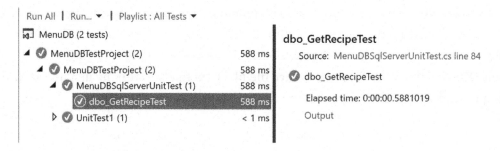

Figure 11-9. *Passed Unit Test*

Now that the unit test has run successfully, I can be confident that my new T-SQL code is working as intended. There are other unit testing options available for database projects. I propose you investigate several alternatives and collaborate with your coworkers to determine which method works best for your environment.

Integration Testing

While it is good to know that a single piece of database code is working as expected, most T-SQL code does not exist in isolation. The very nature of relational design infers that items in the database are related to one another. We normally think of the relationships between tables. However, stored procedures access data that exists in tables. If I wanted to verify an insert of data, I may run a unit test. This would confirm that the data I expected to be inserted has been inserted.

Issues can arise when there is more than one way to access the same data in the database. Oftentimes, these queries were written at different periods in time. This can cause the logic in the queries to be slightly different. I have also seen instances where different business units in a company have different calculations for the same data. If a calculation for one business unit is reused for another business unit, it can cause what appears to be inaccurate results.

This brings up a question as to how to keep our T-SQL code and query results consistent across multiple different database objects. This is where integration testing can be useful. Integration testing is the term used to indicate testing that is designed to work with more than a single piece of code. If you are using an application to insert data and you want to verify that the data is inserted correctly, that could be considered integration testing. You would be testing both the application's ability to connect to SQL Server and the T-SQL code to insert the data into the database.

This is only one scenario where integration testing can be used. A common situation I find myself in is working with two stored procedures that are intended to pull back generally the same information. There are times that changes to one of the underlying tables or code in one of the stored procedures may cause these two stored procedures to return different results. Unfortunately, these differences in results are not usually found until well after the T-SQL code was deployed. This causes an overall loss of confidence in the applications.

While it is preferred that these intertwined stored procedures would be documented or better yet re-factored down to a single stored procedure, this is not always an option. There are costs associated with having multiple versions of similar code, but there are also costs with having multiple processes relying on the same code. For the rest of this chapter, we will assume that the T-SQL code cannot be rewritten to get rid of the dependency.

Just like unit testing database code, you can begin your integration testing manually by using T-SQL queries. The biggest factor in your integration is understanding how your environment works together. Sometimes this is found by accident like when something breaks. Other times, you may be a subject matter expert and already know the interactions. Either way, in order to begin integration testing, you first need to have at least two things to test.

You could begin by testing a data insert along with a data select of the same table(s). You could also use integration testing to compare the results of two queries. This could happen if you have one query where you return all values and another query where you search for a specific value. While these two stored procedures would not match for every record, they may have matching results for a specific record. This type of integration testing would confirm that the values returned in the columns were consistent between one another.

If I start working on making changes to a stored procedure that selects data, I may want to test the insert of the data along with the select for that same data. I may be working on updating the stored procedure dbo.GetRecipeAndIngredientByMealTypeID to only return active recipes. I can unit test this stored procedure by creating a unit test for inactive recipes and a unit test for active recipes. I can also use integration testing to confirm that this stored procedure will still return expected results after creating a new recipe. This type of testing may be considered trivial now, but as the application grows and matures, they may become increasingly useful. I have found that there are times the business needs answers faster than they can be provided. This sometimes causes database objects to be used in ways they were not originally intended.

My integration test will consist of inserting a new recipe into dbo.Recipe tables. After inserting the record, I will execute the dbo.GetRecipeAndIngredientByMealTypeID stored procedure to verify that the new recipe is returned. The stored procedure used to insert the record into dbo.Recipe is shown in Listing 11-5.

Listing 11-5. Insert Record into dbo.Recipe Table

```
CREATE OR ALTER PROCEDURE dbo.InsertRecepie
        @RecipeName         VARCHAR(25),
        @RecipeDescription  VARCHAR(50),
        @ServingQuantity    TINYINT,
        @MealTypeID         TINYINT,
        @PreparationTypeID  TINYINT,
        @IsActive           BIT,
        @DateCreated        DATETIME2(7),
        @DateModified       DATETIME2(7)

AS

        INSERT INTO dbo.Recipe
        (
                RecipeName,
                RecipeDescription,
                ServingQuantity,
                MealTypeID,
                PreparationTypeID,
                IsActive
        )
        VALUES
        (
                @RecipeName,
                @RecipeDescription,
                @ServingQuantity,
                @MealTypeID,
                @PreparationTypeID,
                @IsActive
        )
```

Now that I know how I will be adding the recipes to the database, I should also get a better idea of what stored procedure I will be using. In Listing 11-6, you can see the stored procedure dbo.GetRecipeAndIngredientByMealTypeID.

Listing 11-6. Select Recipe and Ingredient by Meal Type

```
CREATE OR ALTER PROCEDURE dbo.GetRecipeAndIngredientByMealTypeID
     @MealTypeID      INT
AS

     SELECT
          rec.RecipeName,
          ingr.IngredientName,
          ingr.IsActive,
          ingr.DateCreated,
          ingr.DateModified
     FROM dbo.Recipe rec
          INNER JOIN dbo.RecipeIngredient recingr
          ON rec.RecipeID = recingr.RecipeID
          LEFT OUTER JOIN dbo.Ingredient ingr
          ON recingr.IngredientID = ingr.IngredientID
     WHERE rec.MealTypeID = @MealTypeID
     ORDER BY rec.RecipeName, ingr.IngredientName;
```

In order to perform integration testing, I need to write some code so that I can insert the recipe. Afterward, I will run the second stored procedure. I can insert these results into a temporary table then verify that the recipe that was created from the first stored procedure exists in the results from the second stored procedure. In the example in Listing 11-7 below, I will also need to add some ingredients to the recipe so that the dbo.GetRecipeAndIngredientByMealTypeID stored procedure will be able to pull some results back.

Listing 11-7. Manual Integration Testing

```
DECLARE @RecipeID INT
DECLARE @MealTypeID INT

EXECUTE dbo.InsertRecepie
```

```
    @RecipeName = 'Eggplant Parmesan',
    @RecipeDescription = 'A recipe to make eggplant parmesan',
    @ServingQuantity = 6,
    @MealTypeID = @MealTypeID,
    @PreparationTypeID = 1,
    @IsActive = 1
```

```
EXECUTE dbo.InsertRecipeIngredient
    @RecipeID
```

```
INSERT INTO @RecipeMeal (RecipeName, IngredientName, IsActive, DateCreated,
DateModified)
EXECUTE dbo.GetRecipeAndIngredientByMealTypeID @MealTypeID
```

```
SELECT RecipeName
FROM @RecipeMeal
WHERE RecipeID = @RecipeID
```

When determining what you should be integration testing, think about any dependencies related to the T-SQL code that you are writing.

Some T-SQL code has a more obvious need for integration testing than others. One of the scenarios I have found that need the most integration testing involves different database objects that return the same data. This can be two different stored procedures. It is also possible that the integration testing can compare the results between functions and stored procedures or views and functions. While these database objects may return different columns in the result set or in a different order, the columns that are the same can be compared.

Other times you may have T-SQL code where one database object depends on the data handled in a previous step. You may have a stored procedure that updates a value in the table. A view or stored procedure may only return a specific subset of values. Using integration testing can allow you to execute the first stored procedure where you will update a lookup value in the table. Depending on the testing required, you can execute the stored procedure and confirm the record appears. Unless the record should no longer appear, then you can use integration testing to confirm that the record no longer appears.

A common situation where this can occur is when you want to soft delete or disable a data record from your application. You can use one set of T-SQL to disable the record. There may be one or more database objects that should then be tested to confirm that the disabled records no longer appear. Creating a way to keep all your integration testing scenarios together and making sure that they are repeatable is what will protect your applications in the future. Integration testing your code now confirms that your current version of T-SQL code will pass. However, automating and repeating your integration testing going forward will allow you to continue to verify that new bugs have not been introduced into your T-SQL code.

Depending on the design and complexity of your system, you may have data that is entered in one application and is sent to or used by another application. Throughout the business activities, this data may end up in different databases or different tables. This can involve different stages of data throughout your business. This can also include using integration testing between the transactional databases and a data warehouse. Using integration testing in this manner can help make sure that the data entered in your applications remains consistent when it is migrated into a data warehouse.

There are more graceful methods around that can help with integration testing. However, I have found that most of these reference unit testing. The only difference for using these tools with integration testing is how the tests are written. This means you can use the unit testing functionality within Visual Studio as shown in the preceding section. There are other tools you can use for your unit and integration testing, but they will not be covered in this book.

Load Testing

Another aspect of working with SQL Server is handling large data sets quickly. It is often easy to hope that T-SQL code that is functionally correct will also perform well. However, that is not always what happens. While we can use execution plans to get a good idea of the relative performance of a query, that does not guarantee that the code will perform well under a heavy load. If we want to get an idea of how the T-SQL code will perform under stress, we will need to perform load testing.

Load testing presents some very special issues. One challenge is that the hardware is often between the load testing environment and Production. In addition to hardware differences, there is usually a difference in the data that exists in the lower environments. This can be anything from having less data in lower environments to the data in the lower environments being cleansed and having different statistics. Additional differences can include data that has been entered in the lower environments that does not match Production. In many cases, these differences cannot be resolved.

Unless you have the exact hardware and the exact Production databases, your load testing will not match Production with complete certainty. It is still beneficial to try and load test your T-SQL code. Even if you are unable to create the perfect load testing environment, you can still compare relative performance of T-SQL code in your load testing environment. The next step is to figure out how to implement load testing. A simple but not very reliable method is to create T-SQL scripts to generate dummy load testing data. This method will give you a general idea of performance, but without significant analysis of existing Production data, it will not accurately reflect Production performance.

There are several third-party tools available for load testing and many of them are free. These tools should make it simpler to begin load testing. However, you are faced with the same issue that these tests may not accurately reflect Production activity. Another option is to use distributed replay to collect the transactions from Production and replay them in your lower environments. While implementing load testing is an important aspect when developing your T-SQL code, the steps needed to load test are outside the scope of this book.

Static Code Analysis

Creating standards for formatting and developing T-SQL coding standards is only a start when it comes to writing T-SQL code. Back in Chapter 3, I wrote about standardizing your T-SQL code. T-SQL Coding Standards were covered in Chapter 9. These standards are only useful if they are followed. Many times, the standards are lengthy and can be difficult to remember. There are better ways to ensure these standards are followed than trying to remember all the rules. Static code analysis can be used to confirm that your standards are being followed.

As discussed previously in this book, there are benefits to standardizing how you and your coworkers write T-SQL. This can make the code easier to read and save time debugging issues in the T-SQL code. Unfortunately, the benefits of standardization cannot be realized if the T-SQL code getting checked into source control does not match the formatting standards. This is one situation where static code analysis can help.

The static code analysis allows you to write T-SQL code. This code can be saved and checked into source control. Prior to deploying the database code, static code analysis is used to verify that the checked in T-SQL code meets the coding standards. There are options to enforce T-SQL formatting, but the main option that is used is a third-party tool.

In addition to using static code analysis for standardization of formatting for database code, you can use static code analysis for your database coding standards as well. There is built-in functionality in Visual Studio 2017. You can find the window in Figure 11-10 by selecting the Code Analysis option from the Properties menu.

Configuration: Active (Debug)   Platform: Active (Any CPU)

☐ Enable Code Analysis on Build

Rules	Treat Warning as Error
✓ ☑ Microsoft.Rules.Data.Design	☐
☑ SR0001: Avoid SELECT * in stored procedures, views, and table-valued functions.	☐
☑ SR0008: Consider using SCOPE_IDENTITY instead of @@IDENTITY.	☐
☑ SR0009: Avoid using types of variable length that are size 1 or 2.	☐
☑ SR0010: Avoid using deprecated syntax when you join tables or views.	☐
☑ SR0013: Specify values for output parameters in all code paths.	☐
☑ SR0014: Maintain compatibility between data types.	☐
✓ ☑ Microsoft.Rules.Data.Naming	☐
☑ SR0011: Avoid using special characters in object names.	☐
☑ SR0012: Avoid using reserved words for type names.	☐
☑ SR0016: Avoid using sp_ as a prefix for stored procedures.	☐
✓ ☑ Microsoft.Rules.Data.Performance	☐
☑ SR0004: Avoid using columns that do not have an index as test expressions in IN predicates.	☐
☑ SR0005: Avoid using patterns that start with "%" in LIKE predicates.	☐
☑ SR0006: In the comparison, simplify the expression that includes indexed columns.	☐
☑ SR0007: Use ISNULL(column, default value) on nullable columns in expressions.	☐
☑ SR0015: Extract deterministic function calls from WHERE predicates.	☐

Figure 11-10. *Code Analysis in Database Projects*

You can select code analysis to be run every time you build the database project. You also have the option of selecting which items should be included as part of your code analysis. These options include best practices and items that can help affect the performance of the T-SQL code. In addition, there is the option to escalate some of these rules to error and fail instead of sending a warning message.

The benefit of static code analysis is that it automates the process of ensuring that the T-SQL code is meeting your business' coding standards. This can help code rejections feel less personal, and the code is being reviewed and rejected as part of the overall build process. The build process will also communicate the warning or error message in a consistent method.

Getting your database code into source control is only half of the issue. The real challenge can come when trying to deploy database changes that are only saved in source control. Determining how you want to deploy your code will help you determine what method to use to save your T-SQL code. Deploying T-SQL code from source control will be discussed further in Chapter 12.

Deployment

Throughout the course of developing software, there will come a time where you need to implement new functionality. One of the prevailing issues with new functionality is implementing that functionality in a manner that does not affect current performance. For many businesses today, the need to have applications up and running 24 hours a day is critical. This creates a scenario where any form of downtime or loss in current functionality can be incredibly expensive. While the deployment method used can help minimize the overall risk associated with new functionality, there are other options that can be used when writing new code.

A frequent issue that comes up is related to how software is developed in correlation with how code is deployed. In the case of many projects, the amount of time needed to implement new functionality is greater than the frequency with which T-SQL code is deployed. Determining on how source control is managed can mitigate some of these risks. There are different ways T-SQL code can be deployed. Understanding these methods and the best times to use them will help improve your database deployments. There are also some options available when it comes to how your users interact with the database code.

Feature Flag

You may be asked to make some changes to an application that will require many different user stories. To put it differently, you may be re-factoring an application where that process is expected to take months. At the same time, you know your business may deploy database code every 2 weeks. The issue becomes how you develop T-SQL code where you can confirm the code works in the existing database structure but also make sure that those database changes do not end up in Production before they are ready.

This is a question not only many database developers but also software developers have asked themselves. At the heart of the issue is how I can write database code that can

© Elizabeth Noble 2020
E. Noble, *Pro T-SQL 2019*, https://doi.org/10.1007/978-1-4842-5590-2_12

be turned on and off. One method that attempts to handle this is the use of feature flags. There are many ways to implement feature flags. The goal remains the same, to create database code and database objects that can be configured to work in one scenario or another.

When using feature flags, you have the option to enable or disable new functionality at will. This method of managing your database code can allow you to write code, deploy the code to production, and enabled the new functionality at a later time chosen by the business. In addition to being able to determine exactly when to enable new functionality, you also get the added benefit of being able to roll back changes almost instantaneously by updating a single value in a database. There are some foundations you want to have in place before fully embracing feature flags. For instance, you want to be accustomed and in the habit of unit testing your database code. When it comes to feature flags, you will not only need to unit test when the feature flag is enabled, but you will also need to unit test when the feature flag is disabled to confirm that your applications are using the pre-existing database logic.

I would suggest you wait until you have fully implemented source control for your databases before embracing feature flags. One of the reasons for this recommendation is that there is additional effort in managing your feature flags. When you create feature flags for your database objects, you will need to create some additional logic to allow your applications to use the pre-existing T-SQL code or the new database code. This will not only require discipline as you write your T-SQL code, but you will need to have defined processes to determine when to remove the feature flags from your database code. While feature flags will work great for database objects like stored procedures, functions, or views, feature flags are not the solution for everything that you are developing. Some changes such as changes to database columns cannot be toggled on and off. To manage these types of changes to database objects, we will discuss some solutions at the end of this section.

When using feature flags for your T-SQL code, you have a couple options to determine what feature flags are enabled at any given time. There are two main solutions I've heard proposed when it comes to feature flags and databases. The first one may be more application code based. That is supplying the feature flag values in a configuration file. The second option is more of a T-SQL-based solution. This solution involves creating a table to store the feature flags in their current status such as enabled or disabled. There are benefits and downsides to each option. Using application code to manage feature flags may be easier to implement and manage. However, it may be more difficult for the database administrators to support these feature flags. If you keep the feature flag values in the database, you will need to be disciplined in managing those feature flags and removing them. It can become very easy to end up with a table that is cluttered with deprecated feature flags. The downside is that only users with access to the database table can see the value associated with each feature flag.

When you deploy your database code, you can deploy the feature flag as disabled. Once you are ready to enable the new functionality, you can set the feature flag to enabled. You will want to define a process on how to determine when it is time to switch entirely to the new functionality. When you are ready to operate entirely on the new functionality, you will want to remove the previous T-SQL code. You will also remove any reference to feature flags as part of this process. The challenge with this method is it can become easy to skip over the process of removing the prior database code. If your T-SQL code is not cleaned up on a regular basis, this can greatly diminish the manageability of your code going forward.

If I need to update a stored procedure to use new logic, I can use feature flags in order to deploy this change whenever I want. Looking at Listing 12-1, you can see the original stored procedure that has not been modified.

Listing 12-1. Original Stored Procedure

```
/*-------------------------------------------------------------*\
Name:           dbo.GetRecipe
Author:         Elizabeth Noble
Created Date:   April 20, 2019
Description: Get a list of all recipes in the database

Sample Usage:
    EXECUTE dbo.GetRecipe

\*-------------------------------------------------------------*/
CREATE OR ALTER PROCEDURE dbo.GetRecipe

AS

    SELECT
        RecipeID,
        RecipeName,
        RecipeDescription,
        ServingQuantity,
```

```
        MealTypeID,
        PreparationTypeID,
        IsActive,
        DateCreated,
        DateModified
    FROM dbo.Recipe;
```

This stored procedure pulls various information about all recipes. In the preceding T-SQL code, the stored procedure does not differentiate between active and inactive recipes. Information about all recipes are returned. I may find out that this stored procedure was only supposed to return active recipes. While I need to update this stored procedure to only return active recipes, there may be a business reason why this code change cannot be enabled as soon as it is deployed.

In this case, I would need to use something like feature flags to allow me to have the flexibility to create these changes in the stored procedure and control when these changes are available to the application. When working with feature flags, you will need a way to determine whether a feature flag is enabled or not. This is how you and the database code will know which T-SQL code should be executed at a given time. One option is to create a table to store the information about the feature flags. You can create a table like the one shown in Listing 12-2.

Listing 12-2. Create Feature Flag Table

```
CREATE TABLE dbo.FeatureFlag
(
        FeatureFlagID      INT,
        IsActive           BIT,
        DateCreated        DATETIME,
        DateModified       DATETIME
);
```

The preceding table is simple. There is an integer value for the feature flag, a value that indicates if the feature flag is enabled, a date when the feature flag was created, and a date when the feature flag values were last updated. This table will allow us to store information about what feature flags are enabled. In order to use this feature flag table, I will need to enter information about this feature flag into the table created in Listing 12-2. The INSERT statement in Listing 12-3 shows an insert into the dbo.FeatureFlag table.

Listing 12-3. Insert Feature Flag Record

```
INSERT INTO dbo.FeatureFlag
(
     FeatureFlagID,
     IsActive,
     DateCreated,
     DateModified
)
VALUES (947,0,GETDATE(),GETDATE());
```

I have inserted a record for Feature Flag 947. At the time of the insert, the feature flag is disabled. The goal is that the existing stored procedure will continue to return the same results as it did before the feature flag was added. In the stored procedure in Listing 12-4, I have added logic to allow the stored procedure to return different results depending on whether Feature Flag 947 is disabled or enabled.

Listing 12-4. Stored Procedure with Feature Flag

```
/*--------------------------------------------------------------*\
Name:              dbo.GetRecipe
Author:            Elizabeth Noble
Created Date:      April 20, 2019
Description: Get a list of all recipes in the database

Updated Date:      May 20, 2019
Description: Add feature flag. If feature flag is enabled, only
     Show active recipes. Otherwise, show all recipes.

Sample Usage:
     EXECUTE dbo.GetRecipe

\*--------------------------------------------------------------*/
CREATE OR ALTER PROCEDURE dbo.GetRecipe

AS

     IF ((SELECT IsActive FROM dbo.FeatureFlag WHERE FeatureFlagID = 947) = 1)
          BEGIN
```

```
            SELECT
                    RecipeID,
                    RecipeName,
                    RecipeDescription,
                    ServingQuantity,
                    MealTypeID,
                    PreparationTypeID,
                    IsActive,
                    DateCreated,
                    DateModified
            FROM dbo.Recipe
            WHERE IsActive = 1;
        END
    ELSE
        BEGIN
            SELECT
                    RecipeID,
                    RecipeName,
                    RecipeDescription,
                    ServingQuantity,
                    MealTypeID,
                    PreparationTypeID,
                    IsActive,
                    DateCreated,
                    DateModified
            FROM dbo.Recipe;
        END
```

The first portion of this query will now only return results if Feature Flag 947 is enabled. For any other scenario, the stored procedure will return the results from the second query. The original state for the feature flag is to be disabled. When the feature flag is disabled, all recipes will be returned. Once this code has been deployed to Production, there will come a time where you are ready to enable the new functionality. When that happens, running the T-SQL code in Listing 12-5 will enable the feature flag.

Listing 12-5. Enable Feature Flag

```
UPDATE dbo.FeatureFlag
SET    IsActive = 1,
       DateModified = GETDATE()
WHERE FeatureFlagID = 947;
```

Enabling this feature flag will cause the stored procedure dbo.GetRecipe to now only return active recipes.

Once you are confident that the new code is working as intended and there is no business need to roll back, you will want to update the stored procedure to only return results for the new database code. Removing the feature flag will also protect this stored procedure from returning inaccurate results if the feature flag gets updated in error. The T-SQL code in Listing 12-6 shows the final state of the dbo.GetRecipe stored procedure.

Listing 12-6. Final Stored Procedure

```
/*----------------------------------------------------------------*\
Name:            dbo.GetRecipe
Author:          Elizabeth Noble
Created Date:    April 20, 2019
Description: Get a list of all recipes in the database

Updated Date:    May 20, 2019
Description: Add feature flag. If feature flag is enabled, only
    Show active recipes. Otherwise, show all recipes.

Updated Date:    June 20, 2019
Description: Remove the feature flag. Leave only the new logic.
    The stored procedure now only returns active recipes.

Sample Usage:
    EXECUTE dbo.GetRecipe

\*----------------------------------------------------------------*/
CREATE OR ALTER PROCEDURE dbo.GetRecipe

AS
```

```
SELECT
        RecipeID,
        RecipeName,
        RecipeDescription,
        ServingQuantity,
        MealTypeID,
        PreparationTypeID,
        IsActive,
        DateCreated,
        DateModified
FROM dbo.Recipe
WHERE IsActive = 1;
```

The database code in the stored procedure dbo.GetRecipe has been updated. Before any code changes, this stored procedure returned all recipes. After creating the feature flag, the stored procedure was updated to include logic to either return all recipes or only active recipes depending on the feature flag status. When the changes have been confirmed, you can remove the logic for the feature flag. This will leave the stored procedure in place with only the updated T-SQL code.

Depending on how you manage your branching and merging in source control may determine how frequently you need to deploy database code that is incomplete. You may find yourself in a situation where you are working on developing database code, but it is not complete before your next deployment. It is often easiest to write code in a way that it can be deployed when it is completed. However, with the move toward Agile software development, it has become increasingly important to write T-SQL code in a manner where it can be deployed at any moment in time. This is where the true benefit of feature flags can be realized.

Methodology

Each development environment is different. Before deciding how to deploy T-SQL code, it will help to get a better understanding of how development is handled at your company. You will want to know how many database developers are at your company and how many different development teams use SQL Server. Another factor that you will want to know is how those development teams write and deploy code. Collecting all this information will help you determine the best method to deploy T-SQL code that will work for your environment.

When working with SQL Server, often the risks associated with code issues can be larger than with application code. These risks are compounded when there are multiple individuals accessing the same T-SQL code. If you are in an environment where you are the only database developer, there may be less of a chance of having issues with merge conflicts. If there are multiple database developers or teams that may be writing T-SQL code, there is more of a chance to have more than one person working on the same database code. While some of this can be managed through source control, it is also important to be mindful of how database code is deployed.

There are several different ways that database development teams can manage their workflows. Depending on the methodology that is used can contribute to what type of deployment method should be used. My first job that involved consistently writing database code did not have any strict timelines. The goal was to make changes and deploy them as quickly as possible. This is often because I was creating SSRS reports. Typically, this type of development can be referred to as Kanban. I have also worked in environments where changes to the database were only deployed as part of a full sprint cycle. For these deployments, all user stories in the Sprint were deployed as part of the Sprint. While there are some ways to deploy everything in a Sprint without changing functionality, our code was often not written that way. If your business is trying to move toward being able to deploy changes at any point in time, you want to consider changing how you develop your database code. This change can be a shift in how you think about your solutions and how you write your code. Concepts like using feature flags will help you. Essentially you want to write your T-SQL code in a way that it can be deployed at any point in time and your applications will not break. However, to get to this point requires several fundamental steps. The first of which is knowing how your company develops your T-SQL code. You may want to handle deployments differently if you have many developers working on T-SQL code for a single application than if you have each developer working on a separate application. This will help you determine what method of deployment will work best for you.

Part of determining your deployment method will include understanding the current process you use to deploy your database code. Right now, your business may have scripts that are manually deployed. Depending on your organizational structure, you may have an environment where those scripts can be deployed at any point in time to a specific environment or you may have conditions about what days of the week those T-SQL scripts can be deployed. If there are certain days that you can deploy to various environments, this is known as a gated deployment. You may be using database projects in a version control system. In Chapter 10, the topic of branching and merging was covered. Your company may only use one branch for your database project. All development work by all individuals is done in the same place. On the other hand, your company may utilize branching. This is where your developers use a copy of the main code base and make changes to that copy. Some companies may choose to deploy directly from a branch. This can be particularly helpful if you are not writing your database code to be able to be deployed at any point in time. Other companies particularly those who are writing code to be deployed at any point in time may choose to have all branches merged back to master or the main branch once the work is complete. In this case, all deployments would be from the main branch.

Sometimes how teams manage their workflows is determined by the frequency of their deployments. For many companies, the goal is to be able to deploy frequently. However, that does not mean that every company is ready for that frequency of deployments. For the development teams that are writing code in a more Kanban style, there may be no pattern for when code is deployed to Production. Other teams may have a set cadence or sprint cycle for when they deploy their code. These Sprint cycles can range from weeks to months. If your company is still in the process of determining how often to release code, I would caution against longer Sprint cycles as it often means more changes are being deployed at once. This increases the risk of having issues in your deployment.

You will also want to understand the volume of database changes happening on an average deployment. You may find that on average there are not that many database changes getting deployed every Sprint. If this is the case, you will want to make sure you do not end up having a deployment with a significant number of database changes. When there are multiple changes happening to the database during a single deployment, there is not only a greater risk of having a bug, but there is also the possibility depending on your deployment method that one change to T-SQL code may overwrite another.

Before getting into two of the main methods of deploying database code, there is one additional factor you should consider. While we all want every database deployment to go out and work as expected, there may come a time where you need to undo or roll back one or more database changes from a deployment. I would recommend that if you do not have a rollback strategy in place, now is a good time to start considering a solid rollback strategy. Often when a rollback is needed is not the time that you want to start figuring out how to quickly and effectively roll back your T-SQL code. Having a method to do this repeatedly can significantly help increase the confidence you have in your deployments. Your company may use rollback scripts to streamline when you need to revert to the previous version of database code. If you are using version control, you have the option to revert to a different version of your database code. To build upon that if you are using continuous integration, you may have a prepackaged version of the previous database code that can be deployed against your Production database in a manner of minutes.

This ultimately leads us to consider the deployment methods commonly used for database deployments. One such method consists of bundling all the scripts that will be deployed together. This is considered a migration-based approach; another option is to take everything that is existing in source control and treated as the source of truth for your database. When using this type of method, whatever database you are deploying to will be overwritten to match the database objects that exist in source control. This is commonly called a state-based deployment. The information collected so far about who is developing database code, how those changes are coded and managed, and the frequency of your deployments can help you determine whether a migration or state-based approach is best for you.

Now that we know what the migration-based deployment method is, we can start trying to determine if that is the best method for our deployments. One of the main benefits of using the migration-based approach is that you can control exactly what is deployed to your database. This method of deployment often involves having all the scripts that will be deployed saved in a single location, and these scripts are usually named in a way that allows them to be deployed in a specific order. This can make your deployments easy to manage. You can quickly look at the folder where the scripts are saved and know exactly what is getting deployed.

If you use this deployment method, I recommend that you have a separate folder that keeps track of the rollback scripts that need to be deployed and the order in which these rollback scripts should be deployed. This will not only help if you have to roll back on deployment night, but it should help you quickly find the code that needs to be rolled back if you need to roll back several deployments at once. There are some limitations with the migration-based deployment method. One of the main challenges is if you need to roll back a specific piece of code. Depending on how your source control is managed, it may not be as simple as viewing the history of that database object and restoring a previous version from source control.

Using a migration-based deployment method can be set up manually. The rest of your team and you can write your T-SQL code files and save them in numerical order. This really consists of creating a script in SQL Server Management Studio and saving the file with a specific naming convention. This naming convention would include specifying the deployment order such as prefixing the filename with the step number to indicate the deployment order.

If I were to update the query in Listing 12-1 to match the query in Listing 12-6, I would create a SQL file with these changes. I may choose to name this file 001_20190723-2023_ActiveRecipe.sql. However, I may then receive a request to make additional modifications to the same stored procedure. In this case, I need to remove the date columns from the stored procedure dbo.GetRecipe. In Listing 12-7, you can see the new T-SQL code.

Listing 12-7. Sample Script for Migration-Based Deployment

```
-- <Migration ID="68feb116-9776-4168-9d77-b6d28c0f43f9" />
GO

GO
PRINT N'Altering [dbo].[GetRecipe]...';

GO
/*-------------------------------------------------------------*\
Name:          dbo.GetRecipe
Author:        Elizabeth Noble
Created Date:  April 20, 2019
Description: Get a list of all recipes in the database

Updated Date:    July 23, 2019
Description: Remove inactive recipes

Updated Date:    July 23, 2019
Description: Remove DateCreated and DateModified columns

Sample Usage:
       EXECUTE dbo.GetRecipe
```

```
\*------------------------------------------------------------*/
ALTER PROCEDURE dbo.GetRecipe

AS

    SELECT
        RecipeID,
        RecipeName,
        RecipeDescription,
        ServingQuantity,
        MealTypeID,
        PreparationTypeID,
        IsActive
    FROM dbo.Recipe
    WHERE IsActive = 1;
GO
```

Once I have completed my changes to the database code, I can save this code as a SQL script. I will save this code with the filename 002_20190723_2024_RemoteDates.sql. In order to make sure that my deployment runs smoothly, I can put both files in the same folder. Figure 12-1 shows the two files as they would be displayed in a file folder.

Name	Date modified	Type	Size
001_20190723-2023_ActiveRecipe	7/23/2019 8:23 PM	Microsoft SQL Server Query File	1 KB
002_20190723-2024_RemoveDates	7/23/2019 8:24 PM	Microsoft SQL Server Query File	1 KB

Figure 12-1. *Migration-Based File List*

The first script that I created begins with 001. This is the first script in order by filename. This is also the first script that should be run during the next deployment. The second script that I created begins with 002. This will be the second script that will be run during the next deployment. Writing T-SQL scripts and saving them manually is not the only method that can be used as part of migration-based deployments. You also have third-party tools that can help manage this process for you.

There are many proponents of migration-based deployments. One of the main challenges in developing any database code is managing how the code is maintained when multiple developers are working off the same code base. In Chapter 10, I covered branching and merging. This is the main method used to make sure that everyone developing T-SQL code for the database project can work in a manner that limits inconsistencies when multiple developers are working on the same database object. If you are working with a team that is not accustomed to source control, using a migration-based approach may be more logical. A migration-based deployment process is better suited to handle multiple changes to the data in your database. This can be part of a data cleanup or related to re-factoring database objects. Another advantage of using a migration-based deployment method is that it can be easier to pick and choose exactly what database objects will be deployed. If you make frequent changes to your databases, you may end up with many scripts that may increase the amount of time required for deployment.

Due to these factors, there are some scenarios where you may find a migration-based deployment is more effective than a state-based deployment. Smaller development teams may find a migration-based approach easier to use. If you are using source control for your database, you will still need to make sure that your team frequently pulls down the latest version of database code for their development. The same may also be true for environments that have fewer development teams. If your team is not doing frequent deployments during the same day or has a larger maintenance window available for deployments, then the migration-based deployment method may also work well for you.

The one risk you will need to keep in mind when using a migration-based approach involves database changes that happen outside of source control. You may find yourself in a situation where you need to deploy a change immediately to production. Often these changes are deployed to production without having these changes deployed to the lower environments or checked into source control. If you need to deploy a hotfix or a patch and this code does not end up in your source control, you may end up with your environments being out of sync. While future deployments will not overwrite your changes, you may find inconsistent behavior between your environments.

Migration-based deployments are not the only option available when deploying your T-SQL code. Another popular option for database deployments involves using a source for your database schema and updating your target environment to have that same database schema. This is what is known as a state-based approach. Typically, this is used with source control, but that is all not always necessary. The concept is that the target database will end up looking like the source database or source control once the deployment is complete. This method does not require source control, but it is easier to manage through source control.

Whereas each change is saved individually in its own script file when using the migration-based approach, this is not the case for a state-based deployment. In a state-based deployment, you can have many changes to the same database object, but there will only be one set of T-SQL code that is deployed to your target database instance. This single T-SQL script will combine all the changes into one net change. If the database object is in source control or the source database is different from the target, the change script will be run on the target instance. I also like the fact that I know exactly what state the database will be in once a deployment is complete. The database in the target instance should have the same database objects that exist in the source location after the deployment is complete.

Using the same example as the one for the migration-based approach, I will walk through how this is handled as part of the state-based deployment. The first step will involve going into source control and making sure that you have the latest version. Once you have the latest version, you can open the stored procedure dbo.GetRecipe. When you open this SQL script originally, you will see the code as shown in Listing 12-1. You can make the necessary modifications so that the T-SQL code matches Listing 12-6. After you have made these changes, you can check these changes into source control. Suppose someone else will be making the changes to match the T-SQL code in Listing 12-7. This developer will also need to pull down the latest version of source control. They can then make changes to the dbo.GetRecipe stored procedure. These changes can then be merged back into the master branch. When it is time to deploy this code, the source location will have both changes. These changes will be to only show active recipes and to remove the date columns. Instead of deploying these changes one at a time, the stored procedure dbo.GetRecipe will be deployed to the target instance once. This single update to the stored procedure will include both changes.

Working with many developers or many different development teams there may be a benefit from using a state-based deployment method. This is due to the frequency of changes that may be happening in the overall database project. While the state-based migration can work for database projects that have a few or many changes, this deployment method is better at managing frequent changes. When using the state-based approach, you can be confident that any changes in your source location will exist in your target location after the deployment is complete. This also means that if there are many changes made to Production that were not put into source control, then these changes will be overwritten during the next deployment. If your team is performing frequent updates especially throughout the day, you may find the state-based approach takes less time for a deployment. At the very least, this is since there are usually less changes being deployed through the state-based approach when there are frequent deployments.

One of the largest challenges in using the state-based approach has to do with deploying data manipulation changes. The state-based approach is excellent for comparing the overall database schema. However, there are limitations when it comes to changing the data within the database. In most cases, this is done through manual files that may be executed after the deployment. If you are using source control, these can be managed through the pre-deployment and post-deployment scripts. There is only one pre-deployment and one post-deployment script if you are using source control. This can make the process of changing data somewhat more complicated as you will either need to write your T-SQL code to be able to run once and then be ignored or go into source control and frequently change either your pre-deployment or post-deployment script.

Automated Deployment

There are many ways to handle your database deployments. You have various options available to you to help automate these deployments. There are not only different tools you can use to automate your database deployments, there are also different deployment strategies that you can use. Determining what method to use for your database deployments depends on what types of issues you are trying to prevent or resolve. Some of these deployment strategies will depend on what type of T-SQL code is being deployed. Other methods of deploying database code involve deploying your database in a way that can help you catch issues in production before the changes are deployed everywhere.

There are ways to streamline and automate deploying T-SQL code using SQL Server Management Studio, Visual Studio, or PowerShell. If you want to try to automate your database deployments without having your database in source control, you will want to take some additional steps to protect your database. Your T-SQL code should already be written in a way to allow your database code to be run more than once. This may not be the method that you are using now, but you should consider what would happen if someone accidentally tried to deploy the same scripts again. Write your scripts so that they will run successfully no matter how many times they are executed. If you are using source control already, your source control should manage this functionality for you.

When deploying T-SQL code as part of a migration-based deployment, the process may function differently if you are not using source control. For migration-based deployments, you will usually have a set of scripts that need to be run for your deployment. I have found that when you are not using source control, the most complicated step can sometimes be determining exactly what should be deployed. When you are ready to deploy your T-SQL code, ideally the scripts will be saved in the same folder. At this point, you can either manually run all these migration scripts or see what you can do to automate running the scripts. If you choose to run the scripts manually, you will need to open each script and make sure that you are connected to the correct instance of SQL Server. There are other options you can use to improve the consistency and speed of deploying these migration scripts. Using batch files or PowerShell can help you automate these deployments.

If you are using a state-based migration approach and you are not using source control, it can be a little trickier to manage your deployments. The process of having a state-based deployment without using third-party tools consists of using data-tier applications also known as DACPACs. These DACPACs can be generated from a database that already exists and an instance of SQL Server. There is a tool that comes with SQL Server that will help you generate these DACPACs. The tool that you will be using is an executable file named SQLPackage.exe. When using SQL package, you can generate a DACPAC from an existing database. SQL Server has the functionality that allows you to compare this DACPAC to a different database. Depending on how you choose to work with DACPACs, you can either have the target database updated to match the code from the DACPAC or you can create a script file based off the differences between the DACPAC and the target database.

The easiest way to move towards a fully automated deployment is to use third-party tools. However, that is not the only option available to you. If you are interested in migration-based deployments, there is at least one free third-party tool available. This would be DbUp. While this tool may be helpful for managing migration-based deployments, I will not be covering DbUp as part of this book. Be aware that if you are going to use migration-based deployments and source control, you will need an extension or another tool like DbUp.

If your database is in source control and you are using state-based migrations, you have several alternatives you can use to deploy your database changes. You have the option of deploying the changes directly from Visual Studio to your target database instance. However, this does not get you any closer to automating your deployments. Without using third-party tools to automate your deployments, you will need to work on creating PowerShell scripts to create the DACPAC or SQL script file and deploying those files to the target instance.

In the previous section of deployment methods, I went over migration-based and state-based deployments. When deploying changes to the data within a database, you often want to make certain that you cannot accidentally update this data more than once. While we may want to make sure that every script can be written in a way where they could not update the data more than once, there may be times where it is not possible to write a script to prevent this from happening. If this happens, you can use a similar concept to the feature flags. This is where you create a table to record when a data modification script has been run. The first time this script completes, the table can be updated with a value indicating that all records were updated. The script that is run can also check to make sure that this value does not exist in the table prior to running the script. This table can also be checked and populated either as pass or fail for the entire T-SQL script or each individual record can be recorded when the update is complete.

You may also find that there are times where database code is ready to be deployed but the business is not ready to enable the new functionality. Earlier in this chapter, we covered how feature flags can help us control whether applications use the current state or future state of database code. There is a deployment method that can help in these situations. The largest advantage here is that you can deploy database code without having your applications use this new T-SQL code. Depending on the database objects that are changing, this can be relatively easy or difficult to manage.

When you want to deploy T-SQL code changes, but you are not ready for those changes to be released to the Production environment, you can use a deployment method to help you. The deployment method you will want to use is referred to as dark deployment. This method will use a feature flag or a similar concept. You will deploy T-SQL code so that the database code continues to function as it always has. When you are ready to enable the new functionality, you can enable the feature flags. This will switch how the database code works so that it uses the new functionality instead of the original database code.

The beginning state of the application and the database is shown in Figure 12-2.

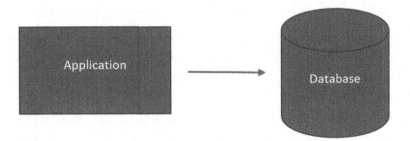

Figure 12-2. *Unmodified Application and Database*

The next step in a dark deployment is to update the database by deploying the SQL scripts. If you are using feature flags, the feature flags should be disabled. The database in Figure 12-3 has been updated with the new database code.

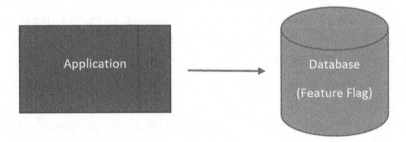

Figure 12-3. *Deploy Database Changes*

After the T-SQL code with feature flags has been deployed, you are now ready to deploy the application. Once you deploy the application and enable the feature flag, your application and database will be in the same state as Figure 12-4.

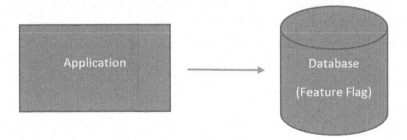

Figure 12-4. *Deploy Application and Enable Feature Flags*

These steps can allow you to deploy your database changes dark.

There are many risks involved with database deployments. These risks can involve T-SQL code or application code that no longer work as expected. There are also risks that the same code may appear to work but does not work as expected. In some cases, this issue may be cosmetic. There are other times that a bug that is introduced into database code may negatively affect the quality of the data that is saved in the database. This can include altering the data in a way that the data is no longer usable. In order to avoid these types of scenarios, there are different deployment methods that can be used to protect the database and the applications.

One potential deployment method is where one set of hardware is swapped out for a set of hardware with the updated software. This type of deployment method is known as blue-green. This can work well for applications, but this can be more difficult when databases are involved. If your application is only using a database to read data, you can use the blue-green method as is. However, since the concept is to replace the code entirely, this does not work well for databases that need to allow for write activity. There is a modified version of the blue-green method that can be used for databases. In this method, you would still have two sets of applications: the original application and the new application.

During the time that users were connecting to the original application, you would deploy any scripts that could be updated and still allow the original application to work as intended. If you were using feature flags, you could deploy those database objects that were using feature flags. Once you were ready to start using the new application code, you could update the stored procedures to start using the feature flags for the new application code. After you were confident that the updates to the applications and the database code were working as intended, you could remove the feature flags. At this point, you would have transitioned entirely over to the new application code, and all feature flags would be removed from the T-SQL code.

The initial state for your blue-green deployment is shown in Figure 12-5.

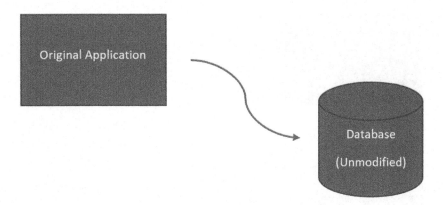

Figure 12-5. *Unmodified Application and Database*

The application and the database are both unmodified before the deployment. The next step in a blue-green database deployment is to deploy the database changes that will work for either the original or new application. An image of the database having some changes applied is shown in Figure 12-6.

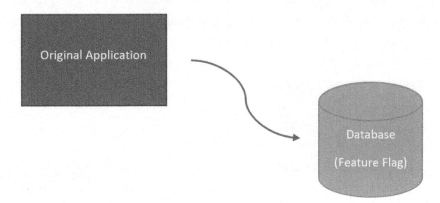

Figure 12-6. *Deploy Database Changes*

The original application will continue to connect to the modified database. The blue-green deployment method is based on the concept of replacing code not overwriting code. In order to follow this deployment method, you will want to stand up the hardware and software needed for the new application. Figure 12-7 shows the state of the database and the updated application.

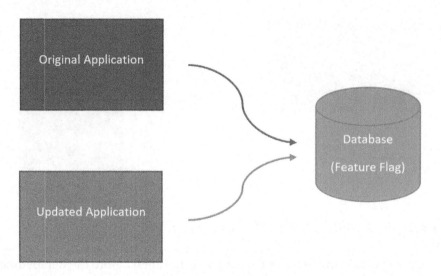

Figure 12-7. *Deploy New Application*

With the feature flags in place, both applications will continue to function in the same manner as the original application. Now that the application code is ready, the feature flags can be enabled in the database. The image in Figure 12-8 shows the updated application connecting to the updated database.

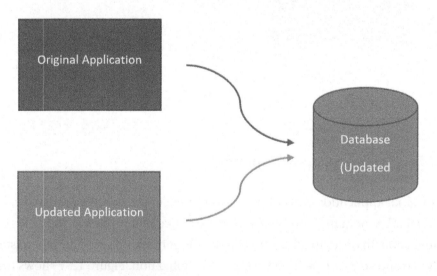

Figure 12-8. *Remove Feature Flags*

The updated application and database are up and running, and the original application has been decommissioned. The new state looks like the image in Figure 12-9.

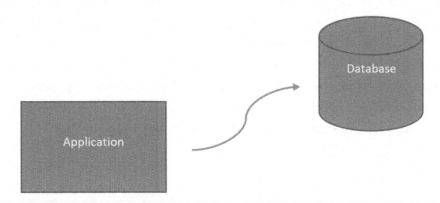

Figure 12-9. *Remove Original Application*

This is the process that you can use for a blue-green deployment. This deployment method lets you manage how you deploy and enable your new database code.

While impacting the quality of the data is one issue, there are also concerns related to the performance of changes that are made to the database code. In some cases, database objects may be added or modified in a way that causes a severe degradation of performance. Depending on how the applications are configured, this can cause the applications to fail. There are some deployment strategies that can be implemented to help identify potential performance issues before they are visible to the end users.

You may also want to try to test your new code before letting everyone use the new T-SQL code. It is possible to get a general idea of the performance of your T-SQL code by using a separate database where the changes to the T-SQL code have been applied. Due to the nature of SQL Server at this time, you will only be able to test read transactions on this secondary database. When you use this method, you are using a canary deployment method. The concept is that the application will connect to both databases. The second database will only perform read transactions. With additional hardware, you can have most of the transactions sent to the original database and a small portion of the activity sent to the second database. As you gain confidence in the new T-SQL code, you can increase the volume of activity sent to second database.

When designing code that is deployable, you want to start at the very beginning. You must understand how your teams are structured, your development cycle, and when your code is deployed across your environments. The goal is to write maintainable and manageable T-SQL code. You can choose to deploy your T-SQL code using a migration-based approach where you can control exactly what is getting deployed to your environments. You could instead choose to use a state-based deployment method where you control what your database will look like after the deployment. You also have the option to determine how to handle developing code that is not ready to be deployed. Using branching and merging strategies, you can keep the code that is in development separate from the code that will be deployed. There is also the option of using feature flags so that you can deploy code at any point in time and control when the new functionality is enabled. Regardless of the methods you choose, you will want to determine a deployment strategy that can be defined and is repeatable.

PART IV

Building Maintainable T-SQL

CHAPTER 13

Functional Design

Over the course of this book, we have covered many different topics. Most of these chapters involve best practices. These best practices involve naming conventions, formatting T-SQL code, or designing database objects. Despite your best efforts, you may find yourself in a situation that is outside the scope of best practices. These times can correlate to periods of high stress or tight deadlines. The goal of this chapter is to help you prepare for the situations when you must make quick decisions about complex topics.

Designing database code for applications that are created to let users insert or update data can be challenging. You may find yourself dealing with applications where you need to disable permissions or functionality. When dealing with legacy application code, there may be additional challenges particularly if those applications are using ORM software. As organizations grow, there may be a need for additional reporting, but there may not be the time required to develop a data warehouse. Within SQL Server, there is the ability to make your T-SQL code more flexible, but you will want to ensure that you do not sacrifice functionality at the cost of flexibility.

Inserting and Updating Data

There are a variety of scenarios where you would want the ability to pass in a set of values. If the records do not exist, you may want to insert the information, but if the record does exist, then you may want to update that record. Often when we are under pressure, we look for the fastest, easiest way to do things. Other times, we may be focused more on T-SQL code readability than what is best for the database engine. While it is important to ensure that your database code can be understood by others, it is equally as important to consider the performance of your database code when writing T-SQL.

© Elizabeth Noble 2020
E. Noble, *Pro T-SQL 2019*, https://doi.org/10.1007/978-1-4842-5590-2_13

This can be equally true when using T-SQL to insert or update database records. It may be easier and more straightforward for an application to execute the same stored procedure regardless of whether the user is inserting a new record or updating an existing record. This type of action can also be referred to as an upsert. It does not matter how you find yourself in the situation; the important thing is to design T-SQL code that works reliably and effectively.

There is T-SQL database code that can make the process of performing an insert or an update simple to write. This functionality is called a MERGE statement. The benefit of using this MERGE statement is that the logic is straightforward. However, there are many known issues with the MERGE statement. I would suggest not using a MERGE statement unless you are willing to accept those potential issues. In Listing 13-1, there is an example of a MERGE statement.

Listing 13-1. Stored Procedure with a Merge Statement

```
CREATE PROCEDURE dbo.RecipeUpsert
     @RecipeID INT,
     @RecipeName VARCHAR(25),
     @RecipeDescription VARCHAR(50),
     @ServingQuantity TINYINT,
     @MealTypeID TINYINT,
     @PreparationTypeID TINYINT,
     @IsActive BIT,
     @DateCreated DATETIME,
     @DateModified DATETIME
AS

MERGE dbo.Recipe AS [Target]
USING
(VALUES
     (
          @RecipeID,
          @RecipeName,
          @RecipeDescription,
          @ServingQuantity,
          @MealTypeID,
          @PreparationTypeID,
```

```
            @IsActive,
            @DateCreated,
            @DateModified
      )
) AS [Source]
      (
            RecipeID,
            RecipeName,
            RecipeDescription,
            ServingQuantity,
            MealTypeID,
            PreparationTypeID,
            IsActive,
            DateCreated,
            DateModified
      )
ON ([Target].RecipeID = [Source].RecipeID)
WHEN MATCHED THEN
      UPDATE SET
            [Target].RecipeName = [Source].RecipeName,
            [Target].RecipeDescription = [Source].RecipeDescription,
            [Target].ServingQuantity = [Source].ServingQuantity,
            [Target].MealTypeID = [Source].MealTypeID,
            [Target].PreparationTypeID = [Source].PreparationTypeID,
            [Target].IsActive = [Source].IsActive,
            [Target].DateCreated = [Source].DateCreated,
            [Target].DateModified = [Source].DateModified
WHEN NOT MATCHED BY TARGET THEN
      INSERT (
            RecipeID,
            RecipeName,
            RecipeDescription,
            ServingQuantity,
            MealTypeID,
            PreparationTypeID,
```

```
            IsActive,
            DateCreated,
            DateModified
            )
    VALUES (
            [Source].RecipeID,
            [Source].RecipeName,
            [Source].RecipeDescription,
            [Source].ServingQuantity,
            [Source].MealTypeID,
            [Source].PreparationTypeID,
            [Source].IsActive,
            [Source].DateCreated,
            [Source].DateModified
            );
```

The preceding MERGE statement updates a recipe if the recipe already exists in the dbo.Recipe table. The logic for this MERGE statement is easy to follow, and the format can be easy to write. There are several known issues with using MERGE statements. You will want to be aware of these issues before implementing MERGE statements in your environment.

I once implemented MERGE statements before fully understanding the issues these statements presented. When I tried to replace the MERGE statements, there were concerns that the logic would be too difficult. To replace the logic from Listing 13-1, you can write a query like the one in Listing 13-2.

Listing 13-2. Store Procedure to Insert or Update

```
CREATE PROCEDURE dbo.RecipeUpsert
    @RecipeID INT,
    @RecipeName VARCHAR(25),
    @RecipeDescription VARCHAR(50),
    @ServingQuantity TINYINT,
    @MealTypeID TINYINT,
    @PreparationTypeID TINYINT,
    @IsActive BIT,
```

```
        @DateCreated DATETIME,
        @DateModified DATETIME
AS

IF EXISTS (SELECT RecipeID FROM dbo.Recipe WHERE RecipeID = @RecipeID)
      BEGIN
            UPDATE dbo.Recipe
            SET    RecipeName = @RecipeName,
                   RecipeDescription = @RecipeDescription,
                   ServingQuantity = @ServingQuantity,
                   MealTypeID = @MealTypeID,
                   PreparationTypeID = @PreparationTypeID,
                   IsActive = @IsActive,
                   DateModified = @DateModified
            WHERE RecipeID = @RecipeID
      END
ELSE
      BEGIN
            INSERT dbo.Recipe
            (
                   RecipeID,
                   RecipeName,
                   RecipeDescription,
                   ServingQuantity,
                   MealTypeID,
                   PreparationTypeID,
                   IsActive,
                   DateCreated,
                   DateModified
            )
            VALUES
            (
                   @RecipeID,
                   @RecipeName,
                   @RecipeDescription,
```

```
                @ServingQuantity,
                @MealTypeID,
                @PreparationTypeID,
                @IsActive,
                @DateCreated,
                @DateModified
        )
    END
```

Replacing the logic from the MERGE statement, you can use an IF... ELSE statement to control the flow of actions inside the SQL Server query. In Listing 13-2, if the recipe exists in the dbo.Recipe table, the record will update all fields except DateCreated. Otherwise, a new record in dbo.Recipe will be inserted.

MERGE statements are not limited to inserting or updating data in a target table. Using MERGE statements can be expanded to handle other scenarios such as inserting or deleting data. MERGE statements can also be created so that missing records are inserted, changed records are updated, and orphaned records are deleted as part of a single statement. While the data modifications can be combined as part of single statement, you should use caution when using MERGE statements as MERGE statements can be prone to performance issues and data inconsistencies. Due to the ease of writing MERGE statements, it is possible to compare data between two tables in a way that is not efficient for SQL Server. While the tables are only being compared once, if the comparison is not efficient, this can have significant impact on the performance tables being compared. There have also been instances where the unique key violations can occur when using filtered indexes. MERGE statements can also create foreign key constraint violations in specific circumstances. This includes using two tables with foreign key constraints where the foreign key is set to NOCHECK and then rolled back. I suggest researching known issues with MERGE statements and performing adequate testing to confirm the T-SQL code will work as expected. The code in Listing 13-2 shows that it is not overly complex to write code that can handle either an insert or an update. Prior to SQL Server 2019, either the code in Listing 13-1 or Listing 13-2 may have been subject to parameter sniffing. Now that SQL Server 2019 has adaptive joins, this should be less of an issue.

Disable Functionality

When designing applications often the first goal is to focus on meeting the specified requirements. In many cases, the product owners or business units are asking for functionality that they need right now. However, the same individuals do not have your knowledge of application and database development. Therefore, the same people may not request the ability to enable or disable specified functionality upon their request. In this case, functionality can either be considered the ability for a user or a role to perform an action or for an application to behave in a certain way. It may be that they are counting on you to know how they may want to use the same applications in the future.

One of the most frequent things that can be overlooked when designing a new application is the ability to enable or disable certain functionality for a user role. You can tell you are in this situation if the existence of a record in a table means that it is available to the application. For this example, table dbo.Recipe would be created using the T-SQL statement in Listing 13-3.

Listing 13-3.   Create dbo.Recipe Table

```
CREATE TABLE dbo.Recipe
(
        RecipeID            INT         IDENTITY(1,1)       NOT NULL,
        RecipeName          VARCHAR(25)                     NOT NULL,
        RecipeDescription   VARCHAR(50)                     NOT NULL,
        ServingQuantity     TINYINT                         NOT NULL,
        MealTypeID          TINYINT                         NOT NULL,
        PreparationTypeID   TINYINT                         NOT NULL,
        DateCreated         DATETIME2(7)                    NOT NULL,
        DateModified        DATETIME2(7)                    NOT NULL,
        CONSTRAINT PK_Recipe_RecipeID PRIMARY KEY CLUSTERED (RecipeID),
        CONSTRAINT FK_Recipe_MealTypeID FOREIGN KEY (MealTypeID)
              REFERENCES dbo.MealType (MealTypeID),
        CONSTRAINT FK_Recipe_PreparationTypeID FOREIGN KEY (PreparationTypeID)
              REFERENCES dbo.PreparationType (PreparationTypeID)
);
```

In Table 13-1, you can see the records in the dbo.Recipe table.

Table 13-1. *Recipe Table Data*

RecipeID	RecipeName	DateCreated	DateModified
1	Spaghetti	01/02/2018	02/05/2019
2	Lee's Burgers	01/03/2018	02/05/2019
3	Spinach Frittata	01/03/2018	03/16/2019
4	Dinner Rolls	02/01/2018	03/17/2019
5	Brandin's Fried Rice	04/16/2019	06/23/2019

For instance, if a recipe was displayed in an application because it was in the recipe table, this would be a case where you could not control how an application interacted with recipes. The only option you would have to keep a recipe from being used by an application would be to delete the recipe record. This action is referred to as a hard delete.

Depending on what tables you need to delete a record from will depend on whether this deletion may be prevented by foreign key relationships. In these scenarios, you would only have a couple options available. One option would be to drop the foreign keys and then delete the specified record. For this table design, if you wanted to remove Dinner Rolls from being an available recipe, you would need to drop any foreign keys referencing the dbo.Recipe table and then delete the record. The query in Listing 13-4 would drop the foreign key.

Listing 13-4. Drop Foreign Key

```
ALTER TABLE dbo.RecipeIngredient
DROP CONSTRAINT FK_RecipeIngredient_RecipeID;
```

Once any foreign keys that referenced the dbo.Recipe table have been dropped, you would need to remove the recipe record to make sure that it is no longer available. In Listing 13-5 is the statement to remove the specific recipe.

Listing 13-5. Delete Recipe Record

```
DELETE FROM dbo.Recipe
WHERE RecipeName = 'Dinner Rolls';
```

The resulting table would have the records shown in Table 13-2.

Table 13-2. *Recipe Table After Deleting Dinner Rolls*

RecipeID	RecipeName	DateCreated	DateModified
1	Spaghetti	01/02/2018	02/05/2019
2	Lee's Burgers	01/03/2018	02/05/2019
3	Spinach Frittata	01/03/2018	03/16/2019
5	Brandin's Fried Rice	04/16/2019	06/23/2019

There is a significant issue with this method. You should take caution when you are faced with the decision to drop foreign key relationships between tables. This can not only negatively affect query performance but can also affect your data quality. Foreign keys are one of the final pieces that can help ensure that data between your tables remains consistent.

Another possibility would be to insert a dummy record into the table with the foreign key relationship. You can add a recipe to the dbo.Recipe table with the name Inactive Recipe. This can be inserted using the query in Listing 13-6.

Listing 13-6. Insert Dummy Recipe Record

```
SET IDENTITY_INSERT dbo.Recipe ON;

INSERT INTO dbo.Recipe
(
     RecipeID,
     RecipeName,
     RecipeDescription,
     ServingQuantity,
     MealTypeID,
     PreparationTypeID,
     DateCreated,
     DateModified
)
```

```
VALUES
(
    0,
    'Inactive Recipe',
    'Deactivated recipes',
    0,
    0,
    0,
    GETDATE(),
    GETDATE()
);

SET IDENTITY_INSERT dbo.Recipe OFF;
```

Inserting this dummy record into the dbo.Recipe table is only the first step. You would need to update the records in the dbo.RecipeIngredient table for Dinner Rolls to use the RecipeID for Inactive Recipe. The update would be written as shown in Listing 13-7.

Listing 13-7. Add IsActive Column to dbo.Recipe Table

```
UPDATE dbo.RecipeIngredient
SET RecipeID = 0,
    DateModified = GETDATE()
WHERE RecipeID = 4;
```

This may not prevent your application from showing the specific value unless your application has been configured in such a way to always ignore that value. If neither of these options can be used, there is another option available. With this table design involved, another option is to remove the ingredients associated with the recipe Dinner Rolls.

Due to these limitations, the concept of a hard delete may not be ideal for your environment. There are other options available to you. It is possible to design your tables so that you can toggle whether the recipes or ingredients are active. This allows you to enable or disable functionality without deleting the data record. To use this option, you would need the dbo.Recipe table to include a column such as IsActive. To change the table created in Listing 13-3, you would need to execute the query in Listing 13-8.

Listing 13-8. Add IsActive Column to dbo.Recipe Table

```
ALTER TABLE dbo.Recipe
ADD IsActive BIT
CONSTRAINT DF_Recipe_IsActive DEFAULT '1' NOT NULL;
```

This would usually be a value that would indicate a true or false. For SQL Server, that is often represented with a one for true and a zero for false. If you set the IsActive to true and ran a query that filtered results where the IsActive value was true, then you would only see a listing of active recipes. Once you have added the IsActive column to the dbo. Recipe table, you can modify your T-SQL code to display either active or inactive recipes based on how they are written.

You have the option to only show results based on the value assigned to IsActive. When the IsActive value is set to 1, the value is true. If you wanted to only show active recipes, you would modify your T-SQL code to use `IsActive = 1` in the WHERE clause. This also gives you the added ability to have some screens that would only show active recipes and other screens that would only show inactive or disabled recipes.

In addition to disabling or enabling functionalities for users or roles, there are also occasions where you would want to be able to control how an application works. Companies often want to change how their business operates over time. This can usually be done by adding, changing, or removing functionality in the applications that the business uses.

For instance, if a business wants to expand outside of their current market, they may choose to add new functionality to their existing applications. The easiest way to add this new functionality is to add new application code. However, the business may find that this new market or new line of business is not working the way that they intended, and the company decides to roll back this new functionality. Depending on how the code was written, this may be a complex change requiring another code rewrite or a simple change allowing the application to use a different part of the code.

Depending on your business environment, you may find that it is easier to manage the changes in functionality through the database instead of the application code. This is even more likely when you may want functionality to change based on seasonality or by region. This allows you the option to exert finely tuned control that can be changed rapidly. You will want to carefully consider the best place to manage this functionality.

The best advice I have received is to keep business logic in the application when higher-level management will need to sign off on any changes. For business logic that can change rapidly and with little oversight, it may be best to leave the business logic in the database.

If you want to manage some of your application business logic from within the database, you will want to create a table to manage whether certain features are enabled. This table is similar in concept to the table created for feature flags in Chapter 12. If you want to manage the functionality in the database, you may want to create a table like the one in Listing 13-9.

Listing 13-9. Create Application Rule Table

```
CREATE TABLE dbo.ApplicationRule
(
      ApplicationRuleID IDENTITY(1,1) INT        NOT NULL,
      ApplicationRuleDescription       VARCHAR(50) NOT NULL,
      IsActive                          BIT         NOT NULL,
      DateCreated                       DATETIME    NOT NULL,
      DateModified                      DATETIME    NULL,
      CONSTRAINT PK_ApplicationRule_ApplicationRuleID
          PRIMARY KEY CLUSTERED (ApplicationRuleID)
);
```

If you are creating rules for a single, centralized application, this table design will work for your needs. If you are managing multiple applications, you will want to consider how these rules are used by applications. If most or all rules are unique per application, you may want to add a column to this table to indicate the application affected.

There could be a business reason why you may want to toggle your application to show only active recipes or show all recipes. This scenario could happen if there were justifiable business reasons why the application may need to show all recipes or only the active recipes. The value for this rule could be stored in Table 13-3.

Table 13-3. *Application Rule Table*

Application RuleID	ApplicationRule Description	IsActive	DateCreated	DateModifed
1	Show only active recipes	1	04/12/2019	04/12/2019

The entry in this table indicates that only active recipes will be shown when this application rule is enabled. If you want the same application to show all recipes, you would need to update the IsActive value to false. While you could update all your database code and stored procedures to use IF... THEN statements depending on when this application rule is enabled, I would suggest handling this functionality within the application.

This is where it becomes important to develop your code to be flexible. While the topic of this book is not an application code development, you will need a database that works with your application code to handle these scenarios. Conceptually this can work similarly to feature flags as discussed in Chapter 12. This is where you could make a table to store a reference to the specified functionality. In some environments this may be referred to as application rules.

Support Legacy Code

One of the key issues in software development involves dealing with technical debt. Applications are developed over time, and depending on how the applications are developed will determine how easy it can be to maintain them over time. For many organizations, applications are initially developed with a timeline in order to meet the current business needs. This can cause applications to be developed rapidly without having the time to plan for how this application will be supported in the future. This often becomes the single source of tension between development and the database administrators.

The real challenge is that when an application is developed, it usually is not well documented. If the application is not well documented, this can make supporting legacy code even more difficult if the T-SQL queries are saved directly in the application code. If the database code is in the application, it will require more effort not only to locate the specific database code but also to get the database code updated. This is because it is not merely as simple as altering a table or stored procedure to increase the flexibility and maintainability of the T-SQL code.

As businesses grow and change, the same application may need to be modified to handle new functionality. This new functionality may require storing new information. To store this information, you may want to add a column to a table or create a new table entirely. The challenge becomes trying to understand all the items that depend on this table. While you can verify dependencies between database objects, the issue is that you do not know how the application is currently accessing this table. Your applications may be accessing the data table through prepared statements and ad hoc queries. If your application is using prepared statements or ad hoc queries, you may have to change your application code when adding a new column to a table especially if your coding standards do not specify that column names must always be specified with your T-SQL queries.

The concern is how to modify this table without breaking the entire application. There are strategies that can be used to allow you to add new columns to an existing table without breaking existing code. You are looking for a way to both allow existing code to reference the table as is and store this new information in a manner that works with your existing standards. The options that will be discussed in this section are intended to support new functionality on a short-term basis. It is recommended that you update your application code and database objects to remain compliant with best practices.

The simplest option that you can use to allow for additional columns in a table is to create another table with the same primary key as the table you want to modify. In this scenario, you will also need to rename the existing table. In order to prevent existing applications from breaking, you would create a view with the same name as the current table. All queries that would access the original unmodified table will now access this view. When you are ready to update all the application code, the view can be dropped and the table can be renamed back to its original name.

These new columns can be added to this second table. You may find that due to how legacy application code was written, you cannot implement the change from Listing 13-8. You may want to add the IsActive column to the dbo.Recipe table, but your application may have embedded T-SQL queries within the application. Therefore, you may not be certain what will break if you add that new column. Creating a new table dbo.RecipeIsActive in Listing 13-10 is one option.

Listing 13-10. Create Copy of dbo.Recipe Table with IsActive Column

```
CREATE TABLE dbo.RecipeIsActive
(
       RecipeID          INT         IDENTITY(1,1)     NOT NULL,
       RecipeName        VARCHAR(25)                   NOT NULL,
       RecipeDescription VARCHAR(50)                   NOT NULL,
       ServingQuantity   TINYINT                       NOT NULL,
       MealTypeID        TINYINT                       NOT NULL,
       PreparationTypeID TINYINT                       NOT NULL,
       IsActive          BIT
```

```
            CONSTRAINT DF_RecipeIsActive_IsActive
                    DEFAULT 1                                NOT NULL,
    DateCreated       DATETIME2(7)                           NOT NULL,
    DateModified      DATETIME2(7)                           NOT NULL,
    CONSTRAINT PK_RecipeIsActive_RecipeID
            PRIMARY KEY CLUSTERED (RecipeID),
    CONSTRAINT FK_RecipeIsActive_MealTypeID
            FOREIGN KEY (MealTypeID)
            REFERENCES dbo.MealType (MealTypeID),
    CONSTRAINT FK_RecipeIsActive_PreparationTypeID
            FOREIGN KEY (PreparationTypeID)
            REFERENCES dbo.PreparationType (PreparationTypeID)
);
```

You can move all the data from the dbo.Recipe table to the dbo.RecipeIsActive table. To allow the applications to continue to insert or update the data records, you will need to drop the dbo.Recipe table and create a view with the same name. An example of the view is available in Listing 13-11.

Listing 13-11. Create View to Match Original Schema of dbo.Recipe

```
CREATE VIEW dbo.Recipe

AS

    SELECT RecipeID,
            RecipeName,
            RecipeDescription,
            ServingQuantity,
            MealTypeID,
            PreparationTypeID,
            DateCreated,
            DateModified
    FROM dbo.RecipeIsActive;
```

Existing application code can reference the view to select or modify data. This is not an ideal long-term solution and is intended to allow you to move toward the goal of re-factoring your applications to use the new table over time. If you have database code written directly in the application, the transition period needed to drop the view and rename the table back to dbo.Recipe may require additional effort to manage. When determining how to modify your database objects while allowing existing code to function, you want to focus on implementing a solution that will allow you to easily continue to develop T-SQL code going forward.

Besides views, you also have the option to make a new object with the desired specifications. This would be making the same table as in Listing 13-10. You can then add a trigger to allow any data modifications for the original table to be passed into this new database object. You would need to create one DML trigger each for the insert, update, and delete actions. Listing 13-12 shows an example of what the insert trigger would look like.

Listing 13-12. Create Trigger when Records Are Inserted into dbo.Recipe

```
CREATE TRIGGER RecipeInsertRecipeIsActive
ON dbo.Recipe
FOR INSERT
AS

INSERT INTO dbo.RecipeIsActive
(
        RecipeID,
        RecipeName,
        RecipeDescription,
        ServingQuantity,
        MealTypeID,
        PreparationTypeID,
        DateCreated,
        DateModified
)
SELECT
        RecipeID,
        RecipeName,
        RecipeDescription,
        ServingQuantity,
        MealTypeID,
        PreparationTypeID,
```

```
        DateCreated,
        DateModified
FROM inserted;
```

This will allow you to continue using the original database object for all your application code. You can leave this additional table and trigger in place until you are ready to start using the new table in your database code.

In addition to adding new columns, you may want to use some other strategies to refactor tables. This can include increasing the normalization of your databases. It is quite common to come across legacy tables with many more columns than would be expected for a database with a high level of normalization. By creating a space where you can modify the table design and create an abstraction layer, you can modify your database objects without affecting application performance.

Sometimes it is easier to start with your end goal in mind. In this case, we are trying to redesign one legacy table into two or more normalized tables. The idea is to accomplish this while allowing your applications to function as normal. For this example, we have a table like the one from Listing 13-13.

Listing 13-13. Original Denormalized Table

```
CREATE TABLE dbo.Recipe
(
        RecipeID             INT          IDENTITY(1,1)    NOT NULL,
        RecipeName           VARCHAR(25)                   NOT NULL,
        RecipeDescription    VARCHAR(50)                   NOT NULL,
        ServingQuantity      TINYINT                       NOT NULL,
        MealTypeName         VARCHAR(25)                   NOT NULL,
        PreparationTypeName  VARCHAR(25)                   NOT NULL,
        IsActive             BIT
              CONSTRAINT DF_Recipe_IsActive
                    DEFAULT 1                              NOT NULL,
        DateCreated          DATETIME2(7)                  NOT NULL,
        DateModified         DATETIME2(7)                  NOT NULL,
        CONSTRAINT PK_Recipe_RecipeID
              PRIMARY KEY CLUSTERED (RecipeID),
);
```

Once you know which table you would like to normalize, you will want to design the tables you will use to replace this original table. Listing 13-14 below shows an example of the tables that can be created so that you can transition to more normalized data tables.

Listing 13-14. Normalized Table

```
CREATE TABLE dbo.MealType
(
        MealTypeID          TINYINT              IDENTITY(1,1) NOT NULL,
        MealTypeName        VARCHAR(25)                        NOT NULL,
        MealTypeDescription
                            VARCHAR(50)                        NOT NULL,
        IsActive            BIT
            CONSTRAINT DF_MealType_IsActive
                    DEFAULT 1                                  NOT NULL,
        DateCreated         DATETIME2(7)                       NOT NULL,
        DateModified        DATETIME2(7)                       NOT NULL,
        CONSTRAINT PK_MealType_MealTypeID
            PRIMARY KEY CLUSTERED (MealTypeID),
);

CREATE TABLE dbo.PreparationType
(
        PreparationTypeID
                            TINYINT              IDENTITY(1,1) NOT NULL,
        PreparationTypeName
                            VARCHAR(25)                        NOT NULL,
        IsActive            BIT
            CONSTRAINT DF_PreparationType_IsActive
                    DEFAULT 1                                  NOT NULL,
        DateCreated         DATETIME2(7)                       NOT NULL,
        DateModified        DATETIME2(7)                       NOT NULL,
        CONSTRAINT PK_PreparationType_PreparationTypeID
            PRIMARY KEY CLUSTERED (PreparationTypeID),
);
```

```
CREATE TABLE dbo.RecipeModified
(
    RecipeID            INT             IDENTITY(1,1)    NOT NULL,
    RecipeName          VARCHAR(25)                      NOT NULL,
    RecipeDescription   VARCHAR(50)                      NOT NULL,
    ServingQuantity     TINYINT                          NOT NULL,
    MealTypeID          TINYINT                          NOT NULL,
    PreparationTypeID   TINYINT                          NOT NULL,
    IsActive            BIT
        CONSTRAINT DF_ RecipeModified _IsActive
                DEFAULT 1                                NOT NULL,
    DateCreated         DATETIME2(7)                     NOT NULL,
    DateModified        DATETIME2(7)                     NOT NULL,
    CONSTRAINT PK_ RecipeModified _RecipeID
        PRIMARY KEY CLUSTERED (RecipeID),
    CONSTRAINT FK_ RecipeModified _MealTypeID
        FOREIGN KEY (MealTypeID)
        REFERENCES dbo.MealType (MealTypeID),
    CONSTRAINT FK_ RecipeModified _PreparationTypeID
        FOREIGN KEY (PreparationTypeID)
        REFERENCES dbo.PreparationType (PreparationTypeID)
);
```

In the preceding example, if we know that there will be no data modifications to the dbo.MealType and dbo.PreparationType tables, we can also use a view to interact with the dbo.Recipe table. In Listing 13-15, I have created a view to use these new tables.

Listing 13-15. View using Normalized Table

```
CREATE VIEW dbo.Recipe

AS

    SELECT rec.RecipeID,
        rec.RecipeName,
        rec.RecipeDescription,
        rec.ServingQuantity,
```

```
        mtp.MealTypeName,
        prp.PreparationTypeName,
        rec.IsActive,
        rec.DateCreated,
        rec.DateModified
    FROM dbo.RecipeModified rec
        INNER JOIN dbo.MealType mtp
        ON rec.MealTypeID = mtp.MealTypeID
        INNER JOIN dbo.PreparationType prp
        ON rec.PreparationTypeID = prp.PreparationTypeID;
```

Like the logic in Listing 13-11, you can create a view with the name dbo.Recipe so that the applications can interact with the new table going forward. Depending on the purpose of the original and new tables, you may not be able to update all code to use these new tables. If so, you may have to rely on triggers to update these tables.

Reporting on Transactional Data

Most databases used by applications are designed to handle a large volume of transactions. The overall design of these databases is referred to as online transaction processing or OLTP. These databases are usually designed to store and retrieve data quickly. This type of behavior involves many writes to the database. However, your business may ultimately decide that it needs information from this same database that is running one of your applications. Ideally, you would only have your applications accessing databases on your transactional servers. You will want to have a good understanding of your business and the impact your queries will have on application performance. You may be able to run very simple SELECT statements that are only accessing a small set of data without negatively impacting your applications. You should do everything in your power to limit the additional load put on SQL Server for data requests outside of your applications. When large quantities of data are accessed for reporting purposes, this can cause performance degradation of your applications. This includes additional CPU resources to generate execution plans that have been flushed from the cache to make way for running queries for reporting workloads. You may also have issues with application data that exists in memory getting cleared from the buffer pool after large quantities of data have been moved to memory for reporting. These issues can cascade into a scenario where your application performance is affected by reporting workloads. If you find yourself in the situation where you need to report directly from a transactional database, communicate with your management team what kind of impact reporting may have on your applications.

When you need to access data for reporting, you need to have a high number of reads from this same database. This type of behavior happens when you need to report on the data in this database. Aside from the fact that a transactional database is not designed for handling reading large quantities of data as well as it can handle reading very small sets of data, there are other challenges that can happen when using your transactional data for reporting.

In some cases, gathering this reporting data can be simple. There may be a small number of joins or the underlying logic may not be very complex. I have found that you can end up writing a single report, and due to the quality of the report, you may be asked to create additional reports. These additional reports may involve many tables or the overall logic for these queries may be more complex. This can often be because these tables were not designed with reporting in mind. In some cases, you may find that you are being asked to report on data that does not exist.

To develop reports quickly, it is often easiest to write specific logic for each individual report. Over time this can cause you to end up with a significant number of reports that should return the same or similar results but may not. The best-case scenario is that the results are similar but that the underlying code is different. This can get even more complex as the business may change the functionality of some applications. It may be easy to identify some reports that will need to be updated while other reports are missed and start returning inaccurate results.

At some point in time, you may receive a request to generate a report from your transactional data. Often these requests can start out as a simple one-time request for data. In our scenario, a user may want to be able to access the recipe and ingredient information for making spaghetti. While this may start as a request to run a query and get some data, you may find that eventually your users want this report available to be run any time or by a select group of people. At that point in time, you may write a query like the one in Listing 13-16.

Listing 13-16. Spaghetti Ingredients

```
SELECT
     rec.RecipeName,
     rec.RecipeDescription,
     rec.ServingQuantity,
     recing.IsActive,
     ing.IngredientName
FROM dbo.Recipe rec
     INNER JOIN dbo.RecipeIngredient recing
     ON rec.RecipeID = recing.RecipeID
     INNER JOIN dbo.Ingredient ing
     ON recing.IngredientID = ing.IngredientID
WHERE rec.RecipeName = 'Spaghetti';
```

While the specifics of report development is outside of the scope of this book, I have seldom worked in an environment where some type of reporting data was not regularly requested off the transactional databases. The preceding query does not show a stored procedure, but you could just as easily use a stored procedure to select this data. The issue with the query in Listing 13-16 is that it is hard-coded to only return results for the recipe Spaghetti.

Over time, businesses often need different or additional information when it comes to analyzing data. This can come in the format of needing a new report showing information about another recipe. In our example, our users have asked for a report with information about Spinach Frittatas. This could have also been a request to replace the report for Spaghetti with a report for Spinach Frittata. In either scenario, you would need to create a query like the one in Listing 13-17.

Listing 13-17. Spinach Frittata Ingredients

```
SELECT
     rec.RecipeName,
     rec.RecipeDescription,
     rec.ServingQuantity,
     recing.IsActive,
     ing.IngredientName
FROM dbo.Recipe rec
```

```
        INNER JOIN dbo.RecipeIngredient recing
        ON rec.RecipeID = recing.RecipeID
        INNER JOIN dbo.Ingredient ing
        ON recing.IngredientID = ing.IngredientID
WHERE rec.RecipeName = 'Spinach Frittata';
```

While we have met the requirements for creating one report for Spaghetti and new report for Spinach Frittata, we have also added additional overhead to maintaining our reports. The queries from Listings 13-16 and 13-17 are maintained separately. If there are changes to how data is pulled from one report, you would need to remember that the other report may also need to be changed. Our next step would be to analyze these two reports and see if we can create one data set for both reports.

If you find yourself in this situation, the next step is to figure out how to start collapsing the data sets in your reports. You will first want to identify which reports return similar results. These can be reports that deal with the same business application or the same functionality. You will want to create a query that returns all relevant information for that application or functionality. This will be the base data source that you can use to update your existing reports. The query in Listing 13-18 shows one way to write a query that can be used for both reports.

Listing 13-18. Recipe Ingredients from Several Joins

```
DECLARE @RecipeName VARCHAR(25)

SELECT
        rec.RecipeName,
        rec.RecipeDescription,
        rec.ServingQuantity,
        recing.IsActive,
        ing.IngredientName
FROM dbo.Recipe rec
        INNER JOIN dbo.RecipeIngredient recing
        ON rec.RecipeID = recing.RecipeID
        INNER JOIN dbo.Ingredient ing
        ON recing.IngredientID = ing.IngredientID
WHERE rec.RecipeName = @RecipeName;
```

In the preceding query, we are using a parameter @RecipeName. This parameter allows us to set a value for the @RecipeName variable. This value can be changed depending on which report is being run. When it comes to using Report Server, the value for @RecipeName can be set for each report. This type of query can allow you to use a single set of code for multiple types of report. This allows you to use the same query for Spaghetti and Spinach Frittata or a report request for a specific recipe.

Creating the query in Listing 13-17 allows your overall code to be reusable. This can solve one of the issues related to generating reports off transactional data. Another issue that can occur when reporting off transactional data is the intricacy of the logic between the tables. In Listing 13-19, the information about recipes and ingredients has been flattened to more closely align with how a data warehouse is designed.

Listing 13-19. Recipe Information

```
CREATE VIEW dbo.MealTypeInformation

AS

SELECT
      mel.MealTypeName,
      mel.MealTypeDescription,
      prp.PreparationTypeName,
      prp.PreparationTypeDescription,
      rec.RecipeName,
      rec.RecipeDescription,
      rec.ServingQuantity,
      recing.IsActive RecipeIngredientIsActive,
      ing.IngredientName,
      ing.IsActive AS IngredientIsActive
FROM dbo.Recipe rec
      INNER JOIN dbo.MealType mel
      ON rec.MealTypeID = mel.MealTypeID
      INNER JOIN dbo.PreparationType prp
      ON rec.PreparationTypeID = prp.PreparationTypeID
      INNER JOIN dbo.RecipeIngredient recing
      ON rec.RecipeID = recing.RecipeID
      INNER JOIN dbo.Ingredient ing
      ON recing.IngredientID = ing.IngredientID;
```

Like the query in Listing 13-18, the query in Listing 13-19 is designed to allow your T-SQL code to be reusable for a variety of scenarios. The design will decrease the complexity of the logic required for your queries or reports. The query in Listing 13-20 has the same functionality as the query in Listing 13-18.

Listing 13-20. Recipe Ingredients from a View

```
CREATE PROCEDURE dbo.RecipeByRecipeName
     @RecipeName VARCHAR(25)
AS

SELECT
     mtp.RecipeName,
     mtp.RecipeDescription,
     mtp.ServingQuantity,
     mtp.RecipeIngredientIsActive,
     mtp.IngredientName
FROM dbo.MealTypeInformation mtp
WHERE mtp.RecipeName = @RecipeName;
```

The main difference between these two queries is that the overall logic required for Listing 13-20 is much simpler and more straightforward. This can allow less technical users the ability to create reports off this same data set. While this can help keep data consistent and easy to access, this method may not have the best performance. When using this method to access your data for reporting, be sure to monitor performance and confirm that the reports are returning data without timing out.

This base data set can then be used throughout all your reports. Once you have updated the reports to use this base data set, you are now confirming that this data set will be able to handle your reporting needs going forward. This gives you an idea of the structure of the data that you will need if you would like to move toward a data warehouse.

Dynamic SQL

Depending on what T-SQL code you are trying to write, you may find it difficult to write your database code to use set-based design. In those situations, it may be tempting to write your code in a way that is more iterative. You may want to write T-SQL code that is highly variable and can be modified depending on the parameters and values passed into it. Using dynamic SQL may seem like the solution you have been wanting. In most cases, the drawbacks of dynamic SQL can far outweigh the benefits, but there are times where dynamic SQL can be one of the right solutions.

Previously in Chapter 7, I covered how you can read execution plans. When using dynamic SQL, a new execution plan will need to be calculated each time the query is executed. This causes additional strain on the database engine.

Most of the cases where you would want to use dynamic SQL involve times when you need additional flexibility. Many of the times where dynamic SQL is desirable relate to database administration activities. Most of these activities involve performing the same actions on more than one database on the SQL Server instance. There is some additional functionality available with dynamic SQL that can make using dynamic SQL especially appealing.

When executing T-SQL, you cannot use a database name or a table name as a variable in standard T-SQL. Using dynamic SQL gives you the option to write queries that can be executed on more than database object. The query in Listing 13-21 shows an example of dynamic SQL.

Listing 13-21. Dynamically Retrieve Data from Tables

```
CREATE PROCEDURE dbo.TableByDynamicValues
    @TableName VARCHAR(100),
    @ColumnName VARCHAR(25),
    @ColumnValue VARCHAR(25)
AS

DECLARE @ObjectID INT;
DECLARE @ColumnList VARCHAR(500);
DECLARE @Query NVARCHAR(1000);

SELECT @ObjectID = OBJECT_ID(@TableName);
```

```
SELECT @ColumnList = STRING_AGG (ISNULL([name],'*'), ',')
FROM sys.columns
WHERE [object_id] = @ObjectID
      AND [name] NOT IN ('IsActive','DateCreated','DateModified');

SET @Query =
      'SELECT ' + @ColumnList +
      ' FROM ' + @TableName +
      ' WHERE ' + @ColumnName + ' = @ColumnValue';

EXECUTE sp_executesql @Query,
      N'@ColumnName NVARCHAR(25), @ColumnValue NVARCHAR(25)',
      @ColumnName = @ColumnName,
      @ColumnValue = @ColumnValue;
```

The preceding query allows a user or application to pass in a table name. This is the table name that will be queried for values. The other two parameters allow a column name and a column value to be passed in as part of the query. This column name is what will be used to filter the data out. There are some examples of how this code would function in Listing 13-22.

Listing 13-22. Execute Store Procedure with Different Values

```
EXECUTE dbo.TableByDynamicValues 'Recipe', 'RecipeName', 'Spaghetti';
EXECUTE dbo.TableByDynamicValues 'Ingredient', 'IngredientName', 'Tomato
Sauce';
```

There are two occurrences of the same stored procedure in Listing 13-22. The first execution will return results from the Recipe table. The second execution will return results from the Ingredient table. Executing the queries in Listing 13-22, you will get the results in Table 13-4.

Table 13-4. *Application Rule Table*

Recipe ID	Recipe Name	Recipe Description	Serving Quantity	Meal Type ID	Preparation Type ID
1	Spaghetti	Pasta dinner	8	2	1

Ingredient ID	Ingredient Name
2	Tomato Sauce

The first set of data returned are the columns from the Recipe table for the RecipeName of Spaghetti. The stored procedure in Listing 13-21 excludes the columns IsActive, DateCreated, and DateModified. All other columns in the table are returned. The values in the second data set is the record from the Ingredient table for the IngredientName of Tomato Sauce. From a software development perspective, this may seem like the ideal method to use when writing database code.

However, this method of using T-SQL does not take how the database engine executes a query into considerations. This will cause SQL Server to generate a new execution plan each time the stored procedure is executed as the data being requested can change dramatically between each execution. While it may seem like dynamic SQL can help make your application code more flexible, there is a cost to this method of writing T-SQL. In general, I would avoid using dynamic SQL for most scenarios when I would need to write T-SQL code. Trying to write your code without dynamic SQL will encourage you to practice writing database code in a manner that uses the strengths of the SQL Server database engine.

Using dynamic SQL can also increase the risk that additional T-SQL code is executed beyond the purpose you originally intended. This type of behavior is referred to as SQL injection. The concept of SQL injection is that additional T-SQL code is inserted, or injected, into the original statement. The additional T-SQL code that has been inserted allows for functionality that was not originally intended for the query execution. This can include viewing data that should not be accessible to this user. That same user may also be able to modify data or database objects through SQL injection. If you want to use dynamic SQL, you can minimize the risk of SQL injection by using parameters to pass values to the dynamic SQL. The method of parameterizing the dynamic SQL will make it more difficult for users to view or modified data in ways that you did not intend.

When writing T-SQL code, you want to write code that is functional and effective. This means writing code that is readable and maintainable. Writing code that can grow with your business is also a critical skill. If you are writing code to handle inserts and updates or variety of data modifications, you want to make sure you are writing code that is easily understood and supported going forward. During application development, consider how you want to handle disabling permissions or application functionality. If not, you will want to consider strategies that will allow you to deactivate data values in a way that does not break relationships between the tables in your database. You may also have to support legacy code. One of the challenges with supporting legacy code is making changes without breaking existing functionality. There are times you may need to pull data for reporting from your transactional database. Try to design your queries to allow for flexibility and reusability. While flexibility is good, also use caution as to how much flexibility you implement in your T-SQL code. After improving the functionality of your database code, you may find that you want to determine how to track changes to your data.

CHAPTER 14

Logging

During your time working with SQL Server, you will get a wide variety of requests from your company. Some of these requests may involve changing business logic or adding new functionality. There are other times that your company may want to track what happened in the past. There are a variety of third-party tools that can help track performance and other functionality related to database maintenance. However, your business may be interested in tracking data changes or understanding where something went wrong.

This type of logging related to data modifications or error handling can be implemented using T-SQL. When logging these types of changes, you have several options available to you. These options can include minimally logging activity all the way to logging the most granular of activities. You will also want to consider how this information will be accessed and used going forward. This will help you log information in a way that can be beneficial to your organization in the future. This will also prevent you from logging data that ends up never being used.

Data Modification

Choosing a method to track data modifications requires understanding what types of information your organization needs to track. You may want to only log information when something has changed. Depending on your business case, you may need to know not only when something changed but also what changed. There are also a couple options on how you can track these changes. You have the option to either use SQL Server to track these changes for you or you can create database objects that will log this information for you.

One of the things to consider when implementing any sort of logging is the performance overhead. This can be even more critical when tracking data modifications. You will want to make sure that you choose a logging method that allows you to both

345

© Elizabeth Noble 2020
E. Noble, *Pro T-SQL 2019*, https://doi.org/10.1007/978-1-4842-5590-2_14

track the necessary changes and have the expected performance impact. As you may expect, the more detailed logging you implement, the greater the performance overhead.

Out of all the options discussed in this chapter, Change Tracking has the least amount of overhead. If you would like to record more detailed information and you are willing to increase resource utilization, then you may want to consider Change Data Capture. Another possible implementation of tracking change involves using database triggers. While the use of database triggers allows you to more finely tune what is logged and how it is logged, it can come at the cost of even higher resource utilization.

An intermediate option may be using SQL Server Audit depending on the type of data you want to log. SQL Server Audit can be used to track server or database-level activity. In the context of logging changes related to applications, you would want to focus on database audits. The database audit actions within SQL Server Audit can track changes related to all types of data activity including accessing or modifying data. SQL Server uses extended events to monitor the audit activity. The data that can be retrieved includes the time the action happened, information about the user that triggered the audit, and the object affected. It may also be possible to record the statement issued when the audit action took place.

Another minimal logging activity available with regard to data modifications involves logging the most recent time a record was changed and incrementing the number of changes that have occurred for that data record. This type of tracking is handled by Change Tracking within SQL Server. To use Change Tracking, you will first need to enable Change Tracking on the database. Throughout this book, we have been using the Menu database. I will need to run the T-SQL code shown in Listing 14-1 to enable Change Tracking on the Menu database.

Listing 14-1. Enable Change Tracking on Menu Database

```
ALTER DATABASE Menu
SET CHANGE_TRACKING = ON
(CHANGE_RETENTION = 2 DAYS, AUTO_CLEANUP = ON);
```

To enable Change Tracking on the Menu database, you will need to specify the database name and indicate that you want to turn Change Tracking on. The last line in the preceding T-SQL code is optional. These values indicate how long you would like to retain changes and if the retention history should be cleaned up automatically.

Once you have enabled Change Tracking in the Menu data, you are able to configure tables to use Change Tracking. The table where you will implement Change Tracking must have a primary key. If this table does not have a primary key, you will need to add one before you can enable Change Tracking on this table. In our case, I will be enabling Change Tracking on the dbo.Recipe table. Listing 14-2 shows the database code needed to enable Change Tracking on the dbo.Recipe table.

Listing 14-2. Enable Change Tracking on dbo.Recipe Table

```
ALTER TABLE dbo.Recipe
ENABLE CHANGE_TRACKING
WITH (TRACK_COLUMNS_UPDATED = ON);
```

Change Tracking is now enabled on the dbo.Recipe table. Change Tracking can either record that an entire data row has changed or specify that specific columns have changed. When you track column changes, SQL Server will record that a change happened and the specific column or columns that have changed. If you do not specify a value for TRACK_COLUMNS_UPDATED, SQL Server will use the default value of off.

After setting up Change Tracking, you may want to see what kind of information is available or has changed. While the changes in the table dbo.Recipe are tracked by SQL Server, this information is not available from a table that you can see in Object Explorer. Instead, you will need to access the CHANGETABLE associated with the table dbo.Recipe. Once Change Tracking has been enabled, records are initialized and can be found in the CHANGETABLE. The query in Listing 14-3 shows how you would see these initialized records.

Listing 14-3. Query Initialized Records

```
SELECT rec.RecipeID,
       rec.RecipeName,
       rec.RecipeDescription,
       rec.IsActive,
       chng.RecipeID,
       chng.SYS_CHANGE_VERSION,
       chng.SYS_CHANGE_CONTEXT
FROM dbo.Recipe AS rec
       CROSS APPLY CHANGETABLE
       (VERSION Recipe, (RecipeID), (rec.RecipeID)) AS chng;
```

This query will return information from the dbo.Recipe table and information from the CHANGETABLE. Table 14-1 shows an example of the initialized records.

Table 14-1. *Initialized Records*

RecipeID	SYS_CHANGE_VERSION	SYS_CHANGE_CONTEXT
1	NULL	NULL
2	NULL	NULL
3	NULL	NULL
4	NULL	NULL

The records in Table 14-1 are from the CHANGETABLE. There is a column for the RecipeID, the primary key on the table, and columns to track information about the changes. Since none of the data records have been modified, the values are all NULL.

I can modify the records in the table dbo.Recipe. In Listing 14-4, I have updated the DateModified.

Listing 14-4. Update DateModified

```
UPDATE dbo.Recipe
SET DateModified = GETDATE()
WHERE RecipeID = 3;
```

Now that a record has been modified, I can get a better idea of how information is being stored when it comes to Change Tracking. Listing 14-5 shows the query needed to find information about changes to dbo.Recipe that occurred since the last automatic cleanup.

Listing 14-5. Find Changed Records

```
SELECT RecipeID,
    SYS_CHANGE_OPERATION AS ChangeOperation,
    CHANGE_TRACKING_IS_COLUMN_IN_MASK
    (COLUMNPROPERTY
        (OBJECT_ID('Recipe'), 'RecipeName', 'ColumnId'),
    SYS_CHANGE_COLUMNS) AS NameChange,
```

```
CHANGE_TRACKING_IS_COLUMN_IN_MASK
(COLUMNPROPERTY
        (OBJECT_ID('Recipe'), 'RecipeDescription', 'ColumnId'),
SYS_CHANGE_COLUMNS) AS DescChange,
CHANGE_TRACKING_IS_COLUMN_IN_MASK
(COLUMNPROPERTY
        (OBJECT_ID('Recipe'), 'IsActive', 'ColumnId'),
SYS_CHANGE_COLUMNS) AS IsActiveChange,
CHANGE_TRACKING_IS_COLUMN_IN_MASK
(COLUMNPROPERTY
        (OBJECT_ID('Recipe'), 'DateCreated', 'ColumnId'),
SYS_CHANGE_COLUMNS) AS CreateChange,
CHANGE_TRACKING_IS_COLUMN_IN_MASK
(COLUMNPROPERTY
        (OBJECT_ID('Recipe'), 'DateModified', 'ColumnId'),
SYS_CHANGE_COLUMNS) AS ModifiedChange,
SYS_CHANGE_CONTEXT
FROM CHANGETABLE
(CHANGES dbo.Recipe,0) as ChngTbl
ORDER BY SYS_CHANGE_VERSION
```

This version information is needed to find the state of the changes on this table. The query in Listing 14-5 shows you one way that you can use to access this information. Table 14-2 shows the results for the query in Listing 14-5.

Table 14-2. *Change Tracking Result Set*

RecipeID	Change Operation	Name Changed	Desc Changed	IsActive Changed	Created Changed	Modified Changed
3	U	False	False	False	False	True

These results are recorded from the update issued in Listing 14-4.

The RecipeID affected is listed in the first column of Table 14-2. This matches the same RecipeID updated in Listing 14-4. The ChangeOperation is listed as a U for update. This also matches the DML action in Listing 14-4. The final five columns in Table 14-2 were populated using specific functions to unmask the columns indicated in the Change Tracking tables. The function involved returns a true value if the column was modified and a false value if the data was not modified. In the case of Listing 14-4, the only column updated was the DateModified. This matches the result in Table 14-2. The columns NameChange, DescChanged, IsActiveChanged, and CreatedChanged are all false. These values were not changed. However, the column ModifiedChanged is true. This indicates that the column referenced, DateModified, was changed.

There are some potential issues regarding consistency when using Change Tracking. Storing the data does not affect the consistency of the data. The consistency of the data is affected as part of the data retrieval. You can do everything possible to make sure you are looking at the most recent data in the Change Tracking table. This includes checking for the last synchronized version in Change Tracking and confirming that this version is still available. However, if the version in Change Tracking is older than the retention period, this data may be cleaned up before the data can be retrieved. With Change Tracking, you may also have occasions where a data modification occurs after the last synchronization. This can cause additional versions or modified records to be returned. Any of these scenarios can affect the consistency of the data returned with Change Tracking. The best practice to minimize issues with consistency is to use the snapshot isolation level.

If you need to know more than the row or column that was changed and the number of changes that occurred for that record since implementing Change Tracking, you may want to consider Change Data Capture. Like Change Tracking, there are benefits and drawbacks of using Change Data Capture. The single largest benefit is that Change Data Capture will capture the details related to the data record that was changed.

For inserted data, you will be able to see exactly what was added to the table. Similarly, you will be able to see all the columns for a data record that was deleted. When updating data, you will be able to access both the data before and after the update. A downside is that each change to the table requires that at least one record is written to a tracking table. Another downside is that two SQL Server Agent jobs are created for each table that is tracked. As you increase the number of tables under Change Data Capture, the amount of resources used will increase as well. This can cause the performance hit associated with Change Data Capture to be severe enough to prevent you from implementing Change Data Capture.

If you decide to move forward with Change Data Capture, you can update a table in a database to use Change Data Capture. Before doing this, you will need to allow Change Data Capture to occur on your database. You can enable Change Data Capture per database by running the T-SQL code in Listing 14-6.

Listing 14-6. Enable Database Tracking on Menu Database

```
USE Menu;
GO

EXECUTE sys.sp_cdc_enable_db;
GO
```

Now that you have enabled Change Data Capture, you will want to choose a table where you are only concerned with knowing when a record has changed. I will implement Change Data Capture on the table dbo.Recipe. Before enabling Change Data Capture on this table, I will need to make sure that SQL Server Agent is running on this instance. In Listing 14-7, you can see the database code needed to implement Change Data Capture on this table.

Listing 14-7. Enable Database Tracking on dbo.Recipe Table

```
USE Menu;
GO

EXECUTE sys.sp_cdc_enable_table
      @source_schema = 'dbo',
      @source_name = 'Recipe',
      @role_name = NULL;
GO
```

At a minimum you will need to specify the table schema, table name, and the database roles that can access this data. If you specify NULL for the role name, the information recorded by Change Data Capture will be accessible to everyone. Once this table has been enabled for Change Data Capture, I will be able to see the new jobs created in SQL Server Agent. You will receive a message once the T-SQL code in Listing 14-7 completes. You can see an example of this message in Figure 14-1.

```
Job 'cdc.Menu_capture' started successfully.
Job 'cdc.Menu_cleanup' started successfully.
```

Figure 14-1. *Message Showing SQL Server Agent Jobs Created*

The process of enabling Change Data Capture also creates several system tables in the cdc schema. You can see these tables in Figure 14-2, the system tables that were created to manage Change Data Capture.

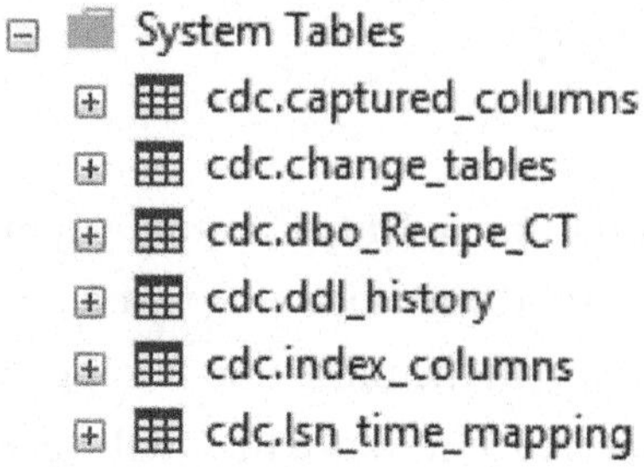

Figure 14-2. *System Tables Created for Change Data Capture*

The table that we will use to track changes on dbo.Recipe is the cdc.dbo_Recipe_CT table.

If you implement Change Data Capture on an empty table, you will be able to track when your data records have changed but you will also be able to track the number of changes that happen since the table was created. In Listing 14-8, I have written a script to insert records into dbo.Recipe.

Listing 14-8. Insert Records into dbo.Recipe

```
INSERT INTO dbo.Recipe
(
    RecipeName,
    RecipeDescription,
    ServingQuantity,
    MealTypeID,
    PreparationTypeID,
    IsActive,
    DateCreated,
    DateModified
)
VALUES
(
    'Lee"s Hamburgers',
    'The best hamburgers',
```

```
      4,
      2,
      1,
      1,
      GETDATE(),
      GETDATE()
);
```

This can work somewhat differently when adding Change Data Capture to an existing table. If you add Change Data Capture to an existing table, you will still be able to track when changes have happened to your data records, but you will only be able to see the number of data modifications that have happened since Change Data Capture was implemented.

Previously in Listing 14-8, I enabled Change Data Capture on the dbo.Recipe table. If I assume that the table was empty and I insert some records into the table, I will be able to determine when these records were added. Executing the query in Listing 14-9 will show you the records in the Change Data Capture table.

Listing 14-9. Query the Change Data Capture Table for dbo.Recipe

```
SELECT  __$start_lsn,
        __$end_lSN,
        __$seqval,
        __$operation,
        __$update_mask,
        RecipeID,
        RecipeName,
        RecipeDescription,
        ServingQuantity,
        MealTypeID,
        PreparationTypeID,
        IsActive,
        DateCreated,
        DateModified,
        __$command_id
FROM cdc.dbo_Recipe_CT
```

You can see a subset of the information that has been tracked about the data records in Table 14-3.

Table 14-3. *Change Tracking Output for dbo.Recipe*

__$operation	RecipeID	RecipeName	DateCreated	__$command_id
2	1	Spaghetti	05/21/2019	1

It may not look like there is much information being recorded, but the information saved in this table can be quite helpful. The column __$operation indicates the action that occurred on this table. The __$operation will tell you which type of activity was performed. If the record was inserted, you will have one entry in cdc.dbo_Recipe_CT with the values that were inserted. If the record was deleted, you will have one entry in cdc.dbo_Recipe_CT with the values that were deleted. If the record was updated, you will have two entries in cdc.dbo_Recipe_CT table. The first record will have the values of the record before the update. The second record will have the values of the record after the update.

If the table had already existed and I had enabled Change Data Capture, you will not see those data records until they had been updated. Once these records are modified, they will show up in the cdc.dbo_Recipe_CT table. While Change Data Capture can be easy for setup and implementation, you should use caution when adding tables to Change Data Capture. Each table added to Change Data Capture causes two SQL Server Agent jobs to be created. There is also a significant amount of logging that occurs as a result of tracking changes on these tables. Both can cause SQL Server to use additional resources.

You can use Change Tracking, Change Data Capture, or database triggers to track data modifications. All these options have their own strengths and limitations. When choosing the right option for your organization, you will want to consider what type of data you need to record and the performance overhead you are willing to incur tracking these changes. If you need better performance, you will generally have to choose less functionality. The more information you would like to collect or the more you would like to customize logging data modifications will come at a cost of increased hardware utilization and potential performance overhead.

Error Handling

In addition to logging data modifications, you may also find that you would benefit from logging certain types of errors that occur within the database. While there are SQL Server specific errors that can occur, that is not the focus of this section. There are also errors that occur as a result of the application interacting with the database. Many of these errors can be logged outside of SQL Server as part of your application development. However, you may find that some issues need to be accessible from within SQL Server.

When considering error handling, you will not only want to consider how that information is logged but also how the application handles errors. One of the more common options from within SQL Server is to use a TRY... CATCH block. This code wraps the ability to try the T-SQL code and perform a specific action if that attempt failed. If the code succeeds, then the T-SQL code will execute as expected. Listing 14-10 shows a TRY... CATCH block.

Listing 14-10. Try... Catch Block to Insert Recipe

```
CREATE PROCEDURE dbo.RecipeInsert
     @RecipeName VARCHAR(25),
     @RecipeDescription VARCHAR(50),
     @ServingQuantity TINYINT,
     @MealTypeID TINYINT,
     @PreparationTypeID TINYINT,
     @IsActive BIT,
     @DateCreated DATETIME2(7),
     @DateModified DATETIME2(7)
AS

BEGIN TRY
     BEGIN TRANSACTION

          INSERT INTO dbo.Recipe
          (
               RecipeName,
               RecipeDescription,
               ServingQuantity,
               MealTypeID,
               PreparationTypeID,
```

```
                    IsActive,
                    DateCreated,
                    DateModified
                )
                VALUES
                (
                    @RecipeName,
                    @RecipeDescription,
                    @ServingQuantity,
                    @MealTypeID,
                    @PreparationTypeID,
                    @IsActive,
                    @DateCreated,
                    @DateModified
                )

        COMMIT TRANSACTION
END TRY
BEGIN CATCH
        ROLLBACK TRANSACTION
END CATCH
```

This block of code will insert a record if there are no errors. However, if an error is encountered, then the transaction will be rolled back. There are some ways to integrate this with your application code so that the user is aware there was an error with the transaction. The goal of using this method is to prevent the application from crashing or prevent the end user from expecting the transaction to save correctly. If the user is aware the action has failed, they have the option to correct the issue and retry the action.

You may find that your application is able to write or update data in the database without any issues. However, you may have a process that sends data from one system to another. There may be infrastructure issues or inconsistencies with data types that can cause failures when sending data from one database object to another. These are also a type of error that you will want to determine how it should be handled. You will still want a method to handle these failures, but you may also need more instantaneous reporting that these records failed to be sent or received. Business today requires a constant state of uptime and successful interactions. You can control your effectiveness in responding to these issues by how you record failures when trying to process data.

Database tables that store information that need to be moved through a system often store a status type column in the data table. Whatever process updates, the status of the record may either have issues updating the record status or update the record status to a failed state. When there is not a large amount of data in the table, finding these failed records can be easy. This would usually require a search of records where the status has not changed in a specified period or where the records are in a failed or error status.

Depending on how we use the information about recipes, we may want to log when each recipe is prepared. We could have an application that would allow us to indicate when a recipe was started and completed. This information could be recorded with a recipe status. I would need to create a table to indicate the recipe history status. An example of the information can be seen in Table 14-4.

Table 14-4. *Data Within the dbo.RecipeHistoryStatus Table*

RecipeHistory StatusID	RecipeHistory StatusName	IsActive	DateCreated	DateModified
1	Started	True	05/21/2019	05/21/2019
2	Completed	True	05/21/2019	05/21/2019
3	Cancelled	True	05/21/2019	05/21/2019
4	Error	True	05/21/2019	05/21/2019

This table includes the status available when recording occurrences where someone has started preparing a recipe. To log each instance of a recipe being prepared, I would need to create a table to store information about when each recipe is prepared. There are several ways this could be recorded. For the sake of this chapter, I will create a single record each time a recipe is started. Once the recipe is started, the recipe can end up in a completed, cancelled, or error status. The query for storing the recipe history can be seen in Listing 14-11.

Listing 14-11. Create dbo.RecipeHistory Table

```
CREATE TABLE dbo.RecipeHistory
(
        RecipeHistoryID         INT         NOT NULL,
        RecipeID                SMALLINT    NOT NULL,
        RecipeHistoryStatusID   TINYINT     NOT NULL,
```

```
DateCreated              DATETIME    NOT NULL,
DateModified             DATETIME    ,
CONSTRAINT pk_RecipeHistory_RecipeHistoryID
      PRIMARY KEY CLUSTERED (RecipeHistoryID),
CONSTRAINT fk_RecipeHistory_RecipeID
      FOREIGN KEY (RecipeID)
      REFERENCES dbo.Recipe(RecipeID),
CONSTRAINT fk_RecipeHistory_RecipeHistoryStatusID
      FOREIGN KEY (RecipeHistoryStatusID)
      REFERENCES
      dbo.RecipeHistoryStatus(RecipeHistoryStatusID)
);
```

This table can store each unique time a recipe is started. An example of the data stored in this table can be found in Table 14-5.

Table 14-5. *Data Within the dbo.RecipeHistory Table*

RecipeHistoryID	RecipeID	RecipeHistory StatusID	DateCreated	DateModified
1	1	2	05/17/2019	05/17/2019
2	1	3	05/18/2019	05/18/2019
3	3	4	05/20/2019	05/20/2019
4	4	1	05/21/2019	05/21/2019

The records in Table 14-5 indicate recipes that have been started and their various statuses. The first record is for RecipeID of 1 with a status of completed. The second record is for RecipeID of 1 with a status of cancelled. The third record is for RecipeID of 3 with a status of error. The last record displayed is for RecipeID of 4 with a status of started.

When there is an error for any of the records, those records will have a RecipeHistoryStatusID of 4 in the dbo.RecipeHistory table. Initially the amount of data in this table will not be very large, and it will be easy to find the recent error records within this table. However, over time this table will grow to a considerable size. This can cause SQL Server to search through many records in order to find any recent error records.

If we plan for the table dbo.RecipeHistory to grow to a size where it will be difficult to search, we may implement error logging differently. There may be other scenarios where you would want to keep all records that have errored in an error status, but you would also want to know what to be able to resolve any issues with recently errored records.

In either of these scenarios, it may be beneficial to create a table specifically for logging recent error records. Before creating this table, you may also want to consider how this table must be managed over time. Unlike the dbo.RecipeHistory table, you would want to make sure that this new table did not get too large. You would also want to only keep recent error records in this table. Keeping a small number of records in the table allows the table to be easily searched. The goal of this new table will only be to alert users of any recent error records. Considering the purpose of this table, you will also want to design a process to purge data from this table regularly.

If you choose to create an additional logging table for error records, you may end up creating a table like the one in Listing 14-12.

Listing 14-12. Create dbo.RecipeHistoryLog Table

```
CREATE TABLE dbo.RecipeHistoryLog
(
      RecipeHistoryLogID      INT         NOT NULL,
      RecipeHistoryID         INT         NOT NULL,
      DateCreated             DATETIME    NOT NULL,
      DateModified            DATETIME    ,
      CONSTRAINT pk_RecipeHistoryLog_RecipeHistoryLogID
            PRIMARY KEY CLUSTERED (RecipeHistoryLogID),
      CONSTRAINT fk_RecipeHistoryLog_RecipeHistoryID
            FOREIGN KEY (RecipeHistoryID)
            REFERENCES dbo.RecipeHistory(RecipeHistoryID)
);
```

Any record that errors on the dbo.RecipeHistory table can have a corresponding record entered to the table in Listing 14-12. In Table 14-5, there was an error record for RecipeHistoryID 2. If we had created the table in Listing 14-12 before that error record was created, we might see an entry like the one in Table 14-6.

Table 14-6. *Data Within the dbo.RecipeHistoryLog Table*

RecipeHistoryLogID	RecipeHistoryID	DateCreated	DateModified
1	2	05/18/2019	05/18/2019

Once we have a record in the dbo.RecipeHistoryLog table, we can generate an alert based on the existence of a record in this table. One option may be to have a stored procedure that is executed every 15 minutes. The purpose of this stored procedure may be to generate an email if there are any records found in the dbo.RecipeHistoryLog table. If you choose this method to create your alerts, you will want to also make certain that you remove data from this table regularly. In this case, you would also need a stored procedure to regularly remove data from this table.

Regardless of which method you choose to implement logging errors between your applications and SQL Server, you should make sure that these errors are tracked somewhere that can be accessible to multiple parties. One of the more difficult issues to troubleshoot is when there is no logging available. The goal of logging errors related to SQL Server is to allow individuals within your organization to quickly find where issues are occurring so that they can resolve them efficiently. You may choose to implement most of your error handling from the application. However, it may be possible to generate automated reports from within SQL Server for errors that need to be corrected promptly.

As part of your application development, you will want to consider what type of logging is necessary for your organization. In industries where there is the possibility for greater theft, it may be more important to track when a data modification occurs and who modified the data. Depending on the information needed will determine what type of logging you implement for data modifications. You will also want to consider how to manage errors associated with the database. These are not errors that are specific to SQL Server but are errors that occur as a result of the T-SQL code that has been written for use by your applications. After determining how to manage logging for your application, you may want to consider how to design your T-SQL code to be reusable.

CHAPTER 15

Managing Data Growth

When a database is first created, for a given amount of time, the tables in the database will remain small. Depending on the nature of the data stored in the table or the amount of time that has passed, you may find yourself in a situation where one or more of your tables have experienced a significant amount of growth since the table was first created. There can be many motivations for managing the relative age of the data stored in a table or how data is stored overall. The goal of this chapter will be to focus on organizing your data in a way that can be managed long term. While many companies also have the goal of improving performance when it comes to managing data, that will not be the focus of this chapter.

SQL Server provides the functionality to separate or sort your data into various groups or categories. When it comes to managing data growth, this data is normally sorted by date. You are not limited to organizing your data by a given date, but for the purposes of this chapter, that will be my focus. You will first want to figure out how to organize your data, not only how the data will be grouped but also how the data will be stored. Setting up the functionality for sorting and storing your data will allow you to start moving your data into those various groups that you have created. There are options available on how to group the data, and you have the possibility of using multiple different ways to store your data. This allows you to design a solution that can support a highly transactional throughput for recent data and allow older data to be designed in a way to support reporting.

Partitioning

Looking at one of your database tables, you may find that this table has grown to a size that has made it difficult to manage. Ideally, you would identify these tables before they had grown to that size. In either scenario, you are looking at a table where you would like to better manage archiving data or maintaining indexes. Conceptually you will want to

© Elizabeth Noble 2020
E. Noble, *Pro T-SQL 2019*, https://doi.org/10.1007/978-1-4842-5590-2_15

think about how you access this data. To make the process of organizing this data more efficient, you will want to choose a column that will always be used when accessing this data. The process of organizing this data by some value is called partitioning.

The first step in partitioning will be figuring out how you want to consistently access your data. I will be working with the dbo.RecipeHistory table. For the purposes of this chapter, this table represents information about when recipes have been used over the past 2 years. I may decide for legal, user experience, or other reasons that I want to start the process of archiving some of this historical information. Since this is a historical table, I will be choosing to partition, that is, organize or sort, this data based upon the DateCreated. Choosing how this data will be partitioned leads to the next decision that must be made.

Once I have decided how the data will be sorted, I also need to decide specifically what data will be sorted together in groups. The groups of data that are sorted together are called ranges. One thing to consider when choosing ranges to be partitioned is to think about how frequently data will be accessed within each range. For most applications, that would mean that recent data was accessed frequently and data that was much older was accessed less frequently. If I had 5 years of recipe history data, there may be a business reason why I would have data for this long of a period, but for day-to-day operations I may normally only access information on a daily, weekly, monthly, or annual basis.

Knowing how the data is accessed in general will allow me to determine the ranges I will use to partition the data. Once you figure out the ranges on how you would like to store your data, you will need to create filegroups. Filegroups can also benefit you by allowing you to choose how you store your data. You can keep more frequently used data in filegroups on faster storage. You can also keep less frequently used data on filegroups in slower storage. This can allow you to change how your data is stored in a way that allows you to save money. The filegroups operate like a logical structure as to how the data will be sorted. When you are using a database that does not have any additional filegroups, you will see that there is a single filegroup named primary. The T-SQL code to create these filegroups is shown in Listing 15-1.

Listing 15-1. Create Filegroups

```
ALTER DATABASE Menu
ADD FILEGROUP RecipeHistory2018;

ALTER DATABASE Menu
```

```
ADD FILEGROUP RecipeHistory2019Q1;

ALTER DATABASE Menu
ADD FILEGROUP RecipeHistory2019Q2;

ALTER DATABASE Menu
ADD FILEGROUP RecipeHistory2019Q3;
```

In this example, I have created four different filegroups. The first filegroup that was created will hold all the recipe history prior to 2019. The next two filegroups are each for the first two quarters of the calendar year in 2019. The third filegroup is designed for the third quarter of 2019. Once I create the filegroups, I will need to create any files that will be used by the filegroups. For the example in this chapter, we will be creating one file per filegroup. You can create these files using T-SQL in Listing 15-2.

Listing 15-2. Add Filegroups to Menu Database

```
ALTER DATABASE Menu
ADD FILE
(
      NAME = RecipeHistFG2018,
      FILENAME = 'D:\SQLData\RecipeHistFG2018.ndf',
      SIZE = 50MB
)
TO FILEGROUP RecipeHistory2018;

ALTER DATABASE Menu
ADD FILE
(
      NAME = RecipeHistFG2019Q1,
      FILENAME = 'D:\SQLData\RecipeHistFG2019Q1.ndf',
      SIZE = 50MB
)
TO FILEGROUP RecipeHistory2019Q1;

ALTER DATABASE Menu
ADD FILE
(
      NAME = RecipeHistFG2019Q2,
```

```
    FILENAME = 'D:\SQLData\RecipeHistFG2019Q2.ndf',
    SIZE = 50MB
)
TO FILEGROUP RecipeHistory2019Q2;

ALTER DATABASE Menu
ADD FILE
(
    NAME = RecipeHistFG2019Q3,
    FILENAME = 'D:\SQLData\RecipeHistFG2019Q3.ndf',
    SIZE = 50MB
)
TO FILEGROUP RecipeHistory2019Q3;
```

Looking at the preceding T-SQL code, I am altering the Menu database and adding a file to the database. When I create the file, I specify the logical name, the filename and file path, the file size, and the filegroup associated with that file.

The filegroups and the files determine where our data will be saved. I must configure how to save that data to those files and filegroups. There are couple different database objects that need to be created in T-SQL before data can be stored in the filegroups. You have already determined how you want the data sorted, and now all you need is to issue T-SQL commands so that SQL Server also knows how to sort this data. This first step is to create a function that tells SQL Server how to sort data for a partition. This type of function is known as a partition function. In Listing 15-3, you can see the T-SQL code to create the partition function.

Listing 15-3. Create Partition Function

```
CREATE PARTITION FUNCTION RecipeHistFunc(DATETIME)
AS RANGE RIGHT FOR VALUES
(
    '01/01/2019',
    '04/01/2019',
    '07/01/2019'
);
```

In Listing 15-3, I specified the range of the function as **RIGHT**. The range is directly related to the values provided as part of the partition function. In the case of a right range, this signifies that the value is on the right-hand side of the boundary when separating your partitions. When using the T-SQL code from Listing 15-3, any value up to January 1, 2019, will end up in the first partition. The second partition will contain all values beginning exactly with January 1, 2019, up to April 1, 2019. However, any data from April 1, 2019 until right before July 1, 2019, will exist in the third partition. As the partition function is currently designed, all data that is created on or after July 1, 2019 will end up in the fourth partition. An example of what right partitions would look like can be seen in Figure 15-1.

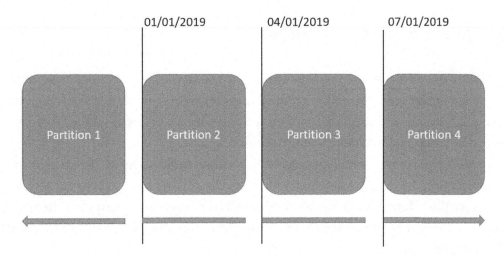

Figure 15-1. *Partition Using Right Range*

The other option when creating a partition function is specifying the range as **LEFT**. If I had specified a left range or not specified left or right, the first partition would include any values up to and *including* January 1, 2019. In Figure 15-2, you can see how the partitions would look if I had used a left range.

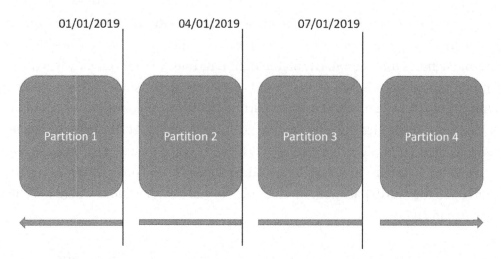

Figure 15-2. *Partition Using Left Range*

With the data we are using, the data type is DATETIME2(7). If I were to use the left range, any data happening 1 millisecond after midnight on January 1, 2019, would have ended up in the second partition. You can see how important it is to understand your data and your data types when creating partition functions.

Creating a partition function is helpful. A partition function lets SQL Server know how to partition the data. However, you also need to indicate how SQL Server should use that partition function. This is where you will want to create a partition scheme. A partition scheme maps a specific partition function to filegroups. You can see the T-SQL code to create a partition scheme in Listing 15-4.

Listing 15-4. Creation Partition Scheme

```
CREATE PARTITION SCHEME RecipeHistRange
AS PARTITION RecipeHistFunc TO
(
    RecipeHistory2018,
    RecipeHistory2019Q1,
    RecipeHistory2019Q2,
    RecipeHistory2019Q3
);
```

The partition scheme has a specific name and references a partition function to use. One difference you can see between the partition function and the partition scheme is that the partition function specified three values. However, the partition scheme has four values. Since we specified that the range on the partition function was right, all values before the first date in the partition function specified will end up in the first filegroup. Reviewing the T-SQL code between Listing 15-3 and Listing 15-4, you can see that the first value specified in the partition function correlates with the begin date for the first quarter of 2019.

Before we get into applying this partition scheme to a specific data table, we will want to get familiar with some additional aspects associated with partitions. Almost any time someone talks about partitions, they also specify that partitions are not necessarily something that is used to improve performance. There are many reasons that partitions may not improve performance, and some of those reasons are because partitions may not always be properly implemented. When considering partitioning, you want to focus on what data column you will be using to partition your data. This is known as the partitioning column. The reason that you will want to be aware of your partitioning column is because this partitioning column will determine how you write your T-SQL code going forward.

The reason that you will want to use your partitioning column in all your T-SQL code is due to how SQL Server uses partitions. Once you have partitioned your data, SQL Server will search through partitioned data differently than non-partitioned tables. Once a partition has been implemented, SQL Server will use the partition to figure out which section of the table has the data that a query is requesting. If I search for a record by date, SQL Server will very quickly know exactly which partition to access to find the data. However, if I do not specify a date and I am looking for information about a specific recipe, SQL Server will look through every partition to find the information I have requested. Selecting a good partitioned column is important when implementing partitioning in your database. If you do not choose a column that is frequently or almost always used as part of your queries, you may incur additional performance overhead associated with having a partition.

It is generally advised that you should not implement partitioning primarily to improve performance. While the overall goal is to simplify managing your data over time, you can implement some functionality in order to increase the possibility of improving performance. One such method is in how you index your partitioned table. You will want to create indexes that are segmented like the partition on your table. These indexes are known as aligned partitioned indexes. Aligned partitioned indexes can be clustered or non-clustered. There are different requirements depending on if the aligned partitioned index is unique. However, the general outcome is the same. Both types of aligned partitioned indexes will include a reference to the partitioned column. In the case of a unique aligned clustered or non-clustered index, the partitioned column must be part of the index. On the other hand, when creating a non-unique aligned index, you do not have to specify the partitioned column. If the partitioned column is not part of the aligned index, SQL Server will add a reference back to the partitioned column as part of the index.

There is also the possibility of creating indexes that are not segmented like your partition. However, these indexes can have their own partition. These are considered non-aligned partitioned indexes. There are some specific cases where you would want to use this type of index, such as confirming that every value in a column that is not the partitioning column is unique. However, I would limit the use of non-aligned partitioned indexes as your queries that rely on indexes may perform worse as the entire table may need to be scanned to find all relevant records. Since the non-aligned partitioned index is not part of the partition function on the table, you do not need to specify the partition column as part of the index.

Ultimately, the goal when using partitioning is to reduce the number of records SQL Server is accessing when trying to read or update data. You can write your queries in such a way that SQL Server can quickly determine exactly which partitions have the data requested. When SQL Server generates an execution plan ignoring specific partitions, this is known as partition elimination. SQL Server can treat a very large table like many smaller tables. In so doing, SQL Server only needs to interact with a subset of the partitioned table. This is your best chance to improve performance as a result of partitioning. However, in order to have your queries take advantage of partition elimination, you will need to reference the partitioning column in your query. Otherwise, SQL Server will not know which partition to access.

Previously in this section, I created new filegroups and added those to the current database. I also created a new partition function and scheme. In Listing 15-5, you can see the T-SQL to add a new partition.

Listing 15-5. Add New Partition to Existing Partition

```
ALTER DATABASE Menu
ADD FILEGROUP RecipeHistory2019Q4;

ALTER DATABASE Menu
```

```
ADD FILE
(
    NAME = RecipeHistFG2019Q4,
    FILENAME = 'D:\SQLData\RecipeHistFG2019Q4.ndf',
    SIZE = 50MB
)
TO FILEGROUP RecipeHistory2019Q4;

ALTER PARTITION FUNCTION RecipeHistFunc(DATETIME2)
AS SPLIT RANGE ('10/01/2019');

ALTER PARTITION SCHEME RecipeHistRange
NEXT USED RecipeHistory2019Q4;
```

In order to create a new partition, I need to take the existing partition function and break the existing partition at a specified point. Before running the T-SQL code in Listing 15-5, the last range in the partition function included all data on and after July 1, 2019. The SPLIT RANGE code on the last partition takes the last partition beginning on July 1, 2019, and breaks it into two partitions. The partition is separated on the date October 1, 2019, provided in Listing 15-5. The previous partition is then split into two partitions. The first of these two partitions includes all dates beginning on July 1, 2019, up to but not including October 1, 2019. The second partition covers all dates on October 1, 2019, and later.

Most of the preceding database code follows the same logic as shown previously in this chapter. I create a new filegroup and add the file to the database. I also need to change the partition scheme to let SQL Server know the next filegroup that should be used as part of the partition scheme. Once that is complete, I can update the partition function. This will allow SQL Server to save data in the correct filegroup based upon the new specifications.

Partitioned Tables

While we have created filegroups, files, partition functions, and partition schemes, none of this partitioning logic has been applied to any data within the databases. We either have the option of creating a new table or partitioning an existing table. For this example, I will start with creating a new table that is partitioned as part of the table creation. You can see the T-SQL to create the partitioned table in Listing 15-6.

Listing 15-6. Create Partitioned Table

```
CREATE TABLE dbo.RecipeHistory
(
    RecipeHistoryID         BIGINT      NOT NULL IDENTITY(1,1),
    RecipeID                SMALLINT    NOT NULL,
    RecipeHistoryStatusID   TINYINT     NOT NULL,
    DateCreated             DATETIME    NOT NULL,
    DateModified            DATETIME    NULL,
    CONSTRAINT pk_RecipeHistory_RecipeHistoryID
        PRIMARY KEY NONCLUSTERED
        (RecipeHistoryID, DateCreated),
    CONSTRAINT fk_RecipeHistory_RecipeID
        FOREIGN KEY (RecipeID)
        REFERENCES dbo.Recipe(RecipeID),
    CONSTRAINT fk_RecipeHistory_RecipeHistoryStatusID
        FOREIGN KEY (RecipeHistoryStatusID)
        REFERENCES
        dbo.RecipeHistoryStatus(RecipeHistoryStatusID)
)
ON RecipeHistRange (DateCreated);
```

In the preceding code, the last line indicates that the table should be created on the partition scheme from Listing 15-4. Once the partitioned table is created in Listing 15-6, the structure of the table will look like Figure 15-3.

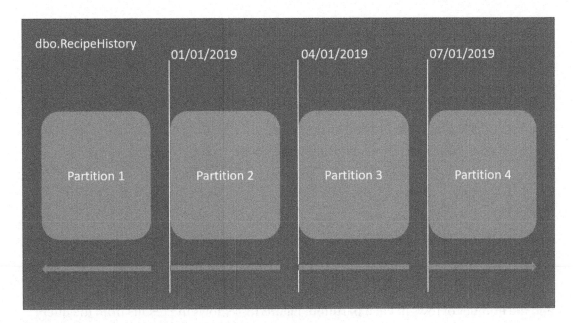

Figure 15-3. *Partitioned Table Data Structure*

Inside of the partitioned table, you can see each partition clearly. Within the partitioned table, you can also see how the right range on the partition function has broken out the data into each partition. You can confirm how the table is partitioned by running the query in Listing 15-7.

Listing 15-7. View Partitions for Partitioned Table

```
SELECT tbl.[name] AS TableName,
      sch.[name] AS PartitionScheme,
      fnc.[name] AS PartitionFunction,
      prt.partition_number,
      fnc.[type_desc],
      rng.boundary_id,
      rng.[value] AS BoundaryValue,
      prt.[rows]
FROM sys.tables tbl
      INNER JOIN sys.indexes idx
      ON tbl.[object_id] = idx.[object_id]
      INNER JOIN sys.partitions prt
      ON idx.[object_id] = prt.[object_id]
```

```
            AND idx.index_id = prt.index_id
    INNER JOIN sys.partition_schemes AS sch
    ON idx.data_space_id = sch.data_space_id
    INNER JOIN sys.partition_functions AS fnc
    ON sch.function_id = fnc.function_id
    LEFT JOIN sys.partition_range_values AS rng
    ON fnc.function_id = rng.function_id
            AND rng.boundary_id = prt.partition_number
WHERE tbl.[name] = 'RecipeHistory'
    AND idx.[type] <= 1
ORDER BY prt.partition_number;
```

The preceding query shows the table name, the partition scheme used on the table, the partition function used on the table, the partition number, value to partition the data, and the number of rows in each partition. Figure 15-4 shows the results from the query in Listing 15-7.

	TableName	PartitionScheme	PartitionFunction	partition_number	type_desc	boundary_id	BoundaryValue	rows
1	RecipeHistory	RecipeHistRange	RecipeHistFunc	1	RANGE	1	2019-01-01 00:00:00.000	0
2	RecipeHistory	RecipeHistRange	RecipeHistFunc	2	RANGE	2	2019-04-01 00:00:00.000	0
3	RecipeHistory	RecipeHistRange	RecipeHistFunc	3	RANGE	3	2019-07-01 00:00:00.000	0
4	RecipeHistory	RecipeHistRange	RecipeHistFunc	4	RANGE	NULL	NULL	0

Figure 15-4. *Data for Partitioned Table*

The preceding results were taken immediately after the partitioned table was created. You can see that the partition scheme used is RecipeHistRange and the partition function is RecipeHistFunc. The preceding boundary values match the ranges specified in Listing 15-3 when the partition function was created. Looking at the value in the rows column from Figure 15-4 above, you can see all the values are 0. This is because there are no rows in the table.

I inserted data from a pre-existing table into the partitioned table. Executing the same query from Listing 15-7, I can see how the data has been stored in the partitions. In Figure 15-5, you can see the number of rows per partition.

	TableName	PartitionScheme	PartitionFunction	partition_number	type_desc	boundary_id	BoundaryValue	rows
1	RecipeHistory	RecipeHistRange	RecipeHistFunc	1	RANGE	1	2019-01-01 00:00:00.000	203493
2	RecipeHistory	RecipeHistRange	RecipeHistFunc	2	RANGE	2	2019-04-01 00:00:00.000	397899
3	RecipeHistory	RecipeHistRange	RecipeHistFunc	3	RANGE	3	2019-07-01 00:00:00.000	427947
4	RecipeHistory	RecipeHistRange	RecipeHistFunc	4	RANGE	NULL	NULL	209109

Figure 15-5. *Data Added to Partitioned Table*

In Figure 15-4, I showed the row counts per partition before any data was added to the dbo.RecipeHistory table. Figure 15-5 shows the number of rows per partition after the table is fully populated. The first partition has 203,493 rows. We know the actual number of rows in the partition, but we may still want to confirm that the table is partitioning data as we would expect. In Listing 15-8, I have written a query to count the number of records by date ranges.

Listing 15-8. Query to Confirm Row Counts

```
SELECT
    SUM(
        CASE WHEN DateCreated < '1/1/2019'
            THEN 1
            ELSE 0
        END
    ) AS Partition1,
    SUM(
        CASE WHEN DateCreated < '4/1/2019'
            THEN 1
            ELSE 0
        END
    ) AS Partition2,
    SUM(
        CASE WHEN DateCreated < '7/1/2019'
            THEN 1
            ELSE 0
        END
    ) AS Partition3,
    SUM(
        CASE WHEN DateCreated >= '7/1/2019'
```

```
                THEN 1
                ELSE 0
        END
    ) AS Partition4
FROM dbo.RecipeHistory;
```

The first column in the query returns a count of records that have a created date before January 1, 2019. Assuming the partition function is partitioning data as we would expect, the number of rows shown for the first partition from Figure 15-5 should match the value returned for column one from Listing 15-8. The query results from Listing 15-8 are shown in Figure 15-6.

	Partition1	Partition2	Partition3	Partition4
1	203493	601392	1029339	209109

Figure 15-6. *Query Results Showing Row Count*

Each column in Figure 15-6 shows the number of records that exist in each date range. The first column represents the number of records with a date created before January 1, 2019. The second column is the number of records with a created date starting on January 1, 2019, up to but not including April 1, 2019. The third column follows a similar pattern for records with a date created of April 1, 2019, all the way until July 1, 2019. The last column is for all records created on or after July 1, 2019. Comparing the values in these four columns to the rows column from Figure 15-5 can help us confirm that our partition function is working as expected. In our case, the value from the rows column from Figure 15-5 does correspond to the column values from Figure 15-6. This confirms that our data is being partitioned as expected.

We have verified that the data is getting sorted into the correct partition. However, we have not confirmed that we have any data that has a value that matches the exact date for our range partitions. One way we can verify this is to run a query, like the one in Listing 15-9, that shows the number of records with the exact date and time as the one specified for our partition function.

Listing 15-9. Query to Confirm Range Function

```
SELECT COUNT(*)
FROM dbo.RecipeHistory
WHERE DateCreated = '1/1/2019'
```

When I run the preceding query, I end up getting 14,720 results returned. This lets me know that my partition function is working as expected. If I had zero results returned, I might not be certain on which partition any records with the exact date and time of January 1, 2019, 12:00:00:00.000 would end up. However, since my partitions show the correct counts by date and time grouping, I know my partition is working as expected.

Previously in this section, we created an empty partitioned table. Once we partition the table, we have are ready to manage the growth of this table over time. This process of managing data growth is not a one-time occurrence but something that will need to be maintained going forward. In the case of the table, we will need to add partitions going forward. This process will be like the one shown in Listing 15-5. Adding partitions to an existing partitioned table is not the only time that we may need to partition tables. You may also find yourself in a situation where you did not originally intend to partition a table, but for any number of circumstances, you may now find you need to partition the table. In Listing 15-10, you can see the T-SQL code required to change a non-partitioned table to a partitioned table.

Listing 15-10. Add Partition to Existing Table

```
ALTER TABLE dbo.RecipeHistory
DROP CONSTRAINT pk_RecipeHistory_RecipeHistoryID;

ALTER TABLE dbo.RecipeHistory
ADD CONSTRAINT pk_RecipeHistory_RecipeHistoryID
PRIMARY KEY NONCLUSTERED (RecipeHistoryID, DateCreated);

CREATE CLUSTERED INDEX ix_RecipeHistory_DateCreated
ON dbo.RecipeHistory (DateCreated)
ON RecipeHistRange (DateCreated);
```

Prior to implementing the partition, all the data in the table is ordered by the primary key. In this case, the primary key is the RecipeHistoryID. However, once we partition the table, we will want the table segmented by the created date. This requires changing how the data in the table is stored. To get SQL Server to update how the data is stored, you will need to drop the original primary key. At that time, you can create a new non-clustered primary key along with the date created. Including the date created as part of the partitioning column on the primary key is necessary for the partitioned table. Once this is done, you can create a clustered index on the date created. This index will be created on the partition scheme. You will want to be aware that adding this non-aligned primary key to the table will prevent you from using partition switching on this table.

If all the data in your existing non-partitioned table exists within one of the partitions on your new table, you have the option to easily move the data from the non-partitioned table to the partitioned table. Listing 15-11 shows the T-SQL code necessary to accomplish this task.

Listing 15-11. Switch All Data Out of Non-Partitioned Table to Partitioned Table

```
ALTER TABLE dbo.RecipeHistory
WITH CHECK ADD CONSTRAINT ck_RecipeHistory_MinDateCreated
CHECK
(
      DateCreated IS NOT NULL
      AND DateCreated >= '08/01/2018'
);

ALTER TABLE dbo.RecipeHistory
WITH CHECK ADD CONSTRAINT ck_RecipeHistory_MaxDateCreated
CHECK
(
      DateCreated IS NOT NULL
      AND DateCreated < '10/01/2019'
);

ALTER TABLE dbo.RecipeHistory
SWITCH TO dbo.RecipeHistoryArchive
PARTITION RecipeHistory2018Q4;
```

To switch the data from the non-partitioned table, you will first need to prove that all the data in the non-partitioned table fits inside of the partition that you will be using on the partitioned table. You will first need to create constraints on the partitioning column that match the range for the partition. Once the constraints have been created, you can switch all the data from the non-partitioned table into the partition specified on the partitioned table.

If I have two partitioned tables, I may want to move a partition from one table to another. This process can be referred to as partition switching. The T-SQL code required to do this is less complex than the code from Listing 15-11. In Listing 15-12, I have written database code that will switch the partition from the current table to a new archive table.

Listing 15-12. Switch Out of Partitioned Table to Another Partitioned Table

```
ALTER TABLE dbo.RecipeHistory SWITCH
     PARTITION 1
TO dbo.RecipeHistoryArchive
     PARTITION 1;
```

For this example, I have moved the records from the fourth quarter of 2018 from the dbo.RecipeHistory table to the dbo.RecipeHistoryArchive table. In order to switch a partition from one table to partition in a different partitioned table, you must specify the partitions for each table. The partition in the target table must also be empty in order for this T-SQL code to execute. This method is a particularly straightforward and easy method of managing your data growth over time. If you create a specific data management plan and move data from your main OLTP tables to an archive table, you can keep all your data but also allow your highly transactional tables to maintain only the most relevant data for your business.

Now that we have covered how to partition new and existing tables, I want to look at what partitioning can mean for query execution. Data is usually recorded in the order that each transaction occurred. This can correlate to a specific time period, but that may not always be the case. In addition, even though data is recorded in a specific order, there are often reasons why the business may want to look at data based on a specific date range. I may want to look at the recipes that were started for a specific date range. Issuing the query in Listing 15-13, I can look at the dbo.RecipeHistory table to find this information.

Listing 15-13. Access Data Before Partitioning Table

```
SELECT RecipeHistoryID,
    RecipeID,
    RecipeHistoryStatusID,
    DateCreated
FROM dbo.RecipeHistory
WHERE DateCreated BETWEEN '10/7/18' AND '10/9/18';
```

After querying the dbo.RecipeHistory table for a specific date range, I can also review how SQL Server executed that T-SQL code to find the data I requested. The execution plan in Figure 15-7 shows how the data was retrieved.

Figure 15-7. *Execution Plan for Unpartitioned Table*

The dbo.RecipeHistory table was not partitioned when this query was executed, and the table was ordered by the clustered primary key. In this case, that is the RecipeHistoryID. While the data may have been stored in the order the records were created, SQL Server has no way to know that is true based on how the table is configured. To make sure that SQL Server retrieves all data based on the date created, SQL Server will need to review each record in the table. This is represented earlier with the Clustered Index Scan operator on the execution plan. Figure 15-8 shows some of the properties associated with the query from Listing 15-3.

Clustered Index Scan (Clustered)

☐ Misc	
Actual Execution Mode	Row
☐ Actual I/O Statistics	
☐ Actual Lob Logical Reads	0
☐ Actual Lob Physical Read:	0
☐ Actual Lob Read Aheads	0
☐ Actual Logical Reads	5654
☐ Actual Physical Reads	0
☐ Actual Read Aheads	0
☐ Actual Scans	5
☐ Actual Number of Batches	0
☐ Actual Number of Rows	33465

Figure 15-8. *Reads Associated with Clustered Index Scan*

The number of total records returned for this query is 33,465. The total number of local reads is 5,654. This represents the total number of pages that were accessed to determine the number of records that met the criteria for this query.

The preceding values represent how SQL Server would execute a query on a non-partitioned table. We can compare the performance of the query in Listing 15-13 between a non-partitioned and partitioned table. We can add a partition to the dbo. RecipeHistory table and compare the results to the preceding non-partitioned table. I will first need to drop the existing primary key and add a new non-clustered primary key like the one from Listing 15-10. Since this table no longer has a clustered index, I will get an execution plan like the one in Figure 15-9 if I try to rerun the query from Listing 15-13.

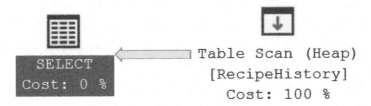

Figure 15-9. *Partitioned Table Without Clustered Index on Partitioning Key*

If you forget to add a new clustered index on the partitioning column including the partition range, you will end up with a heap. In this case, the result is a full scan of the table to find any records that matches the date criteria specified. While you might expect the number of logical reads to be the same for this example and the previous example, Figure 15-10 shows a different result.

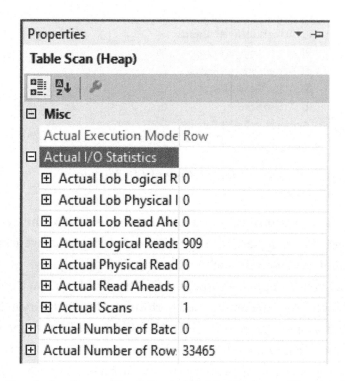

Figure 15-10. *Reads for Query Partitioned Table Without Clustered Index on Partitioning Key*

In the first example, Figure 15-8 shows 5,654 logical reads to find all records in dbo.RecipeHistory that match the date range specified. Partitioning the table and replacing the original primary key with both the RecipeHistoryID and DateCreated has caused the number of logical reads to drop from 5,654 to 909 shown in Figure 15-10. While the number of logical reads has dropped significantly, it is not ideal to perform queries where full Table Scans are required on the partitioning column of the partitioned table. The point is to make sure you have a clustered index on your partitioned table that can take advantage of the partitioning column.

To take better advantage of your partitioned table, you will want to include a clustered index on your partitioned table. This included having a clustered index that is aligned on the partition scheme by the partitioning key. Once you have done this, you can run the T-SQL code from Listing 15-13. You will get an execution plan like the one in Figure 15-11.

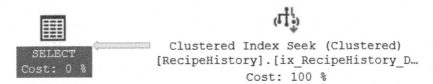

Figure 15-11. *Partitioned Table with Clustered Index on Partitioning Key*

You can see that SQL Server now uses a Clustered Index Seek to find the correct data. We can also look at the properties for this operator to see what kind of impact having a clustered index that includes the partitioning key really has. You can see the I/O statistics and rows return in Figure 15-12.

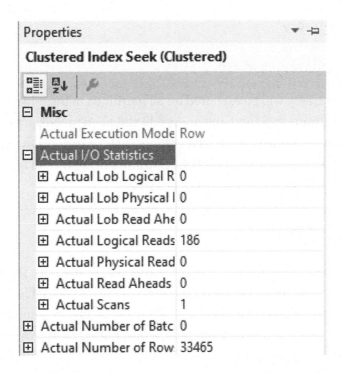

Figure 15-12. *Reads for Query Partitioned Table with Clustered Index on Partitioning Key*

When we originally ran this query on a non-partitioned table, there were 5,654 logical reads. After partitioning table without a clustered index, the number of logical reads dropped to 909. While the lower number of logical reads does not indicate with certainty that the performance will be better, we can confirm that SQL Server will read less data querying a partitioned table with a clustered index on the partitioning column. Now that there is a clustered index on the partition table, the total logic reads has dropped from 909 to 186 logical reads, as shown in Figure 15-12 above.

Creating a partitioned table correctly is only part of the challenge if you want to see improved performance as a result. The main way this can be done is by writing T-SQL code that includes criteria that allows for partition elimination. The data code in Listing 15-14 is an example of T-SQL code that does not specify the partitioning column as part of the criteria.

Listing 15-14. Access Data Without Using Partitioned Column

```
SELECT RecipeHistoryID,
      RecipeID,
      RecipeHistoryStatusID,
      DateCreated
FROM dbo.RecipeHistory
WHERE RecipeID = 4
      AND RecipeHistoryStatusID = 2;
```

As a result, this query will be executed on all partitions in the table. Even if there is an index for the columns specified, the query will still need to look at the data in each partition separately to confirm that all data requested is returned. Once you decide on a partitioning column, you should include the partitioning column in all your queries so that you can take advantage of the partitioned table.

Partitioned Views

You can break a single table up into multiple segments by creating a partitioned table. Conversely, you all have the option of combining several smaller tables together in a way that will allow them to act like one large table. The tables that are joined in this manner can be partitioned or not. Similarly to creating a partitioned table, you also have the option of creating a partitioned view.

Like partitioned tables, you should not expect the use of partitioned views to necessarily mean that you will get better performance from the queries that will use this database object going forward. However, there are some design principles that may allow you to see improved performance. When using partitioned tables, we had the concept of partition elimination. The same sort of concept can be seen with partitioned views. In Listing 15-15, I am creating two tables on the same partitioning scheme.

Listing 15-15. Create Tables for Partitioned View

```
CREATE TABLE dbo.RecipeHistory2019
(
        RecipeHistoryID         INT         NOT NULL,
        RecipeID                SMALLINT    NOT NULL,
        RecipeHistoryStatusID   TINYINT     NOT NULL,
        DateCreated             DATETIME    NOT NULL,
        DateModified            DATETIME    NULL,
        CONSTRAINT pk_RecipeHistory2019_RecipeHistoryID
                PRIMARY KEY NONCLUSTERED
                (RecipeHistoryID, DateCreated),
        CONSTRAINT fk_RecipeHistory2019_RecipeID
                FOREIGN KEY (RecipeID)
                REFERENCES dbo.Recipe(RecipeID),
        CONSTRAINT fk_RecipeHistory2019_RecipeHistoryStatusID
                FOREIGN KEY (RecipeHistoryStatusID)
                REFERENCES
                dbo.RecipeHistoryStatus(RecipeHistoryStatusID)
);

CREATE CLUSTERED INDEX ix_RecipeHistory2019_DateCreated
ON dbo.RecipeHistory2019 (DateCreated)
ON RecipeHistRange (DateCreated);

CREATE TABLE dbo.RecipeHistory2018
(
        RecipeHistoryID         INT         NOT NULL,
        RecipeID                SMALLINT    NOT NULL,
        RecipeHistoryStatusID   TINYINT     NOT NULL,
        DateCreated             DATETIME    NOT NULL,
        DateModified            DATETIME    NULL,
```

```
        CONSTRAINT pk_RecipeHistory2018_RecipeHistoryID
            PRIMARY KEY NONCLUSTERED
            (RecipeHistoryID, DateCreated),
        CONSTRAINT fk_RecipeHistory2018_RecipeID
            FOREIGN KEY (RecipeID)
            REFERENCES dbo.Recipe(RecipeID),
        CONSTRAINT fk_RecipeHistory2018_RecipeHistoryStatusID
            FOREIGN KEY (RecipeHistoryStatusID)
            REFERENCES
            dbo.RecipeHistoryStatus(RecipeHistoryStatusID)
)
ON RecipeHistRange (DateCreated);

CREATE CLUSTERED INDEX ix_RecipeHistory2018_DateCreated
ON dbo.RecipeHistory2018 (DateCreated)
ON RecipeHistRange (DateCreated);
```

While each of these tables is on the same partitioning scheme, there is nothing to limit the type of data that will be stored in these tables. The first table is intended to store data for 2019, and the second table is for data from 2018. However, I need to add constraints to these tables to ensure that the correct records exist in each table. In Listing 15-16, you can see the constraints that will be added to both tables.

Listing 15-16. Add Constraints to Tables

```
ALTER TABLE dbo.RecipeHistory2019
WITH CHECK ADD CONSTRAINT ck_RecipeHistory2019_MinDateCreated
CHECK
(
    DateCreated IS NOT NULL
    AND DateCreated >= '01/01/2019'
);

ALTER TABLE dbo.RecipeHistory2019
WITH CHECK ADD CONSTRAINT ck_RecipeHistory2019_MaxDateCreated
CHECK
(
```

```
        DateCreated IS NOT NULL
        AND DateCreated < '01/01/2020'
);

ALTER TABLE dbo.RecipeHistory2018
WITH CHECK ADD CONSTRAINT ck_RecipeHistory2018_MinDateCreated
CHECK
(
        DateCreated IS NOT NULL
        AND DateCreated >= '01/01/2018'
);

ALTER TABLE dbo.RecipeHistory2018
WITH CHECK ADD CONSTRAINT ck_RecipeHistory2018_MaxDateCreated
CHECK
(
        DateCreated IS NOT NULL
        AND DateCreated < '01/01/2019'
);
```

The table for 2019 now has a constraint that only allows records with a DateCreated from January 1, 2019, up to but not including January 1, 2020. There is also a constraint on the table for 2018 with similar logic so that only records that were created in 2018 can be stored in this table.

You now have tables for two different date ranges, and you have applied constraints to these tables. The next step is creating a partitioned view. The process of creating a partitioned view is relatively simple and consists of adding a UNION ALL between each select statement on the underlying tables. An example of creating a partitioned view can be found in Listing 15-17.

Listing 15-17. Create Partitioned View

```
CREATE VIEW dbo.vwRecipeHistory

AS

-- Select data from current read/write table
SELECT RecipeHistoryID,
       RecipeID,
```

```
        RecipeHistoryStatusID,
        IsActive,
        DateCreated,
        DateModified
FROM dbo.RecipeHistory2019

UNION ALL

-- Select data from partitioned table
SELECT RecipeHistoryID,
        RecipeID,
        RecipeHistoryStatusID,
        IsActive,
        DateCreated,
        DateModified
FROM dbo.RecipeHistoryPartition2018;
```

Notice that the column lists are in the same order for both SELECT statements used within the partitioned view. This is a requirement of creating a partitioned view. You must also specify the full column list of the table when creating a partitioned view. Once the partitioned view has been created, you may want to see how querying a partitioned view works.

Earlier in the chapter, in Listing 15-13, we queried the dbo.RecipeHistory table on the date range between October 7, 2018, and October 9, 2018. We can query the partitioned view for the same date range as shown in Listing 15-18.

Listing 15-18. Access Data Using Partitioned Column

```
SELECT RecipeHistoryID,
        RecipeID,
        RecipeHistoryStatusID,
        DateCreated
FROM dbo.vwRecipeHistory
WHERE DateCreated BETWEEN '10/7/18' AND '10/9/18';
```

The T-SQL code is very similar between Listing 15-13 and Listing 15-18. This shows how easy it can be to shift to using a partitioned view instead of the current table names in your queries. However, what we are really interested in confirming is seeing how the execution plan has changed with the use of a partitioned view. Figure 15-13 shows the execution plan that is generated as a result of running the query in Listing 15-18.

SELECT
Cost: 0 %
Compute Scalar
Cost: 2 %
Clustered Index Seek (Clustered)
[RecipeHistory2018].[ix_RecipeHisto...
Cost: 98 %

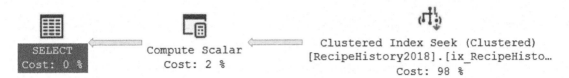

***Figure 15-13.** Execution Plan for Partitioned View*

Like the partitioned table referenced earlier in this chapter, the execution plan for the partitioned view also uses a Clustered Index Seek. Even though the partitioned view includes both the 2019 and 2018 tables, you can see from the execution plan that SQL Server only used the 2018 table when finding the results from the query in Listing 15-18. We can also look at the properties of the Clustered Index Seek in Figure 15-14.

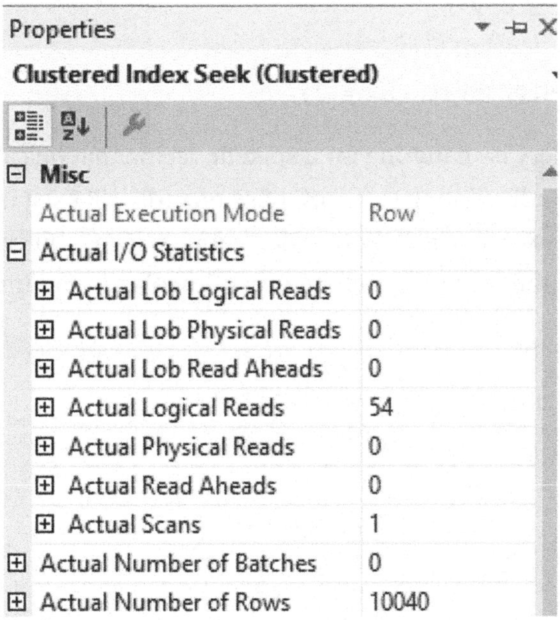

Properties
Clustered Index Seek (Clustered)
Misc
Actual Execution Mode
Row
Actual I/O Statistics
Actual Lob Logical Reads
0
Actual Lob Physical Reads
0
Actual Lob Read Aheads
0
Actual Logical Reads
54
Actual Physical Reads
0
Actual Read Aheads
0
Actual Scans
1
Actual Number of Batches
0
Actual Number of Rows
10040

***Figure 15-14.** Reads for Query Partitioned View with Clustered Index on Partitioning Key*

You can see based on the number of rows returned that the data in the 2018 table is different from the partitioned tables referenced previously in this chapter. You can also see that the relative number of logical reads is low and trends similarly to the partitioned table earlier in this chapter.

The T-SQL code executed in Listing 15-18 accessed the partitioned view based on the partitioned column in each of the tables and on the constraint specified for each of the tables. We saw that SQL Server was able to quickly determine which table to access when querying the data. There may be times where we may want to run a query that does not include the partitioning column like the one in Listing 15-19.

Listing 15-19. Access Data Without Using Partitioned Column

```
SELECT RecipeHistoryID,
     RecipeID,
     RecipeHistoryStatusID,
     DateCreated
FROM dbo.vwRecipeHistory
WHERE RecipeID = 4
     AND RecipeHistoryStatusID = 2;
```

The preceding query is searching for a specific recipe that has a certain status. However, there is no indication that any of these records will exist in a specific table within the indexed view. Since SQL Server does not have the ability to rule out certain date ranges as part of the query, we get the execution plan in Figure 15-15.

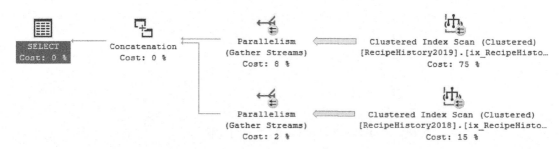

Figure 15-15. *Execution Plan for Partitioned View*

You can see that in this execution plan, SQL Server must access both the table containing 2018 data and the table containing 2019 data. In this example, you can see that there is no benefit on the number of tables accessed as part of this request.

Using partitioned views can help you take more than one table and combine them together into one database object. By accessing this single database object, you can simplify your T-SQL code across multiple ranges. You have also seen that using a partitioned view can be beneficial in limiting the number of tables accessed, but if you do not use the partitioning column as part of your queries, you will still need to access all tables included in the view. While partitioned tables break one table up into multiple segments and partitioned views combined tables together into one database object, you may find advantages to combining them both.

Hybrid Workloads

Companies have been using databases for many years and may have acquired a significant amount of data. Often, these same companies may be generating reports from this data. In many cases, these same companies may not have prioritized building a data warehouse. For these situations, one database is often trying to perform two tasks at the same time. The first role is to continue to store transactional data. However, the second role is to also act as a data warehouse for analytical processing. In many situations, the database design needed for transaction processing does not match the best design for analysis processing. While a company may be willing to move toward a data warehouse some day, you may find yourself in a situation where you need to implement designs that can function well with this hybrid workload.

In combining partitioned and non-partitioned tables with a partitioned view, we can give ourselves some additional flexibility. Using a partitioned view will allow us to use a single database object and name to access any data for a specific purpose. In our example, we will continue to work with the data recorded as a result of recipes being started. Since a partitioned view allows us to combine several tables together, we can investigate how those tables can be created. One advantage of using multiple tables is that each table can use different indexes. This difference in indexes can change both how data is stored and accessed. We can also have the option to make some tables as read only which can also signify that we do not intend to add any additional data to these tables.

We will be creating a partitioned view to access all the recipe history data. The first table we can create is only to hold all the older data that we want to archive. We can also partition this table to allow for partition elimination when searches are performed based on the partitioning key of the table. In Listing 15-20, you can see the T-SQL needed to create our partitioned table for archived data.

Listing 15-20. Create Partitioned Tables for Archived Data

```
CREATE TABLE dbo.RecipeHistoryPartition
(
	RecipeHistoryID         INT       NOT NULL,
	RecipeID                SMALLINT  NOT NULL,
	RecipeHistoryStatusID   TINYINT   NOT NULL,
	DateCreated             DATETIME  NOT NULL,
	DateModified            DATETIME  NULL,
	CONSTRAINT pk_RecipeHistoryPartition_RecipeHistoryID
		PRIMARY KEY (RecipeHistoryID),
	CONSTRAINT fk_RecipeHistoryPartition_RecipeID
		FOREIGN KEY (RecipeID)
		REFERENCES dbo.Recipe(RecipeID),
	CONSTRAINT fk_RecipeHistoryParition_RecipeHistoryStatusID
		FOREIGN KEY (RecipeHistoryStatusID)
		REFERENCES
		dbo.RecipeHistoryStatus(RecipeHistoryStatusID)
)
ON RecipeHistRange (DateCreated);
```

The preceding partitioned table is created like many of the partitioned tables already included in this chapter. Like the partitioned tables created earlier in this chapter, this table was also created on the partition scheme RecipeHistRange. Now that we have a partitioned table, I want to create a non-partitioned table for data that is being actively used by the application right now. The table created in Listing 15-21 is an example of a non-partitioned table.

Listing 15-21. Create Table for Active Data

```
CREATE TABLE dbo.RecipeHistory
(
	RecipeHistoryID         INT       NOT NULL,
	RecipeID                SMALLINT  NOT NULL,
```

```
RecipeHistoryStatusID    TINYINT     NOT NULL,
DateCreated              DATETIME    NOT NULL,
DateModified             DATETIME    NULL,
CONSTRAINT pk_RecipeHistory_RecipeHistoryID
      PRIMARY KEY (RecipeHistoryID),
CONSTRAINT fk_RecipeHistory_RecipeID
      FOREIGN KEY (RecipeID)
      REFERENCES dbo.Recipe(RecipeID),
CONSTRAINT fk_RecipeHistory_RecipeHistoryStatusID
      FOREIGN KEY (RecipeHistoryStatusID)
      REFERENCES
      dbo.RecipeHistoryStatus(RecipeHistoryStatusID)
);
```

The creation of this table does not specify that partition scheme of RecipeHistRange. This table will be a standard table created on the PRIMARY filegroup in the database.

Once the underlying tables have been created, we can create a single database object that can allow us to access both tables. This will be the same as the partitioned view created in the previous section. Listing 15-22 has the T-SQL code needed to create a partitioned view.

Listing 15-22. Create Partitioned View

```
CREATE VIEW dbo.vwRecipeHistory

AS

-- Select data from current read/write table
SELECT RecipeHistoryID,
      RecipeID,
      RecipeHistoryStatusID,
      DateCreated,
      DateModified
FROM dbo.RecipeHistory

UNION ALL
```

```
-- Select data from partitioned table
SELECT RecipeHistoryID,
       RecipeID,
       RecipeHistoryStatusID,
       DateCreated,
       DateModified
FROM dbo.RecipeHistoryPartition;
```

The preceding partitioned view allows us to keep the most recent and highly active data in a table without partitions. This table can be specifically indexed to allow for the best write speeds. Any other tables included in the partitioned view can be indexed based on their usage. The partitioned table included in the preceding partitioned view may only include inactive data. As a result, we may expect this data to only be read going forward. Knowing this, we can use a different strategy to index this table.

Reviewing what we have already covered, I want to show the behavior of SQL Server when querying a non-partitioned table. The query in Listing 15-23 shows a query to find all records for a specific date range in the dbo.RecipeHistory table.

Listing 15-23. Access Data Before Partitioning Table and View

```
SELECT RecipeHistoryID,
       RecipeID,
       RecipeHistoryStatusID,
       DateCreated
FROM dbo.RecipeHistory
WHERE DateCreated BETWEEN '10/7/18' AND '10/9/18';
```

The preceding query will be run on a non-partitioned table. At the time of the query execution, this table is ordered by the original primary key which is the RecipeHistoryID. As a result, the execution plan from the query in Listing 15-23 is shown in Figure 15-16.

Figure 15-16. *Execution Plan for Unpartitioned Table*

Based on the execution plan in Listing 15-16, you can see that SQL Server uses a Clustered Index Scan to find the relevant records. This is because there is no index that includes the DateCreated. With the table not being partitioned by date, SQL Server also needs to go through the entire table to find the data records that satisfy the query in Listing 15-23.

After running this query, we can review additional information about the operators in the execution plan. Specifically, I want to look at the number of logical reads and rows returned for this query execution. Looking at Figure 15-17, you can see the logical reads and number of rows.

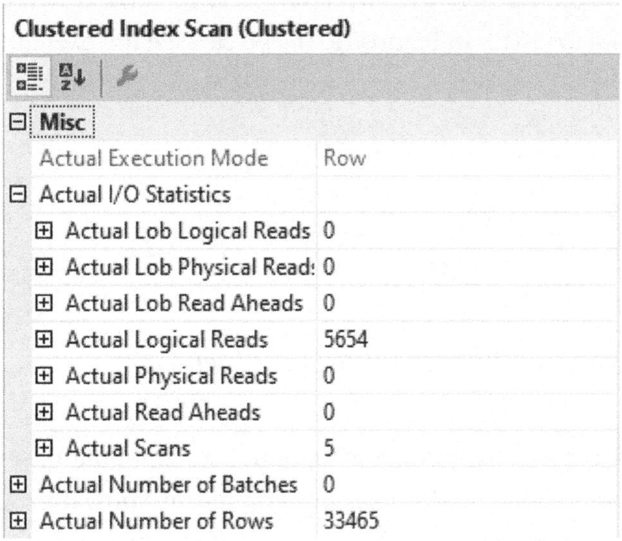

Clustered Index Scan (Clustered)

Misc	
Actual Execution Mode	Row
Actual I/O Statistics	
Actual Lob Logical Reads	0
Actual Lob Physical Read:	0
Actual Lob Read Aheads	0
Actual Logical Reads	5654
Actual Physical Reads	0
Actual Read Aheads	0
Actual Scans	5
Actual Number of Batches	0
Actual Number of Rows	33465

Figure 15-17. *Reads Associated with Clustered Index Scan*

We can see that this query returned 33,465 rows with a total number of 5,654 pages read as logical reads. We will be comparing these values to the performance associated with a partitioned view that contains both a partitioned and non-partitioned table.

Previously, in Listing 15-22, I created a partitioned view that contained a partitioned table for all 2018 data records and non-partitioned table for all 2019 data records. To compare how a partitioned view performs differently than a non-partitioned table, I can run the query in Listing 15-24.

Listing 15-24. Access Data Using Partitioned Column in Partitioned Table

```
SELECT RecipeHistoryID,
       RecipeID,
       RecipeHistoryStatusID,
       DateCreated
FROM dbo.vwRecipeHistory
WHERE DateCreated BETWEEN '10/7/18' AND '10/9/18';
```

The preceding query looks for the same data records as the query from Listing 15-23. However, this query is accessing a partitioned view instead of a non-partitioned table. The partitioned view is composed of a partitioned table for all of 2018 and a non-partitioned table containing data for 2019. In Figure 15-18, we can see the execution plan generated for this query.

Figure 15-18. *Execution Plan for Partitioned View*

One of the important things to note is that this execution plan uses a Clustered Index Seek instead of a Clustered Index Scan. This lets us know that SQL Server could determine where to find the relevant data records efficiently and without having to go through all or most of the records in the table. Another thing that stands out is that the Clustered Index Seek is performed on the partitioned dbo.RecipeHistory2018 table. I can also look at the properties associated with the Clustered Index Seek to get additional information. In Figure 15-19, we can see the number of logical reads and the number of records returned.

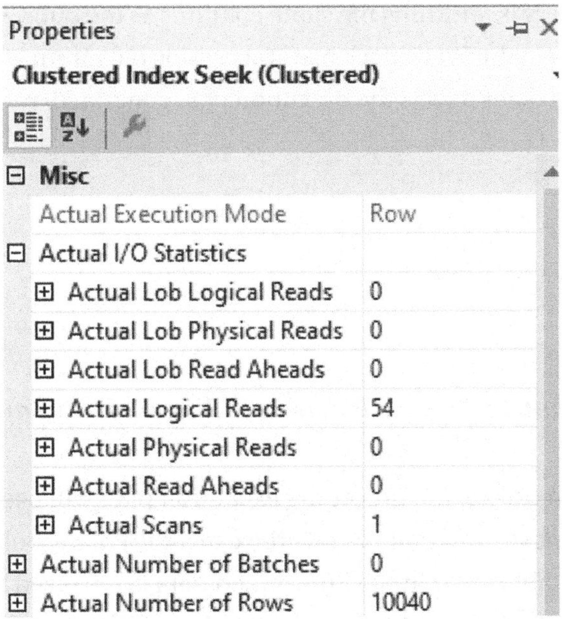

Figure 15-19. *Reads for Query Partitioned View with Clustered Index on Partitioning Key*

The total number of rows returned is 10,040 with a total number of 54 data pages read from memory. The decrease in the number of total data pages read from memory indicates that this query is more efficient at finding the relevant data than the query in Listing 15-23.

We have seen how querying a partitioned view on a column that references a partitioned table performs. The next step is to see how querying a partitioned view works when accessing a non-partitioned table. Listing 15-25 shows a query to access data from the non-partitioned table of the partitioned view.

Listing 15-25. Access Data Using Partitioned Column Not in Partitioned Table

```
SELECT RecipeHistoryID,
      RecipeID,
      RecipeHistoryStatusID,
      DateCreated
FROM dbo.vwRecipeHistory
WHERE DateCreated BETWEEN '5/7/19' AND '5/9/19';
```

The preceding query is returning the same columns as the queries from Listings 15-23 and 15-24. The criteria in the WHERE clause is accessing data from 2019 instead of 2018. To see how this change in dates affects the execution plan generated, we can see the difference in Figure 15-20.

SELECT
Cost: 0 %
Compute Scalar
Cost: 2 %
Clustered Index Seek (Clustered)
[RecipeHistory2019].[ix_RecipeHisto...
Cost: 98 %

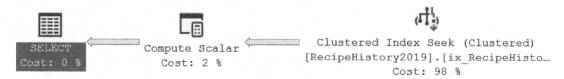

Figure 15-20. *Execution Plan for Partitioned View Not on Partitioned Tale*

Similarly, in Figure 15-20, the preceding execution plan will use a Clustered Index Seek on the dbo.RecipeHistory table. While the execution plans between the partitioned and non-partitioned tables are similar, how much data is retrieved from SQL Server can vary between the two execution plans. Looking at Figure 15-21 can show us how much data is accessed for the query in Listing 15-25.

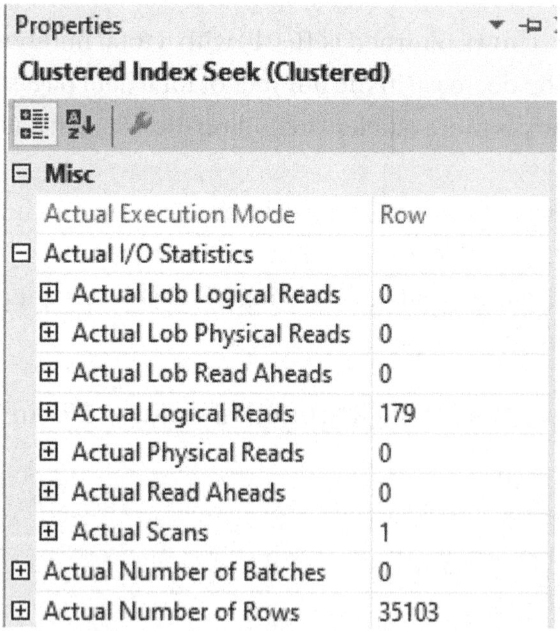

Properties
Clustered Index Seek (Clustered)
Misc
Actual Execution Mode
Row
Actual I/O Statistics
Actual Lob Logical Reads
0
Actual Lob Physical Reads
0
Actual Lob Read Aheads
0
Actual Logical Reads
179
Actual Physical Reads
0
Actual Read Aheads
0
Actual Scans
1
Actual Number of Batches
0
Actual Number of Rows
35103

Figure 15-21. *Reads for Query Partitioned View on Non-partitioned Table*

In Figure 15-21, you can see there are 179 data pages read from memory and 35,103 records returned. This performance is still much better than the performance when all data existed in a single non-partitioned table.

We have confirmed that partitioned views work well for both queries that access partitioned tables and non-partitioned tables within the partitioned view. Like partitioned tables, it is still best to query data using the columns that are part of the partition. In Listing 15-26, I will query the partitioned view using columns that are not part of the partition.

Listing 15-26. Access Data Without Using Partitioned Column

```
SELECT RecipeHistoryID,
       RecipeID,
       RecipeHistoryStatusID,
       DateCreated
FROM dbo.vwRecipeHistory
WHERE RecipeID = 4
      AND RecipeHistoryStatusID = 2;
```

You can see that instead of referencing a date for the preceding query, I want to return all records for RecipeID of 4 that have a RecipeHistoryStatusID of 2. There is no date provided, and SQL Server will need to access all tables within the partitioned view. We can see the execution plan for the query in Listing 15-26 in Figure 15-22.

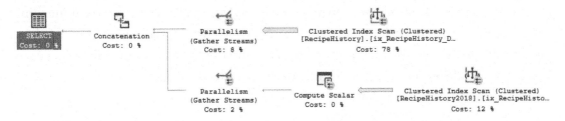

Figure 15-22. *Execution Plan for Partitioned View Not on Partitioning Key*

As expected, the execution plan shows a Clustered Index Scan on dbo.RecipeHistory and dbo.RecipeHistory2018. There is no date range provided in Listing 15-26 which causes SQL Server to access both tables in the partitioned view. The criteria for the query does not take advantage of any indexes on the tables which causes the need for a

Clustered Index Scan. The key point here is to use the partitioning column as much as possible. This gives you the best chance to take advantage of any performance gains associated with partitioning your data.

The longer your applications and databases are in use, you will find yourself facing new challenges in managing the data generated. When working with hybrid workloads, you may find that you need too many different methods to manage and access your data. Combining tables and partitioned tables together in a partitioned view can give you some of the flexibility you need. Breaking your data up into multiple non-partitioned and partitioned tables can allow you to create different indexes on the tables based on how you will be accessing the data within those tables. This sort of strategy can allow you to keep a table with only recent data separate from any data used for reporting purposes. The table containing recent and current data can then be configured to maximize application performance.

One of the options available within SQL Server is the use of partitioning. You have the option to partition information into various filegroups. You can also create partition functions and partition schemes that help SQL Server determine how to segment data. Once the partition scheme is applied to a column on a table, the table is now a partitioned table. The column used for the partition scheme is known as the partitioning key. When queries are designed to use the partitioning key, SQL Server can use partition elimination to find the records that meet the query criteria. In addition to using partitioned tables, you also have the option of using partitioned views. Partitioned views can allow you to combine multiple database objects into a single object that can be referenced by your application code. When running a query, SQL Server will determine which objects need to be accessed to meet the query criteria. You can also combine non-partitioned tables and partitioned tables into the same partitioned view. This method may be able to help you if you find yourself in the situation where your database needs to be able to handle both transactional and analytical based queries.

Index

A

Adaptive joins, 186, 203, 212
Automatic database tuning
    index management, 210
    plan correction, 208, 209
    query store, 208

B

Binary strings, 12
Buffer pool, 126–128, 151–155

C

Clustered Index Scans, 177, 393, 397
Clustered Index Seek, 176, 394, 396
Coding standards
    database design
        ANSI standard, 224
        constraint, 226, 227
        foreign keys, 226
        non-clustered indexes, 226
        normal forms, 224
        primary keys, 225
        table size, 225
        value pair, name, 225
    performance
        implicit conversion, 232
        NOLOCK, 233, 235
        NULL values, 233
        RECOMPILE, 236, 237

        sargeable, 228–231
        select data, 227
        SET NOCOUNT ON, 232, 233
    usability
        BETWEEN, 238
        CASE statement, 240
        CAST, 239
        columns, 238
        cursors, 240
        linked servers, 237
        ORDER BY statement, 240
        stored procedure parameters, 238
        TRY... CATCH, 241, 242
        UNION statement, 239
Commenting
    header, 91
    non-standard practices, 93
    queries, 93
    stored procedure, 94
    view, 92
Common table expressions (CTE)
    creation, 50
    execution plan, 50, 51
    query, 51
    recursive CTE, 52, 53
Complex logic
    comments, 114
    Dynamic Cursor, creation, 112, 113
    header information, 115, 116
    output, cursor, 118
    parameters, 119, 120

399

© Elizabeth Noble 2020
E. Noble, *Pro T-SQL 2019*, https://doi.org/10.1007/978-1-4842-5590-2

E

F

Made in the USA
Coppell, TX
25 August 2020